Selected Poems of
William Gilmore Simms

Residence of W. Gilmore Simms
Woodland S.C.

Selected Poems of

William Gilmore Simms

TWENTIETH ANNIVERSARY EDITION

Edited by James Everett Kibler

The University of South Carolina Press

© 1990, 2010 University of South Carolina

First edition published by the University of Georgia Press, 1990
Twentieth anniversary edition published by
the University of South Carolina Press
Columbia, South Carolina 29208

www.sc.edu/uscpress

Manufactured in the United States of America

19 18 17 16 15 14 13 12 11 10
10 9 8 7 6 5 4 3 2 1

Library of Congress Cataloging-in-Publication Data
Simms, William Gilmore, 1806–1870.
  [Poems. Selections]
  Selected poems of William Gilmore Simms / edited by
James Everett Kibler. — Twentieth anniversary ed.
      p. cm.
  Includes bibliographical references and index.
  ISBN 978-1-57003-914-0 (pbk : alk. paper)
  I. Kibler, James E. II. Title.
  PS2843.K5 2010
  811'.3—dc22

                    2010002597

This book was printed on Glatfelter Natures, a recycled paper with
30 percent postconsumer waste content.

FRONTISPIECE: *Residence of W. Gylmore Simms,*
Woodlands, S.C., Feb. 12, 1852, by T. A. Richards. Graphite
on paper. This is the original drawing from which the
famous 1853 engraving of Woodlands was made.
Collection of William Nathaniel Banks

Contents

EXPLANATORY AND TEXTUAL NOTES

Editor's Preface to the

Twentieth Anniversary Edition

WHEN *SELECTED POEMS OF WILLIAM GILMORE SIMMS* was published in 1990, Simms's poetry was to be found only in rare-book collections and the private libraries of a lucky few. More significantly the volume gathered verse from the entire canon for the first time because *Areytos*, Simms's last collection, published in 1860, could not include works done in the ten years before his death. *Selected Poems* was thus the first consideration of Simms's complete opus, 1822–70. It made his verse accessible again after more than a century and allowed a comprehensive critical evaluation for the first time. The introduction to the volume noted that because more than half the titles in the edition had never been collected before and nearly half were published under Simms's name for the first time, the volume would likely change our assessment of his stature as a poet.

The notice of *Selected Poems* in *American Literature* (March 1991) concluded, "Surely, from now on, we will hear more about Simms as a poet."[1] The reviewer in *Resources for American Literary Study* (1994) declared that the edition opens "a door into the best elements of a major poetical career. . . . Simms's variety as a poet is surprising, occasionally even startling."[2] *Chronicles of American Culture* (April 1993) called Simms "one of our dominant literary voices."[3] The fullest essay, in *Mississippi Quarterly* (Spring 1991), concluded that *Selected Poems* "gives us the equivalent of a new poet. . . . It is now time to evaluate the timbre and quality of that voice."[4] The pronouncement on the original dust jacket by one of our finest living American poets was perhaps the most significant assessment. Fred Chappell wrote that "Simms is a good poet, versatile, accessible, learned, and passionate in feeling. . . . A beautiful sense of tradition informs all his work and an ease of technique makes it inviting."

Favorable notices in *South Carolina Review* (Fall 1992), *South Atlantic Quarterly Review* (May 1991), and *South Carolina Historical Magazine* (October 1991) rounded out the critical reception. Only the daily newspapers in Charleston and Columbia, South Carolina, reviewed the book however. The large establishment organs that make reputations and sell copies nationwide did not.

Despite scholarly calls for reevaluation, the wheels of the academic mill grind slowly. In the nearly two decades since these reviews, the mill machinery has begun to creak into motion with at least nineteen scholarly articles published on Simms's poetry. These include essays by David Aiken, Matthew C. Brennan, A. J. Conyers, Benjamin Fisher, Jason Johnson, James Everett Kibler, James B. Meriwether, David Newton, Charles Sigman, Doreen Thierauf, and John Kerkering. Simms's poetry is also treated in two recent volumes: Kerkering's *The Poetry of National and Racial Identity in Nineteenth-Century American Literature* (2003) and Masahiro Nakamura's *Visions of Order in William Gilmore Simms: Southern Conservatism and the Other American Romance* (2009). A third volume, Brennan's forthcoming *The Poet's Holy Grail: William Gilmore Simms and Romantic Verse Tradition*, will also be of interest to readers.

Of these twenty-one works, perhaps the ones most deserving note are an essay by Kerkering and Nakamura's volume. Published in *Victorian Poetry* in 2005, Kerkering's "American Renaissance Poetry and the *Topos* of Positionality: *Genius Mundi* and *Genius Loci* in Walt Whitman and William Gilmore Simms" appeared in a special issue dealing with the transatlantic crosscurrents in nineteenth-century poetry and thus places Simms on the world stage where he belongs. Nakamura, as the first scholar outside the United States to write a book on Simms, solidifies that position. Kerkering contrasts the wellsprings of Simms's and Whitman's poetic art and intimates that Simms's approach may after all be sounder and more timely.

Kerkering's essay is not without its problems, however, and these need discussing if Simms's poetry is to be taken seriously in certain circles. The central problem concerns Kerkering's unfortunate implication that "Southern" signifies merely a philosophy of white exclusivity, that when Simms sees himself as "local" and finds his identity from the genius loci, he is asserting racial superiority. By extension, Kerkering suggests, if a critic sees Simms as "Southern," he is doing the same.[5]

Professor Nakamura considers this assumption erroneous. He writes persuasively of the falseness of assuming that "Simms as a reflector of the mores and manners of the Old South represents nothing more than a culture . . . obsessed with race."[6] Instead Simms's conservative worldview in poetry and fiction alike warns against the constant disruption of the bonds of society. Nakamura sees Simms as a critic of deracination and a strong proponent of place and "staying put." Simms's view of the importance of the individual's working within society is thus a valuable literary counterpoint to the radical bourgeois romanticism of egocentric and narcissistic individualism seen as the ideological key to human progress.

Another means to counter this simplistic equating of the South and race is the seminal 1979 study *The Poetry of William Gilmore Simms: An*

Introduction and Bibliography. Section 3, titled "The Southern Poet," addresses the Southern reverence for the genius loci in defining the term "Southern" itself. It found in Simms's poetry the following "Southern" qualities: (1) a lyricism and musicality characteristic of fellow Southern poets such as Poe, Pinkney, Legare, Wilde, Cooke, Timrod, Lanier, and others; (2) an oral narrative quality that is the hallmark of the best Southern literature; (3) an emphasis on the human capacity for pity, compassion, sacrifice, and endurance (compare Faulkner); (4) a critique of industrial capitalism, materialism, and a cash-register evaluation of life; (5) a focus on continuity, in other words, not the living for the moment of momentary man; (6) a strong sense of rootedness and place; (7) a valuing of the local, that is, the Virgilian *patria*, or one's own family fields, over the distant *palatia Romana;* (8) the centrality of family, hearth, and home — Nakamura insightfully explores this theme; (9) a faith in a power higher than man; (10) a questioning of scientific empiricism as the only reality; (11) a closeness to nature and praise for the man of the fields; (12) a deep reverence for the genius loci — itself a very Celtic-Southern trait; and (13) a recognition of the importance of the past as shaper of the present. (This brooding sense of the past is seen as a mysterious but almost tangible force ever-present to shape the moment — again compare Faulkner.)[7]

The valuing of the genius loci discussed in Kerkering's essay was and is a trait to be found in the broad span of the Southern literary tradition: It was a concept imbibed from the Latin and Greek classics. It was a Native American given. (Simms said this as early as 1827, writing in *Early Lays,* "When passing any dangerous reef, or point of land, in their frail canoes, the Indians invariably offer to the Spirit of the Place . . . the smoke of burnt tobacco or the weed itself."[8]) It was an African understanding. It was a key Celtic concept. Simms, son of an Irish immigrant and very much aware of his Celtic roots, saw himself as inheritor of the bardic tradition, the *faoin dulraith* and *duchas* of Gaelic poetry. One of the bard's primary duties was to connect legends to particular places and then pass the knowledge of them down to future generations. The process was not intended to replace the locale with the abstract poem, but to lead the listener to view and consider the locale more fully. Simms's Celtic background places him in the Irish / Welsh / Scots-Irish ethnic component that constituted the largest segment of the Southern white population in the Carolinas and to the south and westward. Simms's identity as Southerner was, understandably, tied to his Celtic inheritance.

It is crucial in Simms's case to see that the concept (instinctual and intellectual) of genius loci was a pervasive given that provided Southerners of all races, classes, and degrees of education common ground and a common bond. Simms was, as a social historian, quite acutely aware of this truth. He saw this shared attitude as yet another way in which his South was different from the urbanizing, materialistic, rootless culture of the North, very clearly described by Whitman, as Kerkering demonstrates.

The modern academic's attempt to deconstruct the idea of the South into one word hits a formidable snag in Simms, and particularly in his poetry. As Nakamura points out, to state that a writer's identification as Southern is tantamount to claiming racial superiority is a flawed, even foolish assumption on many counts. Contrary to certain academic disquisitions, Simms's "Southern" means a rich, distinctive, nature-based, hearth- and home-centered, faith-based culture and is a cultural identity that (it may be argued) stems largely from sensitivity to the genius loci. Furthermore, as Simms's poetry clearly details, Southern means a life-embracing, living tradition that stands in contradistinction to the deracination, nomadism, hedonism, abstraction, and money worship that lead to the hollow and dying culture of the momentary men who embrace them. One need only read Simms's poetry to define "Southern." A neophyte seeking a definition could find no better place to begin.

In September 2008 the biennial symposium sponsored by the Simms Society, an institution founded three years after the publication of *Selected Poems*, was devoted to Simms the poet. Eleven scholars from around the world gathered to present papers on Simms's poetry. Ten of these were subsequently published in a single issue of the *Simms Review*.[9]

When I assisted her as a graduate student in the late 1960s, Mary C. Simms Oliphant, Simms's granddaughter, told me that the first thing I should know was that if I was seeking to find Simms the man, I must approach him through his poetry. Two more of his intensely personal lyrics, one on the death of a daughter and another on the loss of his wife, which have never before appeared under his name, join those intimate works of the earlier edition to provide a candid view of the man. Simms was remarkably frank in these poems, franker even than in the copious, impressive letters he wrote to his family and closest friends. Miss May was indeed correct. To know Simms, one must know his poetry and know it well. It successfully opens the door to his inner life.

All the works on Simms's poetry from the 1990s to the present have used the first edition of *Selected Poems* as a text, and most of them as the only text. Nearly two decades after its first appearance, the publication of this expanded anniversary edition is proof of continued progress in establishing Simms as a major poetic voice of his day and as a poet still readable, relevant, and worthy of attention in our time. As attractive as certain facets of his fiction and other prose might be, his poetry, as Simms himself felt, might finally prove to be his true claim to lasting fame. As a poet, he certainly measures up well against his American contemporaries.

NOTES

1. Unsigned review of *Selected Poems of William Gilmore Simms, American Literature* 63 (March 1991): 172.

2. Thomas L. McHaney, review of *Selected Poems of William Gilmore Simms, Resources for American Literary Study* 2, no. 2 (1994): 3.

3. Thomas Fleming, "More Than a Statue," review of *Selected Poems of William Gilmore Simms, Chronicles of American Culture* 36 (April 1993): 25.

4. Terry Roberts, "The Reconstruction of a Poet," review of *Selected Poems of William Gilmore Simms, Mississippi Quarterly* 44 (Spring 1991): 191.

5. John Kerkering, "American Renaissance Poetry and the *Topos* of Positionality: *Genius Mundi* and *Genius Loci* in Walt Whitman and William Gilmore Simms," *Victorian Poetry* 43 (June 2005): 223–48.

6. Masahiro Nakamura, *Visions of Order in William Gilmore Simms: Southern Conservatism and the Other American Romance* (Columbia: University of South Carolina Press, 2009), p. 6.

7. James E. Kibler, *The Poetry of William Gilmore Simms: An Introduction and Bibliography* (Spartanburg: Published for the Southern Studies Program, University of South Carolina, by the Reprint Co., 1979).

8. William Gilmore Simms, *Early Lays* (Charleston: A. E. Miller, 1827), p. 105.

9. *Simms Review* 17 (Summer/Winter 2009).

Introduction

That a tale should live,
While temples perish! That a poet's song
Should keep its echoes fresh for all the hills
That could not keep their cities!
—Simms, "The Lions of Mycenæ"

ANNERS AND CUSTOMS change and cultures themselves
eventually pass, but the songs they produce, if they are
genuine, remain to speak to another time. Such is the case
with Simms's era and his poetic canon.

The poet was born in 1806, in the golden age of the refined old city
of Charleston; and as the son of a woman from an established and
respected family who recently had wed a spirited Irish immigrant, young
Simms found himself in a position auspicious for nurturing an artistic
temperament. The father, a poet himself, a warrior and adventurer, left
the city and his child soon after his young wife died in 1808. Charleston,
as he said, had now become for him a "place of tombs." He went to the
western wilds and left the boy too long with his maternal grandmother,
for when the elder Simms sent for him a decade later, he refused to come.
Even an attempted kidnapping failed on the city streets. Then followed a
court battle for custody, and the judge finally left the decision to the lad.
Young Simms chose to remain in Charleston; and though he was to visit
his father in the wilderness several times before the elder Simms died in
1830, owing to the great distance that separated them, their relationship
was never very close.

Without mother or father, the youth was often alone and became an avid
devourer of books, particularly poetry. Volumes from the best contempo-
rary English poets were in abundant supply in the city, which had from
its infancy been a cultural leader in America. The boy learned to love
nature early, took pleasure in solitary rambles in the lowcountry forests,
and was especially moved by the eerie, moss-hung landscape and deep,
dark rivers. The realistic tales told in the rude cabins of the countryman
also had their appeal. The young man was growing up moody, proud,
eccentric, unorthodox, and certain of his artistic calling. He brooded over
the hurts in his personal life (the loss of his mother, the early desertion
by his father), and began writing poetry at the age of eight and publish-
ing it at fifteen. His first proved poem, a sonnet to his books (here col-
lected), appeared in 1823, when he was sixteen. His initial collection of

poetry, *Lyrical and Other Poems*, was in press by the fall of 1826, when he was but twenty. These works signaled the beginning of his career, one that Simms never abandoned despite discouragement, severe disappointment, and disaster. When he died in the city of his birth in 1870 at the age of sixty-four, he knew he had deserted neither his community nor the high goals of the calling answered in his youth.

This edition is the first to gather poems from the entire canon. His last collection, published in 1860, could not include the works done in the ten years before his death, a decade which produced some exceptional verse, particularly that occasioned by the war and the losses he suffered therein. Neither has any collection attempted to include his personal lyrics, the group which contains his best titles. Rather than a reevaluation of Simms for our generation, therefore, this edition is more accurately described as the first and only real evaluation of his verse since the poet began to publish in 1822. For during his own day, Simms's contemporaries, even those who followed his poetical career most closely, could not know him fully or evaluate him properly because he never revealed to them his authorship of half of the poems; and as for later generations, there has been no edition of his works at all since 1860, and until recently no attempt to identify, locate, and read his nearly two thousand poems, half of which were published anonymously or pseudonymously. This situation has existed despite Simms's continued assertion that his most important contribution as a writer was not his deservedly popular novels and short stories but his verse, which he always clearly considered his forte.

Simms from the beginning had a grand conception of poetry and an exalted view of the poet as "seer," "prophet," and "minister to man." As Aristotle pointed out, the poet, in his use of metaphor and universal analogy, bridges the phenomenal and noumenal worlds. As a result, the true poet has about him what has been called "a certain aura of consecration" because the "practice of poetry amounts in effect to a confession of faith in immanent reality, which is the gravest of all commitments."[1] While still in his teens, he vowed that the true artist had a "mission" to elevate mankind above the corruption of greed and materialism and the too-narrow focus on worldly things which denied the existence of all but empirical reality. People too frequently saw only the surface of things; it was the poet's duty to point out the universal analogies and lead them to the inner meanings. As early as 1824, he swore he would be this "minister" despite the inevitable difficulties it would entail; and in the same year he stated his resolve to remain "unbent" through all the adversities that would work to dissuade him. His lot as poet would be solitary, he would often be misunderstood, he would be viewed as odd and out of step with the times. Certainly, considering the state of the profession in America, he knew he would never be wealthy, perhaps not even make a living at all. He was sure, however, of his vision, his talent, and the importance of the calling. His song would grow out of inspiration, imagination, deep feeling, intuition, learning, and close observation of man and nature and the unity thereof.[2] This high sense of purpose never diminished with age.

His poetry which aims at lifting man and guiding him to better understanding is successful and frequently quite good. Yet, as the poems in this edition should reveal, Simms is more effective in his unguarded moments when he seems to write simply from within, in a spontaneous expression of a great range of emotions presented without theory. The bulk of his poetry therefore falls into two primary categories: philosophical verse and the intensely personal lyric. There are also, however, other major divisions in his wide-ranging and varied canon. For example, the large group of narrative poems contains some of his most memorable achievements, and his dramatic poetry is often vigorous and effective.[3]

Simms's poetry reveals him to be truly an all-encompassing personality, an artist capable of reconciling opposites and of uniting many seeming contradictions. One finds him a good Romantic who has written some of the most realistic poetry of his day, and again a passionate Romantic just as capable of charm, polish, grace, and a delicate touch. He excels in creating the calmly meditative tone as well as the *sturm und drang* of great feeling. He is equally deft at penning the carefully polished sonnet and the jagged lines of spontaneous outburst. He can paint a picture of surfaces or discern the truths beneath them. This edition represents all of these different kinds of poems, as well as other opposites—for example, the comic and the serious, the impressionistic and the objective. The world of Simms is indeed expansive; the scope of his art can in no sense be labeled narrow. In fact, a good case could be made for his being the most richly diverse of all our American poets, old or new.

The types of Simms's poetry also vary widely. He wrote ballads, odes, political and social satire, humorous verse, psychological studies, dramatic monologues, love songs, sonnets, occasional verse, epigrams, adaptations and translations of the masters, war poetry, and works in the larger divisions that he himself designated the "Dramatic, Descriptive, Legendary, and Contemplative."[4] His verse forms and meters are just as varied: traditional ones like Spenserian stanza, ottava rima, blank verse, heroic couplet, and ballad meter, to name only a few; and many forms and skillfully handled meters of his own creation, like, for example, a favorite heptameter with caesura. The product of an obviously versatile talent, the canon has in all respects a range and completeness lacking in the American poets of his day, a fact which alone makes it worthy of note.

A poet whose artistic scope is so broad and whose works are so volu-
minous presents many difficulties for his first editor. Because the canon
consists of nearly two thousand poems, for every one I have chosen to
publish, I was forced to reject at least nine others. Happily, there are good
titles in each category; so the initial object has been to represent all
poetic types and divisions with the best works of each in order to give an
overall view of the canon's scope. It should always be kept in mind, how-
ever, that a volume of this size could be devoted to almost every type and
division, enough to yield at least twelve more volumes the size of this one.

Simms himself stated that there are two ways of judging poetry,
"intrinsically" (or on purely artistic grounds), or as poems "illustrative" of
their time; and he, with his usual solid critical instincts, desired that his
critics use the former.[5] Both these criteria have been utilized in selecting
the poems for this edition, with the emphasis placed on artistic merit,
as Simms himself wished it. The specific criteria used here, in order of
importance, are, therefore: (1) artistic or "intrinsic" merit, (2) thematic
importance or relevance to the canon, and (3) relevance to Simms's life
and times.

Simms, although rightly considered an important figure in literary his-
tory, has not been given his due as artist; hence all the more reason to
have as a major goal the compilation of a poetry edition which shows him
at his artistic best. By "artistic merit" is meant the usual: the successful
integration of tone, diction, theme, figurative language, speaker, setting,
and sound into a work which the reader recalls in a phrase or stanza
when he least expects to, a poem which he wishes to reread for the plea-
sure of hearing it again and because it has meaning for him in a special
way. Simms's verses anthologized heretofore have usually been mostly
rhymed prose devoid of figurative language—essays or descriptions in
rhyme, if you will.[6] If Simms's canon ended here, he must fall into the
category of the very unsophisticated versifier who might well be defined
as one who tries to put prose statements into verse. But in choosing
Simms's best poetry, I have been particularly aware of his use of imagery,[7]
sometimes pedestrian but as often striking, his handling of the speaker
(which frequently involves the first-person narrator whose self-revealed
psychology is more important than the narrative he presents), his lyri-
cism, his effective creation and control of tone and evocation of mood,
his use of sound to reinforce sense, and his ability to create both the real-
istic and imaginative setting. Frequently in my notes to the poems I com-
ment on what I feel to be each work's artistic strengths and weaknesses.

The second most important criterion after artistic merit is actually two-
fold: (1) thematic importance and (2) relevance to the canon, particularly
its chronological development. Thematic importance has been determined

as a result of several qualities: universality, originality, or as examples of Romantic, Realistic, or Existential theory, or departure therefrom. Simms showed himself very early to be in the mainstream of Romanticism, to be abreast of its current European expression and ahead of his American contemporaries in this respect; yet at the same time, his deep-seated pessimism showed him to be looking ahead to the era of late Victorian disillusionment.[8] In the Victorian period itself, Simms seems to have leaped ahead once again, this time into Existentialism. The poems which express these ideas are important works, both for an understanding of Simms's thought and for American literary history in general; the best of their sort are therefore included. A work is deemed "relevant to the canon" if it throws important light on Simms's theories of art and life, or on the meaning of the canon as a whole. Some effort has been made to choose judiciously so as to show development of themes and artistic methods. The chronological arrangement of the edition suggests the significance attached to this effort.

The third and final criterion, "relevance to Simms's life and times," is responsible for the inclusion of poems which reveal the man's emotional life. As such, they present the nearest thing we will ever have to an autobiography. Many of Simms's best works are spontaneous results of a momentary state of mind, the lyric expression of the full range of emotions—grief at death, loneliness, love of a wife, a father's love, love of hearth and homeland, sadness at parting, homesickness, joy in nature, fear of the changes time brings, hope, faith in the rightness of creation, disillusionment, acceptance of defeat. These poems are interesting for what they show about the author, but at the same time are among his highest artistic achievements. In what is otherwise one of the best short critical studies of Simms's fiction, Thomas McHaney states that Simms did not use his experiences as the source of his work: "He lost parents, wives, children, home . . . , but something in him never gave in to these circumstances, and perhaps what would not give in to them, would not . . . or could not use them fully for artistic purposes either. He seems, artistically, never to have driven life into a corner. He never fully expressed its tragedies or its joys or . . . the fullness of strength and spirit which he himself must have understood and possessed."[9] This passage is worth pondering to explain exactly what Simms the poet *did do* in the works chosen as a result of this third criterion, and why these poems which rise from the depths of his feelings about the events of his own life are among his best, and very rare achievements in his day. No poems could be any more honest or intensely personal than many of these. The composition of those frank verses which touch on the very losses enumerated in the quotation above must not have come without causing hurt, a lesser pain which perhaps helped exorcise the greater. Clearly, art for Simms was not an escape from reality but a way of facing it. It has been said that the best lyrical poetry is often the product of the unchecked exuberance of youth. While Simms's youthful Cavalier lyrics are charming and often memorable, his great lyric contribution came in his maturity, particularly in those poems which express love, grief, and loss. These works, precipitated by his own experiences, show that he had indeed "driven life into a corner" in order to face it and deal with it, and that the act of artistic creation was a part of the process essential to doing so. Like much effective art, his poetry was obviously both a means of clarifying the confusions of existence and of expressing life's joys and sorrows "in fullness of strength and spirit." That is largely why they stand as significant artistic contributions. Their rare quality of being unclouded by the slightest trace of didacticism, philosophizing, or theorizing, is an additional strength and shows artistic discernment of no ordinary degree, a trait that marks him as more "modern" than his popular contemporaries like Bryant, Emerson, and Longfellow, to whom he compares favorably in most other respects as well. Some of these personal verses, one might feel, could have been written in our time because they seem so current in their lack of nineteenth-century expositoriness.

As the perceptive poet and critic Allen Tate has remarked, "The trouble with most nineteenth-century poets is too much philosophy; they are nearer to being philosophers than poets, without being in the true sense either."[10] Simms, like his more talented British predecessors Wordsworth and Coleridge, must often fall into the "philosophy" category that Tate describes, but his personal lyrics are totally free of Tate's "trouble" and meet the stipulation that Tate sets for "all great poetry": "personal revelation . . . in the effort to understand [one's] relation to the world" (291). This, Tate goes on to say, is "probably the hidden motive for writing" (292) with the result being a perfectly valid description of this category of Simms's work: there is "no abstract speculation, nor is there a message to society; he speaks wholly to the individual experience" (298). As Simms himself was fond of saying, the true lyric must always be "an involuntary," an "improvisation," a poem "unpremeditated" and then "subsequently refined by art."[11] He understood well the nature of the lyric, and excelled in the form.

Finally, because they are vital responses to his own time, many of Simms's poems reflect Southern life in town, country, and on the frontier. His trips to the Southwest in 1824–25, 1826, and 1831 produced important works, several of which (including "The Indian Village" and "Chilhowee") deserve to be widely known. And Simms's career spanned the period in Charleston's history from the time when the city's power, wealth, and prestige reached its height, through a decline, then into complete eclipse after 1865, when struggle for its society's very survival was desperate. The artist's work charts this course graphically. Many of Simms's most charming poems deal with Southern scenes: for example, the author and his new wife as they walk the plantation, the domestic scene around the plantation hearth in winter, the sea breeze on a summer night as it passes over fragrant orange groves, or of a youth forced to visit his cousins too frequently. There is in the warmth, humor, generosity, ease, and familiarity of these poems qualities missing in the rather cold, narrow, humorless works of other poets of other climes. As Van Wyck Brooks ably noted of Simms: "Large of heart, strikingly handsome, prodigally generous, he was the living emblem in letters of all that made one love the South, its spendthrift energy, its carelessness, lavishness and warmth."[12] With the exception of "careless," these traits describe the canon accurately. The notes to these poems reveal Simms to be far from careless, and instead a tireless reviser and energetic rewriter, not the stereotypical Cavalier of Southern tradition. But the lyrics, particularly those of the first half of the canon, do have a casual grace and sophistication which suggest relaxation and carelessness and which therefore belie their careful composition. True to the old phrase, they embody the Art that conceals Art. In his maturity Simms may have at times maintained the outward fabric of a life of ease, but there is always the indisputable evidence of his obvious devotion to craft in his enormous number of poems, some of which could reach the high quality of those collected here, over a painstaking series of writings and rewritings.[13]

A few of his detractors have sometimes incorrectly assumed that he refused to deal with his own day and that in his "mindless" rush to defend the old regime, he failed to attempt discernment.[14] Poems collected here from the war years should alone contradict this unfortunate notion; these works were immediate responses to specific events. But, more important, from throughout the canon, one constantly encounters such works as "Heedlessness" (1845), "Sonnet—The Wreath" (1858), "Harbor by Moonlight" (1844), and "Promise of Spring" (1860), in which the primary theme itself is that the masses of men usually fail to discern the hard truth beneath the easy surface around them, particularly at their own doorsteps, but that the poet must do just the opposite and point it out. As "Poet-Seer," Simms is fond of saying that the artist's duty is "to extort from every subject its inner secret."[15] One way is to be ever cognizant of the emblematic nature of the physical world, which it is abundantly clear Simms always is, thus yielding such poems as "The Memorial Tree" (1848), "Stanzas to a Lady" (1835), "Flowers and Trees" (1844), "The Prayer of the Lyre" (1836), "The Streamlet" (1829), and a great many others.[16]

Another way to penetrate the surface and discern inner truths is (to quote Simms himself) to "find out the secret in your own soul and you will find out the secrets in other souls"[17]—a statement that serves as an important key to his autobiographical poetry in particular, for Simms is saying here that in discerning meaning within himself, the poet is expressing the universal truths of what it means to be human. Grief, joy, loss, love, inspiration, religious aspiration, loneliness—in fact, as wide a range of the human condition as expressed by any American poet—are all given expression simply by the poet's honest looking within himself. This process, far from superficial and "mindless" in Simms, is an attempt to ascend the heights and plumb the depths of what it means to be alive. If he does so honestly, movingly, and skillfully, what more should one ask of the lyric poet? Further, Simms at his very best (like all great writers) invites an understanding of not only his mind and experience but also our own.

It might be helpful at this point to provide a summarizing overview of the canon by way of a brief survey of some of Simms's chief themes. These show that his response to the world around him is generally most often Romantic. He writes of nature and of nature's manifold roles as teacher, source of inspiration, restorer of a tired spirit, spiritual guide, aid to reflection, nurturer, and symbol of immortality. Nature is at once emblem of the spiritual and a mirror of man's inner being. In typical Romantic fashion, Simms writes of the oneness of all creation, and of how man infuses his own life into nature and is invigorated in return. He often points out the folly of a purely empirical, utilitarian view of nature. A common theme is that modern man has broken his covenant with God by becoming an idolater, by worshipping gold and setting up the temple in the marketplace. He portrays the folly of hedonism, which sees the dead shell of the physical as the only truth of existence. Like many Romantics, he criticizes uninspired science as a "cold blooded demon" that has helped lead modern man to this fallen state. He celebrates imagination, spontacity, wildness, freedom, organicism, and intuition. He attacks strict decorum, artificiality, and orthodoxy and favors Spiritualism and Free-thinking. He emphasizes the past and memory and how human associations invigorate nature with life and meaning.

Another of his primary themes is the transience of all things and that happiness especially is fleeting. Like Keats, he shows that joy can be fully relished only by those who know its opposite and realize its brevity. He goes further than the English poet, however, in possessing a deeper and more pervasive tragic sense of the essential sadness at the core of life. Below its most smiling aspects reside "carnage," "tempest," violence, and utter loss. Many of his works treat the role of the poet as interpreter, prophet, and guide to such understanding. Simms often reveals how men are oblivious to the truths around them, particularly those meanings closest to them. One of his most effective themes is that people often fail to value properly the importance of the local and familiar—an idea that is a natural outgrowth of his literary theory of regionalism. Thus his poems often celebrate the local, familiar, and simple over the exotic. He sees man to be a product of both free will and fate and finds meaning in a chaotic universe through the assertion of that will. Above all, he emphasizes a man's character, duty, and personal responsibility. The way a man behaves in life is more important than what he "achieves." Success, in true Southern fashion, is defined as the "how" rather than the "how much" of achievement and of the triumph of "values" over "interests." Finally, he writes effectively of spiritual yearning, love, and loss. A parent's relationship to a child becomes the central symbol around which many of these themes revolve. Preeminently, he is the poet of family.

This short treatment can only provide the most general and superficial of beginnings for a study of Simms's themes and subjects. Because this edition collects less than a tenth of Simms's poems, the reader can have at best only an imperfect acquaintance with their rich thematic diversity. An attempt has been made, however, to suggest their full thematic range. In order to achieve this goal, I have spent the last twenty-four years identifying, reading, and studying the complete poetical canon. Simms's fugitive verse is scattered throughout dozens of nineteenth-century periodicals, much of it published anonymously or under almost two hundred pseudonyms.[18] Of the 193 poems in this edition, 103 of them (or 53 percent) are collected for the first time.[19] The others appeared in one or another of Simms's poetry volumes published from his first in 1825 to his last in 1860. Of the poems in this edition, 77 of them (or 40 percent) are known to be by Simms for the first time, and thus appear here under his name for the first time. These figures should suggest to the critic the great potential for, indeed the likelihood of, a decided change in our view of the poet.

Simms almost always signed and collected his philosophical, or "contemplative" verse as he called it, and tended to publish his personal lyrics anonymously or pseudonymously. He obviously valued his philosophical poetry as higher creations,[20] as did nineteenth-century writers in general. Yet Simms is a poet who unconsciously rose above the limitations of his era of English verse in the personal lyric which he seemed not to value as much, yet felt it necessary to write nonetheless. Nineteenth-century American poetry is the richer for it. The editor has therefore emphasized this category in his selections.

It is foolish to think that every reader will agree with all choices to include or exclude particular titles. Although a certain amount of purely personal preference is always involved in such an undertaking, I have tried to remain critically objective, basing my choices on the criteria listed here in order to assemble this first modern collection of Simms's verse, a compilation which I hope will present an adequate measure of the author's abilities and significance.

Simms's achievement in poetry is impressive, almost staggeringly so, considering his neglect. What a pity so few have been able to enjoy his work or see the world through his eyes, and that beyond literary historians he is not popularly known. The reasons for this problem are complex and, since they have been enumerated elsewhere, will not be recounted here.[21] Suffice it to say that this edition should remove one major obstacle to an appreciation of his work by making it widely accessible for the first time. The reader of Simms thus stands at a newly opened door; it is only now with our own generation that a fair evaluation of his talents and achievements is possible.

NOTES

1. As expressed by Richard Weaver in *The Southern Essays of Richard Weaver*, ed. George Curtis III and James J. Thompson, Jr. (Indianapolis: Liberty Press, 1987), p. 38.

2. A fuller treatment of Simms's theories of poetry may be found in James Kibler, *The Poetry of William Gilmore Simms: An Introduction and Bibliography* (Columbia, S.C.: Southern Studies, 1979), pp. 5–51. The strongest first instances of Simms's antimaterialism are to be found in his first known prose piece, "Light Reading," *Charleston Courier*, 27 July 1824, where he scorns the "time-plodding mechanics of existence whose only object in life is the attainment of wealth," and in his first known letters, "Letters from the West (1826)," newly printed in *Southern Literary Journal* 19 (Spring 1987): 81–91.

3. Simms himself regarded these two categories highly. In a letter of 15 January 1847, he stated: "I regard poetry as my forte, particularly in the narrative and dramatic forms." *Letters of William Gilmore Simms*, ed. Mary C. Simms Oliphant et al. (Columbia: University of South Carolina Press, 1952–82), 2:257.

4. The subtitle of his *Poems* (Charleston: Russell, 1853). By "Contemplative" he simply meant "Philosophical" in the manner of Wordsworth, whom he deemed "the greatest of all the tribe of contemplative poets" (*Letters*, 4:443).

5. *Letters*, 1:445.

6. Noticeably absent in this edition is such a poem devoid of effective imagery, "The Edge of the Swamp," first anthologized in 1840 and a pet anthology piece ever since, despite the fact that Simms rightly felt it far from his best, though proficient enough as a descriptive piece which evokes a mood. See *Letters*, 5:355.

7. For a treatment of one aspect of Simms's imagery, see James Kibler, "Perceiver and Perceived: External Landscape as Mirror and Metaphor in Simms's

Poetry," in *"Long Years of Neglect": The Work and Reputation of William Gilmore Simms*, ed. John C. Guilds (Fayetteville: University of Arkansas Press, 1988), pp. 106–25.

8. For a treatment of Simms's Romantic theory in his poetry and of his increasing disillusionment, see *The Poetry of William Gilmore Simms*, pp. 5–36.

9. Thomas L. McHaney, "William Gilmore Simms," in *The Chief Glory of Every People: Essays on Classic American Writers*, ed. Matthew Bruccoli (Carbondale: Southern Illinois University Press, 1973), p. 190.

10. Allen Tate, "Emily Dickinson," in *Essays of Four Decades* (Chicago: Swallow Press, 1968), p. 291.

11. *Letters*, 4:431.

12. Van Wyck Brooks, *The World of Washington Irving* (New York: E. P. Dutton, 1944), p. 234.

13. The canon of over nineteen hundred poems is listed by title and first line in *The Poetry of William Gilmore Simms*. Each known place of publication is also given.

14. The most recent is Louis Rubin, in *Long Years of Neglect*, ed. Guilds, p. 232: "He could not view history as something that was happening to him."

15. *Letters*, 6:236.

16. For a study of this aspect of his poetry, see Kibler, "Perceiver and Perceived."

17. *Letters*, 6:236.

18. The precise number for poetry now stands at 194. James Kibler, *The Pseudonymous Publications of William Gilmore Simms* (Athens: University of Georgia Press, 1976) recounts how these pseudonyms were identified and lists all the known works published under them. Since the volume's appearance, I have proved eight more poetry pseudonyms: Boone, Flora De Berniere, Frank, Il Marito Felice, Jonathan, Norma, Percival, and W******. The total pseudonym count for both prose and poetry now stands at 232. New prose pseudonyms since 1976 are Bienami, Bion, Octavian, Quericus, A Reminiscent, and The Wanderer. The first two were proved by John McCardell.

19. Of these 103, 10 are printed from heretofore unpublished manuscripts.

20. In 1854 Simms wrote that he regarded poetry "as the profoundest of human philosophies" (*Letters*, 3:275). In 1858 he stated similarly that poetry is "a proper medium for philosophy; the meditative, contemplative, and social, nay even political; and not merely a musical trifling for the amusement of romantic damsels on moon-lighted waters" (*Russell's*, September 1858). Echoing Coleridge, Simms frequently defined poetry as "wingèd thought."

21. *The Poetry of William Gilmore Simms*, pp. 1–5. For fuller treatments, see John C. Guilds, "'Long Years of Neglect': Atonement at Last?" and John McCardell, "Biography and the Southern Mind," in *Long Years of Neglect*, ed. Guilds, pp. 3–19 and 202–16.

Notes on the Text

SEVERAL BRIEF NOTES on the text are in order before the reader begins this edition. Simms's works in newspapers and magazines were sloppily printed, as he himself lamented time and again, often making the verse sound hopelessly ludicrous. For example, a typesetting error gives wings to a turtle, whereas "The turtle's own pinion" should actually have read "The turtle dove's pinion." Instead of the poet placing his *lyre* inside, he is made to throw his *tire* inside. Instead of saying, "All is vain," a typesetting error forces a speaker to exclaim, "All is rain." The careless missetting of one letter changes Simms's beech tree into a coastal beach with the resulting impossible image of a bird's wing spanning too much real estate. Thus, careful attention has been given to the restoration of Simms's readings.

There has been no attempt to modernize spelling or punctuation; in fact, the housestyled texts of Simms's poems in his collections have been altered to remove any "modernization" or "regularization" by house-styling editors during Simms's own century, so that "recall" returns to Simms's spelling "recal," and "woe" becomes his usual "wo." Simms often published his poems in several places, a fact which has increased the complexity of the task of editing, but has actually been of great value in helping to establish an accurate text. When one source housestyles, perhaps another does not; and becoming acquainted with Simms's habitual practice, particularly in his manuscripts, allows judicious picking and choosing among variants. Absolutely no attempt has been made to normalize or regularize except in restoring demonstrable authorial usage. There has been no normalizing of acceptable historical forms for the sake of tidiness. A listing of each change made to the copy text is given in the discussion of each poem at the end of the edition. All changes made in the text for whatever reason are noted in these lists. Lack of space has prevented the publishing of complete historical collations of the works. I have compiled these, nevertheless, for my own use in preparing the poems' texts.

It has been necessary in most cases to make important choices about which of the various versions of a poem to publish here. The basis of choice has been to select the poem which has the highest artistic merit. Once again, the edition's primary purpose is to collect Simms's best poems, to present the poet in the best artistic light. If an earlier version of a work is better than a later, the earlier is chosen even if it is obvious that the later poem represents the "author's final intentions." Both some early and some later versions appear in the edition for this reason. If two versions have great merit and are different enough to constitute separate poems, or are changed substantially in light of what is going on in Simms's life or society at the time, both versions appear in the edition under their respective dates of composition.

The texts are eclectic only to the extent that later versions incorporate emendations which restore earlier readings when these readings replace housestyling, errors, or editorial tamperings. Or early versions will rely on readings of later ones in order to accomplish the same goal. In neither case, however, will a variant from another version be inserted because that individual variant has been deemed an artistically superior reading from a version of the poem which has been rejected because otherwise inferior. I have, therefore, tried to resist the temptation of (with all the many possible readings which Simms provided) taking a little from this version and a little from that in order to, in effect, write my own poem. Emendations have always been made in order to restore the integrity of the particular version presented, by eliminating errors, housestyling, and editorial tampering, so as to present that specific text as nearly as possible as Simms wrote it.

Because Simms usually recopied these poems each time they were submitted for publication, the normal theory of copy text for "accidentals" does not apply. Punctuation, capitalization, and spelling of the first published version are thus not imposed on later ones because there is no succession of texts printed one from another.

The date or dates in parentheses which follow the poem texts are supplied in the following manner. If there is but one date, it is of the year of earliest known composition and publication. If there are two or more dates, the first is of the year of earliest known initial composition, with subsequent dates listing the years of various versions which figure as important to the establishment of this particular text (with the reasons for the significance given in the textual notes). The poems are arranged chronologically according to initial publication, but not rigidly so. If a poem composed first in 1827 is rewritten in 1832 in light of the death of the poet's wife, the poem is placed in 1832, with both the dates 1827 and 1832 appearing in parentheses following the text. The 1832 text has become largely a new poem, hence its inclusion in 1832 rather than 1827. The reader should always refer to the explanatory and textual notes for an account of the poem's complete history of composition and publication. I have chosen to place all editorial notes at the end of the volume. When footnotes appear in the text itself, they are by Simms. My aim has been to present a text based on both soundest scholarship and textual theories in as simple a form as possible, so as to encourage the reader's maximum enjoyment. It is my hope that the reader in encountering this new artist will experience the pleasure of discovery and the appreciation of a genuine poetic talent and sensibility.

Selected Poems of

William Gilmore Simms

The Poems

SONNET—TO MY BOOKS.

Ye chaste creators of the youthful mind,
    Picture of man in each extreme of fate,
    Nations may fade—but yours no endless date—
For immortality design'd,
Then let me foster with a filial care,
    Your fairy pleasures and historic scenes,
    Where nations long forgot retain some gleams
Of former lustre, new created glare,
Which like the relics in Pompeii found—
    Point out the various beauties there that reign'd,
    And tho' all strew'd with ashes, yet the ground,
The lustre of a former day retain'd!
    Is there, my Books, a charm which ye have not,
No!—When with you, the world is all forgot.

                                                  (1823)

THE EVENING BREEZE.

Battery by Moonlight.

I come from the deep, where the Mermaiden twines
    In her bower of amber her garlands of shells,
Where the sands are of gold, and of chrystal the vines,
    Where the spirit of music unchangingly dwells.
I breath'd on the harp at Eolus's cave,
    And the strain as it rose glided onward with me;
No dwelling on earth, but my home is the wave,
    And my couch is the coral grove, deep in the sea.

Has thy heart ever dreamed of some fanciful bower,
    That ceased on thy waking, to ravish thy sight?
It was I that arose on the wings of the hour,
    And gave to thy senses the visions of light.
Would'st thou have all those scenes that so charmed thy view?
    Would'st thou dwell with the moon that now beams upon thee?
To the hopes and the fears of the earth bid adieu—
    Come rest in the coral groves deep in the sea.

With my breath I will cool thee when noon-day is nigh,
　　The fairest of Mermaids will lull thee to sleep;
She will watch by the couch when the sun passes by,
　　Nor fly when the moon leaves her home in the deep.
The delights of the past shall remain still thine own,
　　The sorrows of Time from thy slumbers shall flee;
Then come with me, taste of the pleasures I've shown,
　　Come, rest in the coral grove deep in the sea.

(1824)

OH! SWEET GUITAR.

Oh! sweet Guitar—Oh! sweet Guitar,
　　That lead'st me thro' the livelong night,
Whilst o'er my pathway hangs no star,
　　To guide me with its lonely light.
Ah! yet more sweet to hear thy sound,
　　Thus streaming from *her* lattice high,
Than wander all the world around,
　　With moonlight ever in the sky.

Oh! sweet Guitar—Oh! sweet Guitar,
　　More dear, because thou'rt touch'd by one
Whose eye is brighter, dearer far,
　　Than all I've ever gazed upon.
Oh, give me heaven, in life's dull round,
　　Where care and grief are all we prove,
That dear Guitar's enchanting sound—
　　That lip, to whisper tales of Love.

(1824)

ADDRESS FOR NEW-YEAR'S DAY.

　Time, as he threw beneath a Poet's door,
His sheet of foreign and domestic lore,
Paus'd at the scene that met his hurried glance—
Once in his life, was captur'd by romance!

There no rich carpet, of imperial pride,
No gorgeous drapery, far extended wide,
No mirror'd toilet bright, no festoons there,
To deck the crumbling wall, all bleak and bare!
There, in one nook, (as wheels within a wheel,
So nook in nook might be, yet not ideal,)
A cot, which boasted but three legs, and they
Were inch by inch, for fire-wood ta'en away—
A chair—but stay, 'twere useless to relate,
The Minstrel's ideal home, and certain state!
But on that cot, a goblet by his side,
The Poet lay—by nectar deified:
"Ha! what is this?" as o'er the vellum sheet
A hasty glance he threw—"a Piece of Plate—
New-Year's Address, &c.—on my word,
Good news indeed, the like was never heard—
A Piece of Plate—mayhap a copious bowl—
The very thought, inspires my listless soul.
'Tis mine—I'll write—I'll write this very day—
The Muses call, and Bacchus leads the way."
To write or not to write, that is the—stay—
That is old Will's—I must not go that way.
Hence, horrible shadow! that with misty cloud,
Dims my mind's eye, and wraps it in the shroud
Of dull prosaic meaning. I would soar
High in the ambient fields, untrod before,
Where the young wizard Fancy, on the gale
Of wild uncertain phantasy dares to sail,
Whilst the dark world, with wondering eye looks on,
Too dull to love, it worships when 'tis gone.

This is a world of shadows—at the least,
Joy is a shadow, take it at the best.
The magic fire that lights the wayward breast,
Time, who shall wing his flight to other days,
Leaves but a faint trace for our wearied gaze,
Where we may roam, whilst memory paints the hues,
Of that the heart has lost, and yet must lose.

The soul's first fire, is soonest to decay;
The heart's first homage, steals with death away;
The light we worship'd when the heart was bright,

Loses its lustre in the robe of night!
Oh, Genius! seldom yet with joy allied,
Tho' worship'd, scorn'd, tho' hated deified;
Go tune thy lyre, it is thy solace, all,
It gives thee joy—and it can give thee gall!
Tho' feeling spreads her rainbow, it will fade,
Tho' sunbeams light thee, yet they have their shade;
Tho' pleasure tempt thee to her magic rill,
Drink of her sweet, but love thy lyre still;
Charm Time's harsh summons with its tuneful strain,
Then, tho' he call thee, he can give no pain.

Go, Time! the veil be closed—no longer stay;
Thou hast thy duties, and hast had thy day;
The curtain falls—he who has play'd his part,
May laugh at Time, nor when he calls him, start.
Be ours the hope that virtuous hearts can give—
May we all merit well, and meriting, receive.

(1824)

THE BROKEN ARROW.[1]

Ye warriors! who gather the brave to deplore,
    And repine for the Chief who shall conquer no more,
Let the hatchet of fight, still unburied remain,
    Whilst we joy in the glory of him that is slain.

Unbounded in soul, as unfearing in fight;
    Yet mild as the dove, when, untempted to smite;
His arm was resistless, his tomahawk true,
    And his eye, like the eagle's, was lightning to view.

Far down in the valley, when evening was still,
    I heard the deep voice of the Wolf[2] on the hill:
And "hark!" said the Chief, as it echoed below,
    " 'Tis the voice of Menawe![3] the cry of my foe!

"He comes not, the coward, to mingle in fight,
    "When the Day-God can offer one streak of his light;

"But in darkness, that emblems his bosom's own hue,
   "He seeks to perform, what he trembles to do!"

The Chief took his rifle, unerring as fate,
   His eye glow'd as proud, as his bosom was great;
I heard the flint strike on the steel, but in vain,
   For I heard not the rifle re-echo again.

Go, sigh not away, as the coward has done,
   The remnant of life, o'er the fields we have won;
But a mournful farewell, to our fruit trees[4] we'll leave,
   They o'ershadow our fathers, and honor their grave.

Farther West! farther West! where the buffalo roves
   And the red deer is found in the valley he loves;
Our hearts shall be glad, in the hunt once again,
   'Till the white man shall seek for the lands that remain.[5]

Farther West! farther West! where the Sun as he dies,
   Still leaves a deep lustre abroad in the skies;
Where the hunter may roam, and his woman may rove,
   And the white man not blight, what he cannot improve!

One song of regret to the wilds that we leave,
   To the Chief, o'er whose grave still his warriors must grieve;
He died as a hero—and equall'd by few—
   Himself his worst foe, to the white man too true!

Farther West! farther West, it is meet that we fly,
   Where the red deer will bound at the glance of an eye:—
And lonely and sad be the strain that is sung,
   For the arrow is broken, the bow is unstrung!

(1825, 1826)

1. The followers and friends of the late Indian Chief Mackintosh, are called the "People of the Broken Arrow."
2. Mad Wolf was the Indian who shot Gen. William Mackintosh.
3. Menawe was commander of the party, about 200 in number, who went in pursuit of the Chief. He, as well as Mad Wolf, are signers to the late Georgia Treaty.
4. The idea of fruit trees being an object of regret to the Indian in leaving his home, may to us appear absurd, particularly, when we consider how many other causes there were for grief, more influential in our view than this. It is, however, less extravagant, when we discover their propensity to fruit of all kinds, particularly plumbs. Their orchards,

probably the site of old towns, are continued even for miles on the road, without order or inclosure.

5. This is literal. I observed to an Indian that was one of those who came under that class in the late treaty, who were to fly farther West, that there were good hunting grounds near the setting sun, and his response was nearly similar—"Yes," said he, with mournful expression of countenance, "Yes, but when the white man sees us living comfortably there, he will want more land, and we will be sent farther yet." They seem to apprehend to its fullest extent, the miseries of leaving the home of childhood, associated so firmly by the ligament of a past eternity.

WRITTEN IN MISSISSIPPI.

Oh! sweet among these spreading trees,
    In noon-day's fervor to recline,
Whilst arching in the cooling breeze,
    We watch the distant waving vine.
And at our feet the rippling stream,
    In gentle murmurs glides along,
Free from the sun's oppressive beam,
    We listen to the Mocker's song.

And nought disturbs the gentle lay,
    Save thro' the pine-tops bending round,
The amorous wind pursues its way,
    Scattering their leaves upon the ground;
Whilst far removed from noise or care,
    Where man has scarcely ever come,
Borne swiftly on the drowsy ear,
    We hark the noisy bee-tree's hum.

Oh! thus remote from worldly strife,
    Without the toil that crowds await,
How sweet to rove the vale of life,
    Unchanged by love, unharm'd by hate.
Where no extreme of joy or ill
    Can urge or clog the steps of youth;
Where all of life, the wild and still,
    But bears the impress stamp of truth.

Swift as the red-deer could my feet,
    Compass the wastes that now divide

Thy form from mine, my more than sweet!
   How soon I'd clasp thee to my side!
Here would we wing the fleeting hours—
   Here taste each joy the heart can see—
Thou finding, at each step, but flow'rs,
   And I, a fairer flow'r in thee!

(1825, 1827)

TO A WINTER FLOWER,

Written in the Creek Nation.

When winter comes with icy mien,
   To silver o'er this brook,
Thy form in loneliness is seen,
   By all forsook.

No shrub upon the fields remains,
   To feed the watchful gaze,
Nor blade of grass the earth retains,
   Nor sprig of maize.

The Indian here shall rest his eye,
   And meditate alone,
That thou, when all his race shall die,
   Will still be known.

Pensive in anxious, thoughtful mood,
   His rifle at his side,
He'll wonder how alone thou'st stood,
   When all have died.

What secret spring of life is thine,
   Or, what art thou, to gain,
Such partial favor, as to shine,
   Last of thy train?

Methinks such lot can ne'er be blest,
   To feel ourselves alone,

On earth the latest, only guest,
   When all are gone.

Then looking up from thee to him,
   That made thy outcast leaf,
Shall wonder that his soul is dim,
   And being brief.

That cannot with the sedgy grass,
   That skirts yon streamlet's blue,
Compare the Indian warrior's trace,
   When life was new.

                            (1825, 1827)

SONG.

"I HAVE NO HEART TO SING."

I have no heart to sing of thee,
   No tongue to speak thy praise,
For well I know the theme would be,
   Too rich for prouder lays;
Yet can I tell, in humble strain,
   Of all thy smiles and love,
And in the offering of my brain,
   My heart's devotion prove.

Take, then, the song, however weak
   The tribute that I bring;
Oh! as I've felt, could I but speak,
   It were not vain to sing—
Such song, decreed by heaven for good,
   Than him who sings, more blest,
Might, in some happy hour and mood,
   Find entrance to thy breast.

                            (1825, 1842)

SONNET.—"IF FROM THE MORNING OF THY DAYS."

If, from the morning of thy days, hath flown
   The sunlight that illum'd them—if thine eye
   No longer brightens with the luxury
Of happiest hopes within thee, and are gone
Those joys that kindle the young heart alone,—
   Then will I weep with thee! I did not come,
   When life was blushing with voluptuous bloom,
But when its wither'd flow'rs are lost, all thrown
Worthless, upon the waters,—gliding down,
   The ocean of past pleasures!—I will now,
Since thou'rt forgotten by the crowd once known
   Bind the sweet fever-balm upon thy brow!
Ah! loveliest in thy sorrow—the sad show'r,
Hath only brought back freshness to the flow'r!

(1826, 1842)

THE SLAIN EAGLE. (SALUDA.)

i

The noble bird! What mighty stretch of wing—
   Seven feet from tip to tip! And what an eye,
That glares in death, as with the will to spring,
   Spurn earth, and rush into the blazing sky!
   What talons!—that shall lift the lamb on high,
And bear it to its heights, nor feel the weight!
   Emblem of power, and might, and majesty,
Yet victim of the feeblest stroke of fate,
Transfixed by Indian shaft, when soaring in thy state!

ii

The eye that stopt thy flight, with deadly aim,
   Had less of fire and beauty than thine own;
The arm that cast thee down could never claim
   Such matchless vigor as thy wing hath shown,
   Yet art thou, in thy pride of flight, o'erthrown:
And the great rocks that echoed back thy scream,

11

As from the rolling clouds thou sent'st it down,
No more shall see thy red-eyed glances stream,
From their wild summits round, with fierce and terrible gleam!

iii

Lone and majestic monarch of the cloud!
    No more shalt thou o'ersweep the mountain's brow,
Mocking the storm, when from its vampire shroud
    It pours wild torrents on the plains below!
    Thou, with thy fearless wing, yet free to go,
All undebarr'd, undaunted in thy flight,
    As scorning, while defying, every foe;
Shrieking, with clarion burst, thy conscious might,
That, for a hundred years, hath kept the unchallenged height!

iv

Thou had'st no dread of danger! Thy great pride
    Kept thee from fear! Breasting the wintry storms,
Thy mighty pinions have stretched far and wide—
    Have triumphed, struggling with a thousand forms
    Of terror! Thou hast felt such strife but warms
The sovereign courage; and with joyful shriek,
    Sang of the rapturous battle—its wild charms
For the born warrior of the mountain peak,
He, of the giant brood, sharp talons, bloody beak!

v

How hast thou, in thy very mirth, stretched far
    Thy wings in flight; with freedom that became
Miraculous in license; still at war
    With winds and clouds and storms, that could not tame
    Thy spirit, nor arrest thy sinewy frame!—
Such power and courage, such a billowy flight,
    Man wonders to behold, and calls it Fame!
His soul, when noblest soaring into light,
But follows in thy track, at once of aim and might!

vi

Morning, above the hills, and from the ocean,
    Ne'er sprang aloft into the fetterless blue
With such a glorious grace and godlike motion,
    Nor from her amber pinions cast the dew

That hung about her path, and dimm'd her view,
With greater ease than thou—resolv'd to steer
   Onward, through storm—hast sped with courses true,
Though winds pipe high, and arrowy lightnings glare,
Thy Day-Star wrapt in shroud, through fathomless fields of air.

      vii

Thus eminent in vision as in wing,
   With ever paramount purpose to achieve
The highest; scorning to keep low, and cling
   To earthy thraldoms; but, by might, to grieve
   The emulous crowds who vainly would conceive
Thy secret, and o'ercome the height and space;
   I find a faith that sways me to believe
Thou wast designed, the model of a race,
For conquest born, like thee, and wing'd for loftiest place!

      viii

Let men but once behold thee in thy sweep
   O'er mountain heights to heaven, and straight they grow
To stature; and the big thought, fond and deep,
   Works in them with a restlessness like wo,
   Till they have put on wings, and felt the glow
Of flight and might, like thine; and with their eyes
   Have sought the secrets of the cloud to know;
And bathing their grand plumage in the skies,
Feel ever, with the will, the wing and power to rise!

      ix

Alas, for thee! Even from the chosen race,
   The antagonist nature, loathing thy estate,
With subtle arts, the virtue of the base,
   Barbs the sharp arrow that becomes thy fate.
   The very bright of glory 'genders hate;
The grandeur of the sun himself will bring
   The clouds about the shining of his state;
And he who hath no moral, but a sting,
Will hound with hate the steps of each superior thing.

      x

And thus it is that such as thou go'st down,
   Even at the highest; thy imperial flight

Stay'd, sudden, in career; when, all thine own,
  The sun had made thee brother of his light,
  And earth and skies maintained no eminent height
Baffling thy pinion; rival wings no more
  Waged conflict; and thy might had grown to right!—
Supreme, o'er sky, and rock, and wood, and shore,
Thine was the sovereign wing, as thine the will to soar!

          xi

Of all the race, from out the ranks of men—
  The million moilers, with down-looking eyes—
Perchance but one, beholding thee, as when
  Thy wing was bathed in beauty of the skies,
  Grew lifted by thy flight, and thence grew wise:
To struggle through the cloud, with emulous aim;
  Achieve the grand condition; and arise,
Through hate and envy, rivalry and blame,
To sway, on loftiest terms, in highest homes of fame.

          xii

How hath he watch'd thy wing, to see how vain,
  From his great central eminence, the sun
Shot forth his brazen arrows to restrain
  Thy triumph!—how the storm, with aspect dun,
  His ice-bolts vainly might they beat upon
Thy buckler!—To their presence didst thou fly,
  And Eblis-like, undaunted and alone,
Thou didst confront the Unknown; his power defy,
And to thy sun-god's face uplift thy rebel eye!

          xiii

And he who watch'd thee then had hope to soar
  Even with a wing like thine. His daring glance
Sought, with as bold a vision, to explore
  The secret of his own deliverance,
  As of his thraldom; eager to advance
To sovereign sway like thine—above his race;
  To rise and rule, the better to enhance
The virtues in their gift, with gifts of grace;
Lifting them proudly up to his superior place.

xiv

He triumphs in his flight; but not in aim!
  He strives for those who, with a resolute will,
Reject the blessing; loathe the very fame;
    Prone to the dust and eating of it still,
    As did the serpent, never having fill!
To the base spirit, obligation grows
    A torture, and all gratitude is shame!
Hate finds increase with sense of what it owes,
And while one hand receives, the other 'quites with blows.

xv

He triumphs, but he perishes, like thee,
  O sun-brow'd eagle!—scales the sovran heights;
Cleaves clouds; mounts tempests; feels his pinions free;
    Wantons in worlds of empire; and, in flights
    That fill his soul with paramount delights,
Endows his race with provinces of pride;
    New thoughts and attributes; new fields and rights;
Then sudden, when on topmost height astride,
Falls—smitten by hand so base that even the base deride!

xvi

O glorious bird! whose wing hath pierced the cloud;
  Nor sun nor storm had barrier proof to thee!
Thine was the soul, magnanimous as proud,
    That stoop'd not; but, majestically free,
    Won heights whose secrets man shall never see.
Ah! where thy spirit now? the wing that bore?
    Thou hast lost wing, and all—save liberty!
Death only could subdue—and that is o'er—
Alas! the very hind who slew thee might deplore.

xvii

The missile sped, the victim at his feet,
  How looks he now, with sense of sudden shame,
At the great vans, the pinions that so fleet,
    Held pace with winds, and on their wings became
    A pioneer to realms that have no name!
Wings broken now: and dim the dying eye,
    Dilating with the effort still to claim

Its summits; straining upward for that sky
Which vainly woos its vans to light and liberty.

xviii

A proud exemplar hath been lost the proud!—
  Oh! he that smote thee in thy fearless flight,
Had wiselier follow'd thee, and fled the crowd,
    That babbling now take measure of thy might,
    Stretch wide thy pinions, and with wondering sight
Compute thy talons! Had he not been base,
    With wretched comrades, he had found delight
To take the lessons of thy nobler race,
And make his way, through thought, to some superior place.

xix

'Tis he should weep for thee; for he hath lost
  The model of dominion! Not for him
The mighty eminence; the gathering host
    That worships; the great glittering pomps that dim;
    The tribute homage and the hailing hymn!
He might have had a life, that, to a star,
    Rises from dust, and sheds the holiest gleam,
To light the struggling nations from afar,
And show to kindred souls where fruits of glory are.

xx

Behold him now, where, clamoring o'er his prey,
  He tells you how his secret shaft was sped:
He lurk'd within the rocky cleft all day,
    Till the proud bird rose surging o'er his head,
    At sunset, when he slew him! O'er the dead
Exults he now; yet, had those eyes their fire,
    Were but those talons unclasped, those vans outspread,
The dastard had shrunk trembling from the ire
Whose very glance had quench'd each foe's most fierce desire.

xxi

How basely do we seek to overthrow
  The thing we are not! The ignoble mind
Thus ever aims to strike, with secret blow,
    The nobler, finer beings of their kind;

In this their petty villainy is blind:
They smite their benefactors; men who keep
   Their homes from degradation; men designed
Their guides and guardians; well, if they may creep,
At last, to honoring shrines, and o'er their victims weep.

     xxii
Farewell, proud bird!—this human homily,
   How vain for those who fall, and those who hate!
Who now shall teach thy young ones how to fly?
   Who fill the presence of thy longing mate?
   Ah! type of Genius, bitter is thy fate!
The shaft of meanest boor may leave them lone—
   Thy eaglets and the partner of thy state:
Shaft from the very fen whence thou hast flown,
And feather from the wing thy own wing hath struck down!

(1826, 1860)

TO THE MOUNTAINS.

     i
Wander, O! wander here;
   Sweet is the sky-born fountain,
Bubbling soft, and lapsing clear
   From old Saluda's mountain;
Fly from the city, fly;
   Pleasures will here delight thee;
Children of forest and sky,
   With song and smile invite thee.

     ii
Hither, away from the crowd!
   What can its tedious measure,
Mix'd of the selfish, the mean, the proud,
   Bring to thy soul, of pleasure!
Hither, where life will spring,
   With a rosy blush to meet thee;
And love rejoice to bring
   His tenderest song to greet thee.

iii

Never a cloud is here,
  Shadowing the noon-day splendour,
And the sun, with a purple rare,
  Crowns the sad dusk with the tender;
Here the fond song that greets
  Your ears with delight at even,
Morning with rapture repeats,
  Even as she springs from Heaven.

iv

Sweetest, O! sweetest, fly!
  Hither, where sun-loved Hours,
Skim along, 'neath a soft-blue sky,
  Over a realm of flowers:
Here shall thy young heart glow,
  Here shall thy bright eye glisten;
Love ever glad to vow,
  Beauty most glad to listen!

(1826, 1858)

THE LOVE OF MACKINTOSH.

I saw the love of Mackintosh, she lay
  Upon the warrior's tumuli, and breath'd
Sad music, such as may be heard to stray
  From mermaid, as her string of shells she wreath'd;
She lay upon the tumuli reclined,
And breath'd her song upon the list'ning wind.

Its tones were low and beautiful, they stole,
  Like the low ripple on the O-co-ne wave,
When winds are sighing over it—the soul
  Of feeling, mingled with the strain, and gave
A rich, and melancholy note, which told,
How all that love had sigh'd for, now was cold.

'Twas in that language, which the Indian deems
  The sole-one in his fabled heaven, behind

The western hills, where rivulets nor streams,
    Shall intercept the chase, or cloud the mind:
Where life shall be all morning, where fatigue
Shall never clog the form, tho' wand'ring many a league.

"And" sung the maiden, "shall the white man pale,
    O'erspread our homes, and from the river's bank,
Pluck the red strawberry, and on hill and vale
    Build the great house, from whence the swift-foot[1] shrank,
And from thy grave the cedar tree remove,
And each memorial of thy latest love!

"Yet, 'tis not this," she sung in wilder mood,
    Tho' nought of feeling stole upon her look,
"Not, that the cedar tree has not withstood
    The ploughshare man, or that the silver brook
Must make the mill-dam, and the red-deer shrink,
No longer in its crystal wave to drink;

"But, that the Indian with the sun must glide,
    To the big waters of the western sea,
And leave the vales and mountains, once our pride,
    And thee, O, desert Arrow, fly from thee;
Where none shall know the story of the brave,
And strangers heedless, trample on thy grave.

Here shall thy spirit seek in vain to find,
    When the pale white man has our land o'erspread,
Aught in the wilderness that may remind,
    And tell thee of the glories of the dead;
The tall pine shall be torn away from earth,
As if it never had, in this wide valley, birth.

It is the morning's dawn, I know it well,
    By the faint ripple on the silver stream,
And op'ning of the red flower's early bell,
    And through the distant woods the faint light gleam;
Another day—Oh! Mackintosh will see
Thy woman wand'ring, from thy grave and thee."[2]

(1826)

1. The Deer. I have never heard it termed "Swift-Foot," but have endeavored to conceive in this, as in other instances, the originality and boldness of their figures of epithet.
2. The party of Mackintosh in the Creek nation are those destined to vacate their homes for others farther west.

THE WILDERNESS.

He whose proud intellect forbids to rove
In nature's wild recesses, nor can taste,
From the deep waters of forgotten times,
Of feeling or of joy, with grateful thirst,
Scorning the deeply cavern'd rock, the stream
That glideth with a prattling whispering
O'er pebbly beds, or dasheth listless down,
From the far precipice, I would not seek
Much converse with. He may own a heart
Of subtler intricacy, more remote,
From nature's open book of fruits and flow'rs,
Which all may be acquainted with, but to me
There is a chilliness in lofty thoughts,
That like the mountain's brow, forever wears
A wreath of frostwork, that forbids approach.
I would mark its base, where falls the stream
And buds make merry with the gliding drops,
That steal into their open bells, at morn,
To hide, from the fierce thirstings of the sun at noon.
There is a melody in waterfalls,
A sweetness of repose in solitude,
In the far windings of untrodden wilds—
Where nature is the same, as at her birth,
I love to riot in. My heart forgets
The chains of social life, and I become
A member of the scene, I but survey!
'Tis a fond mystery to hold converse,
With the sweet warbler, who at noontide heat,
Whispers soft carols to the blushing rose,
That opens by the wayside, yet untouch'd
By wanton or uncaring hands, alone.
Nor is it solitude as man may deem—

But a wide glance at all existing nature,
Who sits within a tangled bower, and speaks
To the reposing earth, who straight casts down
His mantle redolent with flowers and fruits
Of mingled sweetness, and of varying hue.

'Twas a deep Indian forest, where I laid
My form, reposing from the noonday sun
Listless. A lowly green grass-plat, my couch,
And a small tuft of flowers, my pillow form'd
Which, cautiously I press'd upon, as not
To crush them, so delicate and soft they grew.
A torrent tumbling from a neighboring hill,
Incessant murmur'd, as it reach'd the base,
Where straight diverging into several streams,
It found a passage thro' a rising rock,
Furrow'd by time in his irregular course.
The tangled flow'rs and vines, a zephyr fill'd,
Discoursing, as the wind-harp, touch'd at night,
By the soft language of the enamour'd sea;
Holding such pleasant music, that it came,
Like fairy spells upon me, and I slept.
Straightway, transported to a by-gone age,
I seem'd to be—tho' still the scene, the same.
But in the distance could I hear the roar
Of the wide waste of waters, and at length,
My vision more expansive grew, and soon
The far Atlantic, created o'er with foam,
And shining, like the sky with many stars,
Torn from the sun, which the disporting waves,
Leaping continual from their boundless bed,
Divided into brilliants, filled my view.
A speck was seen, tho' scarce perception-noted,
Upon the verge of the pale grey horizon,
Like a hand upon the wall at midnight.
It grew in swift proportion as it rose,
Upon the bounding billow, cleaving on
Its cresting foam, and rising at each leap,
With newer energy, and tenser nerve,
Till o'er the waters, with resistless force,
It bore wide way, as up its yellow sides,
The struggling billows leap'd. The ship drew near,

And now upon her deck, might many a face
Awe-fill'd, and wond'ring at the new found land
Be seen—They look'd around on all;
The sky that wore a different aspect,
A clearer blue, and the wide forest,
That unbounded seem'd, in the blue world
Of distance. The trees of giant height,
Mantled in foliage, and the sparkling sand,
Of Ophir seeming, and the mountains vast,
That the extended eye grew pain'd to search
Their summits capp'd with clouds.

   The Chief he came,
Pensive, but calm, as fill'd with grateful pride,
And prostrate on the earth, to him who gave
That earth, before a waste, untrod, unknown,
He bent his soul in pray'r, whilst all around
Spoke audible the same; accepted then
The voice of nature, thro' her thousand echoes,
Straightway repeated it again, again,
Whilst tears of sweet communion fill'd each eye.

            (1826)

INVOCATION.

Spirit! that dwellest in the opening flow'r,
 And bathest in the morning's earliest dew,
And in the honeysuckle's scarlet bow'r
 Hid'st in thy native elements from view;—
Spreadest rich odours to delight the sense,—
And when the wind with mournful eloquence,
 Speak'st to the soft and budding rose,
That lend'st an airy influence to its tone,
Might well be deem'd, impassion'd Music's own.
Spirit, I call thee from thine airy throne,
 To syllable sweet numbers to my love,
In earnest voice, yet such as would not seem
Unfit to mingle with a spirit's dream—
 Nor such, as thou would'st not thyself, approve.

            (1827)

THE GREEN CORN DANCE.[1]

Come hither, hither, old and young—the gentle and the strong,
And gather in the green corn dance, and mingle with the song—
The summer comes, the summer cheers, and with a spirit gay,
We bless the smiling boon she bears, and thus her gifts repay.
       Eagle from the mountain,
          Proudly descend!
       Young dove from the fountain,
          Hitherward bend—
       Bright eye of the bower—
       Bird, and bud, and flower,—
Come—while beneath the summer's sunny glance,
The green leaf peeps from earth, and mingle in the dance.

Not now reluctant do we come to gladden in the boon,
The gentle summer brings us now, so lavishly and soon—
From every distant village, and from deep secluded glen,
They gather to the green corn dance, bright maids and warrior men.
       Of the grave, the gravest,
          Smiling, now come—
       Of the brave, the bravest—
          Give the brave room.
       Loftiest in station,
       Sweetest of the nation,
Come—while beneath the summer's sunny glance,
The green blade peeps from earth, and mingle in the dance.

Now give the choral song and shout, and let the green woods ring,
And we will make a merry rout to usher in the spring—
Sing high, and while the happy mass in many a ring goes round,
The birds shall cheer, the woods shall hear, and all the hills resound.
       Fathers, who have taught us
          Ably our toil,
       For the blessing brought us,
          Share with us the spoil.
       Spirit-God above us,
       Deign thou still to love us,
While long beneath the summer's sunny glance,
We see the green corn spring from earth, and gather in the dance.

                        (1827, 1833)

1. This is one of the primitive and pleasing festivals common to many of the Indian tribes of North America; and presents a pleasing portrait of the naturally devotional temperament of this savage people. On the first appearance of the green corn from the earth, old and young, male and female, assemble together in their several classes, and, rejoicing in the promise of a good harvest, unite in offering their acknowledgment to the Great Spirit for his beneficence. This is the poetry of truth—of religion; and is one of those fine traits in the habits of every people, however savage, by which they still seem to indicate a consciousness, not merely of a superior being, but of a higher hope and destiny for themselves—a consciousness, which must always, to a certain extent, work out its own fulfilment.

ROSALIE.

1

I seek thy pleasant bow'r,
    My gentle Rosalie,
To win its richest flow'r,
    And find that flow'r in thee.
No more, though Spring advances,
    I seek her shining train;
I only meet thy glances,
    And my heart is young again.

2

Thou art the morn, fair creature,
    That wakes the birds and roses,
Thine, is the living feature
    Where light and joy reposes.
All day, young joy pursuing,
    I've found, when caught, that she
Was the maid I had been wooing,
    The wild, young Rosalie.

3

When first the morning's lustre
    Lights up the fleecy plain,
When first the shy stars cluster,
    When the moon begins to wane;
Then do I seek thy bow'r,
    With a spirit fond and free,

To win its richest flow'r,
    And find that flow'r in thee.

(1827, 1837)

TOKENS AND PLEDGES.

I take the rose thou giv'st to-night,
    Tho' by the morrow's dawn 'twill fade;
I bless the gracious star, whose light,
    This ev'ning guides us through the glade—
Though, by the morning, it will be,
A thing, alone, of Memory.

The blooming flow'rs that round thee grow,
    We love, as they were living things;—
The bird that carols sweetly now,
    Approach, and, lo! his form hath wings;—
For Time, who loves no beauty long,
Will steal both blandishment and song.

These, fate and fortune shall remove,
    The winter blight, the summer sear,—
I claim some better pledge of love,
    More lasting, not less sweetly dear:—
Seal me thy vow, with lips of youth,
That blossom for a heart of truth.

Then shall I see the planet fly,
    The rose's odor, fleet or pall—
Lose the bird's music from the sky,
    And smile at parting with them all—
Thine eyes shall light without eclipse,
And songs and flow'rs are on thy lips.

(1827, 1835)

THE APPROACH OF WINTER.

Now come the premature chills of Winter on,
    And cool airs circle o'er our city's breast;
The bright sun leaves no more, when day is done
    His purple isles of beauty in the West;
The winds grow prouder in their wide career,
And bring with shriller cries the remnant of the year.

And morning comes on heavily, and stirs
    With rougher breath, the few remaining leaves
Of the broad Indias, and the lofty Firs
    That bear out longest, as old winter gives,
(If thro' the summer, they can only hold)
Some promise of their lasting 'till they're old.

And Man, the same, dame Nature doth enrich,
    With like analogy—let him struggle thro'
The varied passions of his bosom, which,
    Now storm, now sun-shine, morning light and dew,
We term the *moral* summer of his life—
He may most stoutly bear with age's wintry strife.

Day is more sluggish—tho' he speeds on still,
    Yet like the sturdy peasant of the soil,
Compelled against the freedom of his will,
    To give to hard task-master all his toil;
There are *few suns* to light him on his way—
And *much* to tempt the wanderer to delay.

From us, in this more comfortable sky,
    Where winter loses something of his sour,
It is no wonder he should hate to fly
    To colder regions—if he had the power,
I make no doubt, he would not leave the space,
(For aye,) which holds the sun in its embrace.

But let day speed along—and come the night,
    The sober night of Winter, when the heart
Contracts its circle of affections quite,
    Nor ventures from the fireside to depart;

When the broad sofa, and the fire's rich blaze,
Afford the best of reasons for delays.

When, free from politics, (oh! curse you all,
　　Mercury, *Gazette*, etcetera, thus to crowd
Your columns with the rabble's ceaseless brawl,
　　The folk who are, and folk who would be proud:)
The social converse wings the blust'ring eve—
And frequent movements made, reluctant still to leave.

Nor, do I love the winter night, alone,
　　Because in grateful converse, I may find
The pure affections of the heart, long grown
　　Congenial with my own abstracted mind;
But that I love the beauties of the sky
When the pale moon and stars are circling by.

For then their looks are brighter, and the blue
　　Of the rich sphere is unalloyed and clear:
And there's a virgin chasteness to the view,
　　Which summer could not bring throughout the year;
Then, when leaves whisper to the wooing breeze,
There's a sweet mystery in the bending trees.

But pray, remember reader, that I then
　　Effect some little changes in my dress!
I put on woollen clothes, like other men,
　　Spite of the "Woollens Bill," I rather guess—
And over-all is usually arrayed,
A robe, more vulgarly call'd, "Tartan Plaid."

For tho' I love to look upon the sky—
　　To watch its silent beauties, as the stars
Are slowly wheeling in their orbs on high;
　　To gaze upon the moon, as nothing mars,
The intense and glorious homage, which the Heaven,
And Earth, and Seas, and all, to Him has given,

Yet, I confess, if not provided well
　　With the *said* evidences of respect,
To Him who binds time in his icy cell
　　Old Winter—then my Muse's vein is check'd—

27

My Fancy's flight is chill'd, in no wise flattering,
And my bones ache, and all my teeth are chattering.

Yet, come with thy cool airs, and with thee bring
   Returning health—and want of ice, that we
May view the virgin belle, like bright eyed spring,
   And rosy cheek, red lip, and smile of glee,
Tripping once more with lightsome step and air,
Thro' Broad-street, King-street, Battery, everywhere.

Come with thy bracing airs, tho' some will curse
   Thy intrusive presence—some who now repose,
In chairs, upon the side walks, thou'lt disperse,
   And to the public ease, no longer foes,
Their weak obtrusive vanity will sigh,
That it can now arrest, no more the fair one's eye.

Broad-street too, unimpeded at Chupein's,
   Will lose its loungers—and your presence bless!
The Yellow Fever, too, will curb its reins,
   And drive off to some other shore express!
The Ball rooms will re-open, and the pretty,
And wise, and good, will crowd once more our city.

(1827)

SERENADE.

To thee—when morn is shining,
   My early homage tends;
To thee, when day's declining,
   My evening song ascends.
When grief is sternly swelling,
   And hope's no longer free,
I fly my humble dwelling
   To thee—to thee!

Come forth—thy step is lightest,
   And watchful eyes may see;
Come forth—thy smile is brightest
   And I am proud of thee—

Come forth—rich lips are parting,
   And thought appears in glee,
And sunny eyes are darting
   To thee—to thee.

To thee—upon the waters,
   I wake the serenade;
Thou sweetest of earth's daughters,
   My gentle southern maid.
Come forth—the moon appearest,
   Our path is bright and free;—
I bring a true heart, dearest,
   To thee—to thee!

(1827, 1829)

SONNET.—THE PORTRAIT.

My portrait!—will it serve when I am dead,
   To bring me to thy memory,—when beside
   Thy cheerful fire, thou sit'st at eventide,
Musingly resting on thy hand thy head;
And, from thy mantle, with unconscious glance,—
   How full of speech to friendship!—I look down,
   To meet thine eye fix'd on me in a trance,
That speaks dear memories of a season known,
Precious to both, and full of a sweet faith,
   That won the heart by fond soliciting,
   To that fresh time in nature, the young spring,
Ere hope has found denial, or love scaith—
And to believe in what we see and hear,
Wins all that hope may seek or love find dear.

(1827, 1841, 1845)

THE MINIATURE.

I've thought upon it long, and to mine eyes,
Howe'er my feet have wander'd, it hath been

The sweet star that hath guided through the night,
And brought me home again. I've worshipp'd it,
Even as the Hindoo maiden her gay boat
Of flowers, her heart's first fond experiment,
Sent down the Ganges. I regard it now—
Though all my flowers have wither'd, and my boat
Been baffled nigh to shipwreck—having loss
Of what the waters give not forth again—
With a beseeming reverence. And 'tis all,
So valued, but an image—one that needs
No color from the artist's brush, to raise
In features sensible. They have been touch'd
In more intense embodyings. Pearl and gold
Are but slight gear, its riches to secure,
And honor by their setting. Would'st thou see?—
It is the picture of a delicate love,
Fair lady, and I've set it in my heart—
There, could'st thou look, thy own unwitting lips
Would murmur, with misgivings, to thy self,
"Where sat I to this painter?"

(1828, 1845, 1853)

SONNET.

I will breathe music in the little bell
  That cups this flower—it shall have a tone
  For every passion that the heart has known:—
Tho' hearts their secrets may not often tell,
Mine is a spell to win them—I will wake
  Notes, which tho' new to men, they will not fail
  To tremble when they hear—as an old tale
Will by surprise the absent dreamer take,
And his young heart shall tingle with delight.
  I will win lovers back to the old lure—
  And (greater charm) I will their loves secure,
And then this rose shall ever more be bright—
Each leaf shall be a harp, and every wind
That sweeps the chords—a newer note shall find.

(1828)

SUMMER NIGHT WIND.

How soothingly, to close the sultry day,
Comes the soft breeze from off the murm'ring waves,
That break away in music. And I feel,
As a new spirit were within my veins
And a new life in nature. My hot frame
Awakes from the deep weariness, that fell
Upon it like a cloud of dust and heat—
A newer nerve, braces my weary eyelids,
I gaze and feel the whisperings of night,
Lifting the hair upon my moistened brows—
As if a spirit fann'd me. Slowly, at fits
The wind ascends my lattice, and climbs in,
And swells the shrinking drapery of my couch,
Then melts away around me. Now it comes
Again, and with a perfume in its wake,
Gather'd from spicy gardens. Some fair maid
Knows not who robs her roses of their sweets—
When, at the morn, she finds them drooping low,
From their nocturnal amours. Is it not
A gentle Providence that thus provides,
With odour like to this, the unfavor'd one,
Who else had never known it. Pleasant breeze,
Misfortune well may love thee. Thou hast fled
From gayer regions, pleasant palaces,
Fair groves and gardens of nice excellence—
To wanton with the lonely. It is meet
That he should rise to welcome thee.
Thou art most lavish, and thou should'st not steal
Thro' a close lattice with but half thy train,
When he would gather all of thee, and feel
Thy energies around him. Thou art sweet—
And comest with a mournful whispering
Among the bending trees and watchful flowers
That maketh a rich music for the heart,
Long jarr'd by restlessness and out of tone
From the distemper'd and oppressive heat
Of the long day in Summer.
                              I will sleep
Beneath my window. Thou meanwhile wilt come

And fan thy wings above my throbbing brow,
And put aside the tangles of my hair
With a mysterious kindness. And I know,
That when thou bringest me the sweets of flowers,
Thou'lt bear away my sighs, and bring them back
Laden with comforters, from fairy groves,
That fling away their loveliness to thee,
That they may win thee to the same embrace
Thou dost bestow upon me as I sleep.

(1828, 1836)

THE STREAMLET.

i

Once more in the old places!—and I glow
   Again with boyhood. Once again renew'd,
My wandering feet have found the rivulet's flow,
   My eyes pursue old vistas in the wood;
My heart partakes their consciousness,—I hear
Long lost, but well-known sounds, salute mine ear.

ii

The voices of the forest and the stream,
   And murmuring flights of wind, that through the grove
Come fitfully, like fancies in a dream,
   And speak of wild and most unearthly love—
Such love as hope prefigures to the boy,
Crowning each hillock with a sunbright joy.

iii

There gleams the opening path, and there, below,
   Glimmers the streamlet sparkling through green leaves;
I catch the distant pattering of its flow,
   In sudden murmurs, ere mine eye perceives,
Complaining, as it takes its tiny leaps,
To the scoop'd basin where it sings and sleeps.

iv

It was my father taught me, when a boy,

The winding way that wins it; and I grew
To love the path with an exceeding joy,
  That heeded not the moments as they flew,
So sweetly were they then beguiled—gay gleams
All green and gold, the garments of youth's dreams.

     v

And, sitting by its marge, my father said,
  That streamlet had a language for his ear,
Though vainly did I bend my boyish head,
  With him, but nothing could I ever hear;
Yet, as we did return, he still would say,
He was a better man, so taught that day.

     vi

Yet, surely was there nothing but the flow
  Of idle waters, evermore the same—
A sweet, sad pattering, as they went below—
  I never heard them syllable a name,
Though much I strove, for in my father's look
I read the serious truth of all he spoke.

     vii

An hundred streams like this the country knows,
  From Santee to Savannah—brooks that glide
Through willow tassels—where the laurel blows
  In triumph, and the poplar springs in pride;
A slender thread of silvery white it went,
Winding and prattling in its slow descent.

     viii

Where, then, the mystery of its voice and whence?
  Like other forests those which round it grew;
In what the source of that intelligence,
  Denied to me, which yet my father knew?
Change had not touch'd its waters,—'twas that morn
As small as in the hour when he was born.

     ix

He too, like me, had from its yellow bed
  Pluck'd the gray pebble, and beneath its wave

Had plung'd, in summer noon, his aching head,
　　Glad of the cool delight that still it gave;—
Then he grew up to manhood,—then became
Agéd,—yet was this little stream the same.

　　　x
His grave is in the forest, and he sleeps
　　Far from the groves he loved—his voice no more
Is in mine ear; yet through my memory creeps
　　Its echo, and the wild and solemn lore
He taught me, when we walk'd beside that brook,
Comes back, as now within its waves I look.

　　　xi
The spells of memory to my side command
　　The shadowy thought, nor desolate nor lone;—
Faint are the images that near me stand,
　　Yet are they images of things well known;
Years gather to a moment and inform
The trembling bosom which they fail to warm.

　　　xii
No longer am I desolate, beside
　　These green and sacred borders: in my ear,
As down I bend, where the fast waters glide,
　　Murmurs from sweetest fancies do I hear;
Hope takes the swallow's accents, and they bring
To glad the gathering years, a rich and green-eyed spring.

　　　xiii
And my old sire, he err'd not sure! I feel
　　As if I were a listener to the spell
Of one whose voice is power! My senses reel!
　　It is his language,—I should know it well,—
He speaks through these sweet waters which he loved
In boyhood, and where still our footsteps roved.

　　　xiv
I tremble with a joy—my heart is still,
　　As, swelling up, the accents break the air;
My spirit, troubled, shrinks, even as the rill

When leaves disturb the sleeping waters there;—
My feet are fasten'd with a subtle charm,
Soothing but startling—full of sweet alarm.

xv

The accents gather to familiar sounds,
  And wake anew a lost and well-loved tone,
I hear the sacred words, while silence rounds
  The enchanted circle, and my breath is gone:
They rise melodious, sad, but softly clear,—
My heart receives the music, not mine ear.

xvi

"I have been when thy father dream'd of thee,
  I shall be, when thou dreamest of thy child;
Thy children shall be listeners to me,
  Whose tones so oft thy father's feet beguiled;
I am thy guardian genius,—from the first
My waters still have slaked thy spirit's thirst.

xvii

"When thou shall be forgotten I shall be,
  And to the race that shall succeed thee on,
I will repeat my counsel, as to thee,
  And like thy footsteps now, shall theirs be won,
From the thick gathering—from the crowded street
With me, within the solitude, to meet.

xviii

"And I shall soothe their spirits, as I now
  Soothe that of him, their sire; my streams shall be
A gracious freshness for each burning brow,
  While my soft voice shall whisper, sweetly free,
Tempering to calm the bosom vex'd and bow'd
By the unfeeling clamors of the crowd.

xix

"Go forth, fair boy, and happy be thy years,
  Forget not soon the lessons, long our theme,
Nor, when the growing Time shall teach thee tears,
  Desert these shady bowers—this sacred stream;

'Twill be my care, when man hath taught thee gloom,
To bring thy worn heart back to all its bloom.

    xx

"Look on these waters when thy mood is sad,
   Fly to these groves, when close pursued by power;
These shall restore thee all that made thee glad,
   And bring oblivion of the present hour;
Mine is the stream that must forever roll,
A memory not of earth, but of its soul.

    xxi

"I keep affections pure—I save the heart
   From Earth's pollutions;—treasured in my wave
Is healing, and the power to make depart
   Bad passions, those worst tyrants; and to save
The victim from himself, and still restore
The angel whiteness of the soul once more.

    xxii

"Oh, when the world hath wrong'd thee, seek me then,
   Though, hapless, from thy better self estranged;
Fly to these waters from the strifes of men,
   And gazing in them shall thy heart be changed;
Though years have risen between, and strife and scorn,
Yet shall thy face, once more, be that thou wear'st this morn."

                          (1829, 1840, 1853)

TO———.

Look on me, am I sad,
   More stern or gloomy now,
Than when I've met thee, warm and glad,
   With freshness on my brow.
If there remain one shade
   Of gloom about mine eye,
Where smiles for thee alone have play'd,
   'Tis not where it should lie.

To thee, however dark
  My gloomy fortunes be;
However other eyes may mark—
  What thou should'st see;
To thee, my looks and heart the same
  As tried long since, must prove;
The one all smiles, the other flame—
  Both harbingers of love!

(1829)

BALLAD.

THE SLEEPING CHILD.

i

My child, upon thy slumbering eye,
  What lovely visions now descend,
  Sweet shapes, that with thy fancies blend,
And woo thee for Eternity!

ii

The smile of gladness on thy face,
  Declares a presence in thy heart;—
  Celestial visitant, whose art
Would make it Love's abiding place.

iii

And pure ideals, fond and warm,
  Are shaping now thy infant thought—
  By these, the latent virtues taught
Grow strong, and eminent of charm.

iv

Glad forms before thee flit and play;—
  The Future, with her promise fair;
  Love that floats free in upper air,
And Friendship, that makes smooth the way.

v

And hallow'd Truth, and genial Hope,
  These bend above, and, with thy dreams,

Twine flowers of fancy, shed the gleams,
That through the clouds the vistas ope!

vi

And how that happy heart pursues
   Each avenue of light, that shows
   Where, in sweet harbours of the Rose,
Sits Beauty, that in worship woos.

vii

She builds thy little Temple fair,—
   And Hope, and Love, and virgin eyes,
   Seize on thy soul with glad surprise,
And raise a joyous altar there!

(1829, 1857)

TO MY FRIEND.

Ambition owns no friend, yet be thou mine!—
   I have not much to win thee,—yet if song
   Born of affection, may one name prolong,
My lay shall seek to give a life to thine.
Let this requite thee for the honoring thought
   That has forgiven me each capricious mood;
   Dealt gently with my phrenzies, school'd my blood
And still with love my sad seclusion sought.
And when the gray sod rises o'er my breast,
   Be thou the guardian of my deeds and name,
   Defend me from the foes who hunt my fame,—
And, when thou show'st its purity, attest
Mine eye was ever on the sun, and bent,
Where clouds and difficult rocks made steep the great ascent.

(1829, 1845, 1853)

THE PEACE OF THE WOODS.

Thou hast enamor'd me of woodland life,
   Good shepherd, for thou showest me, in thy faith,

More than thy argument, how free of scaith
Thy cottage—how secure against the strife
That beats on prouder dwellings. So I glean
   Thy secret from thee, of true happiness,
   Inbred content, and quiet humbleness,
That striving only at the golden mean,
Can never be o'erthrown by soaring high,
And vexeth not the glare of envious eye.
Thy blessings are of that serener kind,
   Which, as they rouse no passions up, must be
   Liked to that breeze benign that strokes the sea
From rages into murmurs. No rude wind
Disturbs thy placid waters, and deforms
The glory of thy peace, with its unreckoning storms.

(1829, 1845, 1860)

CONFOUNDED BORES.

I care not to record the years,
That Time, at each returning bears,
   Far other aims for me—
To meet him, on his rapid flight,
With something, which, however slight,
   He shall not shame to see.

Alas! the rules so oft laid down,
I find neglected for the town—
   My days are not my own;
This one, or that, would try his pow'r
In social confab for an hour,
   And thus the hour is gone.

My wife, inclined to spend the day
Abroad, should surely have her way—
   There's no great harm in that,
Were she contented, so to do
Alone,—but 'husband must go too:
   So bring his stick and hat!'

That day is lost. Luxurious diet
For two more days disturbs my quiet—
   And then, to time mispent,
I'm doom'd to add the greater ill
Of physic and a doctor's bill,
   By way of punishment.

At eight, my study nicely aired,
My pen and paper all prepared,
   I sit me down to write;
When hark! the knocker—to the door
The servant flies—another bore
   Is full before my sight.

With moody brow, and strange grimace,
I meet his broad and busy face—
   He talks of this and that;
The travelling English—men of straw—
And women impudently raw—
   And other slop-shop chat.

His own opinions! —God! how strange—
His penny intellect's small change—
   'I'—'mine'—'we'—'number one!'—
Until my vex'd and fever'd blood
Has roused me to a savage mood,
   Politeness still would shun.

Yet how escape?—In vain he sees
My eyes grow dim—my answers freeze
   Myself—yet touch him not;
Yet all the while, he knows I wish
The devil had him in a dish,
   On coals confounded hot.

Of all the fools that life beset,
At least, of all the kinds I've met—
   Oh hear my prayer, ye Gods!
Preserve me from the monstrous ass,
Whose impudence becomes the pass
   To bore his brother-sods.

(1829, 1830)

AT PARTING.

i

I have no joy when thou art far,
   And if thou need'st must fly,
My soul shall feel perpetual war,
   Till thou again art nigh.
Yet may the seas be quiet seas.
   And may each breeze be fair,
And every cloud, as soft as these,
   Be beautiful and clear.

ii

Thus, should the season haply smile,
   When thy returning prow,
Shall bear thee by old Moultrie's isle,
   Thou passest heedless now;
As stedfast in its faith, my heart,
   With Love's fond fires shall burn,
As now, when first about to part,
   It counts on thy return.

(1829, 1845)

FRAGMENT.

————They've come back
To their old fathers' graves. The desolate
Retread the waste and wilderness once more,
To the rude homes of childhood. They retrace
The well-remembered path-ways,—they ascend
The rough and jagged rock, precipitous,
Gathering a wide and boundless horizon,
To the young eye familiar—making young
The aged eyes that hail it,—they embrace
The ancient pines, and know them for old friends
That gave their sports a shelter. Thus, the men.—
The women sit and weep beside the hill,
They care not to ascend.

Sad outcasts! They are happy, and forget
Their toilsome knowledge of the lonely way,
Their long delay, faint heart and weariness,
And lack of shade and water, when the sun
Shot downward his red arrows,—sad no more,—
Thus blessed at last with the sweet, glimmering sight
Of their old homes—the places of their play,
And days now gone forever.

(1829, 1838)

BALLAD—STANZAS.

i

I loved an eye, a gentle eye,
   I've loved it long, and love it now;
   And still it looks upon my brow,
Unchangeable, unchangingly.

ii

It could not change though it is gone—
   For 'twas a thing all life, and so,
   It could not with the body go
To that dark chamber, cold and lone.

iii

It had a touch, a winning touch,
   Of twilight sadness in its glance,
   And oft it wore a dewy trance
That made me sad I loved so much.

iv

For life is selfish, and the tear,
   Is seldom sought and cherished late;
   And I deplored the heavy fate,
That made a thing of grief so dear.

v

Through sunny hours, and cloudy hours,
   And hours that had nor sun nor cloud—

That eye was wrapt, as in a shroud,
Such shroud as winter flings o'er flow'rs.

vi

It had a language known to me,
   Though hidden from the world beside;
   And many a grief it strove to hide,
Came out at last, and I *would* see!

vii

I could not stay the grief, nor chase
   The moisture from the drooping eye;
   I gave—'twas all—my sympathy,
And Sorrow's hand was on my face.

viii

'Twas on my face—'twas in my heart,—
   And when, at length, the maiden died,
   Whom so I lov'd, I never sigh'd,
And tearless, saw her spirit part.

ix

They laid her coldly on the bier,
   And took me to my home away;
   Nor knew, that from that fatal day,
I had no home, but with her—there.

x

They watch'd my steps and scann'd my face,
   And when they watch'd me I grew stern,—
   For curious eyes have yet to learn,
How Sorrow dreads each finger trace.

xi

Mine was too deep a love, to be
   The common theme of idle tongue—
   And every word they utter'd, wrung
My spirit into agony!

xii

I live a sad and settled wo;—
   I care not if the day be fair,

Or foul;—I would that I were near
The maid they buried long ago!

(1829, 1838)

THE MODERN LION.

"*Bottom.* Let me play the lion too. I will roar that will do any man's heart good to hear me." . . . "I will aggravate my voice so, that I will roar you as gently as any sucking dove; I will roar you an 'twere any nightingale."

i

I am a pretty gentleman,
    I walk about at ease,
My habits are all pleasant ones,
    And very apt to please.
I dress with taste and tidyness,
    My coat's a purple brown;
And with a bamboo in my hand,
    I switch my way 'bout town.

ii

The ladies like me, terribly—
    And 'pon my soul, I'm sure,
My absence were a sad disease
    That I alone could cure.
To me they all refer at once,
    My judgment, it is law;
I fill them all with love of me,
    And that begets their awe.

iii

'Twixt twelve and three I shop with them,
    At four o'clock I dine—
And 'twixt the six and eight I loll,
    Or push about the wine.
Then for the evening coterie,
    And for the evening chat,
I put my lilac breeches on,
    And take my velvet hat.

iv

My visage is remarkable—
    For so they all agree,—
At least, they're all in love with it,
    And that's enough for me.
'Twould do you good to see my face,
    And forehead, I declare;
One half the latter smooth and smack,
    The other black with hair.

v

Two different pictures should you see;—
    My right profile is grand;
The Brigand pattern, savage—sad—
    Most admirably plann'd.
While, on the left—Adonis' self
    Would much his fortune bless,
To own my style of countenance,
    And steal my fav'rite tress.

vi

I have been painted many times—
    But never to my mind;
I think to sit to Inman soon
    As I can raise the wind.
I'll write a book to print with it,
    And in a little while,
Employ the 'Mirror' and the 'Star'
    To show me up in style.

(1830, 1837)

STANZAS AT EVENING.

Written in the Southwest (1831).

Night closes fast around my way,
    And still the cot I seek is far,
Yet, through the forest shines a ray,
    Most welcome, in the evening star.

Mild breezes from the west arise,
   And fan my cheek and stir my hair;
And gazing on these woods and skies,
   My lonely heart forgets its care.

These solemn woods offend me not;
   And these sad murmurs of the wind,
To him who loves the quiet lot,
   Bring gentlest feelings to the mind.

And, lo! the rising moon is bright,
   Far glancing from her eastern throne;
The clouds grow glorious in her light,
   And all that's lovely is her own.

She rises like a dream of love,
   Beguiles the sense, informs the sight,
Subdues the heart and bids it move
   To softest measures of delight.

Visions of other days she wakes,
   The past, with all its joys, is hers;
Sweet thoughts she brings, sad thoughts she takes,
   And blesses all her worshippers.

Benignant still, she prompts the heart,
   With sadness, to such sweet allied,
We would not have the one depart
   To lose the other from its side.

How sweetly does she silver now
   The heaven she fills, the earth she lights,
'Till lovely grows the mountain's brow,
   Whose hoary frown by day affrights.

My steed, whose feet disturb the stream,
   Drives flakes of silver from its bed,
And the long prairie grasses gleam
   With tufted jewels far outspread.

There, rising high to greet her rays,
   Yon giant pine begins to glow;

And now, a shooting beamlet plays,
   Through many a leaf, on groves below.

Dark grow the forests, but mine eye
   Still cheers my warm and lightened heart,
As, stretching far o'er wood and sky,
   I see a thousand splendors dart.

Oh, could it be, that not alone
   My feet might seek my dwelling here,
When life is pure, where cloud is none,
   Where earth is rich and nature fair!

Some chosen spirit could I find,
   My own sweet minister to be,
The kindred creature of my mind,
   The bud of all the bower to me;—

How happy then!—This forest, far
   From human crowd and city strife,
Lit by yon pure and perfect star,
   Gives promise of the sweetest life.

Here, chastened by each soothing ray,
   Without the lure to pride or crime,
Life is a happy child, at play,
   That laughs at place and mocks at time.

And she should make my cottage bower,
   With leaflet green and chaplet rare,
And be, alike, the bird, the flower,
The beam, the song, the blessing there!

                          (1831, 1841)

SONG.

While the silent night goes by,
And the winds have scarce a sigh,
And the hours seem not to move,
Do I think of thee, my love!

And the moonlight's on the hill,
And the voice of man is still—
Silent, in our walks, I rove,
And I think of thee, my love!

Every thing recals thee now,
And I see thy maiden brow,
Large blue eyes that sweetly rove,
While I speak to thee, my love.

In thy maiden bosom's swell,
There is yet a deeper spell;
And its gentle throbbings prove,
All thy truth to me, my love.

Walks thy spirit now with mine,
'Neath the calm and clear moonshine?
Dost thou seek in sleep our grove,
Dost thou dream of me, my love?

(1831)

THE WINTER FLOWER.

i

When winter comes with icy mien,
    To silver o'er this little brook,
Upon its banks thy form is seen,
        By all forsook.

ii

No shrub then lingers on the plain,
    To feed the warm and watchful gaze;
Nor sprig of grass the fields retain,
        Nor blade of maize.

iii

Far as the searching eye may bend,
    O'er gentle slope and bedded vale,
The barren, cheerless plains extend,
        Thou tell'st their tale.

iv

Thou, of the autumn train the last,
   A mournful truth thy form conveys,
Thou lingering relic of the past,
     And brighter days.

v

No other flow'r, that late could vie,
   Superior once in bloom to thee,
May now unfold, beneath the sky,
     Its pageantry.

vi

Struck in the sullen clod too deep,
   Thy roots the wintry winds defy,
And while thy thousand brethren sleep,
     Thou lift'st thine eye.

vii

What secret spring of life is thine,
   And what art thou, pale flow'r, to gain
Such partial favor, thus to shine
     Last of thy train?

viii

Unhurt, when all around are dead,
   Unshrinking, though the blasts arise,
And lifting still thy fearless head,
     In fearful skies.

ix

Such lot, methinks, can ne'er be blest:
   To feel ourselves in life alone,—
A late, and watchful, lingering guest,
     When all are gone!

(1825, 1832, 1860)

BROKEN SLUMBERS.

I named her in my dream, and with the sound
Of that dear name I waken'd, and look'd round,
As if, half-dreaming still, I should espy,
The spirit I had summon'd hovering nigh.
That name dispersed my slumbers, and no more
Might I that night the unwilling dream implore;
Sleep fled my eyes, and, slowly, the sad night,
Gathered the weary hours upon its flight,
And all was calm, except within the breast
From which that spirit's name could rob all rest.
And if, perchance, a moment's slumber came
To still, if not to satisfy my frame;
Dread forms of memory rose, and many a wo,
Stood up before me sternly,—a sad show,
As in the daylight I have seen them stand,
Things of consuming flesh, and skinny hand,
Worn and diseased,—and eyes all glazed and dull,
And cheeks all dead, that once were beautiful,—
Now passing gloomily before my glance,
Whilst fix'd, I lay, as in a spirit trance,
Nor strove to move a limb, nor breathe a pray'r,
To break that spell, so desolate and drear.
And then I saw thee change to what thou wert,
All matchless, as when first upon my heart,
Thy presence had the magic of a spell,
I loved too dearly, not to mourn too well.
Such as thou wert, when to thy rounded cheek,
Like rose-tints to the blossom, came a streak,
Like that of spring; and in thy gentle eye,
With softened grace, there shone a spirit high,
That well became the lofty snow-white brow,
Thou wor'st in life, and wear'st in memory now.
Oh! buried one, and beautiful, and dear,
I trace thee to the skies, and still thou'rt fair,
And in fair company. I look and see
In dreams, a glorious crowd that beckon me—
Sweet phantoms,—and the grave hath for me more
True friendships, than my sad heart knew before,—
A father's watchful eye, a mother's love,

Pure as the angels feel who burn above;
And thou, more dear than all,—and, roused to pride,
I single out full many a form beside,
Of dead affections, 'mongst the pure and good,
Like early roses, blasted in the bud;
Untimely cropt, and leaving on the stem,
The fellow that had better gone with them,
Than thus, a lingerer, when the crowd are gone,
Moaning the many dwindled down to one!

(1832, 1842)

ELEGIAC.

The beautiful, the silent! Do they come,
   At midnight to my couch? Does she return,
With all her early loveliness and bloom,
   Re-animate and glorious, from her urn?
To keep sweet watch above my slumbering brow,
   To paint dear visions to my wandering sense,
To bring me back in dreams, the memory now,
   That cannot sleep while seeking recompense,
For life's remediless ruin. Doth she stand,
   When whispering shadows gather with the night,
Waving them from my couch with guardian hand,
   Making my slumbers then one long delight,—
Of joys it once had been my joy to taste;
   Of beauties it had been my balm to see,
Of hopes that time hath scatter'd all to waste,
   And many a bliss too blessed far for me?
Oh! comes she in the deep night to my side?
   Young, beautiful!—as when in boyhood's hour,
She stood a thing of life, my dream, my bride,
   And hung upon my bosom like a flower!

(1832, 1842, 1858)

STANZAS BY THE SEA-SHORE.

Roll on, ye restless waters!—Roll,
   Dread ocean, to thy drear extreme,
Where hope may never soothe the soul,
   Nor Joy afford a single gleam;
I know no Joy to kindle mine,
   Since all I ever loved hath fled,
And yet, how bootless to repine,
   Unless our tears could wake the dead.

And such, if Sorrow had a spell—
   And such, if Passion held a charm—
And such, if Love could cherish well,
   What Fate could doom to cruel harm!—
Would be the power of many a tear,
   Shed, gentlest blossom, here for thee;
And rising from thy slumbers drear,
   Again thou'dst come, Beloved!—to me.

How could I live to bear thy loss,—
   To watch the dreary hours alone,—
To feel the world's eternal cross,
   Nor turn to meet thy cheering tone;
To hear thy soothing lips repay
   For all earth's bitterness and hate,—
To feel and know that, day by day,
   Thou wast my Angel 'gainst my Fate!

How can I fondly thus recall,
   The all that thou hast been to me,
Thou that hast sweetened Being's gall,
   And in my bonds still made me free;
That cheer'd my heart, that chain'd mine eye,
   That made my soul grow calm and light,
Until, methought, thou could'st not die,
   Thou wert so pure, so good, so bright!

And Desolation reigns alone,
   Where many a blessing found abode;
And, in the place of pleasures gone

The mourner lifts his heavy load;
And Grief is sovereign at his heart;
  And none may bless, and few condole,
And tears are now his only part:—
  Roll on, ye sleepless waters, roll!

(1829, 1832, 1852)

THE FEARFUL MEMORY.[1]

It comes but as a dream, yet is no dream,
And my rack'd soul requires no sleeping hour
To shadow forth its presence. It is here:—
By daylight and in darkness still the same,
Keeping its watch above my desolate heart,
And, when it would escape to other thoughts,
Bringing it back, with stern unbendingness,
To its curst prison, and its scourge and rack!

Some years, and many thoughts we never lose,
Howe'er time changes. This is one of them!—
Seasons on seasons, since that hour is gone,
Have passed away, with many a circumstance,
To root the dreadful token from my soul;—
And yet its fearful memory, freshly still,
Stands by me, night and day;—and, with a voice,
Monotonous as the evening bird, sends forth
One fearful adjuration—one deep tone
Of dread reproach, and omen, and dismay!

It is no flickering shadow on the wall,
That startles me at midnight, and expels,
The sweet sleep and fond quiet, all away—
Fills me with horrid thoughts, with many a dread,
And leaves me wan and spiritless at dawn.
No childish spectre, such as fancy paints,
Sudden, before the trembling criminal,
When the bell tolls at midnight, and the vaults
Of the old minster echo back the sound,
With replication wild—haunts me with scowl

53

Of horrible complexion—a vague spright,
Of chattering teeth, and wan and empty glance,
And stale, lack-lustre semblance!—Would it were—
I were not half the wretch that now I am!

Back to that fearful hour, I need not look,—
The past is ever present! There it stands—
The time, the scene, the dreadful circumstance,
Vividly in my soul, and fresh as when
Each fell particular of thought and deed,
Came to me, as a parcel of myself,
Destined thence, ever, to abide with me!
Let folly, all agape, at some dread mask,
Wonder, with shooting pulse and bristling hair,
At the poor trick of fancy, which invests
Each fleeting, flick'ring shadow on the wall
With spiritual semblance. Nought of this
Troubles my sense, and with unmeasured arm,
Shakes some unshapely terror! I see nought—
'Tis in my soul the fiend hath ta'en abode,
And yields not up his watch. There, all night long,
He tells the monotonous story of my crime;
Paints, in detail, each dread particular,
With horrible recital. On each part,
Dwells with a deep minuteness, loud and long,—
Portrays my haggard fright to mine own eyes,
At mine own work of sorrow; and forbears,
Not even when day has come, and with it brought,
The busy mart, the crowded festival.
There, in the wildest hum, he seeks me out,
Becoming my sole partner. In my ear,
Some feature, even more dreadful than the rest,
With jeering tone and gibbering laugh of scorn,
He whispers—and the sound like rushing fire,
Or, subtlest poison, from the mountains won,
When spirits are abroad—through my chilled veins,
Without arrest, goes sure and fatally;—
And all grows dark around me—and I lose
The crowded presence, and the lights grow dim,
And I behold myself, again, as once—
In that old hall—the long-gone hours restored—
Darkness around me, save, at intervals,

When inauspicious lightnings broke the gloom,
And the foul bat from out his sooty wing,
Shot through the heavy air, a glimmering ray,
That deepen'd the accumulated gloom,
Of that deep gloom about me. Then, once more,
Appears that form of matchless excellence,
Creature of ravishing mould, and grace that came,
From Eden, ere 'twas blasted. Did I then,—
Cold, selfish, worthless,—as even then I was—
Destroy a flower so bless'd and beautiful?—
Bless'd in itself, and more than happy now,
Yet doubly bless'd with me its enemy.
She comes to me again—I see her now—
How glorious every glance—how smooth each limb,
In exquisite proportion, never match'd;
All rich but ruin'd, and the sightless gaze,
The sole perfection dimmed. Could I have seen,
That moment, what, a moment after, stood
Before each sense of my spirit, she had been,
A living creature—I, a happy one!

And yet, I struck her not. The blow that reft
Earth of so fair a creature—lopt away,
Suddenly from its stem, as recklessly,
The ploughshare smites the daisy—was not mine;—
That crime is spared my soul; and yet, the crime,
For which I suffer this pursuing fiend,
Was not less deadly, though less dark and dread.
Yet, in that Gothic hall, as then I stood,—
Scarce seeing—all unseen—save by the God,
Whose minister this demon has become—
Even now I stand, beholding all anew,
With freshest glance; and ever since that hour,
Which brought the doom on her, the curse on me,
The deadly circumstance, the fearful crowd,
Of images, all terrible and stern,
Is present to my soul. Before my eyes,
Limned in the outline, by a scanty gray,
Thrown in the latter aperture, from which,
The broken shutter, creaking sullenly, swings,—
I mark a prostrate form—a silent mass,

No feature marked—no colour, shape or face,
Tone or expression—nothing to the sight,
Worthy the sight's observance; yet to me,—
My soul aroused and with a spirit's gaze—
All's clear—all vivid, bright. Her eye no more,
Sends forth its fine expression—all is dim!—
The dark knife lies beside her—in her hands,
The fatal scrawl that drove her to despair,
Writ in my madness. I can see no more.
But madden as I move, for, at each step,
My feet do clammily adhere to the floor,
As if 'twere clotted blood that bound them there,
Unwilling they should fly—unyielding still.
In vain would I retreat—for as I move,
Wildly, with face turned backward on the scene,
I fain would fly from, down the narrow stairs,
I hear the trickling drops, keeping full pace,
In concert with my feeble falt'ring steps.
Blood—blood!—pursuing wheresoe'er I fly.
And reeking to the heavens, and calling down
This vengeful memory, that, with demon spite,
Inhabits mine own soul, and makes me yield,
A prison of myself—of mine own heart,
A prison meet for mine own punishment.

What further of my story would you hear,—
What boots the name, the deed, the hour, the place,
And each foul feature of what men call crime:
Brief name, to mark a history so long,
So wild, so very fearful as is mine,—
Was hers—is memory's still. It were all vain;
Words are not things, and fail to paint our thoughts,
When they are dark and terrible as mine,
Else, should you hear it all, from lips that now,
Blanch with the recollection. But you see
Its truth in what you see. A little while,
The demon will give up its dread abode,
And still will be the tongue of memory—
Desolate soon must be its dwelling place,
And the torn spirit it has rack'd so long,
Freed from its presence and its bonds all broke,

Will seek—ah, will it find what still it seeks,
The form it crush'd—the spirit it deplores.

(1833)

1. The idea of the following poem was suggested by the perusal of a single and small paragraph, rendered from a German romancer of repute. The object was to furnish a grouping of successive and corresponding images and ideas, in themselves vague and indistinct, which would nevertheless form, when taken together, a perfect narrative, such as, in matters of jurisprudence, may be considered the collected body of circumstantial evidence necessary to the conviction of the criminal. How far I may have been successful in carrying out my design, it is not with me to determine.

THE EXILE.—A BALLAD.

i

Well, though thou hast denied me long, with words of scorn or strife,
And sent me forth in exile far, I love thee more than life:
Thy hills, thy vales, thy streams, thy woods, thy skies of softest blue;
And, though thy sons have done me wrong, I feel I love them too.
They can not rob my heart of that sweet solace, where I go,
To love, in Christian mood and mind, the thing that is my foe;
Nor can they take from me the pride, held dearly through the past,
Whate'er my future lot may be, with thine that lot was cast!

ii

Thou hast had me in thine arms, thou hast borne me on thy knee,
Yet hast thou been, my mother land, but a step-dame unto me;
A thousand sons thou hast caress'd, with kindlier deed and tone,
Yet sent me forth, a thing unbless'd, to sink or swim alone.
No loving word to soothe my heart, no hope to cheer my way,
Unmov'd, thou saw'st my feet depart, and still thy smile was gay;
Thou kep'st the revel in thy halls, while sorrow sate in mine,
Nor heard the last, fond, pleading calls my heart sent out to thine!

iii

Yet did I, with thy favorite sons, heir all that gives thee name;
My fathers bravely struck, with thine, for liberty and fame;
Their blood is on thy battle-fields; their toils have served to raise
Those glorious monuments on which their son no more shall gaze;
Their groans, from prison-ship, I hear;—alas! they speak for mine;

Now poured, at midnight, for thine ear, across this waste of brine.
Ah! little did they think to hear, in homes so bravely won,
The doom of exile, dark and drear, for this their only son!

iv

I see thee on my vision rise, O clime forever dear!
Thy revelry but mocks the pang, in which thou dost not share.
The stranger comes, an honor'd guest; thy proud saloon is bright;
Forms swim in twiring dance and eyes grow glorious in his sight.
A little hour and he forgets—nay, mocks the love that shows
Such homage to the foreign form, of whom it nothing knows;
While at thy knee, thy native sons, unlov'd, uncherish'd, pine,
For, oh! how small the boon of love, so precious as 'tis thine!

v

But yield them *that*, and they will bound, in danger's path, to dare,
With song and sword, to serve and strike, and all thy woes to share.
How true their hearts, how strong their hands—what deeds
    unmeasured done,
To prove their might, assert thy right, and both to render one!
'Tis but to claim them as thine own, with loving pride and care,
Accord the smile for service done, and bid them do and dare;
Watch fondly o'er each infant grace, each germ of goodly pow'r,
And give each noble talent place, and every Muse her flow'r.

vi

Yet, let me not upbraid thee now, whose pride it still hath been
To lift thy name, and win thee fame, though nought from thee I win;
To paint, as I would have thee show, a glorious form and high,
Beyond approach, and worthy all thy sons' idolatry;
Depict the deeds that make thy past a grand romance of pride;
Show how for thee the patriot strove, and how the hero died;
On what near fields, in trial stern, the breast and blade they bare,
And make the foreign foeman learn to honour thee in fear!

vii

How fenced thee against his shaft and hate, and foot to foot in fight,
Pluck'd from his grasp thy shield of state, and sworded it with might!
And from the past, with tongue of fire, speak to the present hour;
Rouse living hearts, with fond desire, to toils of equal power;
Wake patriot love to jealous strife, and patriot will, to aim
At all the arts that win from life, security for fame;

Till, over all, supreme thou stand'st, the world's bright eye, that far,
Wins wond'ring nations to thy feet, their cynosure and star.

viii

No more! no more! the passion fond, which makes the heart
    complain,
Hath birth in something yet beyond, which must not sing in vain:
'Tis love that moans o'er love denied—the privilege to share
That service in a field of pride, which needs to brave and dare.
Even now thy dangers threaten all—thy future as thy past—
The very men who man thy wall, shrink cowering from the blast;
The foe insidious makes his way, with near approach, and arts
That well may rouse the patriot fear in fond and faithful hearts.

ix

Where are the champions now that stood, the favorites in thy grace?
They traffic with the hostile brood, for pension or for place.
The motes that peopled all thy beams, the flies that suck'd thy
    flow'rs—
Are these the things to fling thy flag defiant from thy towers?
Call back thy banish'd sons that knew no favour at thy hands;
Go seek them where with strength they strew the wilds of western
    lands;
And if their love be such as mine—as *theirs*, when bade depart—
There shall not sound one call of thine, in one unwilling heart!

(1833, 1859, 1860)

STANZAS.

Written on the North River in 1833.

i

The hour is still, and from afar,
    Wafted by all that's sweet in night
The tones of some sweet girl's guitar
    Are swelling from yon distant height,—
And many a former thought returns,
    Of all the loved, of all the lost,
'Till memory fills her cherished urns,
    With flowers that long have felt the frost.

ii

Hush! o'er the waters, hark the swell,—
  I see them come, the spirit band,
The joys, in soothing strains to tell,
  Of that remote, that happy land.
They come,—those gentle Southern gales,—
  They lift me up,—they wrap me round,
And bear me to those lovelier vales,
  Where all my earlier hopes were found.

iii

Ah me, I wake! but still the dream,
  Whilst comes that music, lingers yet,—
And still I hope that every gleam,
  That cheered my boyhood, has not set;—
That some survive the tempest's stroke,
  Which in its pathway overthrew
Affection's deepest planted oak,
  And the frail twining ivy too.

iv

Oh! like the wild strain heard by night
  Borne from the Æthiop's lonely boat,
When cheering time's encumbered flight,
  He wins the rude horn's sweetest note,—
So, unknown minstrel, now thy strain,
  Arousing liveliest memory,
Bears my rapt spirit home again,
  And makes the Hudson, Congaree.

(1833, 1837)

SONG.

Oh! with a delicate art, most quaintly taught,
Meetly around thy lattice thou hast wrought,
  In many a mazy twine,
  The flow'ry vine.

Its sweets reward thee, and as Summer comes,
It yields thee up its odors and its blooms,

And folded in thy breast,
Its buds are blest.

Am I less valued than the Summer flower
Whose little life of sweets is but an hour?—
Am I of humbler birth,
And frailer earth?

Thou'st taught my fond affection to entwine,
Folding around thee as that gadding vine,
Oh, take me, with like art,
Unto thy heart.

(1833)

SONG.—I HAVE LIVED IN FANCIES.

I have lived in fancies,
Heart and soul at play,
Dream'd through bright romances,
Night and day!
Loved too well the dreaming
Much to think of self;
Knew no arts of scheming
After power or pelf.

Life with me was loving;
Love the only true;
And, with fancies roving,
Love was all I knew.
To be loved was ever
All my simple art;
To be sure forever
Of one loving heart!

Ah! the worldly fashion,
Sternly mock'd at mine;
My proud, foolish passion
Was not thine.
Thou hast lost the many,

Whom thy spells had won,
And, unloved by any,
  We are both undone!

(1834, 1860)

FAREWELL STANZAS.

On Leaving a Northern City, to Three Sisters,
Cornelia, Caroline and Mary.

Ere many days, ere many days,
  And he who fain would never fly,
Must lose, perchance for aye, the rays,
  That beam from each benignant eye,—
Yet would he know, when far remote,
  Doom'd in some distant wild to pine,
His memory still was in your thought,
  Cornelia, Mary, Caroline.

He would rejoice, in graver mood,
  To turn his thoughts' direction back,
And from the dim and gloomy wood,
  Retrace awhile his memory's track—
And when sad thoughts would o'er him steal
  When all would teach him to repine,
From out the three, he'd choose Corneile—
  Cornelia, Mary, Caroline.

But at another hour, if thought,
  Less grave, should oversway his breast,
And gentler moods, by fancy wrought,
  Should move his heart, nor be repress'd;
Then with a wing as fond as free,
  His soul should seek this land of thine,
And choose the last from out the three,—
  Cornelia, Mary, Caroline.

In wilder hour and livelier mood,
  A laughing spirit should preside,
And from his memory's solitude,

He'd seek a form of fire and pride—
He'd roam the wilds and deserts drear,
   And where the lights of Twelfth-street shine,
Choose Mary from the triad there,
   Cornelia, Mary, Caroline.

(1834)

"COME BACK SOON."

i

'Twas thus she cried, as late I bore,
My footsteps from this happy shore;
   And still within mine ear,
"Oh! come back soon," fond memory sings,
Until my dreaming spirit brings,
   The form that spoke it, near.

ii

And doth her bosom still inspire,
As spake her lips, the dear desire,
   And at the night's deep noon,
Doth she, with straining eye explore,
Where roves my form, that foreign shore,
   And murmur—"Come back soon"?

(1835, 1858)

THE AWAKENING.

i

Thou'st waked me from a pleasant dream,
   And with a single word hast still'd,
Of happy thoughts, the fairest stream,
   That e'er through boyish fancy thrill'd;—
I dream—alas! I sleep—no more,
   But with a phrenzied memory,
Still destined idly to deplore,
   I turn in hopeless pain to thee.

ii

I turn to thee, but turn in vain,
  Thou hear'st me not—thou can'st not hear,
Nor heed, that daring hope again,
  Though idle, yet to me how dear;
Ah! could'st thou but one hour restore,
  That hour would make me more than free;
And yet, though destined to deplore,
  And curse the past, I curse not thee.

(1835, 1846)

STANZAS

TO A LADY WHO ASKED WHY MY

VERSES WERE ALWAYS SAD.

i

The mournful God of Florid's cape,
  Has taught his woes to me,
And all the strains my fancies shape,
  Must share his destiny.

ii

He looks o'er weary wastes by day,
  And with its mournful flight,
To mocking winds and storms the prey,
  He breathes the drearier night.

iii

What other song should then be mine,
  Thus taught by kindred grief,
O'er memory's waste by day to pine,
  Nor find in night relief.

iv

My lyre like his, upon the rock,
  What should its music be,
Thus smitten by each tempest's shock
  That sweeps along the sea.

(1835, 1841)

CAROLINA WOODS.

These woods have all been haunted, and the power
Of spirits still abides in tree and flower;
They have their tiny elves that dance by night,
When the leaves sparkle in the moonbeam's light;
And the wild Indian often, as he flew
Along their water in his birch canoe,
Beheld, in the soft light of summer eves,
Strange eyes and faces peering through the leaves;
Nor, are they vanish'd yet.—The woodman sees,
Even now, wild forms that lurk behind the trees;
And the pine forests have a chanted song,
The Indians say, must linger in them long.

(1836, 1847)

THE PRAYER OF THE LYRE.

i
How gloriously the night,
Dawns, in her silver light,
Shedding gay gleams along the sleeping sea;
While gentle wings that rise,
In the far Eastern skies,
Send to the ear a sweet sad melody,

ii
And silent is the crowd,
The city, vex'd and loud,
That had been death to these glad spells around!
Come, let us seek yon beach,
Where, rich in solemn speech,
The billows wake our thoughts to themes profound.

iii
Night is Thought's minister,
And we, who wake with her,
Err not to seek her in a couch so bright:—
Scene that too soon departs,

Yet, meet for loving hearts,
And, like the troth they pledge, precious in Heaven's own sight.

iv
'Twas in such scene as this,
When, roused to Heaven wrought bliss,
The sacred Bard's quick fingers smote the lyre;
    And, harmonizing Earth,
    Then music sprang to birth,
And claim'd, so sweet her power, a God to be her sire!

v
Then the wild man grew tame,
And from the hill-tops came,
The shaggy-mantled shepherd with his flocks:
    And, as the minstrel sung,
    Old Fable found his tongue,
And rear'd a glittering form on all his rocks!

vi
Is there no hope again,
For the prophetic strain,
That made rocks musical?—when, far and wide,
    From every hill and dell,
    Down-brought by mightiest spell,
Bounding, the Muses came, in joy, on every side.

vii
When, taught by spirits choice,
Each forest-thronging voice,
Made music of its own for thousand listening ears;
    When every flower and leaf,
    Told of its joy and grief,
And wings ascending rose from the less gifted spheres.

viii
When song was common need,
And nature, glad to feed,
From the celestial homes, to wants arose,
    That brought their sure supply;—
    Since, there's a Deity,
For each true craving that our nature knows!

ix

Shall the time never more,
The old sweet song restore,
That made the stern heart gentle; taught to all
The proper thirst—the sense
Of Thought's great recompense,
In music, that still binds in sweetest thrall!

x

And the delicious dream,
That on our souls may gleam,
Bright visions of the eternal, glad and good:
Shaping the soul for flight,
Making the Hope delight,
Filling the mouth of faith with its celestial food.

xi

Oh! for the power that then
Showed spirit forms to men,
And crowned high aim, and led to the superior shrine:
The oracles that wore
Rich robes of mystic lore,
And taught, if not a Faith, at least, a song divine.

xii

Still silent do they keep,
In a cold, death-like sleep,
Nor minister to man, nor soothe him as of old;
Winning him from his sty,
To immortality,—
Making each passion true, making each virtue bold!

xiii

Oh! will they not descend,
Sweet spirits, to befriend;
Bring back the ancient muse, bring back the golden lyre;
Teach us the holier good
Of that more pliant mood,
When self untutor'd came to light Devotion's fire.

xiv

When, yet untaught to build

In some more favor'd field,
His cheerless cabin far from where the rest abode,
  Man had no thought so free
  But his heart yearn'd to be
Bow'd down, with all his tribe, to each domestic God.

    xv

Still keeps the sky as fair,
Still moon and stars are there,
And the winds whisper soft, as if upon them borne,
  Spirits came down to earth,
  Happy, as at its birth,
To rove its shadowy walks, now crowded and forlorn!

    xvi

'Tis man alone is changed,—
The shepherd. He, who ranged,
O'er the wild hills, a giant in the sun;
  His soul, with virgin gift,
  Having eye and wing uplift,
Soaring, in eager search, for loves that might be won!

    xvii

Look on him now—the slave!
What province doth he crave,
Whose sway is love, whose fruits are innocent good?
  The simple joy, no more,
  That the old forests bore,
Nor yet its mystic songs, that charm his sleepless mood.

    xviii

Power's proud consciousness,
That still should strive to bless,
Now prompts alone to cruel selfish strife;
  A sleepless strife to sway,
  And bear that spoil away,
Had been the common stock in the old shepherd life.

    xix

Ah! me, would Time restore
The ancient faith—the Lore,
That taught sweet cares, kind charities and love:

Soothing the spirit's pride,
Making the heart confide,
Lifting the hope until its eye grew fixed above.

xx

Once, once again, the song
That stayed the arm of Wrong;
That checked the savage chief, that charm'd the shepherd rude;
Send it, sweet spirits—ye,
Who bless man's destiny;
Come ye once more to cheer our human solitude.

xxi

We have gone wand'ring wide,
Wilful, from side to side,
Wandering in groves forbid; striving at conquests ill;
Come ye, and turn us back,
On the good ancient track,
Win us with ancient lures to ancient worships still.

xxii

Teach us that strife is wo,—
The love of lucre low,—
And but high hopes and thoughts are worthy in our aim:
Teach us that love alone,
True love, long heavenward flown,
Can bring us that sweet happiness we claim.

xxiii

And, with the sacred lore,
The shepherd loved of yore,
Rouse ye the frolic beat of the love-licensed heart;
When, gathering in the grove,
Young maidens sang of love,
And no cold Bigot came to chide the minstrel's art.

xxiv

Then were there teachers still,
This moon, yon rugged hill,
The sea, the grove, the swelling breeze that brings,
With every hour like this,

Still a fresh dream of bliss,
With healing for the sad heart on its wings!

XXV

Oh! then the mighty strain,
    Of the old Bard again,
Would bless the sylvan sport, and cheer the cottage fire,
    Then would the young and pure,
    Find all affections sure,
Hallow'd to service meet by nature's antique lyre.

(1836, 1864)

LANDSCAPE.—SALUDA IN MIDSUMMER.

When to the city's crowded streets
    The fiercer spells of summer come,
Then for thy calm and cool retreats,
    Saluda, may the wanderer roam.

Then should he seek thy guardian haunts,
    Thy rocky stream, thy shady tree,
And while the plain below him pants,
    From all oppression find him free.

Above him towers thy giant form,
    Rock-throned, and rising like a king;
Around him rides thy summer storm,
    With cooling freshness on his wing.

Beside him, borne o'er craggy steeps,
    From dells that never see the light,
Thy sun-bow'd cataract roars and leaps,
    In joyous gush and headlong flight.

Below him—what a scene is there!
    The hallowed, sweet repose of home,
The sheltered green, the waters clear,
    The sylvan sway, the cottage dome.

Gathering above, the noonday clouds
   The sun's intenser fires would chide,
His glories edging still their shrouds,
   Palls not unmeet for princely pride.

And far in sight the streamlet goes,
   With ceaseless chaunt of grateful cheer,
Glad in escape from hungering foes,
   And singing but in friendly ear.

See where the hunter speeds his bark,
   Not as the Indian chief of old,
Bound on some errand, wild and dark,
   Whose legend still remains untold,

But bent to cross the foaming straits,
   And win the woods of yonder shore,
Where, hid in thicket, one awaits—
   She knows not why—yet feels the more!

How changed the strife for sweet repose;
   No more the red man scouts the wood;
The hunter through the thicket goes,
   Nor dreams of hostile hate and blood.

The wolf with mournful howl departs;
   The panther's spotty hide makes gay
The cot, where woman's gentler arts
   Woo young affections forth to play.

And safe within the cottage shade,
   The song birds, with a generous strain,
Teach Nature's music to the maid,
   Who pays them back with song again.

The prowler hawk no more infests
   Their home; and o'er the sacred place,
They pour from glad and grateful breasts,
   Their raptures for the guardian race:

Crown home with grace, make lonely cot,
   For humble hearts, a home of joy;

Such as makes sweet the lowliest lot,
    And glads the dream of man and boy.

Oh! not alone a dream, while here
    That Nature well achieves her part,
And in her colors, bright and clear,
    Prepares the holier dawn of art.

Hence, to the city, well transferr'd,
    Our poet-painter bears the scene:
We see the landscape, hear its bird,
    Dance with its groups, and feel its green;

Joy in the gush of living streams,
    That bound from prison forth to light,
And feel, all quivering through our dreams,
    The music which they make in flight;

And hear, with reverent awe, the roar,
    From gathering winds, through many a dell;
Of heights we may not oft explore,
    That rush, a wondrous tale to tell.

Oh! but to dream beneath the rocks,
    And hear that song so wondrous sweet,
While Fancy every door unlocks,
    And brings us, Nature, to thy feet!

                                    (1836, 1855, 1860)

DEAR HARP OF THE FOREST.

i
    Dear harp of the forest, in gladness,
With my rude hands I clasp thee again,
    Though we parted but lately, in sadness,
And sorrow was mix'd with thy strain;
    The dew-weeping moss was upon thee,
And weighed thy frail strings to the earth,
    While the spirit that gloomily won thee,
In thy master's own sorrows had birth.

ii

But the night of my sorrow is over,
And the gloom from my spirit is gone;
  I seek thee once more, as the lover,
Seeks fondly some desolate one;—
  I have found thee, though silent and shaded,—
Thou art mine, and I strike thee again;
  Not a note hast thou lost, nor has faded
One memory of love from thy strain.

iii

No more, in the wild wood forsaken,
Thou pourest thy desolate song;
  I have found and again I awaken,
Each feeling note treasured so long;
  To the exile, what strain can be dearer,
Than that which he heard in his youth;
  To the lover, what sweeter or clearer,
Than the song of affection and truth!

(1836, 1840, 1846)

THE BROOKLET.

A little farther on there is a brook,
Where the breeze loiters ever. The great oaks
Have roof'd it with their arms and affluent leaves,
So that the sunbeam rifles not its fount,
While the shade cools it. You may hear it now,
A low faint murmur, as through pebbly paths,
In soft and sinuous progress it flows on,
In streams that make division as they go,
Still parting, still uniting, in one song,
The sweetest mortals know, of constancy.

  Thither, ah, thither, if thy heart be sad!—
That song will bring thee solace. Or, if hope
That may not yet find name for what it seeks,
Inspires thee with a dream whose essence brings
Fruition in its keeping,—still, the strain

That's murmur'd by yon brooklet, is the best,—
Having a voice for fancy at its birth,
That keeps it wakeful on its own sweet wings.
And thou wilt gather, for whatever mood
That makes thee fond or thoughtful, a sweet tone
Beguiling thy best sympathies, and still
Leaving in thy keeping, as thou seek'st thy home,
A kindlier sense of what is in thy path.

Beside these banks, through the whole livelong day,
Ere yet I noted much the flight of time,
And knew him but in ballad books and songs,
Nor cared to know him better,—I have lain,
Nursing delicious reveries that made
All being but a circle of bright flow'rs,
With love the centre, sov'ran of that realm,
And I a happy inmate, with the rest.
There, with sweet thoughts, all liquid like the stream
That still inspired their progress, clear and bright,
I lay as one who slept, through happy hours,
Unvex'd by din of duty, unrebuked
By chiding counsellor to youthful cares,
That ever seeks to plant on boyish brow
The winter that has silver'd all its own.
And thus, in long delight, with the rapt soul
Shaping its own elysium of the peace
That harbor'd in the solitude, the eye
Grew momently familiar with sweet forms,
That offer'd to the genius of the place,
Making all consecrate to gentleness.
How came the thrush to whistle as he drank,
Heeding not me, and darting through the copse,
Only to bring his loved one on his wing,
To gather like refreshment; squirrels dropt
Their nuts adown the bankside where I lay,
And, leaping to recover them, ere yet
They rolled into the brooklet and away,
Swept over me, and with fantastic play
Drew up the feathery brush above their heads,—
And their gray orbs, with bright intelligence,
Cast round them, while from hand to hand they frisk'd
The prize, which none might covet but to feed

Such nimble harlequins. The dove at noon
Couch'd in thick bristly covering of the pine,
Sought here its sweet siesta, wooing sleep,
By plaintive iteration of sad notes,
That might be still a sensible happiness:—
And sometimes, meek intruder on my realm,
Through yonder thick emerging, half in light
And half in shadow, stole the timid fawn,
That came down to the basin's edge to drink,
Now lapping, and now turning to the bank,
Cropping the young blade of the coming spring
And heedless, as I lay along unstirr'd,
Of any stranger—sauntering through the shade,
Even where I crouch'd,—having a quiet mood,
And not disturbing, while beholding mine.

    Thou smil'st; and on thy lip the speaking thought
Looks still like censure—deems my hours misspent,
And saddens into warning. A shrewd thought,
I will not combat with an argument,
But leave the worldly policy to boast,
That such an errantry as this life of mine,
Hath found its fit sarcasm, well rebuked.
And yet there is a something in the life
Thou mock'st, as idle still and profligate,
Something to life compensative, and dear
To feelings that are fashion'd not by man.
Ah! the delicious sadness of the hours,
Spent by this brooklet—ah! the dreams they brought,
Of other hopes and beings—the sweet truths,
That still subdued the heart to patientness,
And made all flexible in the youthful will,
That else had been most passionate and rash.
I know the toils that gather on my path,
And I will grapple them with a strength that shows
A love for the encounter, not the less
For hours thus wasted in the solitude,
And fancies born of dreams—and 'twill not more
Impair the resolute courage of my heart,
Wrestling with toil, in conflicts of the race,
If still, in pauses of the fight, I dream
Of this dear idlesse,—gazing on that brook

So sweet in shade, thus singing on its way,
Like some dear child, all thoughtless, as it goes
From shadow into sunlight and is lost.

(1836, 1849, 1853)

COTTAGE LIFE.

It is a quiet picture of delight,
This humble cottage, hiding from the sun,
In the thick woods. We see it not 'till now,
When at its porch. Rudely, but neatly wrought,
Four columns make its entrance—slender shafts—
The rough bark yet upon them, as they came
From the old forest and dame Nature's hand,
Who did not grudge her gift. Prolific vines
Have wreathed them well, and half obscured the rind,
Unpromising, that wraps them.—Crowding leaves
Of glistening green, and clustering bright flowers,
Of purple, in whose cups throughout the day
The humming bird wantons boldly, wave around,
And woo the gentle eye and delicate touch.
This is the dwelling, and it is to me
Quiet's especial temple. No rude sound
Breaks in upon time's ancient ordering,
Save the occasional mill clack, and the hum
From yonder bee tree—the still busy tribe,
Lightening their labors with a song of thrift,
Harmonious with the good wife's spinning wheel.

I know not what may move me to the thought,
But I do think, that life might glide away,
Nor feel itself at parting—cloistered here
In calm seclusion from the bustling world,
Untroubled by the doubt and the despair,
The intrusion, and the coil of crowded life;—
Soothed, when the erring pulses do beat high,
With the sweet catches of the vagrant birds,
That, perching on your eaves, win you away
Into the stillness of more gentle thoughts.

The woods at morn have life—the winds at eve,
Play, whispering at the shutter—stealing in,
To counsel slumber—waving o'er your couch
Their leafy winglets, strewing the blossoming airs
Won from the forests they have all day swept!
The skies—I know not why, but, in the vale,
Secluded thus, and o'er our cottage roof—
Wear a perpetual face of gentleness,
Smiling in sunshine—and when clouds are there,
They come as seasonable friends to bring
The unobservéd showers, that freshen all,
Yield life and verdure to the drooping plants,
And bid the young and shrinking flowers rejoice.

The hills are natural tombs, and we shall sink
Quietly, in their bosoms, at the last,
Nor leave our homes less peaceful. The soft hands
Of the twin-sister seasons, shall unite
To bend the green shrubs o'er our graves in turn—
And then we know that spring will bring her flowers,
And, like a maiden who thus mourns her love,
Plant them above our silent resting place.

(1828, 1836, 1838)

THE SHADE-TREES.

God bless the hand that planted these old trees,
Here, by the wayside. While the August sun
Sends down his brazen arrows on the plain,
They give us shelter. Panting in their shade
We gaze upon the path o'er which we came,
And, in the green leaves overhead, rejoice!
Far as the eye may reach, the sands spread out,
A granulated blaze, pain the dim sense,
And vex the slumberous spirit with their glare.
Like some o'erpolish'd mirror, they give back
The sun's intenser fires. The green snake writhes
To run along the track—the lizard creeps,

Carefully tender, o'er the wither'd leaves,
And shuns the wayside, which, in early spring,
He travell'd only;—while, on the moist track,
Where ran a small brook out, a shining group
Of butterflies fold up their wearied wings,
Mottled with gold and purple, and cling close
To the dank surface, drawing the coolness thence
Which the gray sands deny. A thousand forms,—
Insect and fly, and the capricious bird,
Erewhile that sang so gayly in the spring
To his just wedded partner,—forms of life,
And most irregular impulse,—all seem press'd,
As by the approach of death; and in the shade,
Hiding in leafy coverts and dense groves,
Where pines make natural temples for fond hearts,
And hopeless mourners,—seem in dread to wait
Some shock of nature. Summer reigns supreme,
With power like that of death; and here, beneath
This most refreshing shelter of old trees,
I hear a murmuring voice from out the ground,
Where work her agents; like the busy hum
From out the shops of labor, or, from far,
The excited beating of an army's pulse,
Mix'd in some solemn service.
                                 'Twas a thought
Of good, becoming ancient patriarchs,
Of him who first, in the denying earth,
Planted these oaks. Heaven, for the kindly deed,
Look on his errors kindly! He hath had
A most benevolent thought to serve his kind,
And felt, in truth, the principle of love
For the wide, various family of man,
Which is the true religion. Happy, for mankind,
Were such the better toil of those who make
The sacred text a theme for bitterness,
Who clamor more than pray, vexing the heart
With disputation. Better far, methinks,
If seated by the wayside, they beheld
The sorrows of its pilgrims; raised the shade
To shelter in the noonday; show'd the way
To the secluded fountain; and brought forth

The bread, and bless'd it to the stranger's want,
Who might, even then, be on his way to heaven!—
How fortunate for him who succor'd then!

(1856, 1853)

MORAL CHANGE.

Darkness is gathering round me, but the stars,
Silent and unobtrusive, stealing out,
Lend beauty to the night. The air comes cool
Up from the fountain; and the murmuring breeze,
Gushing through yonder valley, has a song
Spelling the silence to such mystery
As mingles with our dreams. It is the hour
When sad, sweet thoughts have sway;—when memory,
Triumphant o'er the past, waves her green wand,
And bids the clouds roll back, and lifts the veil
That had been closed behind us as a wall,—
And the eye sees, and the heart feels, and lives
Once more in its old feelings. I retrace
The homes of past affections, and dear hopes,
And dreams that look'd like hopes, and fled as well.
This is the spot—I know it as of old
By various tokens, but 'tis sadly changed.—
Men look not as they did; and flowers that grew,
Nursed by some twin affections, grow alone,
Pining for old attendance. Thus, our change
Brings a worse change on nature. She will bloom
To bless a kindred spirit; but she flies
The home that yields no worship. She is seen
Through the sweet medium of our sympathies,
And has no life beside. 'Tis in our eye
Alone that she is lovely—'tis our thought
That makes her dear, as only in our ears
Lies the young minstrel's music, which were harsh,
Did not our mood yield up fit instrument
For his congenial fingers.
                    It is thus,—
The beautiful evening, the secluded vale,

79

The murmuring breeze, the gushing fountain, all
So exquisite in nature to the sense,
So cheering to the spirit—bring me nought
But shadows of a gloomy thought that rise
With the dusk memory—with repeated tales,
Censuring the erring heart-hope with its loss:—
Loss upon loss—the dark defeat of all
The pleasant plans of boyhood—promises
That might have grown in fairy land to flowers,
And were but weeds in this. They did but wound,
Or cheat and vanish with deluding glare:
Having the aspect of some heavenly joy,
They also had its wings, and, tired of earth,
Replumed them back for the more natural clime,
And so were lost to ours. Hopes still wrong
And torture, when they grow extravagant—
Youth is their victim ever, for they grow,
With the advancing season, into foes
That wolve upon him. 'Tis a grief to me,
Though a strange pleasure still, thus to look forth,
Watching, through lengthening hours, so sweet a scene,
And winning back old feelings as I gaze.
Boyhood had drawn a picture fair like this
On fancy's vision. Ancient oaks were there,
Giving the landscape due solemnity—
A quiet streamlet trickled through a grove,
And the birds sang most sweetly in the trees—
But then the picture was not incomplete,
Nor I alone, as now.

                                                    (1836, 1853)

THE INDIAN VILLAGE.

Nature and Freedom! These are glorious words
That make the world mad. Take a glimpse at both,
Such as you readily find, when, at your ease,
You plough the ancient military trace,
From Georgia to the "Burnt Corn" settlements—
Or, higher up, if, happily, you speed,

Where the gaunt Choctaw lingers by the swamps
That fence the Yazoo, or the Chickasaw
Steals his hog nightly from the woodman's close,
And gets a furlough from all service thence,
In a keen bullet at an hundred yards.—
—Uplift thy glass, and tell me what thou seest.

A screaming brat that lash'd upon his board
Hangs rocking in the tree—the dam beneath,
A surly drudge that never once looks up,
But hills and hoes her corn, as if her soul
Lay clamoring there for sudden and strong help,
And perish'd in her pause—an ugly cur,
Mangy and most unclean, that, yelping, runs
For shelter at our coming—two green skins
That clothed the brown deer of the woods last night,
Wrapped now about the oak, beneath whose boughs,
Their owners browsed at evening, ere the tribe
Sent the young hunters forth—and lo! a group,
Women and children, in that happy state,
Ere Adam wore his fig leaves, and became
A tailor for the nonce—that round one hole
Bend down, clay digging for their pots and pans,
The baking fire at hand—and then the huts,
They fill the background—linger not to look,
Or, in rebellion, justified of man,
Our nostrils will rise up and nullify.
A more legitimate picture for good taste,
And the heroic, basking in the sun,
Behold the chiefs—five warriors of the wild,
That may be sung in story—vigorous men,
Ready for strife and trial, scalp and stroke,
But monstrous lazy. There is "Turkey-Foot"—
Not slow to run;—Achilles-like, his heel
Is sadly mortal. There's "Fat Terrapin,"
No runner he, I ween. A braver man
Than the "Gray Weasel" never sought the fight,
But then he loves fire water, and even now,
Not scrupulous to meet the stranger's eye,
See, his head dangles on the unsinew'd neck,
And bobs from side to side. "The Crooked Path,"
A double-dealing rogue as ever lived,

Looks like a cutpurse, and among the tribe
Such is his high renown. No counsellor
Can deal with him in subtle argument,
No fox-like politician double so,
In getting round the wild "Cape Positive,"
To channel "non-committal;"—happy he,
To steer between those breakers "yes" and "no,"
Yet leave no furrow on his sinuous path
As guide point to a troublous enemy.
Last of this group, behold old "Blazing Pine,"
Though but a pine knot now. His seventy years
Have all been tasted, yet his limbs are strong,
And bear him still in the chase. His keen eye
Not often fails to mark—his steady hand,
Still sends the bolt, with most unerring stroke,
Into the brown deer's flank.

               These warriors brave
Will all be drunk by night. The sober now,
Drunk with the drunkest. The already drunk,
Mad—looking for their weapons in the dark,
Beating the winds, the walls, striving with trees,
And one another—impotent but fierce,
And foaming with the fury unappeased—
Till, in their madness, with their emptied bottles
They'll break the old squaw's head, and she will fly
Howling for vengeance. She will swim yon stream,
Her blood still streaking, as she scuds along,
The wave that washes gainst her shatter'd scull.
Seeking for safety 'mong her kindred tribe
Of the "Mud Turtles," she will head a war,
And they will lose their scalps with infinite grace
To one another. War, with its long train
Of toils and injuries, will rive their fields,
Destroy their little maize crops and frail towns,
And leave them starving. Want will then produce
The peace that came not with prosperity,
And they will link their arms, and, in small groups,
Steal nightly over to the opposite shore
And rob the squatter's farm yard. Cows and calves
They'll drive across the stream. The young corn
They'll burst from its green column, and the pigs—

They barbacue as well at an Indian camp
As at a white man's muster. What comes next?
The squatter goes against the savages,
And drives them—a most sad necessity,
Much mourned by modern-mouthed philanthropy—
Into yet deeper forests. Five years hence,
And the foul settlement we gaze on now
Will be a city of the paler race,
Having its thousand souls. Churches will rise,
With taverns on each hand. To the right, see,
A gloomy house of morals, called a gaol,
And, from the town hall, on the opposite square,
You yet shall hear some uncombed orator,
Discourse of freedom, politics, and law,
In tones shall make your blood bound, and your hair
Start up in bristles. Turning, you shall see,
"Fat Terrapin," "Gray Weasel," and, perchance,
The aged "Blazing Pine,"—all christians now,
Cowering, bewildered, 'mong the heedful crowd
Which hangs delighted on the patriot's words—
Heedful, delighted, drunk as any there!

(1837, 1838)

FIRST DAY OF SPRING.

Oh! thou bright and beautiful day,
    First bright day of the virgin spring,
Bringing the slumbering life into play,
    Giving the leaping bird his wing.

Thou art round me now in all thy hues,
    Thy robe of green, and thy scented sweets,
In thy bursting buds, in thy blessing dews,
    In every form that my footstep meets.

I hear thy voice in the lark's clear note,
    In the cricket's chirp at the evening hour;
In the zephyr's sighs that around me float,
    In the breathing bud and the opening flower.

I see thy forms o'er the parting earth,
  In the tender shoots of the grassy blade,
In the thousand plants that spring to birth,
  On the valley's side in the home of shade.

I feel thy promise in all my veins,
  They bound with a feeling long suppress'd,
And, like a captive who breaks his chains,
  Leap the glad hopes in my heaving breast.

There are life and joy in thy coming, Spring,
  Thou hast no tidings of gloom and death,
But buds thou shakest from every wing,
  And sweets thou breathest with every breath.

(1837, 1853)

BOY LOST IN THE WOODS.

i

You've been a boy. Forget your toils awhile,
And be a boy again. Look back, and listen,
While in the evening sunset, where we sit
Aneath the lengthening shadows of the trees,
Your fancy leads you to the by-gone hours,
The ancient play-places, the time-worn haunts,
Sacred to youth, and dear to thousand sports
You shall not know again, save in some tale
Of erring childhood, such as now you hear.

ii

'Twas in my time of boyhood—happiest time
In every life, however low its lot—
So full of sweetest certainty—so full
Of pleasant change to sweeter certainties—
My heart grows young as I remember it.
I feel the season, like a gentle ray
Of moonlight o'er my soul; and, as some billow
That leaps and glows beneath the mellow beam,
My bosom's pulses freshen with the fancies
That bring me back my boyhood.

84

iii

                    It was then
I was an erring youth—a lone one too,
Whom nothing seemed to love, yet loving all,—
I strayed into the forests, far away
From the close city,—far beyond the suburb,
Until I lost the glare of the white houses,
And heard no din; and round me rose the woods,
Dense, green and spacious, and my freedom grew,
From consciousness to action, while I caper'd,
And shouted 'till the forests rang again:
For I was ever fond of unrestraint,
And wooed the liberty I seldom won,
Save when a truant. I had heavy tasks
Which I had fled from. There were my relations,
Three aunts and thirty cousins, whom my mother,
Despatch'd me, in each school recess, to visit,
And taught me thus to hate them. Thus I fled
The streets, the city, man, my aunts, my cousins,
And my own mother—fled into the woods,
Glad to escape, and rushing recklessly
Into their wildest haunts, in my sad rambles,
Which, as they grew more frequent, grew most far
For a mere boy to venture—though I grew
Before my season, up into a man.

        iv
    The hours went round, and the day came at last
When schoolboys hold their saturnalia,
And in licentious freedom balance well
The trammels of the week, now flying fast.
It was that delightful season of the year,
When birds have birth in the late coming spring—
When berries ripen, and the birds above,
Chide you with sudden cry and angry note
From the suspended nests, that overhead,
Hold their unfeather'd offspring—'till your eye
Detects the prey, which else had been unseen.

        v
    Flying from care, I cared not where I flew,
And wander'd on, won, wooed at every step,

By the gay tribute which the season brought.
I chased the birds—I followed sinuous paths
That loiter'd, and were lost in circling woods—
Plucking wild flowers for beauty—casting them down
To find still lovelier, and discard them too,
With an indifferent hand; and with a mind
Capricious as the season, or the birds,
Taking the paths they counselled, with no thought,
And all unheeding, wheresoe'er they led.

vi

On some few berries, gathered as I went,
That jutted forth from every wayside bush,
And tasked but little toil to gather them;
I did amuse my appetite to want,
And then I hungered. To be far from home,
And hungry, is an evil—so I stray'd
Still farther onward, in the hope to share
The few-word courtesy of some low boor,
Which is the pleasantest, even though it come
But in attendance on a sweet potato.
Onward, still onward for another hour,
And then I turned for home. For home, indeed:
The woods were changed around. The paths look'd strange,
And grew bewildered at each step I took,
'Till I was lost. Oh, most unmanly loss—
Fairly confounded with the crossing paths,
The crooked trees, the over-crowding thickets,
That led, misled, now right, now left, now forward,
Yet wrong, though going right, still left, though forward,
And going backward, even when forward bent,
And losing ground at every step I gained.

vii

Certainly lost! Yet could I not be lost
In the great volume of my self-esteem;
For I was wild and ventrous—well I knew,
(Such was my erring fancy in that day,)
Each glen and valley, and uprising hill,
Old grove, or stunted thicket, to discern
When nights were dullest, and the untrodden path
Was festering in its weeds. I did not heed,

At first, my danger; erring still, went on
'Till the wild woods grew wilder, and the trees
Like frowning giants, with out-stretching arms,
Stood boldly in my path, and threaten'd me.
Vines caught my feet, in heaviness set down;
Branches and brambles met me, and assailed,
And through their roofing tops, an angry cloud
Look'd down in storm that blacken'd all the scene,
And to the sad confusion of my mind,
Brought terrors that confounded me the more.
A guilty spirit mocked me as I flew,
And punishment, in hundred gloomy forms,
Shook her gaunt fingers and berated me.

viii
I fled from my own fancies—wildly fled,
Blinded and trembling, plunging farther yet
Into the mazes of the wilderness.
All thought was drown'd in terror—I had lost
The goodly wits that might have work'd me out;
And after a long hour of fruitless toil,
I laid me in the long grass 'neath an oak,
And sobb'd until I sobb'd myself asleep.

ix
I slept away my hunger. When I woke,
The lengthening shadows of the trees were cast,
Like old men's dreams, upon the longer past.
Sweet lay the deepening forest in the sun—
That brighten'd into glory—one might watch
As it grew fainter; while he lingering gazed
Upon the scene he hallowed, and I thought
There was a gathering sadness in his smile,
As if he sorrow'd still, that he must leave,
Though for a space so brief, this beautiful earth.

x
The forest—which he sweetly lighten'd still,
In slant rays and in broken glances, falling
Through patches in its tufted tops, and where
The woodman's axe had linger'd with a death—

Wore a deep gloom, more fearful, as beside
The sinking glory I had gazed upon;
And this aroused me into care anew.
Where was my home—the night was coming on—
Where should I turn—what kindly hand would guide—
What gentle spirit, guardian of the wood,
Watchful of those who loved its devious ways,
And worshipp'd the sweet thought in solitude,
Would look upon me now? I shouted loud,
And the dull echoes mocked me with response,
Feeble as childhood's.

   xi
         With a resolute thought
I took my manhood on, and strove once more
My pathway to retrace. My marks were lost,
Or multiplied in mockery. Each side
Possess'd conflicting claims. There was a tree
Hollow and rotten, tott'ring to its fall;
By that old tree I came, and rounded it
On the left hand—yet, lo! there is another
As like it, as if both had sprung together
From the same hand and model. Yon ravine,
I thought a sure guide, has a fellow to it
Not twenty yards to the right—and both are left
To others yet beyond—there's choice enow
To him whom one would better satisfy.
Confusion worse confused: with doubt grown sick
I look'd upon the sun, and saw him sink
In a full blaze of glory through the trees,
Still leaving, as I thought to comfort me,
A wreath of rosiest robes upon the sky,
That seem'd to gladden in the generous gift!
Then did I look upon the deep dread shade,
That grew around me to a solid gloom,
'Till I despaired once more, and moan'd and wept,
As if the last hope had forever gone.

   xii
I thought—I had a multitude of thoughts—
I thought upon the dinner I had lost,

The vacant chair I had so often fill'd,
The knife and fork just suited to my mouth,
The good beefsteak, or mutton, goose or fowl,
Ham, turkey and accompaniements and all,
That my long legs had lost my long desire.
How cheerless did I feel without my chair,
And what a goose was I to fly from goose!
Oh, cruel thoughts, that grow the more acute,
Unlike my appetite, when exercised—
They bring before my sight the calm outline
Of the enticing supper—"cold baked meats,"
That now could furnish nothing cold to me:
And so I chew'd the cud of my reflection—
Ah me! 'twas every thing I had to chew!

xiii
How goodly to my sight, in that sad hour,
Seem'd then the home I fled from. In my grief,
The ugliest crone of an aunt, the lankest cousin
That ever vex'd before, had then been grateful
To my sad eyes. I had jump'd up and kiss'd them,
Thrown my fond arms, with apt hypocrisy,
Round their lean necks, and swore in sweetest measures
Never, henceforth, to miss one Saturday,
Unmarked by my most punctual visitation.

xiv
Oh nature! Neither aunt nor cousin came
Howe'er I wish'd them; but a mocking fiend,
That took their shapes, forever taunted me:
" 'Twas for my truancy that I was punish'd—
"I fled from them—I did not joy to see them,
"As still good nephews and fond cousins should,
"And so the Providence had punished me."
'Twas thus they spoke, and with malicious skill
They drew before mine eyes the joys of home
At the blest eventide. They showed my mother,
Like a good housewife, busy with the tea things.
There was the hissing urn—there the round table,
Chairs ready placed, and cakes awaiting me;
And in my quicken'd ears, I heard the tone,
So sad yet gentle, sweet yet unaffected,

Of my fond mother, asking for the truant,
And asking vainly—"where can William be?"

xv

Then came a glimpse of bed time, and her sorrow
To apprehension grown; and my heart trembled
With newer grief, thus thinking upon hers.
I shrank from the reflection. Not as bad
Yet most annoying then, was the next picture:
There was the chamber of your humble servant,
The bed and bed clothes, neatly turn'd and ready
By the good mother's hand, awaiting me.
Alas! my bed that night—so thought I then—
Must be the heath—my canopy the sky,
And my close curtain—close enough to keep me—
The rough big trees that had no sympathy,
And grew more black with each increasing hour.
Then, images of danger and affright
Clustered among the shadows, and around me
Dark, frowning enemies that lurked and waited
For the increasing night, when I was drowsy,
To leap upon their prey. Such were my fears,
'Till hope itself, the destitute's last jewel,
The one we save from wrecks and burning houses,
And hide with secret joy within the bosom,
Glad all's not lost—hope's self deserted me:
Gloom fill'd my soul—the big, the swelling shadows
Successive chased each other through the wood,
'Till night reign'd there in solemn majesty;
And I, like some poor criminal, sank down
Despairing, at her footstool, to my fate,
Almost resign'd, whatever it should be.

xvi

At length, dame Fortune, of her sport grown tired,
Or, pitying the sad state she brought me to,
Sent her redeeming messenger, in the shape
Of a rough woodman, late returning home
From his employment, felling the old trees.
He found me at the bottom of a hill
Squat 'neath a clump of pines, sullen and sick,
Half crazed with hunger, half enraged by fear.

His presence cheer'd me. With a hearty laugh
He heard my story—by a sinuous route
He led me to his cottage—some three miles—
I found them six and better—in the wood.

xvii

His cabin was of logs, not squared, nor yet
Properly round—a single room it had,
And but one window; but the chimney took
Ample allowance of the northern side.
His wife received us, sitting at the door;
Three urchins filled the chimney—a large dog,
Rugged and mangy, sat before the hearth,
In close communion with a fearless cat,
That might have been a wild one on a visit,
Striving at manners for good company.
Man, wife, dog, cat, and the three chimney-children,
Spoke or look'd welcome; and I felt at home—
A feeling without limit, when I heard
The signal made for supper. Truly would it seem
Our home depends upon our appetite,—
The native place of all supreme affections
Is when we feed them. As I heard the clatter
Of plates and dishes, cups and clinking saucers,
I straight forgot my aunts, my thirty cousins,
And my poor mother's tears and apprehensions.

xviii

I ate a hearty supper. 'Twas a meal
Most homely; but I had an excellent sauce,
That made it luscious. I was monstrous hungry—
Hungry as thirteen Indians on a scout
In winter, when the woodrats eat the venison—
But not so patient. There was bread of corn,
Made on a hoe—from thence it took its name,
Domestically, "Hoe-cake,"—bacon fried,—
(I have a faith in ham will never leave me
While I can get it,)—some two dozen eggs,
And some fried cabbage. Of this mess—this mass,
I am inclined to think, on this occasion,
I ate my portion, and a trifle more.
Necessity is Freedom's parent. Ho!

How I love a proverb when it helps me.
I took good counsel from this noble axiom,
And ask'd no better rule for appetite.
The good old woodman, though he did express
Repeated wish that I should eat my fill,
Was not,—I'm sure from his lugubrious smile—
Was not quite sorry when he saw me stop.

xix
'Till a late hour, he kept my spirits up
By telling me strange stories. Some there were
Unwonted, but most pleasantly conceited—
Strange with cross lights, fearful with warring shadows,
With gloom and glare, conflicting, yet commix'd,
And dress'd with a complexion from the truth,
Which made them queerly happy. I have kept
Some of these stories in my memory—
I cannot help but keep them—and will tell them
Some of these days, if I can pluck up courage
To shake a printer's hand, or with more daring,
Encounter that most awful tribunal,
Where sits, upraised on sculls of slaughtered authors,
The mighty monster call'd an Editor.
These would you hear? 'Twill pleasure me to tell them
Even as I heard them, in the self-same language
From the old woodman, nor abate a jot
Wherein his speech was rude, for any ear.
If then you be not warp'd away from nature
By the insidious art and changing fashions,
Those legends wild, by timorous fancy wrought,
And not by rash romances, will delight you—
And you will give me thanks for having told you.

xx
Sweetly I slept that night, with dreams of home
All pleasant—all inviting—all deceptive.
I dream'd my mother let me off my visits,
And I was *minus* all my aunts and cousins.
Rapture, Oh! rapture! wherefore wert thou born
So soon to perish? Dreams are fleeting things.
Soon as the grey-eyed messenger of light
Leapt forth, and with his fleet steed hurried on

O'er his far eastern summits, through th'expanse,
Unchained now, which late was night's own chamber,
I leapt up too, and thought on my own journey.
I did not wait for breakfast. The good woodman
Led me upon my way—show'd me the path,
And gave me 'God-speed' as I darted off.
I soon reach'd home, and to perfect my wo,
And cap the climax of my cruel fate,
Got a sound whipping from my tender mother,
Making me not less tender. By my faith
And flesh, a day had strengthen'd her,
And her blows told in terror. Monday came,
And I was sent to school, bearing a missive,
Which begg'd the ascetic master to repeat
Her humble effort to improve the moral,
(As cooks make tender stubborn steaks,) by basting
The shrinking flesh of the poor animal.
This was intended to create a taste
For the enjoyments of my loving home,
But failed most strangely. I ran off again,
Play'd truant—robb'd the orchards of my cousins—
Fibb'd to escape—was then detected—punish'd,
And fled again—again from punishment;
Each day grew worse than ever—'till they all,
Schoolmaster, mother, cousins, aunts, agreed
To leave me to my fate—all well assured,
(And anxious to secure the fame of prophets
By seeing what they said,) that when I grew up,
I should be pilloried, perhaps, or hung:
But so far I've defeated them—*sub-rosa*—
Their tyranny—like tyrannies in general,
Upon the victims—have but strengthen'd me.
It made me what I am—though it may bring me
To block or halter yet—a fearless patriot,
Ready to stand by any hapless urchin,
Doom'd to three aunts, and thirty ugly cousins.

(1828, 1837)

LINES

IN THE ALBUM OF THE LATE MISS M. T. R——, NOW MRS. ——, OF SOUTH CAROLINA.

As one who may not see again
   The form of her who asks his song,
Invokes some blessing in his strain,
   To crown with joy and keep from wrong;—

So, in thy book of blooms and flow'rs,
   Sweet maid, the wanderer notes his pray'r,
And calls down health, and happy hours,
   To keep thee young, and good and fair—

To win thee joys that may not fade,
   And hopes that will not vex nor fly;
A spirit, like its Maker's made,
   A happy home, a quiet sky;—

Nor these alone,—the sunny dreams,
   That glide o'er Eden flow'rs, and prove
Etherial airs, immortal gleams
   That crown with heav'n, and come with love.

And if, within thy maiden heart
   There lurk a warm and secret flame;
Oh, be it, of thyself a part,
   And well-adored and love its name:

Nor felt in vain;—for at thy shrine,
   Oh, may the loved adorer stand,
With spirit formed to mate with thine,
   And feed its fires with gentle hand.

(1837)

ANACREONTIC.

i

Wilt thou then leave me, ere the hurrying hours,
  Have yet gone by when sleepless souls should meet;
Wilt thou then leave me, when in these love bowers,
  Time lingers, wrapt in joys forever sweet?—
Oh, break not thus away, with trembling spirit,—
  It is not true that rapture can be wrong;
And hours of joy like this, so few inherit,
  Have never yet been found to linger long.

ii

Love can reward, and still awhile remaining,
  Some joy, before unknown, shall touch thy heart!—
Ah, me! thy own, unto my bosom, straining,
  If thou didst love like me, we should not part;—
Thou would'st still pause, and with a fresh affection,
  Reclasp the hand, unite the lips that burn;
And, when in fear, thou break'st the sweet connection,
  Return and linger, linger and return.

(1837, 1841)

TWILIGHT MUSINGS.

1

Stilly falls the boatman's oar,
  Faintly sounds the evening bell,
As from off the dusky shore,
  Soft the evening breezes swell;
Oh! how sweet at such an hour,
  O'er the yellow sands to rove,
Rapt the full soul, 'neath the pow'r
  Of youthful love!

2

And 'tis sweet, when youth has gone,
  When the eye of man grows dim,

Still to wake, in memory's tone,
    Love's first dewy vesper hymn;
Bringing back each happy note,
    That in early hours we knew,
And while still in dreams they float,
    Believe them true.

3

Oh! even thus the buried joys,
    Our boyhood's faded hopes and fears,
The all that cruel time destroys,—
    Returns, awhile, to bless our years:
Thus do the pure affections come,
    Each gushing rapture to restore,
Bidding the lone and sad heart bloom,
    Beloved once more!

(1837, 1842)

ASHLEY RIVER.

i

Still, still, thou gentle river,
    A long, a last farewell:
I fly from thee forever,
    In other climes to dwell;
And never more, thus roving,
    Along thy banks, shall I,
Behold a stream so worthy loving,
    Beneath the blessed sky.

ii

Thou hast bless'd me with a beauty
    Like a smile from the Most High;—
Thou hast cheer'd me with a murmur
    Of music melting by—
I have seen thee in thy glory,
    When the loved ones saw thee too,
But we see them now no longer,
    To them and thee, adieu.

iii

Sad parting with thy waters,
  Sweet waters of my youth;
When every hour was gladness,
  When every tone was truth—
Dark clouds have come about me,
  Thou, too, hast felt the change,
And thy billows only flout me,
  With a murmur stern and strange.

iv

Yet, well my heart has loved thee,
  And, alas! it loves thee still;
It cannot soon forget thee,
  Let me roam where'er I will—
Thou still art to my spirit,
  Like a smile from the Most High—
Thou art still most worthy loving
  Beneath the blessed sky.

(1838)

THE HUNTER OF CALAWASSEE;
A LEGEND OF SOUTH CAROLINA.

i

When bites, in bleak November, the blast that rives the tree,
And scatters wide the yellow leaves, so sweetly sad to see,
Its voice's moaning murmur, borne through the trembling wood,
Awakes the heedful hunter up, and stirs his drowsy blood;—
In ancient times a summons meet,[1] for all who struck the deer,
He will not be the last to heed, who's still the first to hear;
He plucks the rifle from its rest, he winds the yellow horn,
And sweet the music of the sound through all the forest borne.

ii

'Way down where ghostly cypress and dodder'd oaks spread free,
By the winding fen of Calawass, and on to Ocketee,
The mellow notes go searching far, the bloodhound's bay is full,—
Shame light upon that hunter now whose bosom's beat is dull!

There's life within that bugle note, steeds snort and riders shout,
And life, in every bound they take, is gushing gladly out;
A spirit rends the thicket,—upstarts the couchant deer,
Shakes from his sluggish flanks the dew, and bounds away in fear.

iii

"Now sound your horns," cried Kedar, "and let the hunt be up,
And bring me, ere we start, my boy, a strong and stirring cup;
The air is keen and searching, and sadly, in my breast,
The blood, that should be bounding still, lies lazily at rest;
Not long to rest, for, by my soul, and all the saints! I swear,
This day I perish, or I kill the buck that harbors here,—
That one-horn'd buck;"—"Nay, swear not so, dear master," thus he
     cried,
The aged slave, who then drew nigh and stood by Kedar's side.

iv

"Now, out upon thy coward soul!" cried Kedar to the slave;
"Thou wast a man upon a time,—my father thought thee brave;
But age has dull'd thy spirit—thy limbs have need of rest,
This air's too keen for such as thou—go, harbor in thy nest;
Fool-fears have quell'd thy manhood, and, in this buck I seek,
Thou find'st a foe whose very name 'twould white thy lips to speak;
But though he be the fiend himself, and stand before my eyes,
This day I hunt him down, I say, and deer or hunter dies!"

v

Then sadly spoke that aged slave—"Oh, master, swear not so—
Leave hunting of this one-horn'd buck, that's like no beast we know;
He makes no slot,[2] no entry[2] leaves, though through the closest
     brakes
Of bush, or cane, or thicket swamp, his headlong course he takes:
Still bears the same erected port, and never frays a head;[2]—
Two seasons have you hunted him, and still with evil sped;
Some grievous chance hath ever happ'd when on his scent we came,
The first"—"Now, fool," then Kedar cried, "be still for very shame!"

vi

"Sound, hunters, ere this idle tale arrest the sluggish blood,
And lend to braver hearts than his yon aged dotard's mood;
It is my oath this day to track that buck unto his den,
And we shall see if he or me shall live for hunt agen;—

Two seasons hath he baffled us, 'twere shame if still he may,
And I am sworn, and heed my oath, to end the toil to-day;
And Lauto, you shall stay behind—I would not have you drive;
If such the fears that fill your heart, the hunt can never thrive."

vii

"I'll go, my master," cried the slave, with sorrow in his tone,
"If fears are in old Lauto's heart, they're fears for you alone;
Here, Willow, Wand, and Wallow!"—three dogs of famous breed,
That had a boast from Rollo's pack, the Norman's, to be seed:—
He sounded then most cheerily, that aged slave, and cried,
'Till, from the kennel, all the pack, came bounding to his side;
He took the route his master bade, and with a heavy heart,
That shook with fears he could not name, did Lauto then depart.

viii

'Twas standing in a cypress grove, that, by the Ocketee,
Kept crowding shadows that forbade the searching eye to see,
Young Kedar waited long to hear the music of the hounds,
That told the hunt was up, and fill'd the wood with cheering sounds;
No sound he heard, yet, on his sight, that one-horn'd deer arose,
As speeding on, he left behind, in secret, all his foes:—
"But me he shall not baffle thus," cried Kedar as he came—
And lifting up his rifle then, he stood with ready aim.

ix

Three strides the buck hath taken, his single horn on high,
And then he stay'd his forward flight, and look'd with steady eye;
He look'd upon the cypress grove where Kedar watching stood,
Then, turning, took his easy way toward the distant wood.
This madden'd Kedar then to see, and to his steed he gave
Free rein and rashing spur, and went as if some devil drave;
With shriek and shout he bounded on, and wonder'd to behold
How easy was the gait he went, that deer, along the wold.

x

And still nor horn nor hound he heard, and nothing did he see,
Save that one deer that, fleeing, seem'd as not to care to flee;
This vex'd young Kedar to behold—a madness fill'd his blood,
And shouting as he went, he flew, with fury through the wood;
He heeded not for stop or stay—he look'd not once behind,

His soul was in that fearful chase—his spirit on the wind;—
A twilight shade came o'er the earth, and through the wood a moan,
Yet nothing did he see or hear, but that one deer alone!

xi

The cypress groves he leaves behind, where, with impatient heart,
Three goodly hours he watch'd that day, from all the rest apart;
The long pines gather round him now, and now the thicket stays,
Yet on, with headlong haste, he goes, through wild and rugged
    ways;—
The deer, still willing as he wends, keeps ever in his sight,
Yet indirect his forward course, as careless still of flight;—
More furious grew that hunter then, to see his mocking pace,
And feel at last, his noble steed was failing in the race.

xii

No warning sign like this he heeds, but with his oath in mind,
Young Kedar, in that keen pursuit, is striving with the wind;
The rowel tears his charger's flanks until they glisten red,
The thong now smites his burning sides and now his aching head;
Yet docile still, in all his pain, though fainting with the chase,
He strives, that noble beast, to keep, unfailing, in the race; —
The madness grows in Kedar's soul, and blinds his thought and will,
Such madness as must vex the heart of him that's doom'd to ill.

xiii

And he that has no eye to see his weary charger's pain,
As little heeds the baffling wood through which his feet must strain;
The giant pines have faded far—the knotted thicket shakes
Its purple berries round his brow at every bound he takes;
The swamp is nigh, the horse's hoofs in ooze are plashing fast,
God save him, if he mean to save—such chase can never last!
The river's edge is nigh, and dusk, its solemn shadows rise,
And what a heavy silence hangs and broods along the skies.

xiv

Before him sleeps the sluggish swamp that never sees the day,
And through its bosom, bounding on, the deer still keeps his way;
Another leap he gains the stream—another effort more—
And deeply in the charger's flanks, the rashing rowel tore;—
A sound is in young Kedar's ears—his hounds are close behind—

And 'tis old Lauto's cry that cheers upon that sudden wind;—
A warning cry that vainly seeks to drive the spell away,
And check the fiend that lies in wait and hungers for his prey.

      xv

Mad shouts from Kedar answer'd then old Lauto's kindly cry,—
"Ha! ha! I have him now!" was still the hunter's wild reply;
"I have him now—that one-horn'd buck—our path lies fair and free,
He sinks—he can no farther run—he lies by yonder tree;—
Upon him, Cygnet!—he is ours—one goodly effort more,
By death and all the saints, he's mine!—ha! ha! our hunt is o'er!"
And still the noble steed obeys, and through the swamp he goes,—
The swamp is past, and, round his feet, the dark Che-che-see flows.

      xvi

The dark Che-che-see flows along, in tribute to the main,
But stops not Kedar's rash pursuit—he spurs his steed again;
And breathing hard, the patient steed now takes the gloomy stream,
While roll'd the thunder cloud above, and sunk the westering gleam.
Old Lauto reach'd the river's edge, with dim and straining eye,
And something like a struggling steed, a moment did he spy;
But soon the waters closed above—he look'd beyond, and there
Still went, a failing shadow now, with easy pace, the deer!

                            (1838, 1853)

1. The fall of the leaf was always the signal for ancient hunting. It is, perhaps, to be regretted, that it is not more generally observed at present. Our game would then be less harrassed and more plentiful than now.

2. Old Lauto is somewhat more learned in his terms than most of the *drivers* of the southern country; and, for the sake of his brethren, some little explanation may be given here. These are all terms of the chase in ancient English hunting; and are furnished to me, at second hand, from Gascoigne's "Commendation of the noble Arte of Venerie." The *slot* is the print of a stag's foot upon the ground; *entries* are places through which deer have lately passed, by which their size is conjectured; *frayings* are the pillings of their horns; and a deer is said to "fray a head" when he rubs it against a tree to cause the outer coat to fall away in the season of renewal. These nice traits of the hunt, by which the hunter learns all that is desirable to know of the game he seeks, form, however, but a small number of those in the collection of the experienced in this "noble arte."

SONNET—THE WREATH.

This is a pleasant wreath, but you have gone
   Too far to seek it. I could venture now,
You have been much too choice, and left alone
   Some that had set much better on the brow.
These flowers are sweet—yet, were there but a few,
   I should regard them with more calm delight.
   Their gay and gaudy hues do pain my sight
And seem to crowd upon me while I view.
I mark me, when I was the playfull'st boy,
   I sought one day for roses in a wood—
'Twas a wide wood; and so my taste was coy,
   And when I had gone through it, lo! I stood,
With a poor bunch—the poorest of the flowers,
Whose lovely shapes and hues had won mine eye for hours.

                         (1838)

MEMORY.

There is a moonlight in the heart,
   A lonely, sad expanse of light;
Cold as the meteors that impart,
   Strange lustre to the wintry night:
A vacant being, which though lit,
   By gleams that haunt it from the sky,
Still feels cold phantoms o'er it flit,
   The shapes of those who should not die.

These are the memories of the past,
   Gray watchers on the waste of years,
Shadows of hopes that could not last,
   And loves, forever born in tears.
The mellowed music that they bring,
   Falls sweet but sad upon the heart,—
Around whose brink they sit and sing,
   Of death,—and will not thence depart.

                      (1838, 1848)

INVOCATION.

Come, Chevillette, my own love, come with me,
  No idle pomp, no bustling world, I seek;
Enough, if in the shadow of the tree,
  I watch thy glistening eye and glowing cheek.

Enough, if in thy gentle heart and eye,
  Mine own may find a warm, responsive flame,
Enough, if in thy murmur and thy sigh,
  Breathed out from love's own lips, I hear my name.

Thy hand in mine, thy spirit watchful still,
  Of what mine own hath spoken, and thy heart
Fill'd with that hope which love can best fulfil,
  We feel how sweet to meet, how sad to part.

Come, be a dweller in this quiet grove,
  And teach the wild vine how to gather round,
While, with thy lips, still breathing songs of love,
  To the deep woods thou lend'st a genial sound.

Things gentle shall be won to gather near,
  Solicitous of all the sweets thou bring'st,
And the young mock-bird, bending down his ear,
  Shall emulous listen whensoe'er thou sing'st.

Toward eve, the frisking rabbit 'neath thine eyes,
  Shall overlay the grass plat near our cot;
The squirrel, as from tree to tree he flies,
  Fling the dismember'd branches o'er the spot.

Thy gentle nature, winning as their own,
  Theirs all unwronging, shall a favorite be;
And they will gather round thy forest throne,
  And own thy sway, and love thy chains, like me.

Come, be a dweller in this quiet grove,
  Sweet heart! and with thy spirit true as fine,
Attune the sleeping chords of life to love,
  Till the high harmonies shall kindle thine.

Shut out the world's coarse discords, till no more
  Thy heart shall hear of violence or grief,
And heaven, in mercy to our lot, restore
  The bloom of Eden, blissful, but how brief!

(1838)

TAMING THE WILD HORSE.

Last night he trampled with a thousand steeds
The trembling desert. Now, he stands alone—
His speed hath baffled theirs. His fellows lurk,
Behind, on heavy sands, with weary limbs
That cannot reach him. From the highest hill,
He gazes o'er the wild whose plains he spurn'd,
And his eye kindles, and his breast expands,
With an upheaving consciousness of might.
He stands an instant, then he breaks away,
As revelling in his freedom. What if art,
That strikes soul into marble, could but seize
That agony of action,—could impress
Its muscular fulness, with its winged haste,
Upon the resisting rock, while wonder stares,
And admiration worships? There,—away—
As glorying in that mighty wilderness,
And conscious of the gazing skies o'erhead,
Quiver for flight, his sleek and slender limbs,
Elastic, springing into headlong force—
While his smooth neck, curved loftily to arch,
Dignifies flight, and to his speed imparts
The majesty, not else its attribute.
And, circling, now he sweeps, the flow'ry plain,
As if 'twere his, gathering up
His limbs, unwearied by their sportive play,
Until he stands, an idol of the sight.

He stands and trembles! The warm life is gone
That gave him action. Wherefore is it thus?
His eye hath lost its lustre, though it still
Sends forth a glance of consciousness and care,

104

To a deep agony of acuteness wrought,
And straining at a point—a narrow point—
That rises, but a speck upon the verge
Of the horizon. Sure, the humblest life,
Hath, in God's providence, some gracious guides,
That warn it of its foe. The danger there,
His instinct teaches, and with growing dread,
No more solicitous of graceful flight,
He bounds across the plain—he speeds away,
Into the tameless wilderness afar,
To 'scape his bondage. Yet, in vain his flight—
Vain his fleet limbs, his desperate aim, his leap
Through the close thicket, through the festering swamp,
And rushing waters. His proud neck must bend
Beneath a halter, and the iron parts
And tears his delicate mouth. The brave steed,
Late bounding in his freedom's consciousness,
The leader of the wild, unreach'd of all,
Wears gaudy trappings, and becomes a slave.

He bears a master on his shrinking back,
He feels a rowel in his bleeding flanks,
And his arch'd neck, beneath the biting thong,
Burns, while he bounds away—all desperate—
Across the desert, mad with the vain hope
To shake his burden off. He writhes, he turns
On his oppressor. He would rend the foe,
Who subtle, with less strength, hath taken him thus,
At foul advantage—but he strives in vain.
A sudden pang—a newer form of pain,
Baffles, and bears him on—he feels his fate,
And with a shriek of agony, which tells,
Loudly, the terrors of his new estate,
He makes the desert—his own desert—ring
With the wild clamors of his new born grief.
One fruitless effort more—one desperate bound,
For the old freedom of his natural life,
And then he humbles to his cruel lot,
Submits, and finds his conqueror in man!

(1838)

LAY OF LEONORA.

i

Old men young maids pursuing,
  How little do they guess,
That every hour of wooing,
  But makes their chances less;
The maid no longer spousy,
  O'ercome with stories long,
To keep from feeling drowsy,
  Must seek relief in song.
And so, with tinkle, tinkle,
  As falling rain to fire,
She soon contrives to sprinkle
  The good old man's desire.
    And so with tinkle, tinkle,
    She soon contrives to sprinkle.

ii

Love hath no long discourses,
  A single smile, a sigh,
These are the sovereign forces,
  That give him victory,—
Thus, while the old man's purring,
  Dull speaking, dully heard,
The young one's stirring, spurring,
  And he carries off the bird:
Ah! then, the tinkle, tinkle,
  Is the church bell from the spire,
To kindle, not to sprinkle,
  The fond bosom with desire.
    Ah! then, the tinkle, tinkle,
    Is to kindle not to sprinkle.

(1841, 1843)

THE LAND OF THE PINE.

i

The land of the pine,
The cedar, the vine,—
Oh, may this blessed land ever be mine;
Lose not in air,
Breezes that bear
Blossoms and odors, the song and the pray'r.

ii

Take not from mine eye
The blue of its sky,
Bid not the soul of its loveliness die;—
Still let me see
The bloom on its tree,
Still bring its blossoms and blessings to me.

(1841, 1846)

MY LOVE, LOVES ME.

i

Seek not the reason for my love,
The best that I can give, d' ye see,
Is, that all other men above
My love, loves me.

ii

She is not beautiful, I know,
No learned dame, no bookworm she,
But then, howe'er the seasons go,
She still loves me.

iii

Tell her that I have nought to boast,
No wealth, no fame, and, heedless, she,
Will smile when you have said your most,
And still love me.

iv

I care not for your brilliant eyes,
  Your subtle wit, your manner free;
I boast, and boast a dearer prize,
  Her love for me.

v

And all I say and all I do,
  Is simply said and done, that she,
Who loved me long, and loves me so,
  May still love me.

(1832, 1841)

SONNET.—I WILL BREATHE MUSIC.

I will breathe music in the little bell
  That cups this flow'r, until it takes a tone,
  For every feeling human heart has known:
Though hearts their secrets do not often tell,
Mine is the spell to win them. I will wake
  Strains, which, though new to men, they shall not fail
  To tremble when they hearken; as an old tale
Will by surprize the absent wanderer take,
Moving his spirit with a strange delight.
  Love will I win from friendship; the old lure
  I will make new; and all the new, secure;
And beauty never more shall fade from sight!
  Such charms—the magic fruit of holiest pow'r—
  May gather in the blue cells of a flow'r.

(1828, 1841)

SOLACE OF THE WOODS.

Woods, waters, have a charm to soothe the ear,
  When common sounds have vex'd it. When the day
  Grows sultry, and the crowd is in thy way,

And working in thy soul much coil and care,—
Betake thee to the forests. In the shade
  Of pines, and by the side of purling streams
  That prattle all their secrets in their dreams,
Unconscious of a listener,—unafraid,—
Thy soul shall feel their freshening, and the truth
  Of nature then, reviving in thy heart,
Shall bring thee the best feelings of thy youth,
  When in all natural joys thy joy had part,
Ere lucre and the narrowing toils of trade
Had turn'd thee to the thing thou wast not made.

(1842, 1853)

LOVE'S TOUR FOR THE PICTURESQUE.

I've linger'd all too long,
  With a much too fond neglect,
Where the glad thousand throng,
  With many a glory deck'd;
Bow'd at too far a shrine,
  Loved with too losing art,
And with too feeble a spirit pine,
  O'er the doom which makes us part.

But I've sworn to better things,
  And I'll run a manlier race,
The hope that sighs and the love that sings
  Shall to nobler things give place.
I will no more serenade,
  I will no more sigh to the moon,
And in search of some foreign aid,
  I shall start on my travels soon.

I'll seek the Tallulah Falls,
  And look on Toccoa's stream,
On the Highwassee make some calls,
  On the cliffs of Mount Yonah dream.
Through the vale of Naugoochie rove,
  Where Guy Rivers once of old,

A smart trade in ponies drove,
    All of which is in history told.

But do not you think, I pray,
    For the picturesque I fly,
If it chance to fall in my way,
    It may chance I will turn an eye.
But the scenes that I most desire,
    And the colours that most I seek,
Are found in an eye of fire,
    And bright on a Georgian cheek.

Let them look where Mount Yonah sweels,
    In the landscape a very gem,
At brawling streams and at fairy dells,—
    Enough that I look at them.
The sense of love, not the sighing,
    Is the doctrine which now I profess,
The living for love, not the dying,
    The delight and not the distress.

So away to Naugoochie's valley,
    Toccoa, Tallulah, and all;
In a week I intend to sally,
    You may look for me back next fall.

(1842)

DREAMING OR WAKING.

Thy hair round my fingers I twine,
And I lay my warm lip upon thine,
And I turn to that eye's dewy bright,
And I sleep in an ocean of light.

Oh, soul of my sleep and my dream,
Shining down like a star on the stream,
I awake from a presence of bliss,
And I melt in the certain of this.

My head, as it droops on thy breast,
Whether waking or dreaming is blest;
And the white arms of snow which entwine,
May be not, though they seem to be, thine.

'Tis the fool that, in dreaming of pleasure,
Would wake to be sure of his treasure,
Methinks 'tis the smallest ambition
To measure one's actual condition.

Could'st thou whisper, methinks I should tell,—
Yet that would be breaking the spell;—
Enough that my dream is divine,
And the arm, lip and bosom seem thine.

(1842)

NIGHT SCENE:

MOULTRIE HOUSE—SULLIVAN'S ISLAND.

i
How still is Nature now,
    How quiet all her sleep!
The dews are on her brow,
    And all her dreams are deep;
Closed darkly is her eye,
    Her breathings soft and low,
As if the spirit, once so high,
In challenge of the earth and sky,
    Would cease to flow.
And out on the black waste of ocean,
    We hear no commotion:
And the billows that lazily break on the shore
    Have a life, but no roar:
And the winds, that were chafing all day with the waves,
    Are subdued into slaves,
That crouch, and but murmur and wait,
As the night, trailing cloud robes, marches on in her state!

ii

Above the expanse of dark,
   That forms her sombre pall,
One star, with glowing spark,
   Looks loving out o'er all;
There spreads a tract of fleece,
   White, in the dusky west:
Like some fair Isle of Peace,
That, when the tempests cease,
   Smiles out on ocean's breast!
And we dream, as we gaze, of old fancies,
   Found in ancient romances:
Of strange dwarfish races, of delicate graces,
   That peopled such places—
To be seen when the sun was at setting,
   On the sands pirouetting;
And who sped, on the star-beam, from islet to sea,
With frolicsome pinion, fantastic as free!

iii

A murmur from the sea,
   A faint and dying strain,
Takes, as the night-winds flee,
   Their parting moan again;
And the twin voices link
   Their pinions for the shore,
Flutter with plaining on its brink,
Then on the sands subside, and sink
   To sleep once more!
And they bury white heads in black pillows,
   Those great rolling billows;
And the vast world of sea, in her bosom,
   Doth lovingly close 'em;
While her murmur of lullaby, soft as the mother's,
   Their deep sobbing smothers;
And the white fleecy isle, that we look'd on erewhile
In the west, passes east, and broods o'er with a smile.

iv

Westward, two rivers wind,
   Sweetly yielding to the deep;

In one embrace they find
    The silvery sway of sleep:
And, from the embosomed bay,
    Ascends a spell, whose chain
Subdues their murmurous play
Of sounds, which melt away,
    As echoes from the plain;
And the skiff that late glided rejoicing,
    With lute-music and mellowest voicing
Now feels the same magic dominion,
    And floats, but with folded-up pinion;
The peace of the sky and the ocean
    Hath hush'd even rapture's emotion,
And the hearts that were stirr'd at each musical word,
Now sleep on their wings as a satisfied bird.

                                        (1843, 1860)

SONNET.—BY THE SWANANNOA.

Is it not lovely, while the day flows on
    Like some unnoticed water through the vale,
    Sun-sprinkled,—and, across the fields, a gale,
    Ausonian, murmurs out an idle tale,
Of groves deserted late, but lately won?
How calm the silent mountains, that, around,
    Bend their blue summits, as if group'd to hear
Some high ambassador from foreign ground,—
To hearken, and, most probably, confound!
    While, leaping onward, with a voice of cheer,
Glad as some schoolboy ever on the bound,
    The lively Swanannoa sparkles near;—
A flash and murmur mark him as he roves,
Now foaming white o'er rocks, now glimpsing soft through groves.

                                        (1843, 1853)

SHAKSPEARE.

The mighty master in each page we trace,
Natural always, never common-place;
Forever frank and cheerful, even when wo,
Commands the sigh to speak, the tear to flow;
Sweet without weakness, without storming, strong,
Jest not too strain'd, nor argument too long;
Still true to reason, though intent on sport,
Thy wit ne'er drives thy wisdom out of court;—
A brooklet now, a noble stream anon,
Careering in the daylight and the sun;
A mighty ocean next, broad, deep and wide,
Earth, sun and heaven, all imaged in its tide!—
Oh! when the master bends him to his art,
How the mind follows, how vibrates the heart,
The mighty grief o'ercomes us as we hear,
And the soul hurries, hungering, to the ear;
The willing nature worships as he sings,
And Heaven is won when Genius spreads her wings.

(1843)

INFANT SMILING IN SLEEP.

Its little lips are smiling in its sleep!
    Alas! lorn stranger in a world of care,
That it should smile, thus born in shame, to weep,
    The very being, fate has formed so fair;—
Sleep on, sleep on! and be your slumbers deep,
    The guilty never sleep as thou dost there;
Yet when thy life shall blossom, what shall be,
The solace of the heart thus born to shame in thee?

Once more it smiles! O! what is there in being
    The soft or the majestic, high or low,
Spell-binding, or heart-soothing, worthier seeing,
    Than that dear innocent so smiling now;
Its little hands from every bondage freeing

Wander and settle on its snowy brow—
No wonder, O! no wonder that the tears,
Of trembling mothers flow, for such, in after years.

(1843)

FOREST WORSHIP.

And whence can the prayer of affection
   More purely ascend to the sky,
Than from temples whose glorious erection
   Still brings the Great Architect nigh?
Deep woods, in whose solemn recesses,
   Tall pines, 'neath whose pillars of might,
The spirit looks upward and blesses,
   And the shadows grow sacred to sight!

Can the prayer that is breathed by devotion,
   Thus hallowed by silence and thought,
And nursed by the deepest emotion
   That ever religion has taught,
Be unworthy God's ear because offer'd
   In a temple whose majesty shames
The proudest that art ever proffer'd,
   For His sacred acceptance and Fame's!

The soul that has drunk from the chalice
   Of sorrow and love, and is bow'd,
Needs none of the pomps of the palace,
   Nor the cold measured rites of the crowd;
It rather implores the dim regions,
   Of shadow and silence; and there,
In the sweet hallow'd twilight, are legions
   Of angels, to sanction its prayer.

There gather, in pity, down-bending,
   The blessedest hopes of the heart;
Dear children, that, never offending,
   Have been bidden, while pure, to depart;
Sweet angels, in shapes that have perish'd,

The mother, the sister, the wife,
All the bright ones that life ever cherish'd,
    All striving to lift us to life!

Their shrine wafts no earthly oblation,
    Their temple, pure, lovely and grand,
Still rises, as when, at Creation,
    It bloomed, the fair work of His Hand;
And well may the devotee falter,
    As he thinks on the races of yore,
The myriads who've bow'd at an altar,
    Where myriads yet must adore.

Ah! vain is that worship, whose vision
    Still craves for the gold on the shrine;
Still looks, with an eye of derision,
    On the rude scatter'd emblems of mine;
More blessed by far, if the blossom
    Of faith may be nourish'd and known,
In the depths of the wood, where the bosom,
    Can feel but God's glory alone!

And think not the prayer of that being,
    O'er whom fortune forever hath smiled,
Can be grateful to him, the All-Seeing,
    As the offering of misery's child;
Though the former, in palace most splendid,
    The rites of acknowledgment gave,
While the latter's frail offering is blended
    With the winds of the desert and wave.

                                                    (1843, 1849)

NOTES FROM BARTRAM.

1. WATER OAK.
The Water Oak whose *hemispheric* head,
Presents the likeness of a mighty grove,
Upon the far Savannah.

2. GOLDFISH AND CRAYFISH.

Here you see
A likeness of the invasion of the Huns,
'Gainst the Italian cities—the beautiful Arts
O'erwhelm'd by the Barbarian. See, where fly
The swarming Goldfish, in their homes assailed,
By foray of the Crayfish—odious foes
Whose very aspect, to the Beautiful,
Is hateful, like their power.

3. THE CYPRESS.

Lo! where the Cypress soars in majesty;—
Gigantic column from an archéd base,
Springing above the swamp—with great flat dome,
Fringed with the Druid moss. It stands aloft,
Meet emblem of the virtues in Old Age,
Which wave paternal arms o'er feebler tribes,
And, bearded with the grey of eld, yet mocks
Decay in humbler forms. The tooth of Time,
Gnaws unavailing on its mighty trunk,
While the storm beats as vainly on its brow.

4. THE SNOW DROP.

Oh! precious, with a crest of pure white flowers,
Showing the blest virginity in Hope,
That, midst the work of Winter's violent shocks,
Promises Spring; and, rising through the snow,
Asserts its triumph, over all assault,
And right to sunshine! And the green spear hedges,
With which it fences its sweet virgin flowers,
Declare the warrior-legions, set to rise,
And guard the shrines she consecrates to love.

5. PAPAYA.

So supercilious in her stateliness
Proud in harmonious beauties—grace in pride!

6. CREEPERS.

Creepers, the emblems of a timid love,
Born of dependence and a sense of fear,
That only seeks *permission.* They will creep,

And climb, and cling, and spirally involve
Their feeble muscles; so to spring at last,
As to take captive; and, in fond embrace,
Bind, close as fate, the stalwart massy form
That never felt their growing, till together,
Their fortunes grew to one.

7. THE SARACENIA.

The Yellow Saracenia, whose bright flowers,
Seem models for a silken canopy.
The yellow pendant petals are the curtains;
The hollow leaves, like Amalthæa's horn,
With lid spontaneous shutting at each draught,
Gather and hide within a cup of waters,
Cool, sweet, refreshing as the morning dews.

8. CANE SWAMP. HIBISCUS.

Here you see,
In best perfection, in a mould so vast,
As shames the architectural shows of Europe,
The glory of the Gothic arch. You stroll
Through grandest avenues of feathery cane,
Enliven'd with the Hibiscus. Its great flowers,
Pale yellow and white, with a deep crimson eye,
Bristling with hair; in contrasts beautiful
With the green verdure of the populous waste,
While spread great forests o'er it making shade,
Even at the noonday, such as mocks the sun,
And flings back every arrow from his brow.

9. THE OAK.

The hospitable oak, whose outstretched arms,
So vast, so patriarchal, draped in moss,
Invite to rest, and shield with confidence.

10. SPANISH CURLEWS.

We have broken the peace,
Of a most beautiful family. Our sports
Mar the domestic joys of tribes that ask
Security alone—and we deny!
See the swift sailing squadrons, how they rise,

The Spanish Curlews, with their robes outspread,
White as the veil which Innocence still wears,
Gleaming bright in contrast with cerulean skies.

11. THE CRANE.

The wary Crane, sharp-sighted, from afar,
Descries our cypress coracle, and speeds,
Shrieking in flight. We might send a bolt
To bring him from his high perch in the air,
But that 'twere pity! See, how beautiful,
His snowy wings now full abreast yon cloud,
That blackens with its thunders.

12. WOOD PELICAN.

Think you we move unseen?
Look, now, where broods yon sad Wood Pelican,
A sentinel, perch'd on topmost height of spire,
That watches, like some venerable sage,
The sports of the unconscious tribes below.

13. ODORIFEROUS SHRUBS OF FLORIDA.

How sweet the sudden scent!—
The shrubs you tread upon, with every breeze,
Weep odors! Strange, that we may win the sweet,
Even by injury! Thus virtue grows,
Most grateful when most trodden; and we bruise
The human sensibility, to win
What's precious in its keeping.

14. THE KALMIA—AZALÆA.

For perfect show of gaiety in childhood,
Look to the Kalmia—to the Azalæa.

15. INDIANS SPEARING SALMON.

The red man that you see,
Reclining on the bank above the stream,
Watches the unconscious salmon as he glides,
Beneath the bluff, and with his arrowy shaft,
Transfixes his bright sides.

16. DIONEA MUSCIPULA.

Would you learn
A fruitful lesson which shall keep your feet
From frequent danger? Study then yon plant,—
Dionea Muscipula—that vegetable,
Most animated, most intelligent,
With faculty carnivorous, and wits,
Instinctive that still manufacture snares.

17. THUNDER STORM.

Within an hour,
Roll up the great black billows of the West,
The birth place of the storm. Even now, behold
Where from his cloudy chasm in angry mood,
And a fierce flame-glance darting from his eye,
Leaps forth the sovran thunder; while his spear,
Edged with the lightning's red and rapid rush,
Clangs on his pondrous shield.

18. THE AROMATIC KALMIA.

19. THE POMPOUS PALMS OF FLORIDA.

How stately rise
These pompous Palms of Florida. Methinks
They tell of virtues in a rugged rind;
And firmness in misfortune; and a strength
To live on little nurture from the soil;
Yet brave the fury of each storm that roars
O'er the blue vast of yon tumultuous gulph.

20. THE BLUSHING CHIRONIA.

21. THE SPIRAL OPHRYS.

Framed for innocence,
With its immaculate white virgin flowers.

22. WINGED SEEDS.

That colonize countries far remote,
A cosmopolitan race, that, gipseying,
Make happy homes in lands however strange,
Nor asks what virtue or what despot rules.

23. THE PRINCELY FISH HAWK.

24. THE FOREST OF AGAVE (VIVIPARA).
  Their tall forms
Spreading into pyramids.

25. PRICKLY FAN LEAF PALMETTO.
Here, a green field, the dwarf Palmetto waves
Her leafy fan in the half drowsy shade,
Screened by the towering water oak and pine.

26. THE BALD EAGLE.
That execrable Tyrant, who maintains,
By rapine and violence, usurping sway,
Extorting tribute from all feathered tribes.

27. THE FAITHFUL DOVE.
Brooding at noon, within the bristling pine,
O'er satisfied affection, fond as true.

28. THE PLUMED PALMS.

29. THE PYRAMIDAL LAURELS.

30. THE SCARLET NYSSA, OR THE OGEECHEE LIME.

31. THE ANNONA.
With its clusters of white flowers,
Plant for the summer festival and show.

32. THE GOPHER.
  Like a Robber from his caves,
Comes forth to prowl by night.

33. ANDROMEDA.
The beautiful Andromeda of Florida,
Loveliest of all its race.

34. THE CRYING BIRD, EPHOUSKYCA.
With faithful watch and sudden cry, alarms,
The flocks that feed below.

35. THE SWEET SUCCULENT GRASSES.

36. THE HOARY GRAY OF TWILIGHT HORIZON.

37. COPPICES.
      The scene so wild,
Checquer'd with Coppices of fragrant shrubs.

38. THE NEW MOON.
The dark eclipse of that maternal star,
Whose light of love, so dear to all that love,
Goes out,—and but a silver thread remains
Untouch'd by dark, about her ample brows.

39. WHITE LILY.
That admirable Lady, the White Lily,
That dwells in shadiest grove with modesty,
Still takes her dwelling where she may receive,
Her tribute of pure breezes from the sea.

40. FOREST LUNCH.
A regal feast! our rural table spread
Beneath the shadow of great palms and oaks;
The odorous Bay in tribute with her sweets,
And the fresh breezes, from the ruffling seas,
Humming in concert with most tuneful tribes,
That make the forests glorious with glad song;
Even as the sea, with choral notes from shells,
Whose twisted cores, imprison the soft air,
Only to teach it music! See, yon bough,
Where sings the painted Nonpareil, a flower,
Animate with a soul; whose regular lays,
Responsive, first and second—always two—
Sweet voices, singing love—delude the house
To dreaming and delight. Ah! they are hushed
By a great master. 'Tis the Mocking Bird,
That silences the forest with such strains
As teach to music's self a sad despair,
Pouring a very cataract of song,
O'er the astounded forest. Never Count
Of Europe, had such music at a feast.

41. PALMETTO ROYAL.

Crested with silvery pyramid of flowers,
Fenced in by thousand swords of glittering green,
A forest of sharp bayonets at your breast.

42. EPHEMERA.

That with the first grey glimpses of the dawn,
Emerge from depth and silence, and march forth
A long procession, to the grassy shores.

43. THE WILD TURKEY.

The wild turkey's chaunt
Of exultation, and a conscious pride,
Repeated by his numerous centinels,
Through hundred miles of forest, till the air
Swells into common shout.

44. ACORN OIL.

The Indian, from the acorn, draws an oil
Which garnishes his rice; or roasts them hot
In the live embers.

45. MAGNOLIA GRANDIFLORA.

Majestically, with a giant spring,
The laurel grows, a pyramid all green,
With milk-white blossoms silvered, as a Prince,
Pearl-dusted, the rich velvet of his robes.

46. WILD TURKEY'S MATING IN SPRING.

From early dawn 'till rising of the sun,
The forest gobler to his modest mate,
Decorous shouts; and all the myriad brood
Through the grey forests, and the mighty tops
Of cypress and magnolia, many a mile,
Echoes the cheering crow! Descending then,
From their high places, on the earth alight,
They spread elate their silver-border'd fans
And dance around their favorites of the flock.

47. THE DRUID MOSS—THE PROPHET-BEARDED OAK.

48. VINES.

The vegetable vagabonds, that stroll,
Profligate, heedless where they spread themselves,
Over green knolls, and twined in airy folds,
With the lithe grasses of the gentle slopes.

49. WATER FOWL.

Squadrons of wild aquatic fowl sail forth
From the lagune, at sunrise, to the lake,
Emerging sudden, but with amorous cries,
From leafy and deep coverts of the shore.

50. CAYMAN—ALLIGATOR.

The Cayman, bellowing at the set of sun,
As at his rising.

51. XANTHOXILON, A SHELTER FROM THE SUN.

The Seminole, retiring from the heat,
Sleeps happy, rapt in odoriferous sweets,
In shade of the Xanthoxilon.

52. PLUMED PALMS.

Palms orb'd with grandly waving and green plumes,
Floating like pennons.

53. CORMORANTS.

Hung above the stream,
From twigs or bending branches, wings outspread,
The brooding Cormorants watch, and as you move,
Drop from their heights into the glassy wave,
And sail away in silence.

54. WILD SQUASH.

From gay green branches doth the wild Squash hang
Her yellow fruits.

55. CRANE.

The stately Crane,
White chief of the Savannah.

56. SEMINOLE DOGS—BLACK.

The faithful black Dog of Seminole,
The guardian watcher of his herds of horse.

57. KEOWEE.

By Keowee's steep side,
Its rocky brow, gray and seam'd with storm,
Flames with the Azalæa.

(ca. 1844, 1858, 1867)

SHADOWS.

A shadow rises on my view
   When gray the mists descend of eve;
It wears the look of one I knew,
   And long have loved, and still must grieve;
Its glance recals the perish'd years,
   The hopes they brought, the joy, the pain;
The all that love to time endears—
   That mournful shadow brings again.

As sinks the pale and crescent light—
   It rises slow beside me now,
Half shaded by the gathering night,
   I see its pure and pallid brow;
So sad, so wan! as if, though bless'd
   In happiest realms where love is sure,
It sorrowed still at my unrest,
   And shared the grief it could not cure.

Sweet spirit! by those heavenly airs
   That, as thou com'st, around have met,
By every pang that still endears
   The sweetest memories to regret;
By all the hopes I may not lose,
   Which yet were only known as lost
I would not, if I might, repose
   Thy sad attendance, mournful ghost.

What though that voice, once mirth and song,
  To me be hushed for aye, and still,
That eye be dim whose light was long
  The charm and impulse to my will;
That breast be cold, whose pure desires
  Had just enough of earth, to wake
An homage meet in human fires—
  Thence, worthy heavenlier, for its sake!

Yet as my heart no longer flames
  With hope and rapture now, as then,
So, to its present humbler aims,
  That seek no more the haunts of men,
Sufficeth well, that in the place
  Of young delights and boyish bliss,
A shadow fills my cold embrace,
  And solitude my soul, like this!

I know thee, and 'tis joy to know,
  Since dread the doubt that overcast
That hour of more than mortal wo,
  When from my grasp thy spirit passed;
When, in the vacant, glassy glare,
  In eyes whose smiles had kindled mine,
I felt, and shudder'd at the fear,
  Lest they no more should on me shine.

That doubt is gone, and all the rest,
  Of sorrow and wo, is small for us;
I know thou livest—I deem thee bless'd,
  Else wert thou not permitted thus;
Then come, as still thou cam'st of yore,
  A form of heaven, a dear delight—
Thou fill'st my fond embrace no more,
  But it is all—thou fill'st my sight.

                                    (1825, 1844)

WITCH OF ELLANO.

i
Damsel wild of Ellano
   Let them never idly tell,
That no more, on earth below,
    Witchery works her spell!
      In thine eyes
      The fountain lies,
Of a magic far more deep,
     Than, of old,
     Subdued the bold,
Made the guardian dragon sleep;
     Mischief play'd
     With man and maid,
Making the one go rage, the other weep.

ii
Likeness of the forest land,
   Where thy infant beauty grew,
Like a palm I see thee stand,
    Beautiful to view.
      Thou hast grown
      In forest lone,
Near a stream of shaded grace;
     And thy bloom
     Cheers its gloom,
Makes all sweetness in the place:
     Thou hast taught
     A charm to Thought,
Till Thought grows one with Beauty in thy face!

iii
Beauty, the secret of thy power,
   And it spells whatever sees;
In thy hair one virgin flower
    Waves o'er mortal destinies.
      And thy glance,—
      Indian lance
Never sped so sharp and well;
     And thy brow,

Like his bow,
Makes each magic arrow tell:
Every smile
Hath its wile,
And all confess the witchery of thy spell!

(1844, 1860)

PARTING.

A FRAGMENT.

My heart must perish when it parts from thee;
  It lives no longer, for its life was made,
Like some fine harp of cunning minstrelsy,
  Of delicate chords that would not sound when play'd
By any but the one whose mastery,
  Born for that office, taught by holiest aid,
Had wrought its secret fibres and had wove,
The many spells that moved it, out of love.

My heart is that same harp, and thine the hand
  Whose over-mastering spell and witching might,
Touching the hidden string with strong command,
  Could wake it into speech, and life, and light—
And now that parting for another strand,
  I lose thee, my Ianthe, from my sight,
Stills the sweet harp whose sounds thy touch set free,
And chills for aye the heart which had its life from thee.

(1844)

FLOWERS AND TREES.

March is profuse in violets—at our feet
  They cluster,—not in pride, but modesty;
  The damsel pauses as she passes by,
Plucks them with smiles, and calls them very sweet.
But such beguile me not! The trees are mine,

These hoary-headed masters;—and I glide,
Humbled, beneath their unpresuming pride,
And wist not much what blossoms bud or shine.
I better love to see yon grandsire oak,
Old Druid-patriarch, lone among his race,—
With blessing, out-stretch'd arms, as giving grace
When solemn rites are said, or bread is broke:
Decay is at his roots,—the storm has been
Among his limbs,—but the old top is green.

THE SAME SUBJECT.

The pine with its green honors; cypress gray,
Bedded in waters; crimsoning with bloom
The maple, that, irreverently gay,
Too soon, methinks, throws off his winter gloom;
The red bud, lavish in its every spray,
Glowing with promise of the exulting spring;
And over all, the laurel, like some king,
Conscious of strength and stature, born for sway.
I care not for their species—never look
For class or order in pedantic book,—
Enough that I behold them—that they lead
To meek retreats of solitude and thought,
Declare me from the world's day-labors freed,
And bring me tidings books have never brought.

(1844, 1853)

RELIGIOUS MUSINGS.

The mighty and the massy of the wood
Compel my worship: satisfied I lie,
With nought in sight but forest, earth, and sky,
And give sweet sustenance to precious mood!—
'Tis thus from visible but inanimate things,
We gather mortal reverence. They declare
In silence, a persuasion we must share,
Of hidden sources, spiritual springs,

Fountains of deep intelligence, and powers,
　　That man himself implores not; and I grow
　　From wonder into worship, as the show,
Majestic, but unvoiced, through noteless hours,
Imposes on my soul, with musings high,
That, like Jacob's Ladder, lifts them to the sky!

(1844, 1853)

SONNET. POPULAR MISDIRECTION.

Would we recal our virtues and our peace?
　　The ancient teraphim we must restore;
　　Bring back the household gods we loved of yore,
And bid our yearning for strange idols cease.
Our worship still is in the public way,—
　　Our altars are the market-place;—our prayer
　　Strives for meet welcome in our neighbor's ear,
And heaven affects us little while we pray.
　　We do not call on God, but man, to hear;—
Nor even on his affections;—we have lost
　　The sweet humility of our home desires,
　　And flaunt in foreign fashions at rare cost;
Nor God our souls, nor man our hearts inspires,
　　Nor aught that should to God or man be dear.

(1844, 1853)

HARBOR BY MOONLIGHT.

The open sea before me, bathed in light,
　　As if it knew no tempest; the near shore
Crown'd with its fortresses, all green and bright,
　　As if 'twere safe from carnage ever more;
And woman on the ramparts; while below
　　Girlhood, and thoughtless children bound and play
　　As if their hearts, in one long holiday,
Had sweet assurance 'gainst to-morrow's wo:—
Afar, the queenly city, with her spires,

Articulate, in the moonlight,—that above,
Seems to look downward with intenser fires,
    As wrapt in fancies near akin to love;
One star attends her which she cannot chide,
Meek as the virgin by the matron's side.

                                        (1844, 1845)

THE NATAL STAR.

There is a pale and solitary star,
    That, with a sudden but a sweet surprise,
Nightly, with little heed of bolt or bar,
    Peeps in upon my couch and opes mine eyes.
The office of so pure a visitor
    Must be for healing. Lovely was the thought
That, in the dreams of old astrologer,
    The fate of star and man together wrought.
Nor, though this presence robs me of my rest,
    And makes me sad with sleepless memories,
    Shall it be curtain'd from my weary eyes:
As my twin-angel, blessing still and bless'd,
I welcome it, and still lament the night,
When storm or cloud denies it to my sight.

                                        (1844, 1860)

PROMISE.

Another yet, and yet another height,
    And still the last most wearisome! But, hark!
    Comes not, like blesséd starlight through the dark,
Hope's confident whisper, that, with sudden bright,
    Makes glad the landscape; cheers the spirit still;
    Mocks at small toil, o'er rocky plain or hill,
And sings a sweet assurance of the joy
    That waits and beckons at the cottage door?
How little then appears the day's annoy,
    And Bliss rewards us when the toil is o'er!

And if in arms that love us, we should tell
   Of the day's labor, wearisome and sad,
'Twill be in thanks and blessings, that so well
   It ended,—in a night so bright and glad.

(1844, 1860)

SONNET.—THE AGE OF GOLD.

These times deserve no song—they but deride
   The poet's holy craft,—nor his alone;
   Methinks as little courtesy is shown
To what was chivalry in days of pride:
Honor but meets with mock:—the worldling shakes
   His money-bags, and cries—"My strength is here;
O'erthrows my enemy, his empire takes,
   And makes the ally serve, the alien fear!"
Is love the object? Cash is conqueror,—
   Wins hearts as soon as empires—puts his foot
Upon the best affections, and will spur
   His way to eloquence, when Faith stands mute;
And for Religion,—can we hope for her,
   When love and valor serve the same poor brute!

(1844, 1853)

AH! TURNING O'ER THE CLASSIC PAGE.

i

Ah! turning o'er the classic page,
   The unbidden tear will start,
Since, musing o'er the heroic age,
   We lose the heroic heart!
That heart which ever beat with glory's tide,
   So fearless, fond and free;
That knew no prouder hope, no dearer pride,
Than when, triumphing as it died,
   It proved its generous truth and matchless loyalty.

The soul at glory's call which sprung,
  The love whose generous youth,
On beauty's slightest accents hung,
  And yielded truth for truth.
Oh! for such soul in these degenerate days,
  For valor such pure flame;
While battling to the last, in beauty's gaze,
Implored no blessing better than her praise,
  And deem'd her smile the very light of fame.

iii

And it is fame! Hearts cherish long,
  Wherever feeling weeps the brave:
And valor lives in beauty's song,
  And constant faith survives the grave.
Still o'er the page that tells of hero deeds,
  The fond heart lingers yet;
Glows with its triumph, in its anguish bleeds,
And, though it weeps the while, weeps on, and reads,
  And never, weeping ever, can forget!

                                        (1845, 1865)

THE LONELY ISLET.

i

  Lift the oar, as silently
  By yon sacred isle we pass;
Know we not if still she sleeps,
Where the wind such whisper keeps,
  In yon waving grass!
Death's a mocker to delight,
  That we know,—and yet,—
There was that in every breath
  Of her motion—in the set
  Of her features, fair and whole—
    In the flashing of her eye,
    Spirit joyous still, and high,
  Speaking the immortal soul,

In a language warm and bright—
  That should mock at death!

  ii
    Silently!—still silently!
  Oh! methinks, if it were true,
  If, indeed, she sleeps—
Wakeful never, though the oar
    Of the well-beloved one, nigh,
Break the water as before;—
    When, with but the sea in view,
And the sky-waste, and the shore,
    Or some star that, sinking, creeps,
Between whiles of speech, to show
How sweet lover's tears may flow,—
    They together went, forgetting,
    How the moon was near her setting,
Down amid the waters low;—

  iii
Then no more should lovely things,
    Moon or star, or zephyr, stoop,—
But a cloud with dusky wings,
    Gloom outgiving, still should droop,
    O'er that islet lone:—
And the long grass by the breeze
Sullen rising from the seas,
    Should make constant moan!
Silent!—Hark!—that dipping oar,—
    Oh! methinks, it roused a tone
As of one upon the shore!—
'Twas the wind that swept the grass!—
    Silently, oh! silently,—
As the sacred spot we pass!

                                        (1845, 1853)

CLARICE.

i

Maidens there are, of grace and light,
  Who, when ye dream about the sky,
Come, ever smiling, strangely bright,
  Between the fancy and the eye;
Ye feel them sweet to soul and sight,
  And sadden as ye see them fly.

ii

And she was one of those that grew
  The image kindred to the theme;
Still present to the mind and view,
  Though still as something in a dream;
I loved her beauties ere I knew
  So well my thoughts did they beseem.

iii

Not long the heart an ideal thrills,
  Lacks comfort from the thing it woos;
For still the generous nature wills,
  That he shall find who well pursues;
The glad soul which a fancy fills
  Soon shapes the creature it must choose.

iv

True to my fancy thus she grew,
  The living thing that was my thought;
The spirit of grace, the woman too,
  That dreams had found for me unsought;
If doubts declared the dream untrue,
  Her smile the perfect faith soon taught.

v

And ever still, in hours of gloom,
  She brought me glimpses of her skies;
Her presence freshen'd earth with bloom,
  And heaven lay star-like in her eyes;
How should I vex me with the doom,
  Still wrought by evil destinies?

vi

Ah! hers were spells we may not feign,
  Born at her birth and fashion'd so,
Ye may not teach, or falsely train,
  By all th' experience taught below;
To me they brought exceeding gain,
  But work'd her gentle spirit wo!

vii

For, to the delicate hearts that take
  Their nurture from another's eye,
There's danger if the breeze but shake
  The lilies in the lake that lie;
She weeps, lest love his perch forsake,
  And dies with dread, lest rapture die.

viii

The smile, that, like a forest bird,
  Starts up with sudden song to cheer;—
The sadden'd tone, that, sudden heard,
  Sounds strange and cold upon the ear;—
The hasty glance, th' impatient word,
  These ever thrill'd her with a fear.

ix

And pleasure's self was like a pain
  So keenly felt was every bliss;
Even though convulsive throbb'd the brain,
  Lest life should bring no more like this;
The very love she lived to gain,
  Brought death when bonded in its kiss.

x

She perish'd in her innocent youth,
  As well beseems the creature made,
Like her, all tenderness and truth,
  Of such pure light, of such soft shade,—
So full of fear, and faith, and ruth,
  And born for love, of love afraid.

(1845, 1848)

ACCABEE—A BALLAD.

It was a night of calm o'er Ashley's waters,
   Crept the sweet billows with their own sad tune,
While she, the fairest of our southern daughters,
   A maid to spell the footsteps of the moon—
      As slow we swept along,
      Pour'd forth her own sweet song—
Ah! song of rapture, not forgotten soon!

Hush'd was our breathing, still the lifted oar,
   Our spirits spell'd, our limbs no longer free,
While the boat drifting silent to the shore,
   Brought us within the shades of Accabee:
      "Ah!" sudden cried the maid,
      Of the dim groves afraid,
Where roves the ghost of the old Yemassee.

And sure the spot is haunted by a power,
   To fix the pulses of the youthful heart;
Never was moon more gracious in a bower,
   With the green leaves delicious in her art,
      Weaving so meekly bright,
      Her pictures of delight,
That much we sorrow'd but to say depart.

"If these old woods are haunted," sudden then,
   Said she, our dear companion, "it must be,
By one who loved and was beloved again,
   And loved all forms of loveliness to see;
      Here, in these groves they went,
      With songs and worship blent,
Their wilder toils forgot in that idolatry."

Slow sped our skiff into the open light,
   The billows grew around us, but no more,
Rose the sweet ditty on our ears that night—
   Silent the maid looked back upon the shore,
      And thought of those dark groves,
      And the wild Indian's loves,
As they had been a truth her heart had dream'd of yore.

(1845)

SYMPATHY WITH NATURE.

We are a part of all we hear and see,—
   We share in their existence—we are taught
   By what they suffer—with their feelings fraught,—
Are bound by their captivity, or free,
   In their fresh impulses;—the earth, the air,
   Master us through our sympathies—we share
The life that is about us, and thus flee,
   From our own nature to a converse strange
With other natures—to the rock and tree,
The bird, and the sleek animal that glides
   Still happy in deep thickets. Thus we range,
Capricious, still obedient to the tides
That chide or soothe our streams, as winds impel the sea.

                                     (1845)

HEEDLESSNESS.

We see the flow'r decaying as we pass,
Pale with the coming cold, and, on the grass,
   Write ruin, with our footsteps, every hour,
   Yet pause not in our progress, though a pow'r,
As much superior to ourselves, as we
   To these dumb suff'rers of the predestined earth,
   Beholds us rapidly passing from our birth,
To a like ruin with the things we see;
And, from our side, as little heeded, goes,
   Drawn by invisible cords, the treasured thing
   That has our heart, in keeping;—yet we sing
As idly as if life were free from foes,
And love were sure 'gainst danger;—there is one,
Who, speaking near me now, of death, is heard by none!

                                     (1845)

THE SOUL IN IMAGINATIVE ART.

i

Methinks each noble purpose of man's heart,
　Declared by his performance, crowns his works
　With a becoming spirit, which still lurks
In what he builds, nor will from thence depart,
Though time bestows it on the solitude,
　The solitude on Ruin, and her gray,
　In moss and lichen honoring decay,
Makes her a refuge where a nobler mood
Had rear'd a temple to diviner art,
　And based its shrines on worship. In the stone
　Dismember'd, sits that guardian shape alone,
Twin-being with the precious trust whose birth
　Brought down a wandering genius to a throne,
And gave him thence a realm and power on earth.

ii

Thy thought but whisper'd rises up a spirit,
　Wing'd, and from thence immortal. The sweet tone,
　Freed by thy skill from prisoning wood or stone,
Doth thence for thine a tribute soul inherit!
When from the genius speaking in thy mind,
　Thou hast evolved the godlike shrine or tower,
That moment does thy matchless art unbind
　A spirit born for earth, and arm'd with power,
The fabric of thy love to watch and keep
　From utter desecration. It may fall,
　Thy structure,—and its gray stones topple all,—
But he who treads its portals feels how deep
A presence is upon him,—and his word
Grows hush'd, as if a shape, unseen beside him heard.

(1845, 1853)

THE BEAUTY OF DEPARTING OBJECTS.

How beautiful, thus fading from the eye,
　Are the sweet things we scarcely saw before;

Scenes that, 'till now, ne'er challenged smile or sigh,
  How lovely seem they, fleeting evermore;
We feel, too late, our blindness and would buy
  From memory, all that memory can restore!
Thus, the o'erburthen'd form, as on the bed
  Of Death, and the last trial, it reposes,
New freshness feels in all around it spread,
  And finds new sweetness in the leaves and roses.
'Till now there had been nothing in the things,
  Most precious near us, and our eyes unfold,
  Even as they close forever, to behold
How dear the gifts of home our blindness from us flings.

(1845)

IMAGINATION.

i

He is a God who wills it,—with a pow'r
To work his purpose out in earth and air,
Though neither speak him fair!—
So may he pluck from earth its precious flow'r,
And in the ether choose a spirit rare,
To serve him deftly in some other sphere;—
And thus it is that I have will'd this hour,
And thou hast heard me, and thy form is here!

ii

Creature of wing and eye,
That, singing, seek'st the sky,
And soar'st because thou sing'st, and singing, still must fly;
Believe me, though I know not mine own voice,
I see thee, and before thee I rejoice;
Thou, precious in both worlds, with thy sole choice
In ours, I bless thee that I knew thee first,
Ere, in the dawn of mortal joys, my heart,
Low-fashion'd by its fond caprice and art,
Had been for thy blest offices accurst;—
Denied the commerce of thy griefs, which bring
The wholesome of Love's sweetness with the sting;—

The love which Sin hath nurst,—
But nursing, could not keep,—
Soothed by delicious dews, the soul that steep,
And circumvent the wing!—
Oh! thou hast heard me;—heard me and com'st down,
Amid the silence and the shade, a gleam;
I see the glimmer of thy golden crown,
I feel thy wing in murmur, and I dream—
Dream of thy pleasant provinces, which lie
Still open to the conqueror, who, no more
May rifle, than resist, thy precious store,
Which grows, the more he spoils, the more beneath his eye!

iii

Oh! thou hast heard me with no jealous grace,—
Hast heard me, and approv'st the daring quest,
Which, heedless of this lowliness of place,
Would build thee here a shrine,—and, to my breast,
Implore thee, that I may be lifted high
To thy vast realms, that still entreat mine eye,
Shining through fields of vision, by the star,
Most sacred, which, at evening and at dawn,
First comes to teach us where the bright ones are,
Each, in his place, upon the heavenly lawn;—
All open to thy wing, that, dusk and day,
Descend'st and risest,—lifting, at each flight,
Some hopeful spirit, that, beneath thy ray,
Grows fitted to a world of more delight!—
Oh! not for thee to censure lowliness,
Save in the soul; which, grovelling as it goes,
Sees not the bright wings that descend to bless,
And will not seek where the true fountain flows!
And he whom man denies,
Hath but to lift his eyes,
Touch'd by thy breath, fresh-parted from the skies,
And the walls tumble outward that did bound,
And, skyward, the blue deepens; and, in air,
A flutter of the happiest wings is found,
Diffusing sweets that earth still finds too rare;—
And faith takes both her wings—
Will, that o'er mortal things

Still sways, as doth the wand o'er hidden springs;
And Love, that, in her trust,
Holds empire over dust,
And lifts to very life the soul to which she clings!
These grow to freedom with thy downward flight,
While the gross earth, bedarken'd in the bright,
That kindles on his sight,
Feels all its pomps grow nought,
Subject to that great thought,
Borne on thy matchless plumes, by which the soul is taught.

     iv

I know my undeserving—know how vain
The poor equivalent of love I bring,
And yet once more I do solicit thee;—
Again! O! yet again!
Sit by me as thou didst, my beautiful!
When life was but a blossom of the spring,
And thou its zephyr—sit by me and sing.
Thy voice of tears will medicine the gloom
That hangs about my spirit, and set free
That bird of faith that only finds its wing
In thy melodious coming. Chase away
These threatening shapes that cloud my lonely room,
And wrap me in their moody grasp all day!
Come,—for thou only canst,—O! come and lull,
With the sweet reedy music of thy tone,
The weary spirit left too much alone
By the gay strollers of this idle time;
Yet, deem me not irreverent when I ask!—
With thee, the creature of the wing and eye,—
A bird-flight not a task!—
'Twere easy to adjure, from stars sublime,
Such mighty sorrows, as, through these old walls,
Would leave a thousand echoes gushing free;—
At every trailing of a spirit's train,
Recalling still that strain,
That woke me to thy presence first, when far
Led by a single star,
And following in the wake of fancies sweet,
I wander'd deep into the mountain halls,

And ever, through the flashes of the storm,
Beheld a flitting form;
And heard, when winds grew hush'd, the sounds of falling feet!

V

I know, with various wing, that thou canst soar
To realms that know no sorrow—that thy flight
Can waft thee to vain regions of delight,
Where wings may rather wanton than explore;—
But not to provinces like these I pray
Thy pinions; nor for me that idle lore,
That only seeks to wile, or win, by art,
The vigilant hours that watch through the long day;—
Those foolish madrigals that chase away,
As old men laugh, time's wrinkles;—the vain joke
That shakes the theatre, while, for the nonce,
The buffoon triumphs in the sage's cloak,
And wisdom, all forgetful of his part,
Grows heedless of the white upon his sconce,
Nor deafens as he shakes his borrow'd bells!—
Nor should you win me when the drama tells
The sportive passions of that wayward God,
Who, riding Libya's lion, yet with craft,
Still wings his wanton shaft,
Subduing mightiest spirits into shame;
Till lowlier men grow scornful of the fame,
That took the name of glory, ere the sport
Of that boy-archer shook their high report!—
As Love is in thy office, let the strain,
That teaches me his affluence, be implored
From the full heart and the sincerest thought;—
As if the captive thus had been restored
To passions of great pride and purest gain,—
Such as, by truth made plain,
Had never partaken of the pernicious fruit
That held the reptile in its core, and brought
Caprice, that ever must the soul imbrute!
Bring me to knowledge of that nobler flame
That never clouds with shame;
That freely may declare its aim and birth,
Nor glow, all doubtful of its proper name,
Impure, unhallow'd, on the hallow'd hearth!

Mine be the creature of a faith that brooks
No fashioning art or offices of man;
But, for its laws and properties, still looks
To the true purpose, first in nature's plan,
Decreed, ere rolling spheres and twinkling orbs began.

vi

Thine is the night, the cloud, the lone, the far;
Thou bring'st to eve her star:
The cloud from thee receives its wing for flight,
And, clothed in purple light,
Goes sailing, richly freighted, to the sea!—
And thou hast cheer'd the solitude for me;—
Hast borne me, when the fetters of earth had worn
Into the soul, its scorpion lash had torn,—
Borne me, triumphant, from my lonely cell,
To freedom, in far empires of the night;—
The freedom of the rugged mountain's height;
The strange companions of the haunted dell;
Great fields of blue, star-lighted,—while the cloud
Lay mantling o'er the city like a shroud,
And all behind was sad, and all before was bright!
Long vistas of the wood were wooing,—gay,
Sprinkt with the droplets which the sun had left,
Fast hurrying, having loiter'd on his way;—
These, in green thick close hid, and rocky cleft,
Made rich the solemn shadows of the wood;
So that the pilgrim, consciously astray,
Might wander still, since all around was good.
Thus night is in thy keeping! Thou alone
Canst take the veil from off her matron brow,
And bid the dreamer gladden in her sight.
Thou mak'st the secrets of her mansion known,
Her mansion, gloomy with excess of bright;—
And, from its wealth, surpassing mortal show,
The starr'd luxuriance of her pillar'd throne,
Thou canst extort her music—a lament,
As if the stars and winds together made
A requiem o'er the glories that must fade,—
Such as might issue, on a God's descent
From some high sphere his presence once had sway'd.
'Tis thine to put a soul into this train,

While earth is sleeping—blasted from her birth
Into unmusical barrenness and dearth,
Such as might move her ne'er to wake again,
Did it not pleasure her vain pride to spoil,
With keen and clamorous coil,
The delicate labors of our secret toil,
To break upon the midnight watch we keep—
Forgetting sleep,
Here, charming night and silence from the deep,
Stars stooping round us ever as they shine,
While wings, from off thy shoulders, grow to mine.

(1846, 1853)

LOVE SONG IN SPRING.

The heart that reposes,
  While Spring brings her roses,
Is sure to be left in the shade, the shade;
  The youth that is wasted,
  Ere love has been tasted,
Is a youth without blossom, dear maid, dear maid.

There still is an hour,
  When, wooing the flow'r,
The sun in his glow seeks the field, the field;
  When, opening her bosom
  To the beamlet, the blossom,
Knows wisely the season to yield, to yield.

Ah! sad, if ungrateful,
  She turns away hateful,
For never, believe me, again, again,
  Will zephyr or sunlight,
  With one love, or one light,
Renew the approach made in vain, made in vain.

Then yield to me, dear one,
  The season's a fair one,
While to love both the sun and the zephyr persuade;

For the heart that still closes,
Though love brings his roses,
Will most surely be left in the shade, the shade.

(1847, 1866)

PROPER UNDERSTANDING.

i

Why meet me with aspect so chilling,
  As if our last squabble were aught
But love, making piquant the willing,
  By a breeze from good policy caught:
Were there nothing but sunshine between us,
  No gusts sudden ruffling our sky,
I'd seek a more changeable Venus,
  And bid your tame beauties "good-bye!"
        Yes, I would!
  Bid all your tame beauties "good-bye!"

ii

Your eyes are quite precious when smiling,
  Yet nothing it vexes me when,
In a miff, they give over their wiling,
  And show me some foul weather then!
But be cloudy or clear, only time it
  So that storm shall not rule through the year;
And be quick in your changes of climate,
  Whenever you're called on "to clear"!
        Yes, be quick!
  You must shift as the wind does, my dear!

(1847, 1859, 1860)

THE MEMORIAL TREE.

Great trees that o'er us grow—
Green leaves that gather round them—the fresh hues,

That tell of fruit, and blossoms yet to blow,
Opening fond bosoms to the embracing dews;

   These, now so bright,
That deck the slopes about thy childhood's home,
 And seem, in long duration, to thy sight,
As they had promise of perpetual bloom;

   So linked with all
The first dear throbs of feeling in thy heart,
 When, at the dawn of summer and of fall,
Thou weptst the leaf that must so soon depart!

   What had all these,
Of frail, deciduous nature, to persuade,
 Howe'er their sweets might charm, and beauty please,
The memories that their own could never aid?

   They kept no tale—
No solemn history of the fruitful hour;
 The lover's promise, the beloved one's wail—
To wake the dead leaf in each lonely bower!

   The autumn breath
O'erthrew each frail memorial of their past;
 And every token was resigned to death,
In the first summons of the northern blast.

   They nourished naught
That to the chain of moral being binds
 The recollections of the once gay spot,
And its sweet offices, to future minds.

   Thou may'st repair—
Thou, who hast loved in summer-eve to glide
 With her whom thou hast still beheld as fair,
When she no longer wandered by thy side.

   And thou wilt weep
Each altered aspect of that happiest home,
 Which saw the joys its memories could not keep,
Save by the sympathy which shares their doom.

Thus Ruin stands
For Ruin—and the wreck of favorite things,
   To him who o'er the waste but wrings his hands,
Proofs of the *fall*, and not the spring-time brings.

      Ah! who will weep,
In after seasons, when thou too art gone,
   Within this grot, where shadowy memories keep
Their watch above the realm they keep alone?

      Who will lament,
In fruitless tears, that she the dear one died,
   And thy surviving heart, in languishment,
Soon sought the grave and withered at her side?

      A newer bright
Makes young the woods—and bowers that not to thee
   Brought fruit or blossom, triumph in the sight
Of those who naught but fruit and blossom see;

      To whom no voice
Whispers, that through the loved one's mould the root
   Of that exulting shrub, with happiest choice,
Has gone, with none its passage to dispute.

      While thine own heart,
In neighboring hillock, conscious, it may be—
   Quivers to see the fibres rend and part
The fair white breast which was so dear to thee.

      Of all the past,
That precious history of thy love and youth,
   When not a cloud thy happy dawn o'ercast,
When all thou felt'st was joy, thou saw'st was truth;

      These have no speech
For idiot seasons that still come and go—
   To whom the heart no offices can teach,
Vainer than breezes that at midnight blow!

      And yet there seem
Memorials still in nature, which are taught,—

Unless all pleasant fancies be a dream,
To bring our sweetest histories back to thought.

A famous tree
Was this, three hundred years ago, when stood
    The hunter-chief below it, bold and free,
Proud in his painted pomp and deeds of blood.

By hunger taught,
He gathered the brown acorn in its shade,
    And ere he slept, still gazing upward, caught
Sweet glimpses of the night, in stars arrayed.

His hatchet sunk
With sharp wound, fixing his own favorite sign,
    Deep in the living column of its trunk,
Where thou may'st read a history such as thine.

He, too, could feel
Such passion as awakes the noble soul—
    And in fond hour, perchance, would hither steal,
With one, of all his tribe, who could his ire control.

And others' signs,
Tokens of races, greatlier taught, that came
    To write like record, though in smoother lines,
And thus declare a still more human flame.

Here love's caprice—
The hope, the doubt, the dear despondencies—
    Joy that had never rest, hope without peace—
These each declared the grief he never flies.

And the great oak
Grew sacred to each separate pilgrimage,
    Nor heeded, in his bulk, the sudden stroke
That scarred his giant trunk with seams of age.

And we who gaze
Upon each rude memorial—letter and date—
    Still undefaced by storm and length of days,
Stand, as beneath the shadow of a fate!

Some elder-born,
A sire of wood and vale, guardian and king
    Of separate races, unsubdued, unshorn,
Whose memories grasp the lives of every meaner thing!

With great white beard.
Far streaming with a prophet-like display,
    Such as when Moses on the Mount appeared,
And prostrate tribes looked down, or looked away!

With outstretched arms,
Paternal, as if blessing—with a grace,
    Such as, in strength and greatness, ever charms,
As wooing the subdued one to embrace!—

Thus still it stood,
While the broad forests, 'neath the pioneer,
    Perished—proud relic of the ancient wood—
Men loved the record-tree, and bade them spare!

And still at noon,
Repairing to its shadow, they explore
    Its chronicles, still musing o'er th' unknown,
And telling well-known histories, told of yore!

We shall leave ours,
Dear heart! and when our sleep beneath its boughs
    Shall suffer spring to spread o'er us her flowers,
Eyes that vow love like ours shall trace our vows.

(1848)

SPIRITUAL SYMPATHIES.

A GROUP OF SONNETS.

The dream is gone from me—the solitude
    Of self and a most humbling consciousness
Once more are mine, and I must haply brood
    On images that cannot come to bless,
As once they blessed me only. Through the night

I conjure the dear spectres into sight,
Dim, flitting phantoms that, with sudden gleam,
   Fling their sad glances on me and depart;
   I call them from the depths of my torn heart,
And then their solemn whispers do meseem—
   Sighs more than speech—to murmur—"It is vain;
   Yours can we never, never be again!
We leave you night and silence, sleep and dream,
   That, even in its solace, must awake to pain!"

Ah! spirits, dearest memories, wherefore break
   These bands of sleep asunder, and, while night
   So softly does her office with delight,
From the sick soul its dream of solace take?
'Twas ye that brought me—leave me to the doom
   Of this so lone condition; let the shade,
Mournful, but not oppressive, of my gloom,
Possess the heart that never did forsake,
   And would not be again by dreams betrayed.
What ye have ta'en ye cannot now restore,
   Nor have ye more to take, unless it be
That wizard sense that calls ye up once more,
   When Will grows absolute and Thought flies free,
And all that death might spare, comes back from Heaven, to me!

How sweetly, yet how mockingly ye rise—
   A little gleam at first, most like the light
   Of a sad glow-worm, rising through the night
From the deep wood, in silence, to the skies—
   A dewy brightness, that, with lessening bright,
   Dilating into form, flits, softly white,
Between my aching vision and the wall,
That darkens yet more deeply, like the pall
That wrapt ye when I followed, striving vain
   To pierce the dense dominion still, and see!
I tremble not to greet ye, nor complain
   That ye have eyes, but not a speech for me!
Ah! wherefore, when I summon ye again,
   Thus vanish, till the gray dawn darkens all?

Yet is the aspect of one presence still,
   Tearful and bright to consciousness—I know

The gentle spirit is near me, and the thrill
  Of a strange terror mingles with the glow
  That once had birth in rapture. Is it so?
And shall we be denied, even when we will,
  And though that will, if sorrow, be no sin?
  Ah! the blind error, not to look within!
While still these eyes with mortal tears o'erflow,
  How should I dream to have thee or to see,
Save in this heart, which, in thy hour of death,
  Straightway, from heavy bonds of earth set free,
Took in new life, as from thy parting breath,
  And since, each hour, hath grown more full of thee!

                                                    (1848)

THE GRAPE VINE SWING.

Lithe and long as the serpent train,
  Springing and clinging from tree to tree,
Now darting upward, now down again,
  With a twist and a twirl that are strange to see:
Never took serpent a deadlier hold,
  Never the cougar a wilder spring,
Strangling the oak with the boa's fold,
  Spanning the beech with the condor's wing.

Yet, no foe that we fear to seek,
  The boy leaps wild to thy rude embrace;
Thy bulging arms bear as soft a cheek
  As ever on lover's breast found place:
On thy waving train is a playful hold
  Thou shalt never to lighter grasp persuade;
While a maiden sits in thy drooping fold,
  And swings and sings in the noonday shade!

Oh! giant strange of our southern woods,
  I dream of thee still in the well known spot,
Though our vessel strains o'er the ocean's floods,
  And the northern forest beholds thee not;
I think of thee still with a sweet regret,

As the cordage yields to my playful grasp—
Dost thou spring and cling in our woodlands yet?
Does the maiden still swing in thy giant clasp?

(1848, 1853)

OH! WELCOME YE THE STRANGER.

i

Oh! welcome ye the stranger,
  And think where'er you rove,
How sweet will sound in foreign lands
  The voice that proffers love.
How sweet when sad delaying,
  Where fate compels to roam,
If stranger lips a welcome give,
  And sweetly speak of home.

ii

Oh! welcome ye the stranger,
  For still, whate'er his gain,
How much, in dear ones lost to sight,
  Must be his spirit's pain.
His smiles but ill betoken
  The heart within his breast,
That silent beats with hopes deferr'd,
  And doubts that will not rest.

iii

Oh! welcome ye the stranger,
  To whom your hearth shall bring
The image of his own, and show
  Each dear one in the ring.
And as your song ascending,
  Wakes music known of yore,
He'll think of her he left behind—
  Whose song hath bless'd before.

(1848)

SUMMER AFTERNOON, IN MY STUDY.

The ailanthus spreads, beneath mine eaves,
   Its palmy shoots of slender stem,
And, in its shade, the jasmine weaves
   Its vines with many a golden gem;

And drooping twice beneath its fruits,
   The modest fig, imploring place,
Sends humbly forth a thousand shoots,
   That meekly fill beneath the space.

Then, as the western zephyr steals
   With searching wing among their holds,
The bright glance of the sun reveals,
   In mystic twines and mazy folds.

His milder rays admitted gleam,
   Beneath their leaves, upon my floor,
In golden patines, each that seem
   To make the wealth of earth look poor.

How, from the embodied volume lifts
   The weary eye, with study sad,
Glad, that in place of mortal gifts,
   Some smiles from Heaven would make it glad.

Oh! to its shelf consign the book;
   Why toil when slumber's self is life,
And on the smile refuse to look,
   Which soothes the grief, and stays the strife!

The heart, though doom'd to doubts that pain,
   May still some respite take from care
And in repose, not wholly vain,
   Forget the daily toils that wear—

That wear, and vex, and would destroy,
   But that some blessed glimpses come,
To cheer, with unexpected joy,
   The soul that only dreams of doom.

The leaf that floats before mine eye,
   The vine that waves so meekly bright,
The breeze that wantons fitfully,
   With flow'rs that murmur to the sight—

These have a voice for human care,
   And still to sweet submission move,
When human lips no more can cheer,
   And human hearts have ceased to love.

(1848)

THE TRAVELLER'S REST.

For hours we wander'd o'er the beaten track,
A dreary stretch of sand, that, in the blaze
Of noonday, seem'd to launch sharp arrows back,
As fiery as the sun's. Our weary steeds
Falter'd, with drooping heads, along the plain,
Looking from side to side most wistfully,
For shade and water. We could feel for them,
Having like thirst; and, in a desperate mood,
Gloomy with toil, and parching with the heat,
I had thrown down my burden by the way,
And slept, as man may never sleep but once,
Yielding without a sigh,—so utterly
Had the strong will, beneath the oppressive care,
Fail'd of the needed energy for life,—
When, with a smile, the traveller by my side,
A veteran of the forest and true friend,
Whose memory I recal with many a tear,
Laid his rough hand most gently on mine own,
And said, in accents still encouraging:—

"Faint not,—a little farther we shall rest,
And find sufficient succour from repose,
For other travel: vigour will come back,
And sweet forgetfulness of all annoy,
With a siesta in the noontide hour,
Shelter'd by ample oaks. A little while

Will bring us to the sweetest spot in the woods,
Named aptly, 'Traveller's Rest.' There, we shall drink
Of the pure fountain, and beneath the shade
Of trees, that murmur lessons of content
To streams impatient as they glide from sight,
Forget the long day's weariness, o'er steppes
Of burning sand, with thirst that looks in vain
For the cool brooklet. All these paths I know
From frequent travail, when my pulse, like yours,
Beat with an ardor soon discomfited,
Unseason'd by endurance. Through a course
Of toil, I now can think upon with smiles,
Which brought but terror when I felt it first,
I grew profound in knowledge of the route,
Marking each wayside rock, each hill of clay,
Blazed shaft, or blighted thick, and forked tree.
With confidence familiar as you found
In bookish lore and company. Cheer up,
Our pathway soon grows pleasant. We shall reach—
Note well how truly were my lessons conn'd,—
A little swell of earth, which, on these plains,
Looks proudly like a hill. This having pass'd,
The land sinks suddenly—the groves grow thick,
And, in the embrace of May, the giant wood
Puts on new glories. Shade from these will soothe
Thy overwearied spirit, and anon,
The broad blaze on the trunk of a dark pine
That strides out on the highway to our right,
Will guide us where, in woodland hollow, keeps
One lonely fountain; such as those of yore,
The ancient poets fabled as the home,
Each of its nymph; a nymph of chastity,
Whose duty yet is love. A thousand times,
When I was near exhausted as yourself,
That gash upon the pine-tree strengthen'd me,
As showing where the waters might be found,
Otherwise voiceless. Thanks to the rude man—
Rude in the manners of his forest life,
But frank and generous,—whose benevolent heart—
Good kernel in rough outside,—counsels him,
As in the ages of the Patriarch,
To make provision for the stranger's need.

His axe, whose keen edge blazons on the tree
Our pathway to the waters that refresh,
Was in that office consecrate, and made
Holier than knife, in hands of bearded priest,
That smote, in elder days, the innocent lamb,
In sacrifice to Heaven!

     "Now, as we glide,
The forest deepens round us. The bald tracts,
Sterile, or glittering but with profitless sands,
Depart; and through the glimmering woods behold
A darker soil, that on its bosom bears
A nobler harvest. Venerable oaks,
Whose rings are the successive records, scored
By Time, of his dim centuries; pines that lift,
And wave their coronets of green aloft,
Highest to heaven of all the aspiring wood;
And cedars, that with slower worship rise—
Less proudly, but with better grace, and stand
More surely in their meekness;—how they crowd,
As if 'twere at our coming, on the path!—
Not more majestic, not more beautiful,
The sacred shafts of Lebanon, though sung
By Princes, to the music of high harps,
Midway from heaven;—for these, as they, attest
His countenance who, to glory over all,
Adds grace in the highest, and above these groves
Hung brooding, when, beneath the creative word,
They freshen'd into green, and towering grew,
Memorials of his presence as his power!
—Alas! the forward vision! a few years
Will see these shafts o'erthrown. The profligate hands
Of avarice and of ignorance will despoil
The woods of their old glories; and the earth,
Uncherish'd, will grow barren, even as the fields,
Vast still, and beautiful once, and rich as these,
Which, in my own loved home, half desolate,
Attest the locust rule,—the waste, the shame,
The barbarous cultivation—which still robs
The earth of its warm garment and denies
Fit succour, which might recompense the soil,
Whose inexhaustible bounty, fitly kept,

Was meant to fill the granaries of man,
Through all earth's countless ages.

"How the sward
Thickens in matted green. Each tufted cone
Gleams with its own blue jewel, dropt with white,
Whose delicate hues and tints significant,
Wake tenderness within the virgin's heart,
In love's own season. In each mystic cup
She reads sweet meaning, which commends the flow'r
Close to her tremulous breast. Nor seems it there
Less lovely than upon its natural couch,
Of emerald bright,—and still its hues denote
Love's generous spring-time, which, like generous youth,
Clouds never the dear aspect of its green,
With sickly doubts of what the autumn brings."

   Boy as I was, and speaking still through books—
Not speaking from myself—I said: "Alas!
For this love's spring-time—quite unlike the woods,
It never knows but one; and, following close,
The long, long years of autumn, with her robes
Of yellow mourning, and her faded wreath
Of blighted flowers, that, taken from her heart,
She flings upon the grave-heap where it rots!"

   "Ah! fie!" was straightway the reply of him,
The old benevolent master, who had seen,
Through thousand media yet withheld from me,
The life I had but dream'd of—"this is false!—
Love hath its thousand spring-times like the flow'rs,
If we are dutiful to our own hearts,
And nurse the truths of life, and not its dreams.
But not in hours like this, with such a show
Around us, of earth's treasures, to despond,
To sink in weariness and to brood on death.
Oh! be no churl, in presence of the Queen
Of this most beautiful country, to withhold
Thy joy,—when all her court caparison'd,
Comes to her coronation in such suits
Of holiday glitter. It were sure a sin
In sight of Heaven, when now the humblest shrub

By the maternal bounty is set forth,
As for a bridal, with a jewell'd pomp
Of flow'rs in blue enamel—lustrous hues
Brightning upon their bosoms like sweet tints,
Caught from dissolving rainbows, as the sun
Rends with his ruddy shafts their violet robes,—
When gay vines stretching o'er the streamlet's breast
Link the opposing pines and arch the space,
Between, with a bright canopy of charms,
Whose very least attraction wears a look
Of life and fragrance!—when the pathway gleams,
As spread for march of Princess of the East,
With gems of living lustre—ravishing hues
Of purple, as if blood-dipp'd in the wounds
Of Hyacinthus,—him Apollo loved,
And slew though loving:—now, when over all
The viewless nymphs that tend upon the streams,
And watch the upward growth of April flow'rs,
Wave ever, with a hand that knows not stint,
Yet suffers no rebuke for profligate waste,
Their aromatic censers, 'till we breathe
With difficult delight;—not now to gloom
With feeble cares and individual doubts,
Of cloud to-morrow. It were churlish here,
Ungracious in the sov'reign Beauty's sight,
Who rules this realm, the dove-ey'd sovran, Spring!
This hour to sympathy—to free release
From toil, and sorrow, and doubt, and all the fears
That hang about the horizon of the heart,
Making it feel its sad mortality,
Even when most sweet its joy—she hath decreed:
Let us obey her, though no citizens.

"How grateful grows the shade—mix'd shade of trees,
And clouds, that drifting o'er the sun's red path,
Curtain his awful brows! Ascend yon hill,
And we behold the valley from whose breast
Flows the sweet brooklet. Yon emblazon'd pine
Marks the abrupt transition to the shade,
Where, welling from the bankside, it steals forth,
A voice without a form. Through grassy slopes,
It wanders on unseen, and seems no more

Than their own glitter; yet, behold it now,
Where, jetting through its green spout, it bounds forth,
Capricious, as if doubtful where to flow,—
A pale white streak—a glimmering, as it were,
Cast by some trembling moonbow thro' the woods!

"Here let us rest. A shade like that of towers,
Wrought by the Moor in matchless arabesque,
Makes the fantastic ceiling,—leaves and stems,
Half-form'd, yet flowery tendrils, that shoot out,
Each wearing its own jewel,—that above
O'erhangs; sustain'd by giants of the wood,
Erect and high, like warriors gray with years,
Who lift their massive shields of holiest green,
On fearless arms, that still defy the sun,
And foil his arrows. At our feet they fall,
Harmless and few, and of the fresh turf make
A rich mosaic. Tremblingly, they creep,
Half-hidden only, to the blushing shoots
Of pinks, that never were abroad before,
And shrink from such warm instance. Here are flow'rs,
Pied, blue, and white, with creepers that uplift
Their green heads, and survey the world around—
As modest merit, still ambitionless—
Only to crouch again; yet each sustains
Some treasure, which, were earth less profligate,
Or rich, were never in such keeping left.
And here are daisies, violets that peep forth
When winds of March are blowing, and escape
Their censure in their fondness. Thousands more,—
Look where they spread around us—at our feet—
Nursed on the mossy trunks of massive trees,
Themselves that bear no flow'rs—and by the stream—
Too humble and too numerous to have names!

"There is no sweeter spot along the path,
In all these western forests,—sweet for shade,
Or beauty, or reflection—sights and sounds—
All that can charm the wanderer, or o'ercome
His cares of travel. Here we may repose,
Subdued by gentlest murmurs of the noon,
Nor feel its heat, nor note the flight of hours,

That never linger here. How sweetly falls
The purring prattle of the stream above,
Where, roused by petty strife with vines and flow'rs,
It wakes with childish anger, nor forbears
Complaint, even when, beguiled by dear embrace,
It sinks to slumber in its bed below!
The red-bird's song now greets us from yon grove,
Where, starring all around with countless flow'rs,
Thick as the heavenly host, the dogwood glows,
Array'd in virgin white. There, 'mid the frowns
Of sombrous oaks, and where the cedar's glooms
Tell of life's evening shades, unchidden shines
The maple's silver bough, that seems to flash
A sudden moonlight; while its wounded arms,
Stream with their own pure crimson, strangely bound
With yellow wreaths, flung o'er its summer hurts,
By the lascivious jessamine, that, in turn,
Capricious, creeps to the embrace of all.

"The eye unpain'd with splendor—with unrest
That mocks the free rapidity of wings,
Just taught to know their uses and go forth,
Seeking range but no employment—hath no quest
That Beauty leaves unsatisfied. The lull
Of drowsing sounds, from leaf, and stream, and tree
Persuades each sense, and to forgetfulness
Beguiles the impetuous thought. Upon the air
Sweetness hangs heavy, like the incense cloud
O'er the high altar, when cathedral rites
Are holiest, and our breathing for a while
Grows half suspended. Sullen, in the sky,
With legions thick, and banners broad unfurl'd,
The summer tempest broods. Below him wheels,
Like some fierce trooper of the charging host,
One fearless vulture. Earth beside us sleeps,
Having no terror; though an hour may bring
A thousand fiery bolts to break her rest.

"How natural is the face of woods and vales,
Trees, and the unfailing waters, spite of years,
Time's changes, and the havoc made by storm!

The change is all in man. Year after year,
I look for the old landmarks on my route,
And seldom look in vain. A darker moss
Coats the rough outside of the old gray rock;—
Some broad arm of the oak is wrench'd away,
By storm and thunder—through the hill-side wears
A deeper furrow,—and the streams descend,
Sometimes, in wilder torrents than before—
But still they serve as guides o'er ancient paths,
For wearied wanderers. Still do they arise,
In groups of grandeur, an old family,
These great magnificent trees, that, as I look,
Fill me with loftiest thoughts, such as one feels
Beholding the broad wing of some strong bird,
Poised on its centre, motionless in air,
Yet sworn its master still. Not in our life,
Whose limit, still inferior, mocks our pride,
Reach they this glorious stature. At their feet,
Our young, grown aged like ourselves, may find
Their final couches, ere one vigorous shaft
Yields to the stroke of time. Beneath mine eyes,
All that makes beautiful this place of peace,
Wears the peculiar countenance which first
Won my delight and wonder as I came—
Then scarcely free from boyhood,—wild as he,
The savage Muscoghee, who, in that day,
Was master of these plains. His hunting range
Grasp'd the great mountains of the Cherokee,
The Apalachian ridge—extended west
By Talladega's valleys—by the streams
Of Tallas-hatchie—through the silent woods
Of gray Emuckfau, and where, deep in shades,
Rise the clear brooks of Autossee that flow
To Tallapoosa;—names of infamy
In Indian chronicle! 'Twas here they fell,
The numerous youth of Muscoghee,—the strong—
Patriarchs of many a tribe—dark seers renown'd,
As deeply read in savage mystery—
The Prophet Monohōee—priest as famed,
Among his tribe, as any that divined
In Ashkelon or Ashdod;—stricken to the earth,

Body and spirit, in repeated strife,
With him, that iron-soul'd old chief, who came
Plunging from Tennessee.

    "Below they stretch'd,
In sovran mastery o'er the wood and stream,
'Till the last waves of Choctawhatchie slept,
Subsiding, in the gulf. Such was the realm
They traversed, in that season of my youth,
When first beside this pleasant stream I sank,
In noontide slumber. What is now their realm,
And where are now their warriors? Streams that once
Soothed their exhaustion, satisfied their thirst—
Woods that gave shelter—plains o'er which they sped
In mimic battle—battle-fields whereon
Their bravest chieftains perish'd—trees that bore
The fruits they loved but rear'd not;—these remain,
But yield no answer for the numerous race,—
Gone with the summer breezes—with the leaves
Of perish'd autumn;—with the cloud that frowns
This moment in the heavens, and, ere the night,
Borne forward in the grasp of chainless winds,
Is speeding on to ocean.

    "Wandering still—
That sterile and most melancholy life,—
They skirt the turbid streams of Arkansas,
And hunt the buffalo to the rocky steeps
Of Saladanha; and, on lonely nooks,
Ridge-barrens, build their little huts of clay,
As frail as their own fortunes. Dreams, perchance,
Restore the land they never more shall see;
Or, in meet recompense, bestow them tracts
More lovely—vast, unmeasured tracts, that lie
Beyond those peaks, that, in the northern heavens,
Rise blue and perilous now. There, rich reserves
Console them in the future for the past;
And, with a Christian trust, the Pagan dreams
His powerful gods will recompense his faith,
By pleasures, in degree as exquisite
As the stern suffering he hath well endured.
His forest fancy, not untaught to soar,

Already, in his vision of midnight, sees
The fertile valleys; on his sight arise
Herds of the shadowy deer; and, from the copse,
Slow stealing, he beholds, with eager gaze,
The spirit-hunter gliding toward his prey,
In whose lithe form, and practised art, he views
Himself!—a noble image of his youth
That never more shall fail!

       "We may not share
His rapture; for if thus the might of change
Mocks the great nation, sweeps them from the soil
Which bore, but could not keep—what is't with us,
Who muse upon their fate? Darkly, ere while,
Thou spok'st of death and change, and I rebuked
The mood that scorn'd the present good—still fond
To brood above the past. Yet, in my heart,
Grave feelings rise to chide the undesert,
That knew not well to use the power I held,
In craving that to come. Have these short years
Wrought thus disastrously upon *my* strength,
As on the savage? What have I done to build
My better home of refuge; where the heart,
By virtue taught, by conscience made secure,
May safely find an altar, 'neath whose base
The tempest rocks in vain? The red-man's fate
Belong'd to his performance. They who know
How to destroy alone, and not to raise,
Leaving a ruin for a monument,
Must perish as the brute. But I was taught
The nobler lesson, that, for man alone,
The maker gives the example of his power,
That he may build on him. What work of life—
The moral monument of the Christian's toil—
Stands, to maintain my memory after death,
Amongst the following footsteps? Sadly, the ear
Receives his question, who, with sadder speech,
Makes his own answer. Unperforming still,
He yet hath felt the mighty change that moves,
Progressive, as the march of mournful hours,
Still hurrying to the tomb. 'Tis on his cheek,
No more the cheek of boyhood—in his eye,

That laughs not with its wonted merriment,
And in his secret heart. 'Tis over all
He sees and feels—o'er all that he hath loved,
And fain would love, and must remember still!
Those gray usurpers, Death and Change, have been
Familiar in his household, and he stands,
Of all that grew around his innocent hearth,
Alone—the last! And this hath made him now
An exile,—better pleased with woods and streams,
Wild ocean, and the rocks that vex his waves,
Than, sitting in the city's porch, to hear
The hurry, and the thoughtless hum of trade!

"The charm is broken and the 'Traveller's Rest!'
The sun no longer beats with noonday heat
Above the pathway, and the evening bird,
Short wheeling through the air, on whirring wing,
Counsels our flight with his. Another draught—
And to these pleasant waters—to the groves
That shelter'd—to the gentle breeze that soothed,
Even as a breath from heaven—to all sweet sights,
Melodious sounds and murmurs, that arise
To cheer the sadden'd spirit at its need—
Be thanks and blessing; gratitude o'er all,
To God in the Highest! He it is who guides
The unerring footstep—prompts the wayward heart
To kindly office—shelters from the sun—
Withholds the storm,—and, with his leaves and flow'rs,
Sweet freshening streams and ministry of birds,
Sustains, and succours, and invigorates;—
To Him, the praise and homage—Him o'er all!"

                                                    (1849, 1853)

THE CASSIQUE OF ACCABEE;

A LEGEND OF ASHLEY RIVER.

A few words, by way of preface, will save us the necessity of burden-
ing with notes the little story which follows. Accabee is the well-known
name of a lovely, but neglected, farmstead, in the neighborhood of

Charleston, on Ashley River. It was in earlier periods applied to a larger district in the same neighborhood. Keawah is the aboriginal name of the Ashley. The tribe of Accabee was probably of the same family with the Yemassees, the Edistos, and other groups, inhabiting the lower country of South Carolina. The Gaelic Chief spoken of in the text was Lord Cardross, who made a settlement at, or near, Beaufort, which, after a brief existence of four years, was destroyed by an incursion of the Indians and Spaniards.

———

It was a night of calm—o'er Ashley's waters
    Crept the sweet billows to their own soft tune,
While she, most bright of Keawah's fair daughters,
    Whose voice might spell the footsteps of the moon,
        As slow we swept along,
        Pour'd forth her own sweet song,
A lay of rapture not forgotten soon.

Hush'd was our breathing, stay'd the lifted oar,
    Our spirits rapt, our souls no longer free,
While the boat drifting softly to the shore,
    Brought us within the shades of Accabee;—
        "Ah!" sudden cried the maid,
        In the dim light afraid;
" 'Tis here the ghost still walks of the old Yemassee."

And sure the spot was haunted by a power,
    To fix the pulses in each youthful heart;
Never was moon more gracious in a bower,
    Making delicious fancy work for art;
        Weaving, so meekly bright,
        Her pictures of delight,
That, though afraid to stay, we sorrow'd to depart.

"If these old groves are haunted"—sudden then,
    Said she, our sweet companion—"it must be
By one who loved, and was beloved again,
    And joy'd all forms of loveliness to see:—
        Here, in these groves they went,
        Where love and worship, blent,
Still framed the proper God for each idolatry.

"It could not be that love should here be stern,
  Or beauty fail to sway with sov'ran might;
These, from so blessèd scenes, should something learn,
  And swell with tenderness and shape delight:
    These groves have had their power,
    And bliss, in bygone hour,
Hath charm'd, with sigh and song, the passage of the night."

"It were a bliss to think so;" made reply
  Our Hubert—"yet the tale is something old,
That checks us with denial;—and our sky,
  And these brown woods that, in its glittering fold,
    Look like a fairy clime,
    Still unsubdued by time,
Have evermore the tale of wrong'd devotion told."

"Give us thy legend, Hubert;" cried the maid;—
  And, with down-dropping oars, our yielding prow
Shot to a still lagune, whose ample shade
  Droop'd from the gray moss of an old oak's brow:
    The groves, meanwhile, lay bright,
    Like the broad stream, in light,
Soft, sweet as ever yet the lunar loom display'd.

"Great was the native chief,"—'twas thus began
  The legend of our comrade—"who, in sway,
Held the sweet empire which to-night we scan,
  Stretching, on either hand, for miles away:
    A stalwart chief was he,
    Cassique of Accabee,
And lord o'er numerous tribes who did with pride obey.

"War was his passion, 'till the white-man came,
  And then his policy;—and well he knew,
How, over all, to plan the desperate game,
  And when to rise, and when to sink from view;
    To plant his ambush well,
    And how, with horrid yell,
To dart, at midnight forth, in fury arm'd with flame.

"His neighbours by the Ashley, the pale race,
  Were friends and allies 'gainst all other foes;

They dwelt too nearly to his royal place,
    To make the objects of their commerce blows;
        But no such scruple staid
        His wild and cruel raid,
When, by Heléna's Bay, the Gaelic hamlet rose.

"And moved by Spanish wile that still misled,
    Our chieftain, in one dark November night,
With all his warriors, darted from his bed,
    And drove the Gaelic chief from his, in flight:—
        Scalplocks and other spoils,
        Rewarded well his toils,
And captives graced his triumph after fight.

"But, when the strife was wildest, and the fire
    Play'd fiercest on the roofs of bough and leaf,
A fair-hair'd child, misdeeming him her sire,
    Rush'd headlong to the arms of the red chief:—
        'Twas not his hour to spare—
        His fingers in her hair,
And tomahawk, lifted high, declar'd his savage ire.

"But, in the light of her own blazing home,
    He caught the entreaty in her soft blue eye,
Which, weeping still the while, would wildly roam,
    From him who held, to those who hurried by;—
        Strange was the emotion then,
        That bade him stay his men,
And, in his muscular arms, lift that young damsel high.

"He bore her through the forest, many a mile,
    With a rude tenderness and matchless strength;
She slept upon his arm—she saw his smile,
    Seen seldom, and reached Accabee at length;
        Here, for a term, he kept
        The child, her griefs unwept,
With love, that did from her a seeming love beguile.

"Daughter of ancient Albyn, she was bright,
    With a transparent beauty; on her cheek,
The rose and lily, struggling to unite,
    Did the best blooms of either flow'r bespeak;

Whilst floods of silken hair,
Free flowing, did declare
The gold of western heavens when sinks the sun from sight.

"Our chief had reach'd his thirtieth summer—she
Was but thirteen; yet, 'till he saw this maid,
Love made no portion of his reverie:
Strife was his passion, and the midnight raid;
The dusky maids, in vain,
Had sought to weave their chain,
About that fierce wild heart that still from all went free.

"But, free no longer, they beheld him bound
By his fair captive; strife was now unsought;
The chase abandon'd; and his warriors found
Their chief no more where fields were to be fought;—
He better loved to brood
In this sweet solitude,
She still in sight, who thus her captor's self had caught.

"She little dream'd her conquest, for he still
Maintain'd her as his child, with tenderness;—
As one who seeks no farther of his will,
Than to protect and with sweet nurture bless;
Such love as sire might show,
Did that dark chief bestow,
When, with a gentle clasp, he met her child-caress.

"She grew to be the blossom of his sight—
For her he snared the fawn,—for her he brought
Gay gauds of foreign fabric;—her delight
Being still the sweetest recompense he sought;—
And, when her feet would rove,
He led her through the grove,
Show'd her its devious paths and all its secrets taught.

"She grew apace in beauty as in years,
And he the more devoted:—until now
His eye beheld her growth and had no fears,—
But soon a shadow rose above his brow;—
That shadow, born of doubt,

Which finds love's secret out,
And, o'er its sunniest bower, still spans an arch of tears.

"This shadow had its birth with our dark chief,
　　When to his home, one eve, returning late,
He saw, with passion still subdued by grief,
　　A stranger with his beauty, in his gate;—
　　　　One of the pale white race,
　　　　Whose presence, in that place,
Brought to his heart a fear that troubled it like fate.

"Yet was he but a pedlar,—he who came,—
　　Thus troubling waters which had slept before;
He brought his glittering wares, and did but claim
　　To show them, and night's lodging to implore:
　　　　And, o'er his pack, with eyes
　　　　Of eager, glad surprize,
Stoop'd our young maid when stept the chief within his door.

"His stealthy footsteps stirr'd no single sound;
　　They knew not of the eyes upon them set—
She, the gay thoughtless girl, in thought profound,
　　Deep in such wealth as had not tempted yet;
　　　　While his—the stranger's—gaze,
　　　　In a most pleasant maze,
Scann'd her bright cheeks, unseen, from eyes of glittering jet.

"A handsome youth, of dark and amorous glance,
　　Showing a grateful consciousness of power,
Yet thoughtless, in that moment of sweet trance,
　　How best to woo and win the forest flower;
　　　　Even at that moment, stood
　　　　The red-man from the wood,
Gazing, with instinct grief, that had its birth that hour.

"Quickly he broke the silence and came forth,
　　While the fair girl, upstarting from her dream,
Hurried his search into such stores of worth,
　　As did on eyes of young Aladdin gleam:—
　　　　Clipping his neck with arms
　　　　That spoke of dearer charms,
The maid Othello loved might she that moment seem.

"And, with a pleased, but still a sinking heart,
    He yielded to her pleading: he had stores,—
Such treasures as the red-man might impart,
    Of precious value, borne to foreign shores;
        Spoils in the forest caught,
        By tribute hunter brought,
Soft furs from beaver won by snares of sylvan art.

"Sadly, the indulgent chief—but with a smile,—
    Gave up his treasure at his ward's demand;
The precious gauds which did her eyes beguile,
    Soon clasp'd her neck, or glitter'd in her hand.
        All had she won—but still
        There was a feminine will,
That led her glance astray beneath that stranger's wile.

"Their eyes commerced beside the blazing fire,
    Hers still unconscious of the erring vein;
The chief beheld, in his, the keen desire,
    And his heart swell'd with still increasing pain;
        Yet, though the sting was deep,
        His passion, made to sleep,
Look'd calm through eyes that seem'd a stranger still to ire.

"His board was spread with hospitable hand,
    Crisp'd the brown bread and smoked the venison steak;
An ancient squaw, still ready at command,
    Pour'd the casina tea, their thirst to slake;
        Then, as the hour grew late,
        With calm and lofty state,
The chief himself, with care, the stranger's couch did make.

"At sunrise they partook the morning meal,
    And then the white-man went upon his way;
Not without feeling—teaching her to feel—
    How sweet to both had been his still delay:—
        The nature, long at rest,
        Rose, pleading, at her breast,
For that pale race from which, perforce, she dwelt astray.

"She long'd for their communion,—for the youth
    Had waken'd memories, not to be subdued,

Of that dear home, and friends whose tender ruth
    Possess'd her still in that sweet solitude;
        And, saddening with the thought,
        Her secret soul grew fraught
With hopes, with doubts, with dreams, o'er which she loved to brood.

"The chief beheld the trouble in her eye,
    He felt as well the trouble in his heart,
And, ere the morrow's sun was in the sky,
    He bade her make her ready to depart;—
        He had a wider home,
        Where love might safely roam,
Nor fear the stranger's foot, nor tremble at his art.

"Cassique among the Edistos, he bore
    His treasure to the river of that name;
He sought the forests on its western shore,
    Millions of acres he alone might claim;
        Where the great stream divides,
        He cross'd its double tides,
Still seeking denser empires to explore.

"At length, he paused beside a little lake,
    A clear sweet mirror for the midnight star;
'Soon, weary one, thy slumbers shalt thou take;
    In sooth, to-day, our feet have wander'd far;
        Yet look, and thou shalt see,
        The wigwam smokes for thee,—
Those fires that gleam through woods show where our people are.

" 'Here shalt thou have fond service—here the clime
    Is sweet and healthful;—buskin'd, with thy bow,
Thou'lt wander forth with me, at morning's chime,
    And I to snare or slay the game, will show:
        Broad are the sheltering woods,
        Bright are the streams, the floods,
And safe the realm that hence thy youthful heart shall know.'

"Thus counselling, he led her o'er the plain,
    Down the smooth hill, beside the lakelet clear;
They tread the gloomy forest paths again,
    'Till sudden, the whole landscape opens fair;

'Look! weary one,' he cries;
      'Our realm before us lies,
Far spread as bird can fly, or speeds by day the deer.'

"In sooth, to one whose heart is all at rest,
      With not a human care to call it thence,
It was a home that rapture might have bless'd,
      Lovely to sight and dear to innocence;
            Great trees, a welcome shade,
            Of beech and poplar made,
Fortress of peace that love might deem his best defence.

"Long groves of pine and cedar led through wastes
      Made lovely by wild flow'rs of every hue;
Through arching boughs and vines the river hastes,
      Still with the song of birds that wander too;
            A fresh green realm, unbroke
            By plough, or woodman's stroke,
Rich in savannahs green, and lakes of skyey blue.

"His was the realm, and at his bidding came
      The tribes that peopled it; beneath his sway
They framed their rude society;—his blame,
      Or praise, sufficient guide to shape their way;
            Still, with the falling leaf,
            The signal of our chief
Prepared them for the chase and counsell'd their array.

"And thus, for many a moon, within that shade,
      Dwelling 'mongst vassals rude but loyal still,
Remote, but not in loneliness, our maid
      Had all that love could sigh for, but its will;
            Submissive still she found
            The gentle tribes around,
The squaws received her law, the warriors too obey'd.

"No censure check'd her walks—no evil eyes
      Darken'd upon her childish sports at eve;
If o'er the chieftain's brow a trouble lies,
      'Tis sure no fault of hers that makes him grieve;
            For her he still hath smiles,

And, in her playful wiles,
He finds a charm that still must artlessly deceive.

"Her wild song cheers him at the twilight hour,
　　As, on the sward, beside her sylvan cot,
He throws him down, meet image of a power
　　Subdued by beauty to the vassal's lot;
　　　　With half unconscious gaze,
　　　　His eye her form surveys,
And fancies fill his heart which utterance yet have not.

"She had expanded into womanhood
　　In those brief years of mild captivity,
And now, as 'neath his glance the damsel stood,
　　Nothing more sweet had ever met his eye;—
　　　　Fair, with her Saxon face,
　　　　Her form a forest grace
Had won from woodland sports of rare agility.

"Her rich blue eyes, her streaming yellow hair,
　　The soft white skin that show'd the crimson tide,
And perfect features—made her beauties rare,
　　That well the charms of Indian race defied;—
　　　　Her motion, as of flight,
　　　　Tutor'd by wild delight,
Brought to her form a grace at once of love and pride.

"And, as he gazed, with rapture ill suppress'd,
　　Inly the chief resolved that she should be
The woman he would take unto his breast,
　　Ere the next moon should ride up from the sea;
　　　　His child no more,—he felt
　　　　His soul within him melt,
To hear her voice in song, her thought in fancy free.

"She felt at last her power upon his heart,
　　As she beheld the language in his eye;
And, with this knowledge, came a natural art,
　　Which bade her glances unto his reply;
　　　　Made happy by her look
　　　　His soul new poison took,
He drew her to his breast, nor seem'd she to deny.

" 'I shall go hence,' quoth he, 'the Hunter's Moon—
   These sticks shall tell thee of the broken days;
When all are gone, I shall return,—and soon
   The beauties that I hold within my gaze,
     Shall bless, if thou approve,
     This heart, and the fond love
That knows thee as the star the ocean stream that sways.'

"And she was silent while he spake—her head
   Sunk, not in sadness, and upon his breast;
Fondly he kiss'd her—other words he said,
   And still, in dear embrace, her form caress'd;
     Then parting, sped afar,
     Led by the Hunter's Star,
Where the bear wallows in his summer nest.

"She had no sorrow to obey the will
   That ruled a nation: true, he slew her sire,
But he had been a gentle guardian still,
   Baffling each danger, soothing each desire;
     The power that he possess'd
     Was grateful to her breast,
And warm'd with pride the heart, that lack'd each holier fire.

"That night there rose an image in her dreams,
   Of the young trader seen at Accabee;
His fair soft face upon her memory gleams,
   His keen, dark, searching eye, still wantonly
     Pursues her with its blaze;
     And she returns the gaze,
And thus her heart communes with one she cannot see.

"It was as if the chief, by the same word
   That told his own fond purpose, had compell'd
The image of the person she preferr'd,—
   And, seeing him in dreams, her soul was spell'd
     With fancies that, in vain,
     She strove to hush again—
She saw their shapes by day, by night their voices heard.

"Saddened by this communion, she withdrew
   From those who sought her; in deep forests went,

By lonely streams and shades, from human view,
   Nursing a vague and vexing discontent;—
      For the first time, a care
      Hung on her heart like fear—
The shadows from a soul not wholly innocent.

"There is a fate beside us day and night,
   Obedient to the voice within our hearts;
Boldly we summon, and it stands in sight;
   We speak not, and in silence it departs;—
      'Twas thus with her, as still
      She roved with aimless will,
Beside the swamps through which the Edisto still darts.

"She spoke aloud, or did not speak, his name,
   Whose image was the sole one in her breast;
But, suddenly, from out the woods he came,
   And mutual glances mutual joy express'd:—
      'Ah! sought so long before,
      I fear'd that, never more,
Mine eyes should see the form that kept my soul from rest.

" 'How have I search'd for you in devious path,
   Forgetful of the mercenary trade!
And now, though perill'd by the redman's wrath,
   I seek you in forbidden forest shade;
      For never, since that night,
      When first you met my sight,
Hath beauty on my heart such sweet impression made.'

"They sat beneath the shade of silent trees,
   Close guarded by a thicket dense and deep;
There, onward, stole the river at its ease,
   And, through the air, the birds made easy sweep;—
      Those bow'rs were sweetly dight
      For safety and delight;—
The stranger won the prize the chieftain still would keep.

"He came, the dark-brow'd chieftain, from the chase,
   Laden with precious spoils of forest pride;
His heart exulting as he near'd the place
   Where the fair Saxon waited as his bride:

But who shall speak the grief
That shook that warrior chief,
When they declared her flight with yester-eventide.

"He had no voice for anguish or regret;—
He spake not of his purpose—but went forth,
With a keen spirit, on one progress set,
Now on the southern stream side, now the north;
Following, with sleuthhound's scent,
The way the lovers went,
Tracking each footfall sure, in leaf, in grass, and earth.

"Nor did he track in vain! They little knew
The unerring instinct of that hunter race;
A devious progress did the twain pursue,
Through streams and woods, to baffle still the trace;
But how should they beguile
The master of each wile,
Each art pursued in war or needful in the chase?

"In fancy safe, and weary now with flight,
The lovers lay at noonday in the shade;
Soft through the leaves and grateful to the sight,
The sun in droplets o'er the valley play'd;
But two short leagues, and they
Should leave the perilous way,
On Keawah secure, in home by squatter made.

"Thus satisfied, with seeming certainty,
Won by the hour's sweet stillness, did the pair,
Shelter'd beneath the brows of an old tree,
Give freedom to the love they joy'd to share;
His arm about her press'd,
She lay upon his breast,
Life's self forgot in bliss that left no room for care.

"They little dream'd that, lurking in the wood,
A witness to the freedom of their bliss,
The fiery chieftain they had baffled stood,
Fierce, with envenom'd fang and fatal hiss;
The lord of death and life,

He grasp'd the deadly knife,
And shook the tomahawk high but rarely known to miss.

"But, ere he sped the weapon to its mark,
　His heart grew gentle 'neath a milder sway;
True, they had left his dwelling lone and dark,
　But should he make it glad were he to slay?
　　Nor, if the man he slew,
　　Could he again renew
The trust he gave the maid as in his happier day.

"Nor could he strike, with stern and fatal blow,
　Her whose fair beauties were too precious still;
A noble purpose came to soothe his wo,
　And crown, with best revenge, a generous will;—
　　Forth strode he from the wood,
　　And ere they knew, he stood,
With weapon bared, and look still resolute to kill.

"As one who at the serpent's rattle starts,
　Sharp, sudden sounded in the covert nigh,
They heard his voice, and both their guilty hearts
　Sunk, hopeless, 'neath the expected penalty;
　　But, stifling his deep grief,
　　With few stern words, the chief,
Declared, though worthy death, the guilty should not die!

"O'erjoy'd at respite scarcely yet believed,
　The girl had risen and rush'd to clasp his knees,
But he whose faith had been so much deceived,
　No homage now could pacify or please;
　　Calm, but with gloomy face,
　　He checks the false embrace,
And still, the crouching youth, with scornful eye, he sees.

"He bade them rise and follow where he led,
　Himself conducted to the dwelling near;
Here, till the dawn, each found a separate bed;
　With morning o'er the Keawah they steer;
　　Still guided he the way,
　　And, ere the close of day,
Once more the three to shades of Accabee repair.

" 'Here,' said he, 'is your future dwelling-place,
    This be, my gift, your heritage of right;
The holy man, of your own foreign race,
    Shall, with the coming day, your hands unite;
      And men of law shall know
      That I these lands forego,
For her who still hath been the apple of my sight.

" 'See that you cherish her with proper faith;—
    If that you wrong her, look for wrong from me:
Once have I spared you, when the doom was death;
    Beware the future wrath you may not flee;
      Mine eye shall watch for hers,
      And if a breath but stirs
Her hair too rudely,—look for storms on Accabee.'

"He did as he had promised; they were wed
    By Christian rites,—and legal deeds convey'd
The heritage;—without a word then sped
    The chief into his forests, seeking shade:
      Months pass'd—a year went by,
      And none beheld his eye,
Where still his thought, with love, through these sweet places stray'd.

"He grew to be forgotten by the twain;
    Or if not wholly by the woman, she
Ne'er spoke of him,—ne'er look'd for him again,
    Though much it might have gladden'd her to see;
      For love had lost its flow'r,
      And soon there came an hour,
When all her young heart's pleasure grew to pain!

"The first sweet flush of summer dalliance gone,
    The first most precious bloom of passion o'er,
Indifference follow'd in the heart that won,
    And scorn found place where rapture woke no more;
      No kindly nurture bless'd
      With love her lonely breast,
And soon even peace had fled the home so glad before.

"And scorn grew into hate, and hate to wrath,
    And wrath found speech in violence;—his arm

Smote the unhappy woman from his path;—
    Submission could not soothe, nor tears disarm,
        The cruel mood, the will,
        True to past passions still,
Which Love and Beauty now, no more sufficed to charm.

"The profligate husband, reckless of her wo,
    Her meek submission and her misery,
Prepared, in secret, still another blow,
    And bargain'd for the sale of Accabee;
        Already had he drawn
        The fatal deed—had gone,
Resolved, in other lands, remote, his wife to flee.

"He little knew that eyes were on his flight,
    That long had mark'd his deeds;—his way led through
The umbrageous groves of Eutaw:—long ere night
    His footsteps to the white-man's clearings drew;—
        Exulting in the dream,
        Successful, of his scheme,
He hails the cottage-smokes of him who bought, in sight.

"But now a voice arrests him as he goes—
    Forth starts the red chief from the covering wood;
At once he knew him for the worst of foes;
    Guilt quell'd his courage, terror froze his blood;
        The horse is stay'd—in vain,
        He jerks the extended rein,
Vainly applies the spur, and show'rs his flanks with blows.

"Stern was the summons—in a single word—
    'Down!'—and he yielded to the vigorous hand;
'I gave thee all!' were then the accents heard—
    'The woman from my bosom, and my land;—
        I warn'd thee, ere I went,
        Of wrath and punishment,
If hair upon her head, in wrath was ever stirr'd.

" 'I know thee, and thy deeds; and thou shalt die!'
    'Mercy!' implored the profligate in vain.
Vainly he struggles—vainly seeks to fly—
    Even as he strives, the hatchet cleaves his brain.

Quivering, he lies beneath,
　　While, from his leathern sheath,
The warrior draws his knife, and coldly scalps the slain.

"Another night, and on the Accabee,
　　Softly the moon was smiling through its grove;
Yet sad the woman hail'd its light, for she
　　No longer warm'd with hope, or glow'd with love:
　　　　Grief, and a wan despair,
　　　　Reign'd in her soul of care,
Whence love, expell'd by wrath, had long been forced to flee.

"She crouch'd beside the hearth in vacant mood,
　　Silence and wo close crouch'd on either hand,—
Life's hope all baffled,—all the innocent brood
　　Of joys, that once had crowded at command,
　　　　Dead—gone like summer flowers;
　　　　Desolate all her hours,
Her life was now one dread, one deathlike solitude.

"With dreary gaze she watch'd the flickering fire,
　　Nor mark'd around the thickening growth of gloom;
She sees, unheeding, the bright flame expire,
　　Nor marks the fearful aspect in her room;
　　　　Beside her rest the brands—
　　　　'Tis but to stretch her hands:
Alas! her desolate soul for light hath no desire.

"But lo! another form, beside her own,
　　Bends to the task;—sudden, the resinous pine
Flames up;—she feels she is no more alone;
　　She sees a well-known eye upon her shine,
　　　　And hides her face, and cries—
　　　　'The Chief!' His silent eyes
Still saddening o'er the shape too long and dearly known.

" 'The man whom thou did'st wed, will never more
　　Lay angry hand upon thee—he had sold
Thy land, and fled thee for another shore;
　　But that I wound him in the serpent's fold,
　　　　And took from him the pow'r

That had usurp'd thy dow'r;
In proof of what I tell thee,—lo! behold!'

"Thus speaking, he, beside her, on the floor,
   Cast down the white-man's written instrument;
Sign'd, seal'd, and witness'd; framed with legal lore;
   Conveying—such the document's intent—
      All these fair groves and plains,
      The Accabee domains,
To one, of kindred race, whose name the paper bore.

"And she had sign'd it, with unwilling hand,
   Ignorant of its meaning, but in dread;
Obedient to her tyrant's fierce command,
   While his arm shook in threat'ning o'er her head;
      'Twas in that very hour,
      His blow, with brutal power,
Had stricken her to the earth, where long she lay as dead.

"He little dream'd that the avenger near,
   Beheld him, and prepared his punishment;
You ask, Why came he not to interfere,
   And stay, ere yet was wrought the foul intent;
      Enough, the red-man knows
      His time to interpose:—
Sternly his hour he takes, with resolute will unbent.

"Unerring, we have seen him in pursuit—
   Unsparing, we have seen him in his blow;—
His mission was not ended; and, though mute,
   He stood surveying her, who, cowering low,
      Crept humbly to his feet,
      As seeming to entreat,—
He had another task, which found the warrior slow.

"But he was firm:—'This paper is your own,—
   Another proof is mine, that you will be
Safe from the blows of him so lately known;
   He hath his separate lands henceforth from me;
      Ample the soil I gave,
      Beside the Eutaw's wave;
In token of my truth—this bloody scalplock see.'

"Then shriek'd the unhappy woman with affright,
　　Revolting at the trophy, dripping yet,
That, down upon the paper, in her sight,
　　With quiet hand, the haughty chieftain set;
　　　'Spare me! Oh, spare!' she cries:
　　　And crouching, with shut eyes,
Backward she crept, as if she safety sought in flight.

"'Fear nothing!' said the chieftain; ' 'twas for thee,
　　I brought this bloody token of my truth,
To show thee, from this moment, thou art free
　　To the possession of thy life and youth;
　　　Still hast thou beauty; still
　　　Thy heritage—thy will;
Go, seek thy kindred pale, secure of love and ruth.

"'From him, who, in thy thoughtlessness of heart,
　　Thou mad'st a master over thee, I save;
I slew thy father—I have done his part,
　　And give thee wealth more ample than he gave;
　　　Henceforth, thou wilt not see
　　　The Chief at Accabee;
Beware again lest passion make thee slave.

"'I leave thee now forever!' 'No!' she cried:
　　'Oh! take me to thy people;—let me dwell
Lone, peaceful, on the Edisto's green side,
　　Which, had I left not, I had still been well:—
　　　Forgive me, that the child,
　　　With heart both weak and wild,
Err'd, in not loving, where she might have loved with pride!'

"'I had believed thee once; but now, too late!
　　Henceforth I know thee, only to forget.'
'Thou canst not!'—'It may be, that thus my fate
　　Hath spoken; but my resolute will is set,
　　　In manhood,—and I know,
　　　Though all of life be wo,
Thus better—than with faithlessness to mate.'

"She crouch'd beneath his feet, incapable
　　Of answer to that speech; and his sad look,

As if his eyes acknowledged still a spell,
   One long, deep survey of the woman took;—
      She still unseeing aught,
      Of that sad, searching thought,
Which, speaking through his eye, her soul could never brook.

Sudden as spectre, waving wide his hand,
   He parted from her presence:—He was gone,
Into the shadows of that forest land;
   And, desolate now, the woman lay alone,—
      Crouching beside the hearth,
      Whilst thousand fears had birth,
Haunting her thought with griefs more fearful than the known.

"Our story here is ended. Of her fate
   Nothing remains to us, but that she sold,
Of Accabee, the beautiful estate,
   And sought her shelter in the city's fold;
      The purchaser, meanwhile,
      Made the dark forest smile,
And crown'd its walks with works most lovely to behold.

"A noble dwelling rose amidst the trees,
   Fair statues crown'd the vistas—pathways broke
The umbrageous shadows,—and sweet melodies,
   Among the groves, at noon and morning woke;—
      And great reserves of game,
      In which the wild grew tame—
And pleasant lakes, by art, were scoop'd for fisheries.

"Here pleasure strove to make her own abode;
   She left no mood uncherish'd which might cheer;
Through the grim forests she threw wide the road,
   And welcom'd Beauty, while expelling care:
      Wealth spared no toils to bless,
      And still, with due caress,
Honor'd the daily groups that sought for pastime there.

"But still the spot was haunted by a grief;—
   Joy ever sank in sadness:—guests depart;
A something sorrowful, beyond belief,
   Impairs the charms of music and of art;

'Till sadly went each grace,
    And, as you see the place,
Gradual the ruin grew, a grief to eye and heart.

"The native genius, born in solitude,
    Is still a thing of sorrow; and his spell,
Whatever be the graft of foreign mood,
    Maintains its ancient, sorrowful, aspect well;—
        Still reigns its gloomy lord,
        With all his sway restored,
Lone, o'er his barren sceptre doom'd to brood."

———

Slow sped our skiff into the open light,—
    The billows bright before us,—but no more
Rose love's sweet ditty on our ears that night;—
    Silent the maid look'd back upon the shore,
        And thought of those dark groves,
        And that wild chieftain's loves,
As they had been a truth her heart had felt of yore.

(1845, 1849, 1853)

STANZAS.

Here, where great oaks overshadow,
    In the well-known walks she roved,
Here we laid the little maiden,
    Whom our hearts so well have loved.
Silent waving, the great branches
    Make a shelter for the form,
Which our love had vainly striven
    To secure against the storm.

Oh! how peaceful—Oh! how quiet,
    Sacred still, her little home,
Where the squirrel loves to riot,
    And the rabbit loves to roam;

With the summer do we leave her,
  With the autumn we'll return;
But with her we lost our summer,
  And with autumn fitly mourn.

(1849)

SOUTHERN ODE.

Once more the cry of Freedom peals,
  From broad Potomac's wave to ours,
The invader's cunning footstep steals,
  Usurping fast our rights and powers.
He proffers love, he prates of ties
  That still should bind our fates in one,
Yet weaves his subtle web of lies,
  To share and leave us all undone.
What bond of faith, however strong,
  Thus taught by lust of pelf and sway,
He would not, in his march of wrong,
  Hurl scornful from his treacherous way?
The bond that's sacred in our sight,
  Made pliant by his arts of shame,
Is but the means to rob of right,
  The race he cannot rob of fame!
But we have seen the serpent's trail,
  Have heard the wolf's base howl, and now,
Taught by the past, we cannot fail,
  To brand his blackness on his brow.
To crush the viper in his path,
Beat down the were-wolf in our wrath,
And severing bonds so idly known,
Strike, though we stand and strike alone!

Oh! they are brethren these, who seek
  To weave their snares about our feet;—
Their prayers how bland, their pleas how meek,
  Most philanthropic all, and sweet!
We see their guile, and when we cry,
  In scorn and anger, at each wrong,

How Christianly they answer—"Fie!"—
　"Brethren!" the burden of their song!
We show our bonds of union broke,
　Each shatter'd tie, each sunder'd string,
And toiling still our necks to yoke,
　How well of "Union" do they sing!
This marriage bond they plead, while still
　In most adulterous arts they strive;
On us bestow its fruits of ill,
　While they on all its profits thrive.
Their bondmen we, who wage the fight,
　Achieve the spoil and win the day;
They, the keen knaves, with trick of sleight,
　The danger o'er, to steal the prey!
Thus, upon Sinbad's back astride,
The Old Man of the Sea would ride,
While preaching, ever and anon,
"Still let us ride together, son!"

Throw by the Harp! 'tis mockery now—
　Decree that dance and revel cease;
The shame spot darkens on your brow,
　And death is in the snares of peace!
It mocks the past our fathers knew;
　To sing the oppressions we must bear;
To swords, not songs, they bravely flew,
　And broke the very chains we wear.
They only felt the wrong, to spring,
　With fury to the desperate fray;
And did not, like their children, cling
　To bonds that crushed their souls to clay.
They too, had ties, long sacred known,
　With loyal hearts they loved the true;
But, when a tyrant filled the throne,
　They trampled throne and tyrant too.
What union firmer knit than theirs,
　With Britain from their earliest hours;
And yet, when Britain moved their fears,
　For freedom, they o'erthrew her powers.
The tie that cunning makes its plea,
To rob the birthright from the free,

Though by our sires with blessings given,
Is fit for Hell, though forged in Heaven!

'Tis peace no more! for peace is rest,
    In mutual faith, so well bestow'd,
That doubt and danger fill no breast,
    And lust and envy never goad.
What hope have we of state like this?
    Who that has seen the fraudful past,
But feels that still the serpent's hiss,
    Our hour of dreaming peace must blast.
Our Union still hath been the plea,
    To strip us of our natural strength,
Our peace—its future ye should see
    In utter deep despair at length.
A dull, dread wearisome repose,
    Low crouching still in trembling hush,
In moment fear of bonds and blows,
    When power feels bold enough to crush!
With, day by day, some birthright lost,
Some pride depress'd, some purpose cross'd,
Cursed with each thought that brings the past,
And utter slaves to knaves at last!

(1850)

FROM *THE CITY OF THE SILENT.*

    With eyes that weep to see, yet weep to lose,
We yield the loved one to his long repose;
With reverent hands the kindred dust we bear,
To sacred shadows of the wood repair,
Far from the crowded mart, the world whose strife
Still mocks at death, and seldom honors life,
There lay we down the form that cannot know
How fond our homage, and how great our woe.
With tender love,—with tearful eyes,—we trace
For his last dwelling some selected place,
Some shady copse, or isle—some spot of green,
By oak and elm secure with leafy screen;

Where the Magnolia towers—where tribute vines
Steal up to clamber o'er supporting pines;—
Some spot most precious to the musing hour
Of him whose relics cold we thus embower;—
Some sunny bank, whence, gazing on the west,
His living eye with all the landscape blest,
It was his wont, from friendship still to crave,
The spot he couch'd on might be made his grave;—
A spot to heart subdued, and cheer'd by faith,
To make the spirit half "in love with death,"—
Peace in the prospect, peace upon the sea,
And sunny smiles about each guardian tree,
No voice of man to vex the solitude,
But breezes softly whispering through the wood.

(1850, 1853)

HORACE IN DISHABILLE.

TO MY MAN TOM.

Ode xxxviii.

Tom, none of your Yankee pomps for me,
Weave me no wreaths from the maple tree;
Nor trouble yourself to please my mood,
To seek where the Quaker roses brood;
The myrtle alone, good Tom, be mine,
With a cheering bowl 'neath the Southern vine;
'Twill not be amiss, if these you bring,
While, under the rose, we quaff and sing.

(1851)

"LA BOLSA DE LAS SIERRAS."[1]

Peace woos us here with flow'rs;—
Peace in the solitude, where Nature still
Looks unpolluted forth from mountain tow'rs,
And takes no shape of ill;

189

Where, fleet through vales that sleep in lakes below,
The deer leaps free in herds and never dreads the foe.

The swan speeds wild in grace,
Through the sweet lakes that freshen all the vale;
A meadowy sea, far as the eye may trace,
Ripples beneath the trade-wind's soothing gale;
Here woods and groves that never lose their green,
Fringe the fair streams, and crown the heights between.

The gay flamingo there,
Marching with crest erect and footstep slow,
Looks down to watch his form in waters clear,
Nor heeds the trooping flocks that come and go;
Legions of white-wing'd innocents, that glide,
Or dart, with sense of joy, and mirth, that sweetens pride.

Pensive, the palms arise,
As if o'er cherish'd graves; the mezquite towers
Through the dense chapparal; a thousand dyes
Blend sweetly, and the aroma of the flow'rs
From thousand shrubs, by ocean zephyrs fann'd,
With music borne afar, makes grateful all the land.

With never-dying song,
The glad winds gather through the blossoming day,
Like truants still, their sportive play prolong,
Forgetful in their pleasures that they stray;
While in the sky the flecking clouds lie calm,
White, soft, as drinking glad from skies below their balm.

Peace! Peace!—the sad heart's cry,
That blossom of security, here finds
Meet echo,—and with voices never high,
Yet absolute in their sweetness, blends and binds
With natural metes her Empire, soft as wild,
Takes from the innocent fear, weds rapture to the mild.

Peace! Peace! the peace of Love,
Serene and sure in favour of the skies,—
Waters that lend their voices to the grove,
Groves singing back to waters;—grateful eyes,

From each, that kindle in requited fires,
Blest in the embrace of sanctified desires—

    Commerce of kindred things,
Whose instincts find communion and rejoice,
    With all that being ever circling brings,—
Each with its power to bless, and each with voice
To answer for the blessing, and requite
The giver in happy song of ever-wing'd delight.

    How swells the common strain;
The Day-star waking ocean; the gay breeze
    That welcomes still the brightness back again,
Skirrs the white beach, and skims among the trees,
Yet whispers to the sea-shell on the shore,
Which thenceforth aye repeats the sweet song o'er and o'er!

    Oh! voices of delight,
Wings of my joy, and blossoming stars that gleam,
    With still a present fondness for the sight,
That once has gloried in celestial dream;
Here still ye find each dear dismember'd part,
That in youth's first fresh fancies bless'd its heart.

    The peace that harbours here
Is that of the soul's infancy,—when first,
    Untroubled with to-morrow-haunting fear,
The young affections into blossom burst,
And found in breeze and sky, and earth and sea,
Realms sacred—homes and haunts where Love goes singing free.

    Enough for happiness
Is here—where Beauty harbours in the shade,
    And asks but privilege to tend and bless,
To come in beams and blossoming charms array'd,
And soothe to slumberous sweetness with a strain,
Once heard, that never leaves the happy heart again.

    One heart shall grow to mine,
Here in the holy wilderness—shall share
    All its sweet treasures, and the peace divine,

That robs the precious rapture of its fear;
Nor sigh for that the mountain in its breast
Holds—which, with lure of hell, would rob our hearts of rest.

Love thus, at last, shall crown
The warfare of long seasons. Born of Peace,
  She will bring soothing. We shall both lie down
Beneath the slender palm, and feel the increase
That fruitfully belongs to natural joys,
Meet toils, pure thoughts and hopes, delight that never cloys.

(1852, 1853)

1. "La Bolsa de las Sierras,"—the Pocket or Pouch of the Mountains,—is the fanciful title given by the Spaniards to a very picturesque and lovely spot in Texas,—the terminus of the ocean-reach, stretching up towards San Antonio, the mines of San Saba, Chihuahua, and the Rocky Mountains. The scene is one of the rarest loveliness. The meadows are clothed with flowers even in February. The waters spread away among groves that relieve the prospect with a constant variety. Here come, wandering along the margin of lakes and waters, that lose themselves amidst the rich grasses of the slopes, the most wonderful flocks of the flamingo and the swan. But the verses must do the work of description.

BALLAD.

For me that song of sorrow,
  Whose 'plainings touch the heart;
First born of melancholy,
  And not of mortal art;
It strengthens though it saddens,
  A love-commissioned thing;
Oh! sorrow's song is holy,
  And thus, I pray thee, sing!

Sing, while the shadows deepen
  Upon yon hill, whose brow
Wears still the flickering sunlight,
  But whence 'tis flitting now;
Sing of the fading beauty,
  Sing of the coming night,
And, as our eyes grow tearful,
  Methinks they must grow bright.

Let him who has not sorrow'd
  With loss of things most dear,
Exult in music's triumph,
  And joy in Hope's career;
But he who weeps the parting
  That made each blessing brief,
Will seek from music only
  The song that wakens grief.

(1852)

HARMONIES OF NATURE.

But yield yourself to Nature, and you drink,
From her abundant fountains as you go,
New life and gladness. 'Tis but to throw wide
The bosom, and absorb, through eye and ear,
The aliment of beauty.

                 But forget
That you have cares and studies, and great thoughts,
Shaping an empire—the ambitious zeal
For conquest, and a life beyond your time;
That men behold your coming with a hope,
And look to your departure with a fear;—
That you're a man of state, from whom the nation
Expects great things;—that you're a man of wealth,
Needing great speculations to increase
The useless treasure, that upon your Soul
Hangs heavy, with an ever-pressing care,
Lest wealth take wings to itself, and flee away,
As with a dream at dawning; that you are poor,
Needing some daily struggle to disarm
The wolf that ever rages at your door,
For wife and precious ones!

               Our tyrannies
Of self, stand over us ever, in some shape
Of persecution; and between our pleasures
And hearts, forever interpose denial;—

And so life pales upon us, and the beautiful
Fades every where from Nature!

                             Would you forth,
Seeking her blessings?

Then depart, forgetful
Of what you are;—deliver yourself to her;
Hearken her counsels only—song or whisper,—
And be a freeman in her fond embrace,
Untrammell'd and unterrified by Self!

    Oh! she is such a charmer, that, but give her
The privilege, and she will, with a whisper,
Steal softly to each warm place in your bosom,
And make it fruitful of delicious fondness,
To keep it warm forever.

                            She will sing you
Through zephyr and leaf, a song shall rouse up fancy,
To uses of her wings; and though she wander,
Capricious as the bird or bee, as happy
In the discovery of honied treasures,
Lurking in rugged tree or simple flower,
Yet will she bring you her discoveries home,
If you but woo her.

                  Drowsing on the bankside,
Half dreaming, she will troop before your vision,
With royal train of beauties;—each with tribute
To satisfy the longings in your bosom,
As these declare for beauty.

                        You shall gather
From this sweet commerce with her goodly train,
Great store of thoughts and fancies, most delicious,
That shall bring recompense in lonely hours,
Long seasons after; and rare melodies
Will haunt your senses with most loving echoes,
From ditties, sinking now into your Soul
Unvoiced, that, when the Hours grow sad about you,

Shall bring you cheering, and make strong your spirit
For the rough troubles of the encroaching world.

Never than Nature was there fonder mother
To him who brings due service and allegiance,
And searches lovingly her haunts of refuge,
Forgetful of vain passions;—still imploring,
With open heart, her counsels with her fondness.
She gives, besides, her blessings, in such fortune,
As wealth may neither buy nor sell; nor fate
Rob from the treasury of a loving heart.

Oh! see, and hearken! with mysterious whisper
The breeze comes laden; murmurs of the brooklet
Body the music dear to innocent fancies,
When love grows first a wooer, aiming fondly
At proper utterance of the flush he feels;
And, with the choral songs of wind and forest,
The very soul grows lifted into stature,
Feeling the effusion of a sovereign God,
And finds great wings that bear it onward, upward,
Until it grows illuminate, in presence
Of the Eternal Beauty, which makes Nature
The type of the Eternal.

                I'm a dreamer
In the world's notion;—but, if these be dreams
They are not less my raptures. I have pleasures
In this mute converse with the woods and waters,
That fertilize all senses, and make fruitful
The whole soul-garden.

                What if I forget
That bread is wanted for the morrow? Now,
I am full-fed! The old gods bring me food;
And in forgetfulness of the physical need,
The spirit drinks of such a nourishment
As clothes each mortal faculty with wings,
To fly to all the gardens of delight,
Where still an angel keeps the gate, and beckons
Each to his proper province, and makes free

To the repast, where evermore the bounty
Excels the appetite, and makes abundance
The future need of memory and of thought!

Ay, 'tis in very happiness of spirit
I feel within me sacred elements,
Here at the board of nature, where I wanton
In glorious fancies, in whose every whisper
Breathes forth a blessing!

                              Won to confidence,
Through love, I wander off with sightless speed,
Borne far in the forest with glad company
Successive troops of wingéd creatures, bent
To do their angel work for joy of earth!
The starry hosts watch brooding as they go
To hallow their performance. Not a cloud
Frowns on the loving ministry; and waters,
Soft stealing through green-fringéd avenues,
Sing sweetly up to zephyrs in the trees,
That echo softlier back each fond refrain.

These are grand harmonies! How sweet the accord
Of stars, to all the voices of the void!
These breathings of the bodiless breeze, that, slow,
Lifts up and spreads aloft its gossamer vans,
Fitfully for a while, then sinks to rest,
On the light billows which its wings have made.

Thus Nature wings us to a spirit world,
Where every voice is music. Hark! the strain,—
If that thy spirit be attuned to thought
Beyond its daily custom;—and thy fancy
Hath shaken off its fetters; Hark, the strain
As of old voices, when the crowding hills
Lean'd forward, with beguiléd sense, to catch
The far sweet tones from other worlds than ours;—
Then, with unconscious effort, and glad burst,
Requited them in echoes, which were full
Of a new hope, that blessedly came down
As meant to link this lowly world with heaven!

And such is Nature; for, in all her realms
Gather innumerous spirits, that but take
Their robes from woods; their voices from the breeze,
And breathe out sweetness to us from the flowers,
By which alone we know them, when we might,
Were we less heedful of material things,
Enjoy more perfect knowledge of that nature,
The commonest thing of being, yet a God,
Which should inform, with perfect sympathy,
Each yearning passion lonely in our hearts.

(1856, 1866)

SONG OF THE SOUTH.

i

Oh, the South! the sunny, sunny South!
  Land of true feeling, land forever mine;
I drink the kisses of her rosy mouth,
  And my heart swells as with a draught of wine!
She brings me blessings of maternal love—
  I have her praise which sweetens all my toil;
Her voice persuades, her loving smiles approve—
  She sings me from the sky and from the soil!
Oh! by her lonely pines that wave and sigh—
  Oh! by her myriad flowers that bloom and fade;
By all the thousand beauties of her sky,
  And the sweet solemn of her forest shade—
    She's mine, forever mine!
    Nor will I aught resign
Of what she gives me, mortal or divine;
    Will sooner part
    With life—hope—heart—
Will die—before I fly!

ii

Oh! Love is hers, such love as ever glows
  In souls where leaps affection's living tide;
She is all fondness to her friends;—to foes
  She glows a thing of passion, strength and pride!

She feels no tremors when the Danger's nigh;
  But the fight over, and the victory won,
How, with strange fondness, turns her loving eye,
  In tearful welcome, on each gallant son!
Oh! by her virtues of the cherished past—
  By all her hopes of what the future brings—
I glory that my lot with her is cast,
  And my soul flushes, and exultant sings
    She's mine, forever mine!
    For her will I resign
  All precious things—all placed upon her shrine;
    Will freely part
    With life—hope—heart—
  Will die!—do aught but fly!

(1845, 1857)

THE CHIMNEY CRICKET.

i

When the dusky shadows glide
Through the porch at even-tide,
And the wintry faggot's blaze
O'er the wall fantastic plays;
And the household forms appear,
Each in the accustom'd chair—
Grandsire old in seat of pride;
Son and wife on either side;
Urchins on the knee astride;
Slender maid, in volume lost,
Reading rapt of true love cross'd—
Ere the evening board is set,
While the urn is hissing yet,
Then—as if the whole were met,
Unto whom his song is bound,
In his circle gather'd round—
Then, with lay of measured mirth,
Sudden, from the silent hearth,
Our chimney cricket chirps refrain,
Fitting the domestic strain—

Singing of the pleasant peace,
And the household's fair increase,
And the quiet gliding on
Of the years, from sire to son;—
Of old house and ancient state,
Not too high to anger Fate;
Modest worth, and working brave,
Which, of yore, the homestead gave,
And maintain it, with a fold,
Growing well, though growing old:
Planted like a rock, and strong
In God's favor, just so long
As the cricket sings his song.

ii

For, 'tis not a fable all,
That predicts the household's fall,
When the cricket leaves the wall.
Household insect—bird that clings
To the roof-tree, while he sings,
Which, for full a hundred springs,
He hath held, and rear'd his young,
Speaking each the self-same tongue,
Of safe homestead, happy still
In the blessing of good will,
And God's bounty;—
    Dog that waits,
Watching nightly near the gates,
Like a sentry—faithful guard
Of the dwelling and the yard;
    Puss, that purring, coil'd up snug,
Keeps the centre of the rug;—
All have instincts fine, that teach
Presciences, we can not reach—
All domestic, all designed
Waiters, watchers on mankind,
With the family allied,
Sharing in its pain and pride,
Shrinking never from its side,
And, by chirp, or howl, or song,
Signalling the threatened wrong—
Hurt, or hindrance; beast of prey;

Sudden tempest; sad decay,
As the household wastes away;
Or, in hours of peace like this,
Chirrupping domestic bliss.

iii

Grateful to my thoughts and ear
Is, at dusk, the song I hear
Of our cricket in the wall,
Timéd well to sober fall;
With a strain monotonous,
Suiting the well-order'd house;
Suiting well the set of sun,
Conflict over, toil well done,
And the pleasant calm which brings
Sweet repose for striving things.
Song of grave solemnity
For his spouse and children three,
As for mine, though more there be—
Three or thirty, which you will—
But a well-train'd household still;
Making, it would seem, a grace
Fitted to the homely place;
Giving thanks for daily food
To the Giver of All Good,
Even as we, who smile, declare
Bounty that receives no prayer—
Needs none, if the thought be there.

iv

By the lonely hearth I sit,
Watching, while the figures flit
O'er the walls; or, in the fire,
See the phantom shapes expire—
Cities, and their domes, in flashes,
Till they fade in the gray ashes—
Start, to hear the sudden shock,
The knell'd hours upon the clock;
But never lose the cricket strain,
Changing seldom his refrain,
Which would seem in purpose vain,
Murmuring;

—"Wherefore all this stir?
Half life's struggle is to err!"
    He, the best philosopher;
Satisfied with lodging small,
But a dry one, in close wall,
And a single burden ditty,
Dull enough to move the pity
Or the scorn of captious city,
Ever bent on insect ranges,
Constant only seeking changes,
With a lizard lust for sunshine;
And, 'twixt mammon, gammon, moonshine,
Showing butterfly propensity,
With scarce butterfly intensity.

                v

"Better," quoth he, "watch the fire,
See sparks kindle and expire,
Than indulge in vain desire—
Half your strifes of men are flashes
That go out in smoke and ashes!
Half your struggles, but a run
Of brown lizard after sun!
Half your pleasures, or your pains,
But a worm's, for silken gains,
The best part of life made bitter,
With its cares, for idle glitter;
And the soul's most noble powers
Flung away, through fruitless hours,
In a fond pursuit of flowers!
Flowers, or phantoms—vainer far
Than the hope to pluck the star—
Prism rays of fancy, gleaming
Through the fairy realms of dreaming!
Every power of virtue wasted—
Flowers tainted soon as tasted—
All because of that vain struggle,
Still pursued through strife and juggle,
To assert, on painted pinion,
O'er still meaner things, dominion;
Moving motes of meaner station
Into vulgar admiration!

vi

"Better far, my evening prattle—
Purr of cat, or low of cattle,
Bark of dog, or chirp of sparrow—
To avert of Fate the arrow;
Take the sting away from being;
Teach your young ones truthful seeing,
And conduct them to the beauty
That lies sure in homely duty!
Here, beside the evening fire,
You shall guide the young desire;
Train the heart, with modest lesson,
And the noble soul, to press on
In the walks, or high or lowly,
Which the endowment renders holy!"

vii

They are sleeping, all my young,
And their mother. Not a tongue,
Save that whose moral hath been sung,
Makes a murmur through the house.
O'er the carpet runs the mouse;
Heedless of the cricket, he,
Though still rather shy of me,
And the cricket's song, but late
Full of meaning, sinks to prate,
The mere click-clack, dull debate,
Such as to the common sense
Offers little recompense.
Yet, methinks, he might have said,
What's been running in my head?
And, with such a notion, he
Shall never be dislodged by me.

viii

Ah! dear drowsy chirper, why
Should I lodging place deny,
Though thy prattlings never cease,
When they promise household peace?
Till the house itself shall fall,
Take the freedom of the wall,
While it pleaseth thee to hold

Tenure in the mantle old!
Rear thy tribes to teach mine own,
When both thou and I are gone!
It would please me much to know
That when hence, perforce, I go,
Thou, or thine, shall sing for mine,
Teaching them the instincts fine,
Which may lead to the divine;
All the sweet morality
Of that constancy in thee,
Which thou still hast taught to me!
They shall keep the household fires,
And home evenings, like their sires,
With a love that never tires!
And a gentle, calm content,
Which, at close of day well spent,
Keeps the evening innocent;
And, with placid mood, surveys
The slow sinking of the blaze,
Till each golden gleam decays!

(1858, 1860)

THE POET.

Thou art a Poet, and thy aim has been
To draw from every thought, and every scene
Psychal, and natural, that serene delight
Wherewith our God hath made his worlds so bright,
The sense of Beauty—the immortal thrill
Of intuitions throned above our Will—
The secret of that yearning, dim, but strong
Which yields the pulse to Hope—the wings to Song.

(1858)

BALLAD.—COME, LET US DISCOURSE.

i

Come, let us discourse of our sorrow,
  The gloom, and the grave, and the night,
For what shall be our waking to-morrow,
  When the loved one no more lies in sight?
When he answers no more to the loving call,
  And pleads no more to the loving ear,
And stark and cold 'neath his desolate pall,
  Nor feels our groan, nor sees our tear?

ii

Oh, wail, wail!—nothing but wail!—
  Words are a mock, since prayer is vain;
The shriek and the moan must tell the tale
  Of our life-long wo, and his mortal pain!—
How, in his agony, panting, wild,
  Raging with thirst, yet still denied,
We watch'd the face of the dying child,
  With hearts death-stricken before he died!

iii

The boy of a thousand loving ways,
  So true, so innocent, fond and sweet,
What had he done, that his fair young days
  Should close so soon in the winding sheet?
What had he done, that the mortal pain
  Should fasten its fangs on his pure young life,
While the gasping cry, and the raving brain,
  Show'd the agony sharp of the deadly strife!

iv

Oh, wail, wail!—nothing but wail,
  Can speak for the pangs of that mortal blow:
The shriek can but feebly tell the tale
  Of the pain he bore and the grief we know!
Vex us no more with the idle strain
  That bids us find solace in agonies o'er;
Teaches that prayer and care are vain,
  That the angel we've lost we shall see no more!

Know we not this? And because we know,
  Is the groan, the moan, and the wailing cry;
It is not forbid that we feel the wo,
  And cry aloud to the far-off sky!
O child of our love! it is something won,
  To feel that thy innocent life on earth
Hath found thee a passport beyond the sun,
  In the blessèd sphere where thy soul had birth.

vi

Yet, wo, my spirit! What else but wo
  At thy pangs, my boy, though they now be o'er?
'Tis something to soften the griefs we know,
  That thy fair young form shall have pain no more;
Yet, oh, the silence, so deep and drear,
  Dreadest of voices, that speak of doom,
And mournfully echo the cry: "Oh, where?"
  As wistful I wander from room to room.

(1858, 1860)

BALLAD.—OH! MY BOYS!

Oh! my boys, my noble boys,
I am sitting 'midst your toys,
But I hear no pleasant noise;
  I shall hear no more
The sweet voices of your joys,
  Ever dear before.

It was only yesterday
Ye were by my side at play,
Bounding gleeful, all so gay,
  Happy, with such cheer,
That our hearts forgot to pray,
  Having no more fear.

Drum and trumpet, top and ball,
With such merry whoop and call,

Making racket in the hall,
   Deafening every ear:
Oh! that I could have them all—
   That I still could hear!

That I still could hear and see,
Shapes and noises of your glee—
My bright Syd—my Beverley!
   Oh, my noble boys,
Voice and form are lost to me,
   Sitting 'midst your toys.

(1858, 1860)

SONNET.—TO W. PORCHER MILES.

O Friend! who satt'st beside me in the hour
   When Death was at my hearth; and in my home
   The mother's cry of wailing for that doom,
Long hovering, which, at last, with fatal power
Descended, like the vulture on his prey,
   And in his talons bore away our young!—
   Thou know'st how terribly this heart was wrung:
Thou cam'st with watch and soothing, night and day,
No brother more devoted!—More than friend,
   Belovéd evermore,—behold me thine!—
   Yet have I little worthy that is mine,
Save love, and this poor tribute; which must blend
With memories of thy watch, and of our pain,
And of those precious boys, we both have watched in vain!

(1859, 1860)

'TIS TRUE THAT LAST NIGHT
I ADORED THEE.

'Tis true that last night I adored thee,
   But 'twas moonlight, the song, and the wine;

The cool morning air has restored me,
   And no longer I deem thee divine;
I confess thou art pretty and tender,
   And when thou canst catch me again,
As last night, on a desperate *bender*,
   Once more I'll submit to thy chain.

The fact is, dear Fanny, I'm human,
   Very weak, I may say, on a *spree;*
And no matter of what sort the woman,
   I'm her slave if she *cottons* to me.
But this curséd sobriety ever
   Undoes every chain of delight,
And my memory, by daylight, has never
   Any sense of what takes place by night.

I'm a man of most regular habit
   When daylight comes round, on my word;
And though loving, by night, as a rabbit,
   With the sunrise I'm cool as a curd;
I'm quite willing in moonlight for capture,
   But she's a bright woman whose skill,
Having spell'd the short hours with rapture,
   With the daylight can fetter me still.

                            (1859, 1860)

RAISONS IN LAW AND LIQUOR.

There needs should be reason for thinking,
To the eyes that are evermore winking,
   But, when eyes gleam with fire,
   What fool would require
A rhyme or a reason for drinking?

Leave books to the sages that make 'em,
And laws for the scoundrels that break 'em,
   But in wine we have saws
   That are better than laws,
And we're infidels if we forsake 'em.

These teach us that thinking's a trouble,
That your glory is only a bubble,
   And that study and care
   Do but end in a snare,
Making innocent students see double.

We have doctrines more genial and better,
Writ in crimson, and not in black letter;
   Madeira for ink
   Gives us freedom, I think,
While your thought only forges a fetter.

The devil take Blackstone and Vattel;
Here's the wisdom that's born of the bottle,
   And the student who drains
   The last drop, for his pains,
Shall never have pains in his throttle.

(1859, 1863)

FRAGMENT.

FINALE OF THE DANDY-LION.

Your Dandy-Lion's but a butterfly,
Most exquisitely languid; who soon tires
Of his own wings; who shows, but never uses,
Their vans; and ever finds the expense of motion,
Exhaustion of his moral! All's not gold
That his wing carries; and, ere many seasons,
He finds the keeping even of that a cost,
If not a care and canker. He soon rusts,
And the gay lacquer of his painted garments,
Will need more wit than haply was his portion,
To win his tailor's ear most suitably
For a new suit. His life's a very hard one,
In conflict with his tastes and appetites;
But, luckily, a short one.
                In brief season,
You find him, as the tailors phrase it, *seedy*,

Spite of all lacquering; and growing oozy,
Subsiding from the garden to the swamp;—
Glad then to happen on discarded flowers,
In precincts, which, last season, were too common
For his so dainty palate. He'll get back,
If fate and the east wind will suffer it,
To some poor spinster flower, upon the rock
Of her own fears and longings;—and be happy,
Simply to find a nest,—a housing shelter,
And plain short commons, and the waste coarse fare,
Which, when his wings were gay with virgin lacquer,
Had only moved his loathing! One short summer,
And the gay flutterer in the palace precincts,
Wriggling 'mongst roses and lilies,—flies them all,
To dwell in cabbage and in kitchen garden;
Happy in refuge where one pot is boiling.

THE FINALE OF THE FLIRT.

Your flirt is ever frisky;—frisky fancies,
Mix'd blood and brain, will keep her fidgetty;
And she will sing you, and with sentiment
Seduce you to the balcony and moonlights,
Only to leave you groping in the dark!
She's but a wriggler of capricious nature—
An eel in moral! Would you fix her fast?
Run a pin through her; as the naturalist
Fastens the bug, or beetle, to the cork!
She's cork-like, and a floater;—beetle like,
She'll do a world of humming for *three* seasons.
You'll have to seek her out, if you would find her.
These seasons over: and you'll find her willing
For any captor—stuck to any cork!

(1859)

PROMISE OF SPRING.

The sun-beguiling breeze,
From the soft Cuban seas,

With life-bestowing kiss wakes the pride of garden bowers;
                    And lo! our city elms,
                    Have plumed with buds their helms,
And, with tiny spears salute the coming on of flowers.

                    The promise of the Spring,
                    Is in every glancing wing
That tells its flight in song which shall long survive the flight;
                    And mocking Winter's glooms,
                    Skies, air and earth grow blooms,
With change as bless'd as ever came with passage of a night!

                    Ah! could our hearts but share
                    The promise rich and rare,
That welcomes life to rapture in each happy fond caress,
                    That makes each innocent thing
                    Put on its bloom and wing,
Singing for Spring to come to the realm she still would bless!

                    But, alas for us, no more
                    Shall the coming hour restore
The glory, sweet and wonted, of the seasons to our souls;
                    Even as the Spring appears,
                    Her smiling makes our tears,
While with each bitter memory the torrent o'er us rolls.

                    Even as our zephyrs sing
                    That they bring us in the Spring,
Even as our bird grows musical in ecstasy of flight—
                    We see the serpent crawl,
                    With his slimy coat o'er all,
And blended with the song is the hissing of his blight.

                    We shudder at the blooms,
                    Which but serve to cover tombs—
At the very sweet of odors which blend venom with the breath;
                    Sad shapes look out from trees,
                    And in sky and earth and breeze,
We behold but the aspect of a Horror worse than Death!

                                        (1860, 1866)

CICADA—THE KATY-DID.

Sing me Summer,
Sweet Cicada!
Chirruping gay in the bristly pine;
Though thy song hath made me sadder,
Yet my heart must thank thee for it!
Were each comer
But as welcome,
With no better song than thine,
What a bit of Eden were it,
In this forest nook of mine!

(1860, 1868)

GUARANTIES.

Oh! the rose is a sweet one thou givest me to-night,
But it dies in a day;
And that star which would hallow our loves with its light,
With the dawn wastes away;
Ah! dearest, the token must be
Much surer, which tells of thy passion for me.

Methinks the sweet bird which is carolling now,
Will too soon spread his wings;
And I always have found that a musical vow
Is the fleetest of things!
Ah! dearest, the token to bind,
Is surely a something of different kind.

Vows sworn by fond lips on fond lips, are, methinks,
Much more rational ties;
And whether one fudge or fidelity drinks,
Matters not to the wise;
But 'tis certain, my dear, when the guaranty's such,
One never can have an assurance too much.

(1860)

THE PALMETTO ROYAL.[1]

Brave at your peril! But to pause were best!
A forest of green bayonets at your breast,
Royal palmettoes, with keen swords arrest!

You may not pass the barrier! Close, they stand,
Meetly arrayed, a congregated band,
Fix'd firm as faith, the guardians of the land.

Each on his mounded battery, full in view,
Loyal as sworded sentries sworn to do;
And beautiful as stedfast! How they woo—

Thus graceful, rising into rounded towers,
Crested with silvery pyramid of flowers,
That speak of blended purities and powers—

With fence of thousand swords of glittering green,
They tell of proud defenders, soon as seen,
And champions by the shore that guard the realm within.

                                        (1858, 1861)

---

1. One of our Southern Poets, long ago, gave us the Emblematic Signification of the Palmetto, as a badge of our Country. It will be well that our gallant boys should read and remember the lesson.

KING'S MOUNTAIN.[1]

The hills lie soft in beauty of the scene,
That gilds the green of trees; and in the vale,
Peace, in the embrace of summer, finds repose
For every hamlet. The delicious sweet,
Spreads over all the season's calm, and lulls
The air, with pleasant mystery, that breathes,
In grateful murmurs, through the oaken groves!

Yet, here, in olden time, grim war hath striven,
With brand and bolt; fierce grapple with stern foes,

When savage welcome was the shout for blood,
That found a thousand echoes through the hills,
As of wild, wolfish herds, by hunger driven
To madness, and down rushing for the plains,
Having no impulse but in appetite!

Here gather'd the brave mountain men to meet
The fierce assailant; and, with weapons rude,
A stern array, they hemmed his legions in,
And smote them on the forehead, till they fell,
Vanquish'd, and cast their weapons down to earth,
And cried for mercy.

       As the hunters gather,
To track the invading tiger;—at his cry,
Swift snatching down the rifle from the wall,
And, with the boarspear, and the knife in belt,
Grasp'd for the keen occasion; our brave men,
Rose at the bugle's summons; o'er the hills
Resounding lonely as an eagle's scream,
In dying, near her ærie; through the dells,
Sad palpitating, a prolonged appeal,
That spoke of vengeance to her mate, and arm'd
His ire for slaughter.

       From their homes, hard by—
Rude cottages, where courage still beguiles,
Requiting love, that asks but happiness,
In peace and in the solitude—they sped;
'Till in yon gorge assembling, from all sides,
Descending, they were mustered in yon grove,
Making swift count of their so prompt array,
And of the enemy's numbers.

       "Few—and yet enough,
For death!" cried the heroic of their band—
"Not many, but enough!"

       Thus bravely arm'd,
With courage, and the will, to do or die,
They rush'd to victory! On every side
They waited the invader on his heights,

And with a girdle of keen steel and fire,
They hemm'd him close within a narrow ring,
Bristling with death!

      In vain the wild halloo—
The desperate shriek of valor—at a gasp,
Laid prostrate; the shrill whistle of the chief,
Raging for victory, if not escape;
And the long line of levell'd bayonets,
Contending for the precipice's edge,
And trebly crimsoned at each desperate charge,
The mountaineers were ever more the Fates,
Still pressing on the enemy's several flanks,
Even as the bloodhound, panting up the heights,
With the sharp arrow sticking in his sides,
Still hangs upon the footsteps of the foe;
That feels, in flight, the inevitable doom,
And staggers in his tracks; and falls, and dies;
Yet feels, ere yet all consciousness be gone,
The savage jaws that tear him at the throat!

So press'd our mountaineers the British foe,
And his base allies; till they fell, and flung
Their weapons down to earth! Our heros tore
His insolent banner, flaunting o'er their heights,
And trod it under foot.

      And thus they made
Their homes secure through all posterity!
No foeman will again presume to scale
Their rocky eminences; or leap down
The hollows, where the cottage fold lies blest
In the sweet confidence of freedom's peace,
And the delicious sunshine of the plain!
And over all there hangs a powerful spell;
The soul triumphing in its noblest parts;
Its highest aspirations; its great aims;
The best of purity; most dear to peace,
And liberty; and all that to the heart
Of the best manhood consecrates a place!
And these shall still inspire, in other days,
For other triumphs; 'till the land, secure,

Grows blest in precious arts and happiest homes!
Of those who died to consecrate this height,
"Williams, and Chronelle, Mattocks, Robb and Boyd,"[2]
And others who have had no monument,
Cherish the fond remembrance. They were men,
Who had the natural hardihood of virtue,
Who could not brook oppression; could not bear,
The assailant, threatening from the heights above;
And, with most precious instincts, who could rouse,
To brave the danger ere it touch'd the door!
Were ever ready when the country cried,
Clamorous in her sorrow, for the succor
Of all her sons!

       Their blood is on these hills,
Their graves below! They keep the place as when
They kept it from the invader! We, who see,
Will reverence their brave virtues; glad to win
Like reverence from the future. So, our blood
Shall freely flow like theirs. And we shall learn,
From them, to gather, at our people's need,
As eagles, when the wolf or serpent dares;
To dart, like them, with death, upon the foe!

                   (1855[?], 1861)

1. While our brave mountaineers are making new records of glory, worthy of their an-
cestors, it may not be unwise to remind them, nevertheless, of the achievements of that
noble past, in their history, from which they may well derive their inspiration in the
present. The following lines were composed, many years ago, on a visit to the battle field,
at the foot of King's Mountain. They have never before been published.
2. The only monument at the spot, is accorded, one side, to the British Col. Ferguson;
the other to Chronelle, Mattocks, Robb and Boyd.

THE CLOSE OF THE YEAR 1861.

i

Now come the premature blasts of Winter on,
  And cool airs mantle o'er the city's breast;
The bright sun gathers, ere the day is done,
  His saffron robes about him in the West;

The winds grow mightier in their wild career,
And bring with harsher cries, the remnant of the year.

ii

And Night, starr'd Empress, sovereign as serene,
   Sways o'er a sullen empire—jewels bright,
Many as beautiful, proclaim her Queen;
   But, o'er a realm that warms not in her light;
She seems not throned so much in love as pride,
And stars grow pale attending at her side.

iii

There is a sober sadness in the sky,
   Despite the glory; there is, in the air,
A murmuring, as of spirits, far too high
   To brook a sovereignty so cold, tho' fair:—
There is a swelling tumult in the floods,
And deep moans issue from ancestral woods.

iv

We share in Nature's portents; and each voice,
   Of wind, or flood, or wood, or star, conveys
Its counsels to the heart. We now rejoice,
   Now weep, scarce knowing why! And glorious days
Lapse into saddest twilight! We arise,
To joys, or sorrows, changing with the skies.

v

Is man thus subject to each wind's caprice,
   Day's and night's changes? Hath he then no power
To will above the winds? Is there no peace
   For the great soul, commissioned with the dower
Of Immortality, and born for sway,
O'er all the inferior tribes predestined to obey?

vi

Shall we, submissive, sink beneath the chain
   Of Circumstance: and feel it, link by link,
Hot in the heart and heavy on the brain,
   Dragging us on to the precipitous brink,
Where the great maelstrom, Ruin, lurks in wait,
Watching to whelm, malignant as a Fate!

vii

The chill winds blight the flower; the mighty tree,
   Goes down before the storm; the shivering beast
Droops 'neath the frost and famine! In degree,
   As man is animal, he, with the least,
Shares in the common dread, and suffering,—grows
Fearful and feeble 'gainst his natural foes.

viii

But, as he rises to the rank of man,
   With all his grand endowments—Will and Thought—
Courage and purpose—resolute to scan,
   The aspect of the danger, and how fraught
With power of harm—he puts his armor on,
Knowing how safer 'tis to seek than shun.

ix

He knows the true conditions of his life,
   Promise no safety, if he doth not use
The qualities which make him fit for strife;
   Or if the animal nature should abuse
The faculties which lift him into power,
And make his state assured from hour to hour.

x

In this, Religion and Philosophy—
   The best possessions of his mortal state—
Both tutor him, and happily agree:
   Soul-will and manly purpose baffle fate;
And, whether we stand or fall, if we but *will*
What the grand wisdom counsels, we must still,

xi

Rise o'er the time's caprice, the season's change
   The animal weakness—hostile hate and aim!
Wide is our province; great the Empire's range;
   Wondrous the working done; glorious the fame!
These give the wing for freedom; these, the power,
For sway, howe'er capricious runs the hour.

xii

Our life is Liberty's, or it is naught,

Worth moral challenging! The will must be
The offspring of the soul-superior—Thought—
    And this alone can make the mortal free!
What's Life?—what Death?—what Change?—what Chance?—what
        Pain?
To him whose thought cries ever—"all is vain!"

   xiii
What's human happiness, that sucks its sweet,
    From the frail shrub tree that each gale o'erthrows?
How vain, when wings of beauty are so fleet,
    In a blind confidence to find repose!
The wife, the child, that make our bliss to-day,
To-morrow we may shroud them in the clay!

   xiv
We cannot build on these, or aught that life
    Yields us of mortal bliss; but must prepare
For constant change and loss, and frequent strife,
    And toil, and seek, and strive, and bravely dare;
Assured that, at the worst, our loss can be,
Such as must follow our mortality!

   xv
Our *gain* is in the assertion of the right
    In self and country; in well-reasoned will;
In manly purpose, in the nerve to fight,
    Though death confronts us from each quarter still;
We *live* but as we *do!*—if *well* we do,
Nor chance nor change can trouble me or you!

   xvi
My country! O my country! with thy day,
    Dawning in glory; with thy noontide sky,
Serene in sunshine, while November's sway
    Softens each beam—with all thy pulses high—
With promise of new dawnings,—and each flower
Waiting to welcome the awakening hour—

   xvii
That thou should'st feel upon thy sacred shores
    The assailant!—that thy enemy should dare

Usurp thy heritage; and that he pours
　　His hate to blacken, and his wrath to scare
Thy day, thy night, thy sleep; the pleasant peace
That made thy suns to shine, thy fields increase.

　　　　xviii
Ah! what remains? What's life?—what day?—what night,
　　Or care, or pain?—We sport a little hour,
And the flesh falls from us, in sudden blight,—
　　And pleasant things lose all their pleasant power!
The *true life's in the thought*; and if the thought
Be pledged no more to freedom, it is nought!

　　　　xix
We can but die at last! The cord, the shot,
　　Old age, convulsion, sickness—these declare
A pang, a moment's pang, perchance—and what
　　Remains? For freedom we may nobly dare
These pangs, these perils—true to what is true,
Face the dark fate, whatever it may do!

　　　　xx
Ay! well I know that through the pleasant land,
　　The storm goes raging! The sweet hamlet now,—
The little flower-clad cottage, set midst grand
　　Groups of ancestral oaks, upon the brow
Of some fair shining eminence—the plain,
Smiling in green and rich in golden grain—

　　　　xxi
The storm is over them—is over all!
　　The wild demonic rages mock the peace
Of innocence! We see the great trees fall!
　　The hurricane strips the fertile field's increase!
There goes the old man tottering from his home,
While maidens weep and fly the blacken'd dome!

　　　　xxii
Let us not shrink because the storms deface
　　Our beautiful landscape! Turn aside and fly,
Because the wolf hath found the sacred place,
　　And howls to ravage! It were better die,

Strangling the wolf—for daughters would remain,
Mothers of future men, by whom all wolves are slain.

xxiii

Let us not faint because the day grows cold,
   And night frowns out the stars; but, with brave will,
Keep closer watch upon each little fold,
   And hunt the savage down, and smile, and kill!
Smooth waters make no seamen. In the strife,
That tries true manhood, only find we life.

(1827, 1861, 1862)

ELEGIAC.

R.Y., JR.

i

We note with pride the sapling's shoot,
   A vigorous stem and glad to grow,
   Erect, as never fearing foe,
And branching wide for promised fruit;

And look with joy to hail the hour,
   When in its liberal wealth of shade,
   We'll crouch beneath the roof we've made,
And watch the growth of fruit and flower;

And find for age a promised peace,
   A genial shelter, safe as sweet,
   Secure of home, a glad retreat,
When Time shall bid our labors cease.

The germ we've planted, sure will shade;
   The bud we've nursed, in time will be
   A vigorous and well fruited tree,
In all its pomp of green arrayed;

And all the toils of life at rest,—
   Of shelter, flower and fruit, secure,

No more at strife—all passions pure—
We dream of day, at closing, blest.

ii

The child we've dandled on our knee,
  The merry, happy, winsome boy,
  A father's pride, a mother's joy,
Pledge of affections, fond as free—

Still closer to our hearts we bind;
  His growth we watch; and, day by day,
  How fondly note his generous play,
And all the workings of his mind.

We hail each eager impulse—trace
  Each whisper of his infant thought;
  And, teaching him, ourselves are taught
The lessons of a nameless grace.

Hope sings of prouder workings still—
  The manly purpose, broad and strong;
  The pride to *do*, eschewing wrong,
And virtue linked to powerful will.

His manhood is our prop for age;
  His strength will shelter;—he will tend
  Our feet;—our feebleness defend;
And, when we pass from off the stage,

A nobler form than ours will stand
  The occupant of place once ours;
  With braver aims and better powers,
Destined to honor in the land.

iii

Alas for hopes—for idle dreams
  Of future pride and promised fruit!—
  The axe is laid unto the root,
And baffles all our mortal schemes!

Sudden, by night, the tempest sweeps!
  Our plains lie desolate! We rise,

And lo! before our anguished eyes,
Our tree goes, hurried to the deeps!

Just when in flow'r, and bright with bloom,
The fruitage reddening in the sun,—
(But one more day, our prize is won!)
Has brought it blight and doom!

The pestilence, on midnight wings,
Broods o'er our roof-tree,—yet we sleep,
Not dreaming we shall wake to weep
The loss of life's most precious things.

And war, that pestilence of hate,
Coated with venomous snakes, will strike
At pride, and love, and hope alike,
And make our fireside desolate.

The tree goes down before the storm;—
The noble boy, with instinct true,
Of what the duty bids him do,
Bares to the venomous foe his form.

Ere yet his cheek has lost its down,
He sallies forth to seek the strife,
And for his sires and people's life,
He gives, in generous blood, his own.

Exulting, at the dawn, to rise,
Among the first to meet the foe,
He wings the bolt, he strikes the blow,
And, in the arms of victory, dies!

What precious blood,—how purely given—
For home and country—free from shame,—
He wins the truest, best of fame,
The only sanctified of Heaven.

And well he sleeps, though in a grave,
Remote yet, in that bloody field,
Which saw the foul invader yield,
In terror from the strokes he gave.

The field of conquest as of fate—
  With victory in his shout of death,
  His last was a triumphant breath,
His soul, amid its pangs, elate!

There let him sleep! The very name
  Of Chickahominy shall be
  A glory for our braves; and he,
Among the first, shall share its fame.

(1862)

ODE—OUR CITY BY THE SEA.

i
Our City by the Sea,
  As the Rebel City known,
With a soul and spirit free
  As the waves that make her zone,
      Stands in wait
      For the Fate
From the angry arm of Hate;
But she nothing fears the terror of his blow;
  She hath garrisoned her walls,
  And for every son that falls,
  She will spread a thousand palls
      For the foe!

ii
Old Moultrie at her gate,
  Clad in arms and ancient fame,
Grimly watching, stands elate,
  To deliver bolt and flame!
      Brave the band,
      At command,
  To illumine sea and land,
With a glory that shall honor days of yore:
  And, as racers for their goals,
  A thousand fiery souls,
  While the drum of battle rolls,
      Line the shore.

iii

Lo! rising at his side,
   As if emulous to share
His old historic pride,
   The vast form of Sumter there!
      Girt by waves,
      Which he braves,
   Though the Equinoctial raves,
As the mountain braves the lightning on his steep.
   And, like Tigers crouching round,
   Are the tribute forts that bound
   All the consecrated ground,
      By the Deep!

iv

It was calm, the April noon,
   When, in iron-castled towers,
Our felon foe came on,
   With his aggregated powers;
      All his Might
      'Gainst the Right
   Now embattled for the fight,
With Hell's hate and venom working in his heart:
   A vast and dread array,
   Glooming black upon the day,
   Hell's passions all in play,
      With Hell's art.

v

But they troubled not the souls
   Of our Carolina host;[1]
And the drum of battle rolls,
   While each hero seeks his post;
      Firm though few,
      Sworn to do,
   Their old city full in view,
The brave city of their sires and their dead!
   There each freeman had his brood,
   All the dear ones of his blood,
   And he knew they watching stood,
      In their dread!

vi

To the bare embattled height,
 Then our gallant Colonel sprung—
"Bid them welcome to the fight,"
 Were the accents of his tongue—
  "Music! band,
  Pour out—grand—
 The free song of Dixie Land!
Let it tell them we are joyful that they come!
 Bid them welcome, drum and flute,
 Nor be your cannon mute,
 Give them chivalrous salute—
  To their doom!"[2]

vii

Outspoke an eager gun,
 From the ports of Moultrie then;
And through clouds of sulph'rous dun,
 Rose a shout of thousand men,
  As the shot,
  Hissing hot,
 Goes in lightning to the spot—
Goes crashing wild through timber and through mail:
 Then roared the storm from all,
 Moultrie's ports and Sumter's wall—
 Bursting bomb, and driving ball,—
  Hell in hail!

viii

Full a hundred cannon roar'd,
 The dread welcome to the foe,
And his felon spirit cower'd,
 As he crouch'd beneath the blow!
  As each side,
  Open'd wide,
 To the iron and the tide,
He lost his faith in armor and on art;—
 And, with the loss of faith,
 Came the dread of wounds and scaith;—
 And the felon fear of death,
  Wrung his heart!

ix

Quench'd then his foul desires,
  In his mortal pain and fear,
How feeble grew his fires,
  How stay'd his fell career!
    How each keel,
    Made to reel,
'Neath our thunder, seems to kneel,
Their turrets staggering wildly, to and fro, blind and lame;
  Ironsides and Ironroof,
  Held no longer bullet proof,
  Steal away, shrink aloof,
    In their shame!

x

But our lightnings follow fast,
  With a vengeance sharp and hot;
Our bolts are on the blast,
  And they rive with shell and shot!
    Huge the form
    Which they warm
With the hot breath of the storm;
Dread the crash which follows as each Titan mass is struck—
  They shiver as they fly,
  While their leader drifting nigh,
  Sinks choking, with the cry,
    "Keokuk!"

xi

To the brave old City, joy!
  For that the felon race,
Commissioned to destroy,
  Hath fled in sore disgrace!
    That our sons
    At their guns,
Have beat back the modern Huns—
Have maintained their household fanes and their fires;
  And, free from taint and scaith,
  Have kept the fame and faith
  (And will keep, through blood and death)
    Of their sires!

To the Lord of Hosts, the Glory,
 For His the arm and might,
That have writ for us the story,
 And have borne us through the fight!
  His our shield,
  In that field;
 Voice, that bade us never yield:
Oh! had He not been with us through the terrors of that day?
  His strength hath made us strong,
  Cheer'd the Right and crushed the Wrong,
  To His Temple let us throng—
   PRAISE AND PRAY!

                                                    (1863)

1. The battle of Charleston harbor, April 7, 1863, was fought by South Carolina troops exclusively.

2. As the iron-clads approached Fort Sumter, in line of battle, Col. Alfred Rhett, commandant of the post, mounting the parapet, where he remained, ordered the band to strike up the national air of "DIXIE," and at the same time, in addition to the Confederate flag, the State and regimental flags were flung out at different salients of the fort, and saluted with thirteen guns.

FANCY IN SIESTA.

"Haply, this life is best,
If *quiet* life be best."

         "—— Our *cage*,
We make a quire, as doth the prison-bird,
And sing our bondage freely."—*Shakespeare.*

        i

Gems from the fountain, cast in air,
A shower of brilliants, each a sphere,
Sun-pierced, an orb as bright and rare
As fairy eye, that 'neath the screen
Of twinkling leaves of glancing green
 Peers out, with sudden sweet surprise,
 As looking love to loving eyes:
While Zephyr, stealing softly, makes
 His murmur won from ocean's shell;

Just stirs the leaves, and gently shakes,
  To strengthen, not subdue, the spell
That mingles thought and dream so well,
  The reverie with such consciousness,
That which is which we may not tell,
  And care not—both decreed to bless!

      ii
Methinks—is it a Fancy moves?
The Caliph's garden!—these his groves,
His fountains; these his petted doves,
  Named Gul and Bulbul! Hark! a strain
  Of song, just murmured, takes the ear,
  A moment—faltering—as in fear
  Lest one should hark who should not hear—
Young Saadi, singing Haroun's loves!

      iii
Sweets from the Fountain!—sweets where'er
The valley spreads with soft and fair;
  Where winds make commerce with the pines,
And, through the long and slumberous hours,
  Drink odors from the wanton vines,
That flaunt gay robes in cypress bowers;
Scarce conscious of the flashing wing,
  Fleet as a shaft that, darting by,
  Between the vision and the sky,
Is in the clouds a vanishing thing,
  Ere Languor lifts her hooded eye.

      iv
Doves moaning low in cedar copse,
Sad brooding o'er delicious hopes;
While, from the great oak's wandering tops,
  With balanced wing, on bending spray,
The mock bird, in capricious vein,
  Flings out a snatch of idlest lay,
Breaks off in middle of the strain,
  Darts wide in wild and wanton play;
And in his pride of flight upsprings;
  Comes sudden down, in song again,
To fold in shade his russet wings.

v

Hark! Housed in drooping sward of green,
Lush grasses 'neath the forest screen,
Heard all through noon, yet never seen;
   The myriad insect drones, with hum,
Rebuking change of mood or measure,
Each winds his horn above his treasure!
   The beetle, with his tiny drum,
Plays bass, and sleeps without a care,
Even while Arachné weaves her snare,
   With subtle eyes for all who come,
And he, beneath, dreams unaware!
   Cicada, beetle, drone—a host—
   In dreaming mood, without a will!
An army, slumbering on its post,
   Yet beating drowsy tattoo still!

vi

What need of care for such as these,
That sing or slumber as they please,
That range at large, or drowse at ease?
   What duty but to welcome sleep?
What need of better Thought than Dream,
Which finds for thought its sweetest gleam,
And guides its bark adown a stream,
   Where alders yield their shadows deep,
With flowers y'blent to soothe the eye,
   Half shut, that only sees, in flight,
The flash, the tint, the shade, the dye,—
   A something wooing, soft though bright,
Just glimpsing, in the act to fly,
   Not waking Thought, or vexing Sight!

vii

Life is not wholly Memory's keep,
   Thought's workshop, Care's own world for strife!
   The better, beautiful realm of life
Lies in the gracious round of sleep,—
In fancies, never so far from dying,
As in the very act of flying!—
And we are not the things we seem,
As vulgar souls of earth misdeem;—

Nor is the real denied the dream;—
Half life is but a dream, and blest
Is he who dreams away the rest.
Let's take the dream for something worth,
    And put each vulgar seeming off,
    Nor heed the churlish, childish scoff,
That prating all it knows of earth,
Makes of the beautiful a mirth,
As if it had no wingéd birth.
Borrow your wings from dream, and trace
The loveliest sylphs that glide through space,
    That "play i'the plighted clouds," and fraught
    With colors from the rainbow caught,
Make pictures for our lowlier race.

      viii
We vex the soul with needless smart,
And 'tis with *Thought* we barb each dart
That goes most keenly through the heart.
The simple passions madly urge,
Goad to the precipice's verge,
Where, trembling o'er the fiery surge
    They hang,—and saved and spared to life,
Still dream the horrors o'er and o'er
    They knew in that most terrible strife.
Though but a moment felt—no more!—
Force by unnatural law, the heart
To service of unnatural art;
Crush Nature into fashions strange
    That clip her shape and spoil her grace;
Deny bold flight—to vision range,
    Twist honest laughter to grimace,
And ever bent on empty change,
    Make "motley" master of the race!

      ix
I would not torture Nature so,—
'Till it is very pain to know,—
But rather let her seek her food
Where, feeding, she may sleep and brood,
And brooding all unconscious grow,
    To perfect freedom of delight—

Where, on no measured purpose bent,
   Her wings unclipt, her eye star-bright,
She soars and sings, all innocent;
Obedient to each mood that calls,
Climbing, at will, cerulean walls,
To hear the dash of waterfalls
   Among the mountains of the moon;
Or waiting not the hush of night,
Lapsing away from Time in flight,
   And drowsing in the groves at noon.

x

Oh! shallow souls! By greed oppress'd,
And by your very gains unblessed,—
Prince, peasant—all alike—arrest,
The proper virtue in each breast;
   Check the free wings by nature given,
And through a life of long unrest,
   Lament that they have toil'd and striven,
   Not for Earth's boons and not for Heaven,
But in perversion of the powers
   Decreed to make our better gain.
They might have worn their simple flowers,
Drank sunshine in the Caliph's bowers,
Rejoiced to welcome summer's showers,
   And in the ripening coolness lain
Their limbs at rest; souls free to dream,
   Had visions bright, in thoughtless brain,
And, with each sudden flickering gleam,
Bird flight, or sun-smile on the stream,
   Won healing from the Care and Pain!

xi

Wake me to Thought, and what is there,
But shapes of Evil, far and near,
Thunders, and Dragon forms of Fear,
   Blood-red, on wings of sable flying,
With desperate shriek and talons bare,
   Exulting in the Dead and Dying!
The charnel vapor clogs the air,
The serpent climbs the chamber stair,
And, in the cradle makes his lair!

xii

Give me escape in sleep! In dream,
Heaven parts, as at a stroke of gleam,—
And every blue sphere shows its beam;
    Opes vistas that beguile to groves,
Where birds sing glad, in carols free,
    Having no commerce in their loves,
No cunning scheme, no selfish plea,
And where the glimpse, the flower, the flight,
Taking each rose-hue from delight,
    Makes Life an Immortality!

xiii

Give me the Lotus! I would glide,
    Adown the stream in little boat,
With never a sail, with never a tide,
    And but a zephyr's wing to float.
White lilies at my hand—great trees
    With branches drooping to the stream,
Whereon, I lie or rock at ease,
    Still cradled in delicious dream,
And seeing only as I please!

xiv

Give me the Lotus! Let me lie
    Beneath mine oaks the noontide long;
Through drooping lid, with drowsy eye,
Catch glimpses of the far blue sky,
And hark to birds that, as they fly,
    Or brood from flight, in fitful song,—
Make,—as for child that sobs for sleep,
    A murmuring stream of lullaby,
    Whose monotone is melody,
To senses that no vigils keep.
With dusk, from placid dream and drowse,
Eye bright for midnight, let me rouse,
    To see the hooded sun go down,
And hear, with bleatings of my sheep,
    The far-off murmurs of the town.

                                    (1863, 1866, 1870)

THE GAME COCK OF THE REVOLUTION.
(SUMTER.)

General Sumter, aroused from sleep by his servants, on the approach of a strong force of British and Tories, took shelter in a thicket, within a few hundred yards of his family mansion. This was at the period when, Charleston having fallen, the enemy, followed, or preceded, by clouds of refugees from Florida—(then a loyal Province, where the tories and foreigners from the other colonies of the South had taken refuge)— were engaged in ravaging the country, making forced marches in all directions, and garrisoning all commanding points. From his retreat in the thicket, Sumter beheld his wife and children ruthlessly expelled from their dwelling and the house set on fire. Alone, feeble, without weapons, his own situation was sufficiently helpless; and we can imagine the agony which he endured, throughout that dreary midnight watch, beholding the sufferings of those he loved, without any power to relieve them. But, from his despair grew his hope. According to the historian, this brutality of the enemy enured to the benefit of the country. It aroused all the fiercer energies of the patriot. It was the mortal spur in the sides of the Game Cock. Emerging from his fastness, when he could do so with safety, he then began that career of partisanship, which has identified his name, and *sobriquet*, with so many of the most admirable conflicts of the Revolution in the Carolinas. Gathering his little squads from regions more or less remote; from swamp thickets where they harbored; from piney thickets and mountain gorges; he commenced a progress, alternating often, now marked by defeat, now by victory, in which the passion for vengeance sharpened the sword of patriotism! He was always "in at the death." If the destruction of a single dwelling may thus convert a single warrior into a flaming instrument of vengeance, how many thousands of such fiery spirits should be roused to eternal wrath, when towns and villages, and great cities, are recklessly devoted to destruction by a bought, brutal and felon enemy, invading peaceful homes with no higher motive than greed, no purer stimulus than insane rage and the tiger appetite for blood? The Past has many lessons which should teach the proper lessons to the Present!

i

In brutal rage exulting,
    The reckless foeman came,
One hand displayed the weapon,
    The other bore the flame.

ii

Crouched in the thorny thicket,
  The game cock watching stood—
Quoth he, "Some day I'll quench this flame,
  And it shall be with blood."

iii

"I'll build a stronger dwelling,
  With rifle, steel and knife,
And will ensure these rascal foes,
  A lodge in it for life!

iv

"I'll place on every door post,
  A hospitable sign;
And make their slumber certain,
  Though they deny mine!

v

"Wife, children, driven to wander,
  Amid this wintry wild;
No shelter for the mother,—
  No covering for the child!

vi

"Oh! for the work of vengeance,—
  The time will yet be given;
For this I've deadly work on earth,
  And a dread vow in heaven!

vii

"Yes! hear me, skies and forests,
  While now I vow and pray,
For the coming of the hour,
  When I may smite and slay!

viii

"Oh then, to smite unsparing,
  Let every chord be strung,
That I may wring these fiendish hearts,
  As my poor babes' are wrung.

ix

"For every tear they shed to-night,
　A score of hearts shall bleed:
For every shivering infant's wail,
　There shall be bloody deed!

x

"Thousands of goodly yeomen,
　Yet harbor in the wild;
I'll bid them welcome to the sport,
　Avenging wife and child!

xi

"I'll show them yonder ruins,
　And where the lintel stood;
They'll see me make new cement
　Of some foul foeman's blood!

xii

"I'll teach them that the felon,
　Who dares free homes invade,
Must quiver in the halter,
　Or perish 'neath the blade!

xiii

"The homes of men are sacred,
　And when the lawless foe
Breaks in the charter'd dwelling,
　He bides the deadly blow!

xiv

"No law to shield the lawless,
　No prayer the wretch to save,
Who seeks to make of precious homes,
　A ruin and a grave!

xv

"No mercy for the felon,
　Who, like the wolf by night,
Prowls round the freeman's dwelling,
　And shrinks by day from fight.

xvi

"Short shrift for the usurper,
  Who seeks to rob the brave;
And sudden cord and mansion deep,
  In dungeons of the grave!

xvii

"For the dread hour of vengeance
  Be swift occasion given;
For this, I have a work on earth,
  And a dread vow in Heaven!"

xviii

And well that vow of midnight,
  Thus murmur'd in the wood,
Was kept by gallant Sumter,
  In many a field of blood.

xix

Bear witness fields of "Cowpens,"
  When Tarleton felt the shock;
Bear witness, crimson currents,
  That flow'd down "Hanging Rock."

xx

Such witness as to ages,
  Unborn, shall ever show,
How best to guard the freeman's home
  Against the felon foe!

(1863)

BALLAD.

"THE DREAMS OF OTHER DAYS."

i

Oh! how the dreams of other days awaken,
  The echoes of each well remembered song,
And all the pulses of the heart are shaken,
  And hopes and joys revive, forgotten long;

236

A sudden gush of starlight hath the power,
    To kindle rapturous dreams of long ago;
A sudden burst of song, in moonlight bower,
    Speaks sweet delusion to the heart of wo!

ii

How dost thou link thyself to these emotions,
    Sad wanderer, sweet as sad, and young as fair;
Between us roll the barrier-heaving oceans,
    And Alps arrest the vision wandering there.
But soul for soul leaves seed whose germination,
    Needs but true faith, fond tendance, loving eye,
And I, the thrall of love, through all creation,
    Still feel thy smile, still send thee sigh for sigh.

(1864, 1870)

THE TEMPLE AT ÆGINA.

Let thine eyes open on Minerva's shrine,
    Whose pillar'd marbles, far above the sea,
Wake wonder, but no worship; still divine,
    Even though no Goddess looks from them on thee.
How grand the site—that spiral eminence—
    To bear but ruins up! Yet, better these
Than the bald rock; and full of recompense,
    Though they but serve to make the landscape please.
Yet have they in them grandest histories
For him who looks below—beyond—and sees
    The power in mightiest Arts, that from the rock
Drew waters—shaped each stubborn mass to form,
And with a soul made passionately warm
    By Genius, did a thousand stores unlock,
Precious to fond Humanity; such stores
As bring us now, glad Pilgrims, to these shores.
    Pagan they were, whose arts are now at strife
To hold their own with Nature; but they knew
    Such Gods as brought them to Immortal Life,
And taught grand lessons of the Great and True!
The Beautiful forevermore in view,

They found the secret of the Grand and Great;
And in their toils for a duration long,
   They challenged all the Fates, and took from Fate
Serenity, in most triumphant song,
   Whose glorious cadences the world still hears,
Happy, in wondering echoes, to prolong;
   While Homer's Heroes brandish still their spears,
Cassandra shrieks the hour of wrath and wrong,
   And Ilium's daughters join Andromache in tears!

                      (1864)

THE STORM PETREL.

Thou little bird, that dwellest on the deep,
   And still around us takest thy mournful way,
   Thou hast a purpose in the dreary play
      Which thou dost keep.

Wond'ring, we ask thee wherefore thou shouldst roam,
   And idly, ignorant of thy natural powers;
   Thy needs, which still our fancy shapes like ours,
      Which long for home!

Thy nature finds thy home upon the seas,
   Still vagrant and a wanderer; this thy choice;
   And that which seems to us thy plaining voice,
      Declares thy ease.

Wing for wide range—an eye for desert space;
   A passion for the salt and stormy deep;
   The impatient love of change that needs no sleep,
      Ever in chase.

Pursuing insignificant bootless prey,
   Still on the incessant, never-wearied wing,
   And with the cry, as of some tortured thing,
      That hastes away.

Here, while we speed, a thousand miles from land,
   No jutting rock lends respite to thy flight;

No lonely islet, at the coming night,
        Thy nest of sand.

Hast thou no sleep—no succor—never rest?
    Nor pause, nor mate, nor commerce with thy kind,
    Born of the spray, in the incessant wind,
        In hour unbless'd?

And what the food bestowed thee, ranging thus—
    And where the refuge when the storm is high;
    Or, whether thou find'st a joy in pleasant sky;
        All's dark to us!

Nor may we, in our vanity and pride,
    Assume thy uses ours—assume thee sent,
    To cheer the gloom of our imprisonment,
        Our course to guide.

It is no mission of thy flight to bring,
    Cheering the mariner, doubtful of his way,
    Tidings of rocky shore and harboring bay,
        And sweet cool spring.

Yet must thy laws, like ours, in every breast,
    Make grateful the due office, wild or strange;
    And whether in adventure wide we range,
        Or keep close nest.

The pleasure, ever found in duty still,
    Compensates for the peril and the pains,
    If each, obeying what the Sire ordains,
        Sinks his own will.

The winds and waves, their desert range, is thine;
    Thy nest of foam receives thee when the day
    Wanes, and the dawning finds thee on thy way,
        Still dash'd with brine.

Though wild and ominous be thy screaming note,
    Yet, doubtless, it brings music to thy young;
    They hear and answer with like desolate tongue,
        From screaming throat.

And seek their home, and find a grateful rest,
  Where we lose ours! The dread deeps of the wave
  Rock them, and where our forms would find a grave,
    They find a nest!

Go, gipsy wanderer, teaching still aright!
  Day over with its pageants, or its storms,
  How small the care where we should cast our forms
    For sleep at night!

(1827, 1847, 1865)

THE BELLE OF THE BALL ROOM.

TO CAROLINE P**** ——*.

" 'Twas surely in the shape of love at first,
That Ahrimanes subtly pierced the egg
Of Ormusd, to the centre; making sin
A seeming virtue."

i

Butterfly, bless'd in a bright caprice,
  The worm forgot in the wing that bears,
'Tis certain thou seek'st no golden fleece,
  Since pleasure alone thy shallop steers.
Well, if thus seeking the sweets of flowers,
  The hunger of heart and soul be fed;
Well, if the sun shall gild thy bowers,
  When some of the gold of thy wing be shed.

ii

Carol and dance in thy wanton maze,
  Conscious alone of thy gilded wing,—
Of the worshiping insects that idly praise,
  Of the giddy circles that round thee swing.
A fate more dark, but welcome, ours,
  In toils of Care, and the Thought that glows,
With the conscious gift of a soul, and Powers,
  Decreed for long conflict with human woes!

(1865, 1866, 1870)

THE VOICE OF MEMORY IN EXILE,
FROM A HOME IN ASHES.

Ever a voice is pleading at my heart,
  With mournful pleading, ever soft and low,
  Yet deep as with an ocean's overflow,
"Depart! depart! Why wilt thou not depart?
Here are no blossoms such as live; no flowers,
  Such as with sacred scent and happy glow,
Recal Elysian homes, and those dear hours,
When with the breezes sporting in our bowers,
And the soft moonlight sweet'ning the old towers,
There was no tree that sheltered not its bird,
  No shrub without its song and summer bloom,
And never a fate was nigh, with threatening word,
  Articulate of the terror and the doom.
Were not the wings contented there in home
  That never lacked its sunshine and its songs?
We did not lack, beneath the grand old dome,
  The joy of solitude, though bless'd with throngs,
Coming and going; blessing as they came,
  And having solace in the bliss they found:
Depart! depart! and ye shall find the same,
  Nor wither in this cold and foreign ground!"
Alas! alas! for the poor home and heart
That still from out their ashes cry "depart!"

(1865)

WHAT'S LEFT.

i

Oh! thus expell'd from Eden's bowers,
  Where all was love and joy before,
Shall I again seek other flowers,
  And peril all my peace once more;
Sink in the lure of luscious eyes,
  Yield to the spell in music's charms,
And dream again of Paradise,
  In woman's love, or woman's arms.

ii

What tho' her smile be starry bright,
    And sweet her voice as music's own,
The soul once reft of loving light,
    Must make its weary way alone.
The victim long in Circean bowers,
    Where wo was through illusion taught,
He well may dread lest other flowers,
    Shall sting with thorns he never sought.

iii

Who, with his memories of the past,
    In midnight hours, a mournful throng,
But trembles lest the tempest blast,
    Shall hush the sweetest spells of song!
Who, with each soft, subsiding strain,
    But feels some memory, stern and sharp,
Nor hears anew the shriek of pain,
    In all the pauses of the harp!

                                        (1865, 1870)

SHADOWS.—I.

When gray the mists descend of eve,
    A shadow rises on my view;
    It seeks me out at midnight, too,
And wears the look of one I grieve.

The hopes of youth, the bliss, the pain,
    The all that time to love endears,
    In progress of the perished years,
That mournful shadow brings again.

As sinks the wan and crescent light—
    It rises slow beside me now;
    I see the pure and pallid brow
Half shaded by the growing night.

Yet with a brightness all its own,
    Expressive through the gloom, o'er all,

It holds me fixed in dreamy thrall,
And fills my soul with all the known.

I cannot doubt the instinct rare,
    That knows without the sight, and feels—
    At once, each portraiture reveals,
And she that once was mine is there!

So wan, so sad! as if, though bless'd,
    In happiest realms where bliss is sure,
    She sorrow'd still at my unrest,
And shared the grief she cannot cure.

Sweet spirit! by those heavenly airs
    That with thy coming, round me spread,
    By each sweet sanction of the dead,
That brings the blessings through the tears:

I give thee welcome, though thy shade
    No more restores that youth of bloom,
    That cheer'd me long through years of gloom,
And all my life's best solace made.

Dearer than any mortal bliss,
    The consciousness that still thou art
    A loving watcher o'er the heart,
That seeks its world no more in this.

                                        (1825, 1865, 1866)

SHADOWS.—II.

What though that voice be hush'd and still,
    The music of that voice in song—
    That eye be dim whose light was long
The charm and impulse to my will;

That bosom cold, whose pure young fire
    Had just enough of earth to make
    My virtue kindred for thy sake,
That school'd to calm each wild desire;

243

Yet, as no more with hope as then,
    My heart, denied fruition, flames,
    So, to its present dreams and aims,
That nothing ask from homes of men—

Sufficeth well, for boyish bliss,
    And young delights, that, in their place,
    A shadow fills my cold embrace,
And solitude my soul, like this!

Nay, not for soul a solitude,
    Of thought or fancy, since I know
    That, past thy own of mortal wo,
Thou comest o'er mine to bless and brood.

Oh! fearful was that dread of mine,
    When in thy vacant, glassy stare,
    I felt, and shudder'd with the fear,
To see no more those eyes of thine.

That doubt is gone, and all the rest
    Of sorrow and dread, is small for us;
    To see thee now, permitted thus,
I know thou livest, I feel thee bless'd!

Oh! form of Heaven, from that dear goal,
    Still come, even dearer than before;
    Thou fill'st my fond embrace no more,
But fill'st, with more than love, my soul.

(1865)

MIDSUMMER FOREST LUNCH.
A SCENE IN FLORIDA.

Only a wigwam of the simplest poles,
Green cypress, with a somewhat Gothic roof
Of shingle, gabled, rising to a peak—
A portico of that Gothic which might be
Quite natural to the Apalachian tribes;

Rude shafts of resinous pine, with all their knots
Bulging, supporting roof, proportioned well
To that which cover'd o'er the lodge itself—
All overrun, from base to parapet,
With native vines; luxuriant, bearing flowers
That won the sun's love at the dawn of March,
And bourgeon'd ever thence till the late autumn
That brought the Indian Summer to its close.

A woodland lodge, close nestled 'mid great trees,
That broke the winter winds, and from the home
Cast off the lightnings. And, beyond, a lawn,
Wide-spread—a natural prairie, once the field
Of mightiest Micco of the Seminole,
Whose warriors, tall and powerful as the prince
Who fell at Gilboa,[1] measured their full heights,
Yet stood as pigmies 'mid their rows of corn.

Our host, that perfect nobleman of nature,
A perfect gentleman, with grace received us—
Grace gracing his simplicity with ease,
And that most rare, becoming dignity
Which blends with grace and ease the elegance
Becoming in the courtier; so that ease,
Frankness not too familiar, yet at home,
With all consideration and due regard
Of all the nice proprieties which make
The best security of the social man—
With cheerfulness in aspect, and such tones
Of voice, so full of sweetness, mingled well,
In him, the gentleman reduced of fortune—
But never showing gloom because of gloom,—
To win approach of others; with like ease
Counsell'd to confidence, that leads to faith,
From which, alike, all love and friendship grow.

He met us at the portals of a tent
Made of green boughs, with rushes carpeted,
In centre of a circle of great oaks
And lofty firs, and shrubs of rarest scent—
All native—while o'er neighboring and broad plains
Our eyes beheld uprising the great tops

Of the magnolia,[2] with the cypress near,
Equally lofty, as if still rebuking
The pride which towers above a realm of death.[3]

Sweet odors, faint by distance, but most sweet,
Reached us from vast savannahs, where the vines
Lock the grand shafts in ever fond embrace;
And little lakelets, glimping on the sight,
Through the long vistas of each natural grove,
Brought tidings of the sea, in swell of waters,
With coolness of a breeze all made of wings.

How, for such tent, so glorious in its green,
Its wild caprice of aspect, and grand forms,
Should host like ours deliver fond excuse
While giving welcome?
                          Wiser grown from loss
He had risen, in few short seasons, to the strength,
Soul-bodied, which in man's simplicity
Finds living truth in nature, and feels rich.

"*Our* world," quoth he, "in its virginity,
Fresh from the hand of God, so nobly fashioned,
So beautiful, and during in its beauty,
That art falls back abash'd, and only pleads
That she may know from nature, and begin
Her studies here, commencing with the *first*,
In fit prostration at each natural shrine,
Self-knowledge, in humility, to ask."

So speaking, forth he led us, in his walks,
Through the grand wilderness, and down by streams,
That, restless, found their way into the lakes,
Which lost them straight—and, by the lakelet's edge,
Where all the blended beauties of the waste
Seized on the several senses with such glow
That Thought forgot her mission, to inform,
And fell to brooding fancies, which had fill'd
Our hearts with dreams of yet another realm,
Hard by the Tigris,[4] but for the greater wealth
Of this more primitive empire.
                          We were stay'd

Beneath the cypress, close beside the swamp,
Gigantic column, from an archéd base,
Soaring above the scene, with great, flat dome
Fringed with the Druid mosses.
                                        There it stood
Erect, and mocked the majesty of man,
In its great, silent grandeur; while its arms,
Significant of virtue in old age,
Were stretch'd paternal o'er the feebler tribes
That crouched, unconscious, in their very growth,
In humbleness below. The tooth of Time
Gnaws, unavailing, on the mighty shaft,
While the storm beats as vainly on its brow.

"Hath it no consciousness that thus it stands?"
Quoth he, our noble host. " 'Twere well if we,
In our own consciousness of state, could be
As silent of our uses and our pride."

So rambling, and so speaking, we pursued
A devious progress through a sylvan realm,
Where Pan might yet, with music of his reed,
Muster his satyrs, with authority
Unquestioned of his tribes. This fertile realm,
Had sure provided for the scene enough
To make Arcadia.
                            But the bugle sounds,
From the gray lodge, and so comes on the hour
To bid us to the feast.
                            Then did our host,
With brightened countenance, and with all the grace
Of the old patriarch-prophet—poet, too—
Address us in an oriental style;
With bidding, which might well have been a chaunt,
Borrow'd from Idumea, in those days
When Job had equal trials from his God,
His friends and enemies—yet kept erect;
The nobler made by humbleness of heart.

I chronicle this invitation chaunt,
For that it makes some pictures to the thought
Which some day we shall see, when Art makes bold

To tread the forest in Floridian wilds,
Shall burn upon the canvas, and make song
A rapt enthusiast on the zephyr's wing,
Floating far off to Aidenne.
                    Thus he spake:

  "I bid you to a regal feast, on cheer
Such as not simply satisfies the wolf,
But wins the fancy and beguiles the taste,
Beyond all creature need, and into realms
Where fancy grows to government, and shapes
The thought's conditions; foreign, on free wings,
Yet native; so that nature lapses glad,
Like gliding waters through accustom'd groves,
Which make the music for the dream, and soothe
All senses to the harmony of hours,
That never lack for wings.

                    "And we shall soar,
While sitting, and be busied best with bliss,
Half drowsing, though we feed.

                    "And in our calm,
Having our visions of the dreamy East,
With blended sun and shade, with scent and flowers
That to all senses minister in turn,
Making the effortless Light a messenger
To gardens of the Houri,—where it droops,
As motiveless for farther flight beyond,
Lapp'd, steep'd, and in its luxuries o'erfraught,
Beyond accumulation of more bliss.

  "Our world, a world shut in from all the world,
Is peace;—and plenty wedded to content,
Is ever fruitful in its promise still
Of worlds of peace beyond.

                    "The restless rage
Of the far nations doth not vex us here;
We've nothing to despoil, that thirst of spoil
Seeks to appropriate, and so the strife
Goes singing by us.

"What we hear but makes
Our gladness, that the storm is ever past,
Still, without waking our accustomed peace.

"Here's plenty, and such cates as well provide
For all the natural tastes and appetites;
This venison, late a burgher of the woods,
These wild fowl, lately sporting in the lakes;
These birds that fattened on our fields of grain;
These viand berries, with a pulp all sweet;
Cream from the herds, and milk from fattest kine
Suffice the lowlier nature.
                              "But we've more;
'Neath these ancestral oaks, while overhead
The song of birds, the flight of paroquets,
And breathings of delicious ocean airs,
Make an abode most like an Eden home,
Which, yielding wings to thought, endow with flight
Each fancy for a province of its own.
We've but to keep the human moods alive
Through books and memories, and society,
To be as happy as the life is long:—
Or long or short, the same, 'tis happiness."

And 'twas a regal feast;
                              Our table spread
Beneath the shadow of great oaks and palms,
The odorous bay[5] in tribute with its sweets,
And the fresh breezes from the ruffling seas,
Capricious, and with happiest bounds of flight,
Commercing with the forests, whose glad tribes
Make them one common concert of gay song
That set their leaves to circling in a dance,
Which might have been the sport of elvish tribes,
Lurking unseen below, and with soft note—
An undersong, mere murmurs of delight
Subdued to dreaming—timing inanimate things
To comprehensive echoes, softly sad,
Such as the sea leaves deep in choral shells,
Whose twisted cores imprison the soft airs,
Only to teach them music.

There's yon bough,
Where, intertwisted, grow the myrtle and palm—
There sings the painted nonpareil—a flower
Animate with a soul!—a flower of wings,
All green and gold, and wearing wings at will,
Only because it sings! The regular lays,
Responsive, first and second, always two,
Tell of a life that hath a lease from Fate,
To dream and sing, and from the dreaming wake
Only for sweet renewal of the song,
That must, perforce, still lapse away in dream,
Which is the birth of new delight, and ever
Wins new delight from birth.

          The nonpareil,
That cannot live or sing in colder skies,
Exiled, is like the Hebrew, who can string
No cord for Babylon's waters.[6]

          Ah! they are hushed,
By a great master.[7] 'Tis the forest Puck,
Our Ariel of the woods, the mocking-bird,
That silences the choir with such a strain
As teaches music's self a sad despair,
Pouring a very cataract of song,
In spray and sunshine, glittering on glad wings,
That bathe in rainbows, and through veils of mist
Fling ruby and opal, fragmented, in air,
For lowlier tribes to gather and pursue.

So, we drank deep of vision—so beheld
A grand procession, born of beams and flowers,
Gliding on wings, through sunshine, over heights,
Each with a starred crown; and so we supt
To surfeit, with companions such as glide
On beams to earth, from earth again to heaven,
Making of songs their chariots.

                                        (1866)

1. Saul.
2. Magnolia Grandiflora.
3. The swamp, where the cypress grows its greatest size as well as the magnolia.

4. Bagdad, and the Caliphate.

5. The Bay, or Dwarf Laurel.

6. The "nonpareil" is an exquisite but tiny song-bird of the South, ranging from the Carolinas to the Floridas, and beyond. He is said to lose his voice utterly when carried North.

7. When the mocking-bird sings the grove is silent.

THE KISS BEHIND THE DOOR.

i

Methinks the stars now shine more bright,
   Than they have ever shone before;
Their beauty born of that delight,—
     My Rosalie,—
   That first sweet kiss behind the door!

ii

While mother keeps a cheerful din,
   And sister sings, and guests *encore*,
Our bliss, undream'd by all within,
     Dear Rosalie,—
   Is in the kiss behind the door!

iii

In greybeard's veins, the blood still glows,
   And back to twenty bounds three score;
What's years, if beauty still bestows,—
     My Rosalie,—
   Her sweetest kiss behind the door!

iv

Ah! damsel of a glad caprice,
   Enough, if I may hope no more,—
That I have had a taste of bliss,
     Dear Rosalie,
   In that sweet kiss behind the door!

(1866, 1870)

"AY DE MI, ALHAMA!"

i

Ah! woe is me, my Dixie Land!
I weep for thee, my Dixie Land!
I weep o'er all that glorious Band,
That bore thy Banner and thy Brand,
From mountain height to ocean strand,
And bled, and died, for thee, O! Dixie Land!
> My Dixie Land! My Dixie Land.

ii

Thy wail of wo, my Dixie Land!
From homes laid low, my Dixie Land,
From plains once glorious in the glow,
Of summer fruits, and blooms of snow,
Speaks for the brave that sleep below,
Thy braves, thy graves, their virtues and thy woe,
> My Dixie Land! My Dixie Land!

iii

Yet not in vain, O! Dixie Land!
Thy Heroes slain, O! Dixie Land!
Thy ruin'd realm, thy blacken'd fane,—
Thy agonies of heart and brain,
If still thy spirit mounts amain,
And sings for Freedom one, the grand refrain
> Of Dixie Land! Of Dixie Land.

iv

Each lowly grave, my Dixie Land!
Where sleeps your brave, my Dixie Land!
Becomes a shrine that yet shall save,
If, keeping faith, your fathers gave,
Ye rend the shackles, which enslave,
And sharp for happier fields your battle glaive,
> Oh! Dixie Land! O! Dixie Land!

v

Though often crost, O! Dixie Land!
No cause is lost, my Dixie Land!

While still remain a generous Host;
That hold the Faith, that keep the post,
And still invoke each glorious ghost,
That was your people's Beauty and their Boast,
                  Oh! Dixie Land! O! Dixie Land!

      vi
Tender and True, my Dixie Land!
Though faint and few, my Dixie Land!
We keep the Faith our Fathers knew,
For which they bled, in which we grew,
And at their graves our vows renew,—
For nought is lost of truth, where Faith keeps true,
                  Oh! Dixie Land! O! Dixie Land!

                                  (1867)

TO MY FRIEND TOM GREENE,

ON HIS DOULEURS ABOUT MISS QUITA.

Fig for your love! all fiddlesticks!
    A sparrow's chirp, a beetle's hum;
Some pretty airs, some petty tricks,
    And you are in your kingdom come!
Don't make a Donkey of your brains,
    Don't make a plaything of your heart;
Your pleasures are but petty pains,
    Your pains, a mere Miss Quita smart.

Go to the desk, the wagon, plough,
    Till ground, trim trees, your muscle ply;
Do something, as you best know how,
    And don't be bug or butterfly.
You're at your studies now, you say,
    Then tax your midnight hours with thought;
Burn oil, even though you drudge by day,
    Lest all your labor come to naught.

Work's the true wisdom! never man
    Were worth a single doit or dime,

Until he does the thing he can,
    In his brief measured term of time.
Suffer no woman on the brain
    'Till with true work you've made a start,
And every muscle bravely strain,
    To get life's lessons all by heart.

ZEKIEL JONES,
Late Planter, now Knife and Scissors Grinder,
7 Smugg Alley, Frog Garden Court.
(1867)

SONNET.—EXHAUSTION.

I am so weary, wounded, scant of breath,
    So dispossessed of Hope. So comfortless,
    That sometimes, in the dread of this duress,
I half persuade myself to fly to death;
But evermore springs up the generous Faith,
Looking a Goddess! and the life renews,
As grasses, sweetly fed by Heavenly dews;
And I again upspring, and to the sky,
Look, glad to bourgeon! Shall it be in vain?
I know that most of pleasures end in pain,
And pain and pleasure in eternity;
And thus we struggle on—so live, so die;
Happy, if yet, upon the blasted tree
There may be fruits 'twould please a God to see.

(1867)

AMONG THE RUINS.

That they should come, though o'er a waste of tares,
These fresh and delicate airs!
    Come, plaining, O! how sweetly, through these towers,
    Dismantled—in their ruins—shorn of flowers,
Once beautiful with every loving twine;—
Come, like fond memories of departed cares,

Born of true loves, dear hopes, and earnest powers,
　　Devote to best affections! They bewail
　　The mournful issue of the sweetest tale
Begun, with such a sunburst on each shrine,
　　As if it had best guaranty from Fate
To end in ruin—this old house of mine,
All ashes and wreck—yet not the less divine,
　　Because, to Memory only, consecrate!

Oh! saddest of sweet winds! To heart of sorrow—
　　Heart buried in its ruined shrines—ye bring,
Perchance, a better dawning of the morrow,
　　With angel hope and healing on your wing!
　　So must the heart believe, and so they sing,
The pious minstrels of each early clime,
From the glad inspiration of a time
　　When faith in God some faith in man still wrought,
　　And love was in each lesson that they taught:
　　Alas! alas! that all should end in nought!

Yet the sad chaunt, that, through these ruined towers
　　Goes fitfully, like plainings of a ghost,
Doom'd still to wander through forbidden hours,
　　And grieve o'er scenes that once had gladden'd most,
Hath yet a soothing speech for the sad heart
　　That long hath listen'd to the dread decree
Which bade each hope, that made its life, depart,
　　And shook each precious blossom from its tree!
　　Alas! the dreary solace left to me!—
　　　　To love the ruin still, despite the wo,
　　　　When nought but Ruin's left for me to know!

How suited is the wailing through these walls,
　　Piercing the rifts of ruin, to the shrine
Which hath no better minister!—these halls,
　　Now desolate, once flowing with red wine,
And swelling with dilating bursts of joy,
　　From minstrels made inebriate with delight!
　　Ye mock me not, ye winds, with hope of bright
　　　　Music, or bloom, or flowers;
　　　　Promise no more the dawn of better hours,
Nor hush the doom that bade the Fiends destroy!

Oh! as each loveliest hope of home takes flight,
   Come forth the dreaded heritor of the place,
   And Gloom usurps the sweet domain of Grace!

The sweetness, in the sadness of your chaunt,
   Oh! saddest of sweet singers, brings to me
Nothing of promise; yet your memories haunt
   Each vacant cell and shrine of memory;
And, with the wine and song of life denied,
   Your wail becomes the fitting voice for all:
   Thus, soughing sadly through the broken wall,
   Swelling in burden through the desolate hall,
Thence on, through dreary avenue to guide,
   Across the brooklet, and adown the hill,
Away to cypress thicket, where your surge,
   With ever-ascending volume, grows in might,
Till, in the diapason of your dirge,
   Among the sacred thickets on the height,
   The graves of my sweet sleepers rise in sight—
     One, two—alas! how many!—I would count,
    But the tears, gushing, overflow the fount!
Enough!—They are all mine! Oh! happier they,
   Thus sleeping, than if conscious now, they stood,
Feeling my ruins!—Conscious of the prey
   Made by the Fiend of all their famishing brood:
The shame that wraps us as a cloud by day,
   The doubt that threats us with long nights of blood!
     Ah! happier far, escaping from the wo,
     Than these most wretched ones that wist not where to go!

The bitter road of exile must be ours,
   Oh! desolate children!—We must leave the home—
These grand old woods, these venerable towers,
These shrines of best affections—the sweet flowers,
   That won all birds of beauty to their bloom:—
The world of pleasant suns and starlight hours—
   And wait on wo, to guide us where to roam!
We were content with this!—to forfeit all—
The shrines, the blooms, the consecrated hall,
And all the uncounted attributes of years,
And memories sainted in affection's tears,
Link'd with material things—that grew to things

Of soul, and put on spiritual wings!—
   Yield all of wealth's possessions to our slaves,
     Nor murmur at the fate;
     Nor pass away in hate;
     Nor yield of heart and hope, with both in thrall:
   Nor how to yield our graves!—
To know that jackall footsteps will pollute
     These sacred hillocks, and the reptiles crawl
     Where we have laid the best-beloved—the ALL!—
And, with foul presence, and irreverent foot,
     Trample the breast and brow!—White breast, white brow,—
Bloom, beauty, tenderest love, and innocent truth,
     Which fix'd our heart's existence in one vow,
Blending all being—life, hope, love, and ruth,
     In one soul-consciousness—that still must be
     Our welcoming presence in Eternity!
Ah! God, that, for the pure Christ, we should see
The Fetisch in his brutal revelry;
And to the obscene rites of despots and slaves,
Yield these, our graves! our graves!

Oh! saddest of sweet winds, ye have your powers;
Wind hither noon and night:
   And though ye nurse no flowers,
Bring pleasant airs and odours on your flight—
   Keep, what we cannot, these dear graves of ours!

                              (1867)

FROM THE STUDY WINDOWS.

My oaks stride out upon the lawn,
   The grand old bearded Druids rise,
Their great brows reddening, as at dawn,
   Beneath the flush of evening skies.

In lovely cirque below, the flowers,
   Sweet trophies from each sun-bless'd land,
Smile ever through the happy hours,
   And walk with Beauty hand in hand.

The alianthus spreads beneath mine eaves
   Its palmy shoots of slenderest stem,
While 'neath its shade the jasmine weaves
   Its vines with many a golden gem.

And drooping twice beneath its fruits,
   The modest fig, imploring place,
Sends out its fond contending shoots,
   That greenly shadow all the space.

Yet, as the western zephyr steals
   With searching wing among their holds,
The bright glance of the sun reveals
   Their mystic twines and mazy folds.

His milder rays admitted, gleam
   Through leaf and flowers along my floor
In golden patines, each a beam
   Of blended weird and angel lore.

And such the soft beguiling hush
   Through groves below, from skies above,
As if the earth, with sudden gush,
   Had found, herself, a voice for love!

How from the ancient volume lifts
   The wearied eye with study sad,
Glad that in place of mortal gifts
   Such gleams of Heaven should make it glad.

Oh! to the shelf consign the book!
   Why toil when just to brood is bliss?
Why waste delicious hours that brook
   No future, in the balm of this?

The heart, though doom'd to doubt that pain
   May yet some respite snatch from care,
Should in repose not wholly vain
   Forget the weight that still must wear—

Must wear and vex, and would destroy,
   But that such gleams and glimpses come,

To wing anew the hope to joy,
  In opening vistas rich in bloom.

The leaf that flutters 'neath mine eye,
  The waving vine so green and bright,
Zephyrs so fitfully that sigh,
  Though drinking from their blooms delight—

These sing with solace to the care
  With missions as from stars above,
When human song no more can cheer,
  And human hearts grow cold to love.

Let mine not lose, with every loss,
  The sense of sweet that life still knows;
Nor, though I falter 'neath my cross,
  Forget that earth still bears its rose!

(1848, 1867)

CHILHOWEE, THE INDIAN VILLAGE.

Exulting, in the sense of a new realm,
Umbrageous, of grand forests, and great plains,
Spreading like cultured meadows; and crown'd hills,
Ascending, tier on tier, till in the sky,
They lost themselves within a kindred blue;—
Speeding, with eager bound, upon a steed,
Full-blooded and buoyant as the billowy waves
Commercing with a joyous breeze at dawn;—
What wonder if I cried aloud my joy,
Exuberant in keen consciousness of life,
In eulogy of nature, and that freedom
Which seemed in her possession of the wild!—
No law, no limit, no perpetual toil,
No striving of vex'd myriads in the crowd;
Foul airs of the great city and sad sights,
Amid its narrow alleys and low courts,
Where poor humanity struggles, day by day,
For the mean boon and narrow privilege,

Simply of breathing and dying, to no end,
Promised of happiness;—what wonder then,
If freed of these, amidst the boundless spread
Of wilderness, I cried aloud my thoughts?

"Ay, this is freedom! Nature, here, supreme
In tangled realm of verdancy, in forests,
Umbrageous, with protection for her tribes,
Is the unquestioned sovereign! At her feet
Lake, wood, and rivulet, bud and bird, and beast,
Tree, flower and leaf, in matchless quietude,
Enjoying perfect freedom. Here the man,
The golden age renews; in a delight
That knows not gold, and never craves for it;
Nature and Freedom being perfect wealth."

So spake I, and my sage companion laugh'd,
Drew up his steed, and merrily replied:

"Nature and Freedom! These are glorious words
That make the world mad. Take a glimpse of both,
Such as you readily find, when, at your leisure,
You tread the ancient military trace,
Through Georgia to the 'Burnt-Corn Settlements'—
Or, farther West, if happily you deign
To make the journeys I have made and speed,
Where the gaunt Choctaw lingers by the swamps
That fence the Yazoo; where the Chickasaw
Steals his hog nightly from the squatter's close,
And gets his furlough from all service thence,
In a swift bullet at a hundred yards.
Nay, you may find your illustration here,
Of nature, and the freedom she bestows,
In full possession of her sovereignty.
We've but to round yon steep acclivity,
Crown'd with primeval pines, and you shall see
Your empire, happy in its golden age."

So rode we, till we circled a steep hill,
When, said the father, with his laughing eyes,
Twinkling with humor consonant to the speech,
Designed to cure the boy's enthusiasm:

"Now, lift thy glass, and tell me what thou see'st."
[It was an Indian village rose in view,]
"Chilhowee!—sounding well in poesy!—
Now, here is nature surely, but of fashion
Such as, I fancy, never once delighted
Dear, delicate Chateaubriand, when he sought
Arcadia 'mongst the Hurons! How one laughs
At these philosophers who finger nature
With gloves of sentiment, and see her features
Through opera glasses; and exult in Romans,
That strut in costume of good Louis Quatorze!

"Could we transfer this picture now to Paris;
Summon St. Pierre—call up that heartless proser,
All sentiment and syllabub, Rousseau;
Nay, the Iconoclast himself, Voltaire,
Who broke all idols down, that he might leap
To all their pedestals, yet foul his own;
And with their fancies and philosophies,
Contrast this portrait, taken from the life;—
How would they shrink abash'd!

                              "Old Rabelais
Would shake anew in his easy chair; Montaigne
Feel justified at the cost of that pretension
That dared usurp his judgment seat and mock
The bitter lessons of his wiser wit—
Still teaching nature in her nakedness,
Or in her prostitution, or in paint!

"You speak of nature as a thing of trees,
Rocks, woods, and waters; beautiful heights and slopes,
And wild flowers that, appealing as you ride,
With loveliest hues, yet yield you no reward,
When you alight to pluck them; being designed
To please the passing traveler, not delay.
You sum up nature in such things as these,
Yet nature's truest representative
Is man; whose properest nature lies in art!
Nature, as you discern it, lies in growth;
Man's nature is development. He lives
To shape all natural objects to his will,

According to endowment; to make trees
Expand to ships, which, crossing wondrous seas,
Bring nations to commune with one another,
In such relations as still profit all.
He prompts attrition thus; compels the thought,
And with expedient multiplies resource,
To the vast uses of humanity. He shapes
The rock into the temple, and discovers
Where the grand statue harbors in the stone.
His genius means discovery. He explores—
Tears out the hidden treasure from the mine;
Finds out the virtue in the mineral;
Bark, tree, and shrub, medicinal; and thus
Developes all their uses through his own!
The nature which does nothing of these things,
Is, in the man, mere savageism; that knows
Nothing of freedom, and can never know!
Man's freedom hath conditions, under law,
Attainable only as he yields to law,
That law being founded in his special gifts,
Work'd faithfully in humility and hope,
That, in due season, freedom shall be sure,
In the just exercise of art, while nature,
Serenely harbors in society.

"The history in this picture which you see,
Is patent at a glance. You trace it all,
Through the few seasons left it to endure;
And nought of the prophet instinct will it need,
To tell you of the fortunes of the race;
While just as little will philosophy need,
To solve the problem which involves their fate.
There's nothing occult here. Note the *coup d'œil*—
All's spread upon the canvas at a glance.
Survey the wretched hovels, twelve or more,
Shrouded in smoke. In front of each behold
A screaming brat, that, lash'd upon his board,
Hangs rocking from the tree; the dam beneath;
A surly drudge that never once looks up,
But hoes and hills her corn, as if her soul
Lay clamoring there for sudden and strong help!
Behold the groups of curs at every den,

Lank, mangy, most unclean; that, yelping, run
For shelter as we come. See, two green skins,
That clothed the brown deer of the woods last night,
Stretch'd now around the oak, beneath whose boughs
Their owners browsed last season, ere the tribe
Went into summer quarters—

                  "Lo! yon group,
Women and children, in that happy state
Which you call nature, which delights in freedom,
Ere Adam wore his fig leaves, and became,
A tailor for the nonce; the first step taken
In *his* art-progress. There, around a pit,
They squat, clay-digging, for their pots and pans,
The sum of all their excellence in art;
Nay, linger not in study of this scene,
Lest in rebellion, justified of sense,
The nostrils of our very steeds shall rise,
Dilating with revulsion.

                  "It may be,
That, with your lessons in romance, you'll find
A more legitimate picture for good taste,
And the heroic, basking in the sun,
Where crouch the chiefs;—five warriors of the wild
Who may be sung in ballads;—vigorous men,
Ready for drink and quarrel, scalp and strife,
But monstrous lazy!

                "There lies 'Turkey-Foot,'
Not slow to run when sober, should the squatter
Press on his rear. Achilles-like, his heels
Are sadly mortal. There's 'Fat-Terrapin,'
No runner he, I ween; but he will sleep,
Having gorged, like a Boa! Never braver man
Than the 'Gray Weasel' ever sought the fight,
But then he loves 'fire-water,' and even now,
See, his head dangles on unsinew'd neck,
And bobs from side to side.

              " 'The Crooked Path,'
A double-dealing rogue as ever lived,

Looks like a model cutpurse. Such his merit
Among his people. Wondrous his renown,
In council with congressional brethren,
For subtle and sharp practice. There is none
Can match with him in cunning argument
To make the worse appear the better cause;
No fox-like politician double better
In working round the rough 'Cape Positive'
To channel 'Non-Committal.' Happy he,
To steer between those breakers, 'Yes and No!'
Leaving no furrow on his sinuous path,
As guide-track to most cunning enemy.

"Last of this group, behold old 'Blazing Pine,'
Though but a pine-knot now. His seventy years
Have all been tasted; but his limbs are strong
To carry him yet in the chase. His small black eye
Not often fails to see; his nervous hand,
Still sends the ball unerring to the mark,
Into the brown deer's flank.

   "These warriors brave,
Your frequent favorite heroes of romance,
Will all be drunk ere night; the soberest now,
Drunk with the drunkest. The already drunk,
Mad,—raging for their weapons in the dark,—
Hidden by the wise precautions of their wives—
Beating the walls, the winds; striving with trees
And one another; impotent, but fierce,
And foaming with their fury unappeased,
'Till, in their rages, with their empty bottles,
They'll break the old squaw's head, and she will fly,
Howling for vengeance.

   "She will swim yon stream,
Her blood, red-streaking, as she scuds along
The wave that washes 'gainst her batter'd scull,
Seeking for safety 'mongst her kindred tribe,
Of the 'Mud-Turtles.' She will head a war,
And they will lose their scalps, with infinite grace,
To one another. War, with its long train
Of strifes and injuries, will rive their fields—

Destroy their little maize crops and frail huts,
And leave them starving. Want may then produce
The peace that came not with prosperity;
And they will link their arms, and, in small groups,
Steal nightly over to the opposite shore,
And rob the squatter's farm-yard. Cows and calves
They'll drive across the river. The young corn
They'll burst from its green columns, and the pigs—
They barbacue as well at an Indian camp,
As at a white man's muster.

      "What comes next?
The squatter goes against the savages,
And drives them—a most sad necessity—
Much mourn'd by modern-mouthed philanthropy,
Into remoter forests.

      "Five years hence,
And the foul settlement we gaze on now
Will be a village of the paler race,
Having its thousand souls. Churches will rise,
With taverns on each hand. To the right, see
That gloomy house of morals called a jail;
And from the town hall, on the opposite square,
You yet shall hear some uncomb'd orator
Discourse of freedom, politics, and law,
In tones shall make your blood boil, and your hair
Start up in bristles. It may be your fortune
To hear his comment on your favorite themes,
'Nature and Freedom;' while your eyes discern
'Fat Terrapin,' 'Gray Weasel,' and, perchance,
The aged 'Blazing Pine,'—all Christians then,—
Cowering, bewildered, 'mongst the clamorous crowd
Which hangs delighted on the orator's words—
Heedful, delighted, drunk as any there!"

                          (1837, ca. 1868, 1869)

THE TWO UPON THE HEARTH.

i

My soul is dark, but with the power,
　Which grief sublimes at last in wo,
To summon from the past each hour
　We once had known and yet would know;
Bring back the scene of joy or pain,
　Each actor, once to life so dear,
The whole long drama bring again,
　That woke the bliss or moved the tear.

ii

The wizard spell is in the soul,
　Where memory sits with wo alone;
And with a power of grand control,
　It calls the vanished long and gone;
And, with the will, I straight command,
　Now, in this drear and dark of night,
That they shall come and round me stand,
　My loved, my beautiful, my bright!

iii

And, all obedient, at the word,
　The duteous memory wakes, and waves
Her wand of power, that oft hath stirr'd
　And brought the sleepers from their graves;
While, at the wizard spell and charm,
　Upon the hearth still crouching low,
No longer able to disarm,
　Down sinks in sleep the hostile wo!

iv

It is the scene again—that grove,
　Of blended orange bloom and pine,
Where young devotion, led by love,
　First found his altar place divine!
She comes;—and I am at her feet,
　With earnest but with flattering prayer;
Again I hear—I feel—how sweet
　It is the voice of love to hear!

v

Now speed the revel—join the dance;—
    The fairy scene, with music blent,
Gives joy her wing'd deliverance,
    In her own happy element.
Love floats in airy realms of song,
    With visions of the sunset rare,
And o'er the young and joyous throng
    There hangs no single doubt or care!

vi

And she, the centre of the scene,
    My queen, my beauty, born of grace,
So sweet, yet stately, so serene,
    With soft and pale, yet blushing face;
The large dark eyes, whose very glow
    Seems kindling ever with a tear;
The sweet rich voice, whose mellow'd flow,
    To love makes music doubly dear!

vii

And O! the group that gradual came,
    To glad afresh the mother's breast,
With each some sweet and sacred name,
    Of well-beloved ones gone to rest;
Oh! how they crowd around me now,
    As eager for the fond caress;
My hand rests on each fair white brow,
    My fingers play in long brown tress.

viii

Ay, ye are here, my treasures—here,
    Dear woman, sweet as when at first,
Thou echoed'st softly back the prayer,
    When love's first language from me burst?
I clasp thee to my breast once more—
    I feel thy cheek with many a kiss;
No longer lonely I deplore,
    In this vast, sudden boon of bliss.

ix

Throng round me, dear ones—joyous girls;

And trip with fairy feet the room;
I string your hair with orient pearls,
    And crown your foreheads each with bloom;
My noble boys!—Ye are not lost;
    'Twas sure a dream that saw ye die;
'Twas but a moment's breath of frost,
    That came between me and the sky.

x

I have ye still! I hear the shout
    From merry voices, wild with glee;
Sing boys, and pour that music out,
    That, for so long, was hush'd for me.
Out to the fields—a horse for each;
    A gun;—we're for a hunt to-day;
To ride—to shoot and hunt, I'll teach,
    While ye shall teach me, boys, to play.

xi

I must sleep now! The wild delight,
    So precious, so acute,—at last
Grows something into kin with fright,
    Lest it should waken all the past:
Methinks they go!—no more I hear
    That murmurous music, soft and deep,
Which kindled from yon fireside, where
    Wo wakes, while *memory* sinks to sleep!

(1827, 1868)

HORACE IN DESHABILLE.

Ode XI. ad Leucone.

TO JEDEDIAH QUIRK, ESQ., POLITICIAN.

Ask not, dear Quirk, with moody brow,
What next the Congress means to do;
Don't bother your brains or mine to know,
    How long the dogs our days decree;
Consult no wizard, nor through *Pass,*

Of Mesmer, prove yourself an ass,
   And try to make an ass of me!

Better, with Patience, grin and bear,
Than, by the question, rouse the fear
Of worse to come another year,
   While Jove in wrath denies
Season and sky of lengthening bliss;—
Enough that, in a time amiss,
If rightly knowing, using this
   We're, for the Present, wise!

Don't bother with the freedmen, Quirk,
Nor give them rations *not* to work;
Them, as the Bureau, let us shirk,
   Send both to Jericho.
And don't you seek the President,
With any *weather-wise* intent,
Of finding out the thing he meant,
   When sneezing months ago.

Quirk, stay at home,—in quiet stay,—
Rack well your wines;—with ice allay;
Ask me to dinner, day by day;
   Live up to all your powers;—
While vexing Thought with future cares,
And watching Congress, as it swears,—
You know not how the season wears,
   And how your liquor sours!

                                (1868)

THLECATHCHA; OR, THE BROKEN ARROW.[1]

It was a voice of wail, and yet a song—
Such song as wells from soul of bitterness,
That finds no adequate voice in common speech,
And yet *must* speak; and from its agony
Draws its best music.

Through the forest rang
That strange, sad chaunt—that might have been despair,
But that exulting memories of old days
Blent pride with agony; and lifted up
The spirit, through its sorrows, into Hope!
Look through the pines, where, droopingly, they wind,
In sad procession, gloomy as the waste,
Whose shades primeval shroud them as they go—
A thousand warriors of the wild, strong men,
Lithe and well sinew'd; but with drooping gait,
As of the falcon wounded in the wing;
Yet, with a fiery glare in each dark eye
Dilating, that looks battle to the last,
And asks for grand revenges.

By the side
Of each stern warrior, see, a woman glides,
Slowly as sadly; yet, with foot as firm
As if the ancient plain o'er which she treads
Might yet be called her own. One hand conducts
A boy, with bended bow within his grasp,
The little shaft made ready on the string,
As if for mimic battle. On her back
She bears a muffled infant, whose black eyes
Peer o'er her shoulder—lively, full of light,
As curious of the progress, all unknown.

So journey on the melancholy group;
Long, winding trains; peoples of several tribes;
The fragments of a nation torn with strifes,
And now divided; sunder'd, cut in twain
By subtlety, and the treacherous arts of men,
Who, in the guise of Christian love and peace,
Brought poison to the camps of the wild race,
And drug'd their veins with passions born of hell.

They skirt the hill; they wind throughout the plain;
And now they crowd together, in a *cirque*,
Around a gloomy realm—a mystic haunt,
Sacred to ancient memories, and the dead
Of the lost ages of long centuries.

'Tis the performance of a sacred rite,
Ere yet they take their way from the old homes,
To seek, in exile, for a strange abode,
Unnatural, and never to persuade
The old affections of the birthplace born,
To any living exercise of Hope.

That wailing chaunt, that pauses and subsides,
To find renewal, most irregular;
Discordant, passionate, wild, yet still subdued,
As, in obedience to the moment mood,
Now rises into diapason deep,
As of the gathering eagles of the rocks,
Because of some dark destiny, that made
Their rocky realm a dread, and doomed their flight
O'er unknown tracts of ocean.

                    Never a tear
Swells in the great eyes of the warrior men;
Nor do the women weep, how e'er they wail!
Sadly, but sternly—desolate, but strong—
These stoics of the forest and the wild,
Have reached the ideals of philosophy,
Without its books or teachers—taught by nature
How little the tear may profit the strong man,
Or soften fates, he may no longer brave!

The circle opens wide; and, in the midst,
Even as the stern, monotonous, sad chaunt,
Hath reached its utmost volume, there is seen,
On a rude bier, the *Micco* of their race,
The mighty chief—colossal—he who stood,
With head and shoulders taller than the rest!

"Thlecathcha!"—ominous name, which, in our tongue,
Denotes the "Broken Arrow!"

                    Stretched at length,
He, broken lies!—

                    The tall and muscular form,
Reposes, as in sleep, in warrior garb,
As when he went to battle!—

                          On his head
A feathery circlet, with a single quill,
Fresh plucked from out the mountain eagle's wing!
His right hand grasps the tomahawk—his left
The sheaf of *broken* arrows.
                          On his breast
Hang medals, tributes from the pale white race,
To him, the red chief, whom they held a brother,
Having led his tribe to battle in their wars!

Cold and unconscious, he will lead no more
His braves to battle. He will teach no more,
With voice made sweetly subtle for all senses,
His chiefs in the Great Council; never more
Persuade to peace, or with wild eloquence
Inspire their rages for the work of war!

He had been their patriarch! In his fall they lose
Their country!
                    From his death their exile flows—
And, with the moment-growing consciousness
Of what he had been, and can be no more,
Swells the deep chaunt anew.
                    Well may they wail,
For broken is the arrow from their bow;
Their mightiest overthrown, and—all is o'er;
And we but rescue from their parting song,
In feeble strain, of our less passionate tongue,
The fond memories of that burial rite:

Ye warriors, who gather the brave to deplore,
With a wail o'er the chief who shall lead you no more,
Let the hatchet of fight still unburied remain,
While we joy in the glory of him that is slain.

Unfettered in soul as unfearing in fight,
In council and conflict still greater in might;
In battle the tiger, in peace the young fawn,
Whose footstep scarce brushes the dew from the lawn.

Saw ye not, in the thick of the battle's affray,
While the warm blood, like rain, o'er the smoking grass lay,

How the Seminole braves from his tomahawk fled,
While the best of their warriors beneath him lay dead.

How long did their women in agony mourn,
Looking forth for their chiefs who shall never return,
For their scalps the full swell of his legs have embraced,
While their corses, unburied, still cumber the waste.

And when did the braves of the Cherokee dare
To sing their proud war-song in sight of his lair?
He had tracked them through thickets that never knew path,
Till they crouched and did homage to soften his wrath.

Not in vain were his triumphs, though now we deplore
That he leads us to triumph in battle no more;
He has fought the good fight to the last, and now goes
Where the Great Spirit crowns him with sway o'er his foes.

His death-song was grand as the storm wind that leaps
Like the torrent that sudden bursts high o'er the steeps;
Its echoes poured down the great valleys, 'mid cries
From the people who roar when the great chieftain dies.

Not for him be the wail, as we gaze on the face
Of the bravest and best that e'er died for his race;
Our right hand hath perished that gave us the might,
And the arrow lies broken that won us the fight.

Heard ye not his proud speech at the closing of day,
When he knew that the wolf was all hot for the fray;
When he dream'd how the snake from the covert would steal,
Yet sounding no rattle, to strike at his heel.

Had he given but warning, how quick were the blow
To crush with the hatchet the head of the foe,
Had they sought him by day, though with hundreds to one,
How greater than all were the deeds he had done!

Far off, through the forests, when evening grew still,
We heard the long howl of the wolf on the hill—
And, "hark!" cried the chief, at the hiss, soft and low,
" 'Tis the tongue of Menawe, the snake, from below.

"They come not, the cowards, to brave me in fight,
While my people look on, with the Day-God in sight,
But sly, through the covert, as subtly as base,
The heel they would sting, always fearing the face.

"They have gathered their hosts, all with hearts full of hate,
They would gird me with fire, and o'erwhelm me with fate;
But I've lived a long triumph; if now it be o'er,
Nor I, nor my people, have cause to deplore.

"I have rear'd them grand pillars on heights that shall last,
That rise like great smokes o'er the hills of the past;
These shall lead them to valor, where the eagles make song,
Singing ever to the warrior, 'be fearless and strong!' "

———

Then the chief took his rifle and whetted his knife,
And went where the wolf lay in wait for the strife;
He knew, by the howl and the hiss, where they stood,
Wolf and serpent, both eagerly panting for blood.

Here his voice, like a trumpet, rang out on the air;
But the rifle-shot sped from the wolf in his lair!
There came up a clamor of death to the hill,
And a wail as of women—and all was then still!

And the chieftain lay dead in his gore! but his hand
Still clutched the long knife, buried deep in the sand.
They dared not come nigh him, though dead where he lay,
And they tore not the scalp from his forehead away!

Oh! fling not aside, though the arrow be lost,
The bow we still keep at such perilous cost;
We may find a fit shaft for the string when afar,
And go with the Sioux and Dogskin to war.

Farther west! farther west! where the buffalo roves,
And the red deer still wanders, o'er plains that he loves,
Our hearts shall be glad in the hunt once again,
'Till the white man shall seek for the lands that remain.

Farther west! farther west! where the sun, as he dies,
Still leaves his red robes o'er the couch where he lies;
There the red man shall roam, and his women shall rove,
And the white man not blight what he cannot improve.

One song for our hero—not now of regret—
The song of a sorrow for a sun that has set;
A wail o'er the hills and the valleys, and one
For the great arrow broken—the nation undone!

Farther west! farther west! it is meet that we fly,
Where the red deer still bounds at the glance of an eye;
Yet, slowly the song of our parting be sung,
For the great arrow broken—the great bow unstrung.

(1825, 1868)

1. "Thlecathcha," or the "Broken Arrow," was the name of a district, or precinct of country, some forty years ago, among the Muscoghees of Georgia. It was also one of the names borne by the once celebrated Indian chief, or half-breed warrior, known better among the people of the United States as General William Mackintosh. Mackintosh sided with the peace party of the nation when the war party, or "Red Sticks," proposed to make war upon the whites; and when the war was precipitated by the young warriors, and the hatchet was taken up, Mackintosh rallied a portion of the nation, and allied himself with the whole forces under Jackson, rising to command, and doing good service under the flag of the United States. Subsequently, when peace was restored, it became necessary, in order to secure its continuance, that the Muscoghees should make a cession of their lands, and proceed further West. Mackintosh, still in the interest of the whites, favored the cession, for which he was denounced by the young chiefs, and many of the old ones, who were jealous of his superior influence, both with the red men and the white. A party of some three hundred warriors, led by Menawe, the Mad Wolf, and other chiefs, calling themselves "Law-menders," undertook the punishment of this powerful "Law-breaker." They surrounded his plantation residence near Cowetah, in the night, and summoned him to surrender. Mackintosh threw on his hunting-shirt, seized his rifle and fearlessly presenting himself at the entrance of the dwelling, was about to address his assailants; but the rival chiefs well knew his eloquence of speech, and feared its effect upon their followers. Before he could utter a sentence, he was shot through the head by "Mad Wolf," a fierce warrior and vindictive personal enemy of Mackintosh. He, as he fired, shouted to his victim to prepare to die by the law which he had himself made as well as violated. This law, solemnly made in council, where Mackintosh was one of the chiefs, sacredly pledged them all, under the penalty of death, to make no further cession of the lands of the nation. He died accordingly by the law. His sympathies were, no doubt, more certainly with the white than with the red men, as his genius was undoubtedly derived mostly from his Scotch fathers. Chilly Mackintosh, his son, with a considerable part of the nation, was compelled to emigrate and separate the Mackintosh faction from the great body of the people. The poem which follows, is designed to illustrate these events; the writer having passed through the Muscoghee country, and the immediate vicinity

of Cowetah, within a week after the assassination of Mackintosh, when the excitement was still very great and lively, and when all the particulars of the event were fresh in the mouths of all parties.

HEART-OMEN.

Ever a voice is pleading at my heart,
    With mournful pleading, ever soft and low,
    Yet deep as with an ocean's overflow—
"Depart! Depart! Why wilt thou not depart?
Why, wilful, thrust thy bosom 'gainst the dart;
Why make thy couch in ashes;—bend thy knee
    On little hillock of the lone, cold sod,
    With cry of thy great agony to God,
When, with a will for freedom thou art free.
Thou mak'st the memory of thy joys a grief,
For which no prayer can ever bring relief.
    Depart! Depart! Depart!
    Seek out some better refuge for the heart,
    Than in these ruins. Far, in other lands,
    Find newer uses for thy head and hands,
'Till they grow braver in some fresh belief!"

Soothly thou speak'st, thou voice of saddest truth,
And lovingly—and yet thou dost not soothe.
I know that these are ruins; that the cloud
Still hangs above in waiting but to shroud.
Here are no blossoms now, that live—no flowers,
    Such as with sacred scent and happy glow
Recal the Elysian home, and those glad hours,
When with the breezes sporting round the towers,
And the soft moonlight glinting through green bowers,
    The heart forgot the spectral form of wo,
    Nor saw the sword outstretching for the blow!

Ah! God! but it was beautiful and bless'd,
This refuge of Love, with happiness and rest,
By each dear creature of the group possess'd.
There was no tree that shelter'd not its bird;

No shrub without its song and summer bloom,
And never a Fate drew nigh, with look or word,
   Articulate, of the Terror and the Doom!
Were not the wings contented there in home
   That never lack'd of sunshine or of songs;
Nor did we lose, beneath the grand old dome,
   The joys of solitude, though bless'd with throngs
Coming and going;—blessing as they came,
   And taking blessing from the bliss they found!
And yet, depart we! we shall find the same
   In some far, foreign, undistinguish'd ground,
Having no lure to bait the felon eye,
   No altar which the serpent slime may shame;
God still above us in sun-lighted sky,
And purest breezes wooing to delight,
   While birds of orient plumage swim around,
Or, darting wide in circles of gay flight,
   Make the glad air all musical as bright!
Ah! still that ominous voice within the heart!
"Why linger longer in this realm of blight,
When every ruin'd chamber cries 'Depart!'"

                            (1865, 1868)

SKETCHES IN HELLAS.

I.

ARCADIA.

Now should wé, with an inspiration meet,
Caught from the antique chronicles, that rise
In wreck of marble round us, straight compel
The *Genius Loci* to ascend his throne,
The spirit to resume his garb of flesh,
The Homes to brighten with their family fires,
The din of the great multitude to pour
Its music through these mighty avenues,
In clink of hammer, and performing toils,
That make Humanity wondrous:—now recal
The solemn white-stoled Priesthood, while they pass
In grand procession through mysterious groves,—

Each hallowed by its own Divinity,—
To mystic temples, towering on yon heights,
With half their heads in Heaven!
                              Here, the *old Gods*
   Vouchsafed great oracles to credulous hearts
That grew through *Faith* to *Power*. Here, mighty lyres
Discoursed grand musical thoughts to loving echoes,
That prison'd them straightway in these iron rocks,
Where still you hear them murmuring to escape
To other shores, fullfilling that decree
Which makes them Catholic voices for the world!
   We gaze upon Arcadia—to the West—
Pinnacled on her summits,—with high towers,
And frowning Ruins;—while, on slopes below,
She looks on lengthening line of browsing sheep,
And dotted domes of white, where Peace abides,
With the poor Cottager. Arcadian still,
He knows not of his losses in the Past,
Has no impatient memories, which rebuke
His present fortunes—the degenerate soul,
Which knows no sleepless consciousness of shame
Irking him ever to the noble strife,
That seeks Arcadia in re-peopled towers,
And welcomes even their ruin with a shout,
If thus it saves the *State!*
                              The sacred hill,
Lycæus, you behold, yet towering high,
As pregnant still with births, and brooding deep,
O'er possible heavings of Humanity,
Commencing with the Gods; that yet shall make
His height as sacred as, when bless'd of Heaven,
It glow'd with tribute fires that flamed of old
To the Olympian Sovran; or with fruits,
Golden and red, and luscious in the sun,
Deck'd rustic altars to the rural Pan,
While virgins in the shade danced to sweet strains
Of choral pipes of satyrs in the woods!

                                             (1858, 1862)

II.

SALAMIS.

There are quick instincts that declare the Past,

When it is glorious,—ere the chronicler
Can mumble o'er his records. Did we need
That the rude sailor should tell us—

                    "Here—where, now,
Flows silently the sea, and on its shores,
As silently rise groups of pleasant homes—
Once sate the *Persian Despot,* while below
Ranged his proud fleets!"

                    The deed of glory or shame,
In lines of ineradicable depth,
Is written on the rocks. The mighty sea,
Declares it, in the voices of her waves,
By day and night eternally. The skies
Keep all its echoes; stars by night still sing
The high achievements; and the incessant winds,
In tones sonorous ever 'gainst the heights,
Bellow their loud approval or reproach;
While subtler spirits, hovering o'er the scene,
Appeal to human instincts, with a touch
Electric, that informs the eager soul
With the imposing history, which becomes
The tutor of that brave Humanity,
That glows with emulous yearnings to perform,
For conquest or defence.

                    Oh! Gulph of Salamis!
What wonders hast thou witnessed—fleet with fleet
Contending—the fierce Satrap 'gainst the Greek,
More fell than fierce! The calm unconscious seas
Suddenly gored by hostile keels—the sky
O'ercast with darts and fire—the trembling air
Rent with the shout and shriek of agony
Blended with triumph!

                    On this very spot,
Where now we sit, the desperate Despot sate,
In state, on gilded throne, while all about him
Ranged servile vassals. At the first, his soul
Exulting in the dream of conquest sure,—
His myriads o'er the few—his barbarous hordes
Of sleek and sycophant homagers, in mail,
'Gainst naked breasts of freemen, clad in proof
The best, of virtuous courage and true faith

In their own mission and most powerful Gods!
    Not long the Despot sate in state, and dream'd,
Serenely vain, of triumph! Soon he starts,
And pales, as rolling upward from below
Swells the Greek Pæan! Suddenly, his shriek
Echoes the fearful cries that from the sea
Tell him of fearfuller Fates among his ships,
Than strive in armor. Now he flings aside
His robes; now rends his hair; and to the steep
Rushing, he cries to those, who yet below,
Fight 'neath his banner! But they hear him not.
Too fiercely followed by the avenging Greek,
To hearken their own monarch, wild their flight,
But urged in vain. The sharp beaks of their foes,
Dart through the thin sides of his painted ships,
And the seas follow; and their billows heave,
With thousands drowning in their desperate fear;
Or struggling with the waves, are downward thrust
By the Greek spear and javelin. All in vain
Their prayers for mercy as their deeds in fight:—
The eager conquerors, like the Furies speed,
In the hot chase of blood; now doubly sworn
For carnage, as they hear, from neighboring shores,
The cries of women, in their ravaged towns,
Which tell them of the havoc in their homes;
Polluted; given to the flames; or red
With blood of innocence;—in every cry,
A trumpet voice of vengeance to their hearts!

                                                    (1862)

        III.

        CASTALY.

    Feel'st thou no sacred thirst, which fires the veins
With ardor—makes the blood tumultuous swell,
In billows, to the brain; and wakes the soul,
'Till it grows conscious of a wing that spreads
From either shoulder?
                        This is Castaly,—
Still beautiful, still bright, though flowing now,
As through a desert,—all the Deities
Gone, that endowed her waters for the muse,

And made them fruitful in delicious song,
Which here awakes new echoes now no more!
   Yet there are murmurs still among her rocks,
As if from harboring voices of the Past,
That chide them for the improvidence that lost
Their treasures;—chide them that they could not keep
Their temples sacred; well assured that they,
Well kept, had still been safe in reverent throngs,
And a grand Priesthood, and a glorious Muse!
   Yet should the very ruins of the scene
Assure us of the Priesthood. Yonder shrine
Was once Apollo's. Its great ruins stand,
Still looking on Parnassus. See the chasm,
Whence rose oracular voices, at which Kings
Humbled themselves in reverence! Prophecy
Here spake the fate of Empire; and, to Heroes,
Return'd significant answers, which gave heart
To marvellous enterprise. And what remains?—
Look west, you see the Stadium. East of it—
There still the cascade falls, fed by the snows
That crowned Parnassus sovereign of the scene!
Escaped the embrace of the precipitous rock,
Panting and flush'd below, her waters make
The Poet's fount of Castaly,—sweet stream,
That fails not, though Apollo's self be gone!
   Oh! beautiful ever, though her streams no more
Shall water the high hills of hopeful song,
Making them tuneful as a liquid voice,
Born of the brook and zephyr! O'er her breast
Bends no indulgent Sovereign of the skies,
Endowing her with soul. The oracles dumb;
Broken the sacred lyre; the altars down;
The mystic fires gone out; and the grey Priesthood
Grown faithless, and their ancient Gods forsworn,
For hostile Deities.[1]
            The glorious soul
Of Grecian Genius—marbled on her rocks,
And musical in her waters;—in her arts
Eternal; and in deeds of mightiest heroes,
Modelling the virtues for far lands remote,
Even beyond Thulé,—hath no more a voice
In her own temples! Rocks, waters—these remain,

But yield no more a shrine. We gaze around
On ruins, which can make no monument!

(1862)

IV.

THESSALY.

Feel'st thou no wild emotions, such as wake
The soul to fancies which o'erride the earth,
Seeking strange Gods?
            We are in Thessaly,
The land of flocks, and herds, and fiery steeds,
Warriors and Battles!
            Here, the hunter grew
To prowess; and in desperate wrestle strove
With monsters of the wild. The shepherd led
His flocks beside still waters, while his pipe
Wooed friendly converse with familiar Pan,
And cheered his satyrs, as, at eve, they drew
Their files, fantastic, into sheltering woods,
To music of the Syrinx.
            Other Powers,
Most potent when most silent, harboring here,
Made all the atmosphere prophetical;
Subduing men to terror, and from strength,
Plucking its sinewy weapons.
            Here they dwelt,
Who could, with powerful magic, spell the winds;
Wake up the storm to hence, and speed
Fierce Demons through the thick and turbid sky,
In phrenzy-guided chariots, bent on wrath,
And most malevolent purpose.
            Here, the Gods
That had the care of Greece, wore sterner brows
Than when they look'd on favor'd Attica!
Her wonderful Genius, when it wander'd hither,
Took a new aspect from the sky and soil—
Grew weird and savage.
            If her magic rear'd
Shapes of beguiling Beauty for young bosoms,
It gifted them with souls, whose fiery passions
Wiled victims to the embraces with a Fate
Too apt to rob them of Humanity—

Nor left them so much consciousness to know
How brutish they had grown.
                                        And yet her spells
Have crowned the rocks with beauty, and a grace,
That mocks the mind's fertility of Thought,
And leaves the Fancy nothing to create,
And nothing to implore!
                                        The Centaur here,
The Cyclops, and the Calydonian Boar,
Had range for seasons; 'till Alcides hither
Came, with his club retributive, and strove
For empire, through the brutal, with the Brute.
    Here dwelt the model wife of that good King,
Admetus:—she who gave herself to Death,
To crown her lord with immortality:—
While yet the crown of Hebe on her head,
And all the grace of Hebe in her steps,
Made Life her own most sweet necessity;
Alcestis,—the fair mother, fond not frail,
Who met the Fates so fearlessly; and pray'd
But for her children;—that no other mother
Should, with ungentle rule, make their young hearts
Too soon to feel the sorrows of her loss!
Hell could not keep a soul so near to Heaven!
And she to Hercules,—and we to one
More powerful still than he,—Euripides—[2]
Owe, that she lives again—still lives—will ever
Live, in the eternal realm of classic song.
    Yet, not all stern, the Muse of Thessaly
Woos us o'er sterile plains of dust and sand,
Through grim defiles of scarce accessible rock,
Where Neptune smote the barrier-chain which link'd
Ossa to high Olympus, and set free
The glad Peneus.
                                        Winding on his way,
We win, through parallel heights of wooded rock,
The Vale of Tempé,—by the Poets famed
Earth's paradise—all peace!
                                        Here, while the Sun
Flames fierce along the summits, we have shade,
Such as beguiles the breezes from the heights
To song and dalliance. As we wander down

The narrow, long defile, our caravan
And the Peneus travel side by side:—
The vale shoots out its flowers, that purpling gleam
From every cleft; fresh fed by bubbling springs,
Which, breaking through the tesselated floor,
Make bright mosaics, serpent-eyed and ring'd;
Superior far, in gay variety,
To all of art in Italy; to all
Of Nature, in whatever clime of love!
Here sings the bird of twilight as of morn;
Late sitter, yet a riser with the dawn;
As is the wont with more ambitious bards,
Who challenge Nature under her own roofs,
And shame her in the strife.[3] The ivy clings
To the o'ershadowing plane trees, which find root
Even in the river; in whose limpid waves,
Their lapsing boughs make murmur as they go,
Loth to be left. The vine creeps up their sides;
While, in profusest fringes, the green banks,
Freshen in shade of lentisk and of Bay—
That sacred Bay, from which Apollo cull'd
The shoot he planted by Castilian rills.
    Noon—and the lonely wood-dove in the copse
Moans softly, brooding o'er her own sad heart!
We, too, will drowse beneath these grand old cliffs,
And if, in sleep, we make a moan like hers,
'Twill be because of Tempé's Muse, that, dumb,
Hath no more song to freshen memory!
'Tis pitiful, alas!—
                    And yet her bird
Still woos!—and yet her vale, still beautiful,
Might well awake, with inspiration new,
Bright Song and Legend, as in days of old!
    Ah! for fresh echoes from the ancient lyre!
That Nature should be young while man decays!—
That streams and woods should freshen with the hours,
While the brave spirit that made great the Past,
Fails in her flight; that rocks should grow to age,
And wear the bloom of a perpetual spring,
While those who found them Gods, and made their shrines,
And knew so well to worship, should lose voice
Even in their loveliest temples!

Thessaly

Still hath her Tempé, but no more *her* boast!
Her Empire, lapt in barrenness for thought,
Hath lost remembrance, as her Bards lost sway;
And, save what's left of the prolific Past,
Shrined in her sepulchre, and in the ears
Of other races, far beyond the seas,
She hath naught left for Tempé!
Sound her sleep,
Lock'd in the embrace of rocks, on which, of yore,
Her magic lighted altars to dread Powers,
That now partake her sleep, if not her tomb!

(1862)

V.

THE TEMPLE OF MINERVA, AT SUNIUM.

What spells arise to freshen the rapt soul!—
What visions, conjured up by antique song,
Inspire the Muse to holiest offices,
At once of song and worship—homage most fond
To the grey Guardians of this holiest realm,
That lacks all mortal guardian—for the spoils
Won from its wealth when Genius first with power
Possess'd the ears of Time.
Long have we drunk
Of the sweet waters from these ancient rocks,
Nor seen their sources,—drunk of memories,
Taught by indwelling voices from these heights,
That now no more find echoes for the Past,
Yet live for all the Future.
What a spell,—
If there be aught in place to make it sacred—
Should warm us now with voices like the Past,
And make a soul of fire inform the clay,
For whom no longer the Prometheus toils
In holy theft from Heaven!
We may not brood
In the great temple of old ages gone,
Nor catch the sacred spirit of the Seer,
Who watched its fires, and, from its mystic caves,
Caught the wild music in its oracles,
And shaped it to the Lyre.

There should be still
A lingering spirit in these crumbling walls,
To prompt and fill our own,—to yield us powers,
Like those they wielded once, when, at their shrines,
From all the States of Greece came worshippers,
Fond in their faith, with valued sacrifices;
Simple, confiding; well assured of Truth,
No less than law, in each oracular speech,
That bade them go in peace, or march to triumph!
The spirit dies not, though the worshipping race
Melts from the landscape. Can the Genius fly
The realms it render'd glorious? No, it lurks,
Hooded in sorrowful silence, that no more
Its spells command an audience!
                         How we doubt
Of our own senses! Have we traveled hither?
Are these things real, or vision? Do we now
Grasp, with material hands, the mighty shrines
We've dream'd of,—glide through noblest colonnades,
That, thousand years ago, echoed the steps
Of Pericles or Timon? Are we now
In Greece, the wonderful mistress of all arts,
And shaping all to purposes of beauty,
No less than Liberty?
                         One month
And we were ranging through a western world,
Where the brave man, in physical strength assured,
Mocks at the old tradition—knows no Muse,
Save that which prompts the pioneer to strokes
That hew down forests—Cyclopean shafts,
That never yet knew offices of Art,
Or fear'd her axe, or rivalry,—and now!—

*   *   *   *   *   *   *   *

We're at the Sunium Cape! Below us spreads
The sea: above us hangs the grand, grey cliffs,
The eternal rocks; and, over all, the sky
Of Greece, as fair and soft as Italy;
With a bright, rising moon, that, through the rocks,
Pours a gay flood of liquid light along
The rippling waves. No lovelier moon than this
E'er lighted Romeo, on his midnight ranges

To Juliet's balcony; or held the light
When Jessica stole off from Shylock's den,
Forswearing Mammon at the shrine of love!

Fit crown for such a steep above the sea,—
Behold, where silent, in her pillar'd state,
Minerva's shrine, abandoned to the storm,
Makes holy still the mountains and the deep!
It looks on both with eye of vacancy,—
Without a voice to answer to their song—
The song of winds and waters,—mightiest notes,
Poured through gigantic trebles of great rocks,
And caverns of vex'd ocean! Doth she hear—
The Goddess—she who once so joy'd to hear,
When all the seas were glittering with gay barques,
That came to do her homage; while the hills
Beheld their grand processions, height to height
Responding, with the voice of one great heart,
Pouring, with thousand throats, a strain of praise
From proud and happy votaries.
                              Silent now
The worshippers—and the Goddess silent too!
Wisdom's dumb oracle! that with no speech
Can warn the precipitate nations of the Fate
That mocks the Empire's greatness—mocks the Arts
That sway'd o'er Empire!
                              How supreme the spell,
Eloquent thus in silence,—to the ears
That lean on thought; and in the solitude
Seek counsel for the populous worlds that still
Struggle on, through strifes and battles, to grim Ruin,
Which seizes realms for apathy, that once
Were sovereign witness of power!
                              How lonely now,—
Yet with what grand, compelling majesty,
A beacon from the land's end o'er the sea,—
That hallow'd wreck! The pale moon honours it
Nightly, with fond and tributary glance;
And, with the day, Apollo, rising proud,
Pours on it floods of gold, that make it smile
Through all its rents of ruin!
                              Even as we gaze,
The Imagination, eager to dispute

Time's province o'er the absolute and dull,
Flings o'er our eyes his spells, and from the cloud
Evokes the Presence! Following close upon,
The nimble Fancy, with her pallet and brush,
Touches the ruined towers with purpling tints,
And o'er the mouldering columns flings her flowers;
While the superior architect rears up
The mighty dome; and, all at once, restores
The populous realm to Light, as well as thought!
The work of restoration still for Thought
Goes on,—the new creation from the old;
And, with the aid of her great ministers,
The subtle Fancy, grand Imagination,
The realm re-peoples with a race that shows
As worthy of their sires! We hear a sound,
Faint and mysterious, swelling from the rocks,
That speaks a work within we soon shall see;
And lo! each gaping crevice, whence the smokes
Rise from a secret altar.

       Hark! a strain
From mighty instruments of antique mould,
That chaunt the language of an olden time,
When there were giants: in a choral burst
Worthy all ages! Wherefore should it die?

 It lives! they live! the masters of the spell,
And all their classic heroes. See, they come
Across the sea, in flocks of painted ships,
That purple-dot the billows. See the hosts
That, in procession solemn, climb the peaks
Of the grey mountains. Lo! the rock itself
Springs up into the temple! Lift your eyes
To where its shrines grow glorious! Mark the crowds,
The populous Greece, with all its demigods,
Ascending to the altar,—the High Priest
Ready, with bared and sacred instrument;
And, at his feet, with neck begirt with flowers,
The patient lamb awaiting sacrifice!

             (1862)

VI.

THERMOPYLÆ.

"Oh! friends, we stand upon Thermopylæ,

The pass that led into the heart of Greece,
But gave no passage save to greater hearts:—
They keep it still! Their graves are at our feet!

"How stood the brave 'Three Hundred' on that day?—
With all the hosts of Persia in their front,
The 'immortals' of the Median in their rear,
Themselves ten thousand, rushing to the charge!—
How stood the Greeks of brave Leonidas?

"We know the story well! They stood and fell,
Self-consecrate to Freedom. But they felt
Their better immortality begun
In the conviction of their own grand will
To perish, that their country still might live.
Love and great memories kindling each brave soul,
Nerved them for sacrifice!
                    "It did but need,
That he, their chief, Leonidas, should say:

'There rises Œta, from whose sacred brow
The heroic soul of Hercules took flight
For the Olympian Heavens!

                    'He was your sire:
We'll sup with him to-night!

                    'Even now, his shade,
Down from yon summit, bends his eager eyes,
To note who best remembers what ye are,
And from what loins descended!—
                    'Shame him not,
Nor bring perdition, and the loss of Heaven,
On your own souls!
                    —'By Hercules, set on!' "

                                        (1865, 1868)

VII.

THE PEACE IN ELIS.

  Taÿgetus, with its rugged mountain range,
Fit barrier for the stern Laconian race,
Need chain our eyes no more. Look farther south:

You see Corona, and the tribute waters
Of the Messenian gulph. Northwest, behold
A lovelier picture. There, below you, spread
The fruitful plains of Elis:—name most dear
In sweet associations to all hearts
Whom Peace delights,—with choral song and dance
Winning her way to Beauty.

Opening wide,
To the persuasions of the fond Alpheus,
Olympia's breast,—luxurious, yet as chaste
As Love in the first gush of innocent youth,
Implores you to her side.

Hallow'd are these bounds
Beside the glad Alpheus, and beneath
The sacred olive shade:—in the old time
More hallowed far than now; and yet, perchance,
Not a whit lovelier. The sacred realm,
Honor'd then by fond observance—unprofaned
By thoughtless office or irreverent step—
Though Pagan rites unto the Christian eye
Seemed sin no less than sorrow.
Yet the sin
Were surely venial when it led to virtue,
And school'd to meet humanity the hearts
That other schools made savage.

Here, in Elis,
By dread decree of the Olympian Jove,
Men held perpetual Peace; and to his shrine
Beguiled—their arms thrown by, their rage subdued—
The warrior chiefs of Greece in sportive games
Proved strength and skill, agility and art,
In amity, and to mutual admiration;
While eager youth look'd on with emulous eye,
And caught each trick of art, and felt the soul
Glow to white heat of ardor as they heard
The several cries of cities and of States,—
Arcadia now, Laconia, Attica,—
As each in several triumph won the prize
Decreed to the best manhood.

These were games,
Though dress'd in peace, which taught the art of war:
Power, free of passion, imaging the conflict,
Without its venom. So the tribes were taught
By the recurring practice to prepare
For conflict, in whatever terrible shape;
Forever ready, lest the enemy come
And find them weaponless, without a chief.

But Peace must reign in Elis, and beneath
Olympia's olive shade; and never a plea
Of the most plausible necessity
Might give pretext to human appetite,
Evasive of the Law.
           The rival heroes,
But late in opposite ranks, in deadliest strife
No longer raged;—here met in warm embrace,
And eyed each other with an envious love
That sought compassion; watch'd and weigh'd and felt
Each sinewy arm, and measured well the height,
The bulk, the bearing, muscle, eye, and port,
Nor stinted in the proper admiration
Which said—
      "This is a man that was my foe!"
And so, embracing, they together sped
In generous conflict;—in the wrestle, race,
On fiery steeds of Thessaly, or, stript,
Hied their own sinewy thews and limbs afoot,
While eager thousands, hailing as they ran,
Shouted the war-cry of the kindred tribe,—
All shouting as the conqueror reached the goal,
Yet with no mock for those who well had striven.

The full moon was the herald through all Greece,
Proclaiming peace on earth. Soon as she rose,—
Bright, calm, in matron-like maturity,
Full bosomed, making perfect the great heavens,
That, till she came, hung void with all their eyes,—
The shouts of the glad peoples tore the air
With echoes flung from mountains to the seas.
Then armies ceased from leaguer of the cities;
Then gates of cities were thrown open wide,

And all the bolts withdrawn; while the late foe,
Unhelmed, and with his battle-axe in sheath,
Strode in, to generous welcome and glad rites;
While fires of jubilee from all the hills
Declared glad tidings of the general joy,
And grand processions o'er the highways passed,
With choral song and dance and festive flowers,
Seeking the common goal.

        Along the banks
Of Alpheus, see the myriads as they track
The Olympian plains, all garlanded and glad,
Marching to music. Some are driving herds,
Flower-decked for sacrifice. Chariots now, and horse,
Chosen for the contest, famous in all States,—
Spartan, Thessalian, Thracian. With one heart,
Beating with hope of the magnanimous triumph,
The athletes, charioteers, and horsemen march
To Dorian music, which, with fall and swell,
And soft melodious cadences, makes all
Most sensible of joy—all confident
Of the sweet auspices of Peace, assured
By the Olympian Sovran.

        Beautiful still
The plain, the winding river, and the isles
Its loving arms enclose; the sloping banks
Shaded with plane trees; while the pastoral fields
Spread far with verdancy, dotted with white herds,
Whose keepers nestle underneath yon hill,
Mount Cronius.
         In that shade the Stadium rose;
Beyond the opposite slope, the Prytaneum,
Gymnasium, Theatre. The sacred grove,
Altis, in front; most wonderful in the grace,
Blended with grandeur, which invites, yet awes.
And, on the right, behold the Hippodrome,
Half buried in bright clumps of olive and pine.

Ten treasuries—so many States of Greece—
Stood where we see but silent hillocks now;
And each of these, a temple in itself,

Had its grand statues—works of exquisite art,
And gifts and trophies, offerings to the gods.
Central amid the sacred grove, arose
Jove's own especial temple, towering high,
Rich in elaborate art; and, chief o'er all,
That famous statue of the Olympian lord,
Chryselephantine, gold and ivory, wrought
By hands of Phidias, which upon the eyes
Flashed out electric fires, as lighted up
By Jove himself, so that the gazer felt,
And bowed his eyes from looking in his awe,
He gazed upon divinity.

                But, hence!
While we go wander to the Hippodrome,
Seeking Endymion's tomb, which should be found,
As the map shows us, on the northern side,
Near the Aphesis, whence the steeds were sped
In concourse for the goal.

              It *should* be found,
If that the ever-fair Selenæ smiles
Upon her lover's grave, as on those tombs
Which cover thousands for whose living fate
She felt no loving cares.
              To him she came
Nightly, and kissed him to delicious sleep,
On Latmos; and withdrawing at each dawn,
Left him still sleeping, in ecstatic dream,
That made his life but sleep, till night again
Brought new fruition to his dreams of bliss.
And still he sleeps, though nothing of his couch
May we discover; doubtless, with the kiss
Of the fair widow press'd upon his mouth,
And all her pale bright beauties on his breast,
Making his mountain couch as beautiful
As Love had made it happy.
                Let him sleep!

                                (1865, 1870)

VIII

SCENE AT ACTIUM.

These vulgar day-by-day necessities—
Repair of waste in flesh, the satisfaction
Of food and sleep and thirst, and low occasions—
Bring down the immortal from his solar flight,
And leave him wingless.
                              The fine eye no more
(Contracted to the limits of his shadow)
Sees where rise the snow-clad peaks beyond,
Each crowned and glorious with a noonday star,
And wooing onward.
                              Here, as now we rest,
Stretched on a rusted cannon of the Turk,
And busied with our sandwiches and wine,
We half forget the Ambracian gulph below,
Spread glowingly in the sunlight; while, beyond,
The mountains limn themselves in shadowy lines,
Irregular, like battlemented walls
Sun-buried in the sea.
                              We half forget
Those wondrous histories, those swollen events,
Which, 'neath these mountain shadows, on this gulph,
Have made a people's glories and their shame.
Yet here, now near two thousand years ago,
The fate of the ancient world suspended hung,
From rise to set of sun.
                              Here Apollo stood—
So fabled the ancient Poets, who still link'd
(Despite their Pagan worship) deeds of men
With actual will and presence of their Gods—
On his own Actium; and, with quiver charged,
Drove with his arrows far, in shameful flight,
The shameless Roman:[4] by a woman 'slaved,
To loss of Rome and honor.
                              Morning saw
His grand array of ships, great floating towers,
And banner'd myriads, to the slaughter come
As to a festival; and, in midst of all,
The golden barge of the lascivious Queen:[5]
His fate, and her own ruin.

Never before
Had ocean borne upon his billowy breast
Such proud-fraught vessel. Purpling in the sun
Her sails; her thousand bannerets to the breeze,
Each speaking for a kingdom. The great waves
Bounding, as gladdening 'neath the precious burden;
While amorous breezes, won by exquisite odors,
Played round, with rapturous motion of delight,
As sworn to love and service.

But not for *us!*
None after Shakspeare! Let *him* paint the picture.
Here—take the volume: read for us, Melissa.

"The barge she sate in, like a burnished throne,
Burned on the water. The poop was beaten gold;
Purple the sails, and so perfumèd that
The winds were love-sick with them. The oars were silver,
Which to the tune of flutes kept stroke, and made
The water which they beat to follow faster,
As amorous of their strokes. For her own person,
It beggar'd all description. She did lie
In her pavilion—cloth-of-gold of tissue—
O'erpicturing that Venus where we see
The fancy outwork Nature. On each side her
Stood pretty dimpled boys, like smiling Cupids,
With divers-colored fans, whose wind did seem
To glow the delicate cheeks which they did cool.
Her gentlewomen, like the Nerèides,
So many mermaids, tended her in the eyes,
And made their bends adornings. At the helm,
A seeming mermaid steers. The silken tackle
Swells with the touches of those flow'r-soft hands,
That yarely frame the office. From the barge,
A strange invisible perfume hits the sense
Of the adjacent wharves." [6]

Out upon Time!
Who'd rob us of our pictures in the real
But for our Shakspeares, who link hands with Nature,
And rescue from the ravages of seasons
Fruits for their generations.

Still we may see,
If fancy quicken thought into the painter,
The barge of Cleopatra, limn'd in light,
Trim, darting o'er the Ambracian gulph as when
It bore the fate of Antony, and led
Her sixty ships from battle and in flight.
    With morn, how grand the picture!
                                But, ere noon,
Moved by some gay and profligate caprice—
A change of wind perhaps, a jewel's loss,
A damsel's negligence, a feather's fall;
Not by her fears or passions—she spread sail,
Leading her mighty war-ships in her train,
Out of the battle;[7] and the desperate Roman,
Fatuitous, pursued her headlong flight,
To loss of fame and fortune, State and life,
Army and Empire.
                        Terrible the scene
That followed, when the light triremes of Cæsar
Grappled the great hulks of the Egyptian ships,
And flung their flaming javelins at their sails,
And tore their sides with fire.

                                Shakspeare's tale
Lacks not in the catastrophe.
                                Dryden too,
Audacious, following close on Shakspeare's track,
Hath justified his boldness by his merit;
Building his art on that of the great master,
And not in vain.
                        Look to him for the sequel,
The rest of that sad story of defeat,
Despair and Death—the "World Lost for Love;"[8]
Lost, and not well or wisely.
                                Not for Love,
But the insanest passion of the blood,
That, reckless in its lusts, o'ergrows the brain,
Robs manhood of his best securities
In virtue, and makes dull that better reason
Which shapes its arguments by happiest method
To meet the needs of the most noble heart.
    Hark to Ventidius—that fine Roman model—

How with sweet art and proper reverence
He warps the accents of a generous courage,
To win the prostrate hero back to Honor.
   Alas! too late!
                The star that once hath fallen
Knows never again the height's security
In place and lustre it departed from.

Happy for us that have the Poets left us:
Subtle, and grand, and musical, like Shakspeare;
And Dryden, brave and strong, who, in the Drama,
So well asserts his powers—maturer thought
Leading him back, long erring with the vulgar,
To the true walks of Shakspeare and of Nature.

                        (1862, 1870)

IX.
THE LIONS OF MYCENÆ.
  Unwearied, with the memory still in play,
Feeding on grandest histories, we ascend
The site of that Acropolis which still
Frowns o'er the Argolic gulph. Here, at a glance,
Your eye takes in a thousand years of tale,
Drama and poesy. South, behold the bay,
Where Danaus, with his daughters, first made land,
Sailing from Egypt. On its western edge
You see the Lernean pool; and here, below,
Nearing our feet and the old city's walls,
Flows Inachus, the famèd stream. Look forth,
And on the northern margin of the plain,
Mycenæ rises: visible yet the site,
Even from this distance. Let us now retrace
The footsteps of Pausanias, and explore
Those wondrous ruins which Thucydides
Gazed on with reverent awe;—in ruins then,
Though with most evident proofs to show them still
Grandest of all Greek cities. Lo! the Porch,
Which saw processions of the mightiest tribes
That ever made States famous!

               There they rise,
The Lions of Mycenæ—rampant, stern,—

Gigantic triumphs of an elder art
That shames the best of ours;—though Ruin works
Ruthlessly on them, with a mocking smile,
Through lichen and green mosses to persuade
All colors from the rainbow and the sky,
To garnish fondly the gray hurts of Time!

Still stand these famous lions as of yore,
Guardians of dwellings that no more demand
Protection from without. No foe assails
The City of the Atridæ; nor, within,
Clamor those warrior-hosts that once went forth,
Following the King of Men! In vain we seek
The tomb of Agamemnon! Could we find,
We doubtless should behold at dawn of day
The filial shade of his avenging son,
Close tended by the faithful Pylades;
And hear, from out the sepulchre, the cry
Of sorrowful Electra, with her urn!

The tragedy, without a parallel,
Which made this Gate of Lions, and these Courts—
Now shapeless ruins—a dread monument,
Rises to vision as we gaze upon them.
There Clytemnestra comes, the terrible queen,
With horrid hands, still reeking with red gore,—
While yet she pleads for poor humanity,
In fond excuse for that her husband slew
Her daughter, to "appease the winds of Thrace":—
That child, o'er all beloved, Iphigenia,
"For whose dear sake she bore a mother's pains!"

The Lady Macbeth of Mycenæ, she
Had but one human sentiment to plead
To justify her passions in her lust;—
Even as the Scottish woman stayed the stroke
By her own hands, for that the destined victim
"Resembled her own father as he slept!"

The passions sleep at last! The criminals
Lie in their several dungeons of deep earth,
Resolved to dust; and what is living of them,

Gone to their dead account! Another fate
Works on the crumbling Cyclopean walls:
That worst destroyer, Time! As fell his stroke
As that which in his chamber smote the king,
Great Agamemnon!

    That a tale should live,
While temples perish! That a poet's song
Should keep its echoes fresh for all the hills
That could not keep their cities!—should preserve
The fame of those, thrice honored in their lives,
And at their dying, and in mightiest tombs,
While the tombs perish!

    What a moral's this!—
That the mere legend of a blind old man,
A beggar, outcast, wanderer—all in one—
A chaunter by the sea-side to poor sailors,
Weaving his wanton fancies, skein by skein,
So that no man shall need to weave anew,—
That his mere tale, his name and fame should live,
While cities waste away, and temples blasted
Leave bare the mortal greatness with no tomb!

 "*Vixere fortes ante Agamemnona,
Multi*"—and thousands shall live after him,
Thrice honor'd in their living and their dying,
And in grand shrines and gilded sepulchres:
Yet, if they make not interest with the Bard,
Whose songs shall keep the echoes from their tombs,
They have but bartered living for a death,
And place in the promiscuous mausoleum
Of Nothingness—forever and thereafter!

 O shade of blind Mæonides! and thou,
Great master, Æschylus, of horned brow,
Portentous, speaking mightiest mysteries
Of Fate, no less than Passion,—have ye met
The King of Men? and did he veil to ye,
And bid ye welcome as the best of friends,
And makers of the only monuments
That give his deeds to man?

Methinks his feasts,
When ye are guests—and that should be as often
As Agamemnon sups—should ever be
Spread in the Apollo chamber;—Iphigenia
Serving the wine, and sad Electra singing
That song which ever is a song of joy,
Which tells of sorrows over, and the day
At dawning, glorious, after a long night.

(1864, 1870)

---

1. The spring of Castalia is now dedicated to St. John. Over its source a chapel has been erected in his honor. He seems here to be as silent as Apollo.
2. See the "Alcestis," one of the dramas of Euripides.
3. See the beautiful poem of Ford, in his drama of (we believe,) "The Broken Heart," where he describes a contest of music, in the Vale of Tempé, between a musician and a nightingale, in which the bird, defeated, drops down dead on the instrument of the musician.
4. Mark Antony.
5. Cleopatra.
6. Shakspeare's *Antony and Cleopatra*, Act 2, Scene ii.
7. See Virgil's description of the scene in that of the Shield of Æneas.
8. See Dryden's tragedy of *All For Love, or the World Well Lost*, one of the best of his blank verse dramas, after he had renounced what he had long obstinately asserted and ably defended, the propriety and superiority of the rhyming heroic in the tragic or classical drama. In this play, as an avowed imitator of Shakspeare—and Dryden's powers of imitation were wonderful—in respect to vigor of style, and a manly, energetic, and appropriate utterance in simple, direct and proper language, he is not unworthy of his model in those plays of Shakspeare in which he handles the subjects of Roman history. We need not say how little Dryden's genius possessed of the subtlety, spirituality, flexibility of Shakspeare, his melodious varieties and the depth and grandeur of his conceptions. But avoiding all comparison with the great master, the genius of Dryden was very noble, his learning great, and he merits far more consideration from the literary student than is now accorded him. A course of Dryden, after Milton and Shakspeare, would be useful.

UNDATED POEMS

UNTITLED.

This self-complacent Christianity:
　Great God, which garbs itself in form and state,
　And keeps its pious hours, in pride elate,
Yet turns the deaf ear to humanity—

———

Better, ay better, thousand times to be,
　The Pagan, on some Sodomitic shore,
　And take for granted, when the billows roar,
Some unknown God is rising from the sea.

———

Some simple even fond one with a faith,
　Ingenuous, honest; any faith, if true,
　Believed and kept; the Gentile or the Jew,
And we might conquer this our living death,

———

Where we are only to ourselves a fraud,
And nothing to Humanity or God.

———

EPIGRAMS.

1
TERESA'S EYES.

"Teresa's eyes, so brilliant are and black,
That your own fail you at the first attack!"
"Black should they be," a suffering victim spoke,
"If but in mourning for the hearts they broke."

2
CELIA'S BOSOM.

Think not with modesty oppressed,
The gentle Celia hides her breast,

Tis not the heart she would defend
But the sad want of it, my friend.

3
CROSS PURPOSES.

How different from Louisa's tongue, is fair Louisa's eye,
The latter never opes, but forth a thousand arrows fly,
While from the former tinkling thing, though ever on the stretch,
Your ears may carry all the day, but nothing pointed fetch.

4
NELLY'S SEX.

Let not the story I tell ye vex,
    For no one in Gotham disputes it,
Nell never remembers poor Nelly's sex,
    Except when she prostitutes it.

5
ANCIENT DAMSELS.

These ancient damsels, since the world began
Have growled and grumbled at their fortunes still.
They hate the natural sov'reignty of man,
Because he dont subdue them to his will.

6
SHOWING HOW ELLEN'S TEETH MIGHT
BE PATRIOTS.

"True, Ellen's teeth are big, but they might be,
Made quite acceptable to thee and me!"
    "How?" asked his friend, whose ears had just been wrung
By a hoarse ballad which the maid had sung.
    "Would she but use them for the public good,
With proper love for kindred flesh and blood—
With her big teeth bite off her bigger tongue!"

7
CUNNING OF BEAUTY.

Within her breast, more white than snows,
Fair Amaryllis plants the rose;
Not that the flower should fix your eyes,
But the sweet garden where it lies.

8
GOOD EARS.

Meg boasts her ears that catch the farthest sound,
Long in advance of every ear around;—
"Ah!" groans her husband, in his saddest mood,
"Ah!" would that mine were anything but good."

9
ON A LADY WITH RED HAIR.

So coy and cruel was the Lady Jane,
    That in revenge for slighting all his darts,
Cupid, all heedless of her prayer and pain,
    Dyed her soft tresses in her lovers' hearts.

10
BOWS AND KNOTS.

Emmeline boasts two strings to her bow:
    Might I teach her a happier thing—
Then should the thoughtless damsel know
    Better to carry two beaux to her string.

Susan, with luckier judgment led,
    Wisely and silently shapes her lot;
And never with vain delusions fed,
    Soon turns her one beau into a knot.

11
SURFACE VIRTUE.

She eats the fruit without alarm,
Then wipes her mouth—and, where the harm?

12
THE CHASE.

Edgar successful in the chase,
With Susan clasp'd in close embrace,
Repines, and sad with novel pain,
Would rather have the chase again;
Ah! hapless moment of his life,
He can no longer seek his wife.

13

PACUVIUS.

Pacuvius thus lamented to his friend:—
"On the same tree my three wives made their end!"—
His wedded friend had ready sympathy—
"Ah! to my garden pray transplant that tree!"

14

JILTED NED.

Ned sleeps at last, poor Ned who died,
Because defrauded of his Bride.
Fool! had she proved no jilt, her sway,
Had been Ned's death each living day.

15

CHIT-CHAT.

Says Horace to Harry, in talking one day,
"There's a charming young widow just over the way,
With a snug little fortune, a house, and all that;
You have only to walk in and hang up your hat."

"Why yes," replies Harry, "the thing you propose
Is quite to my fancy, as every one knows;
But the fair is so froward, and hard to get at,
I must hang up my *fiddle* instead of my *hat*."

16

BRAVE MEN.

Says Harry to Tom, shooting pistols one day,
    At the heart of the cast-iron figure,
"Why is it the man we are popping at, pray,
    Seems to have no great fear of the trigger?
Give it up? Why the reason's abundantly clear,
    The matter quite easy to settle,
Our friend of the target exhibits no fear—
    Because he's a fellow of *metal*."

17

FAST AND LOOSE.

Young Tibbats would go play at fast and loose,
    And head-long into matrimony run,

And thus, though *haltered fast* in marriage noose,
  'Tis still his grief to find himself *undone.*

18
"FIEL A LA MUERTE."
"Faithful to death!"—'tis what I still have been,
But 'tis your death, and not my own I mean.

19
MY WEAKNESS.
Tis not of woman I complain,
Not that she's fickle, frail and vain,
But of the weakness, heart and will,
Which keeps me bondsman to her still.

20
DEGENERATE DAYS.
I leave this truth for other days to scan,
  Seeing that in ours Nature must have blunder'd,
Of old it took nine tailors to a man
  Now one poor snip can soon achieve a hundred.

21
PEDIGREE.
Jack digging in his garden ground,
Mongst other bones an ass's found;
Treat it, says Dick, with reverent fear,
Your sire, perchance, was buried here.

22
TOM'S OPINION.
Tom holds *me* quite unworthy of *his* thought,
  But such a notion makes me nothing grim,
For, do you see, I all along have taught
  That Tom's best thought was only worthy him.

23
FRIBBLE.
Ah, Fribble's dead! No sighing—
  May the Buzzards spare his bones!
For his having lived, his dying
  In a large degree atones.

24

PHILANTHROPY.

The negro finished with a tail had been,
As fine a monkey as was ever seen;
Philanthropy so labours, tooth and nail,
In the fond effort to restore the tail;
Assured with this, that, in a little time,
The beast will certainly begin to climb;—
He does, but still the farther up he goes,
The more of tail and less of man, he shows;
Philanthropy looks on with rare delight,
To see how well, upon the topmost height,
He ends the play by s—ting on the white.

25

FRAGMENT.

The devil loves church music! I have seen him,
  Sit a whole Sabbath in a damsel's eye,
While she, with fan uplifted, strove to screen him,
  From those who strove as busily to spy;
And all the while her lips, as if to wean him,
  From his snug home, unfold in melody,
With how devout an accent, and sweet quiver,
  As if entreating still—'Good Lord Deliver.'

26

THE CERTAIN EXECUTIONER.

"Your uncle" said you?—The assassin,
  Never physic'd me when ill,—
I never took his medicine,—
  Behold the proof—I'm living still.

27

YOUNG HOPEFUL, M.D.

While o'er Manhattan's isle the plague impends,
  Young Hopeful seeks the scene of misery;
"Many's the death-bed scenes," he tells his friend,
  "This dreary summer, I expect to see."—
"You are too sanguine," cried the friendly few,
  "You look for too much business—that you do!"

28
POLITICIAN.

A shallow mind, a worthless heart,
Concealed and taught by every art—
A soul without a single aim,
Worthy an honorable name—
A spirit prone to petty toils,
And still supreme in tavern broils—
That frets and fever still to be
The vulgar herd's idolatry—
To whom a shout is highest fame,
A vote the thing of fondest aim—
A whiskey speech, where reason reels,
And grammar paces on her heels—
The best performance of the mind
That, dark itself, must others blind—
And yet he bears a human shape,
And has no tail, and is no ape.

29
PROOF OF SENATORIAL WISDOM.

A maxim owned without demur—
  Who speaks but little, wise we call;
How very wise our Senator,—
  He's never heard to speak at all.

30
WISDOM.

Says my teacher, "My Son would you think it
Grass grows not where liquor shall sprink it.
  It will instantly die.—"
  But at once I reply,
Its for that very reason I drink it.

What a pinprick of terror to think on
Of perdition the desolate brink on,
  To hear that one's throat,
  May yield food for a goat—
Oh! brothers, heark wisdom and drink on.

Appendix

A SECOND HARVEST

Of the fifteen new poems that follow, twelve had not been collected in any form, and eight appear under Simms's name for the first time. Two address Simms's Irish heritage. "Wooing" is an addition to the humorous verse, an area reviewers have found congenial, and unusual in Simms's day. "The Dying Child" and "Wail" are additions to the body of Simms's intensely personal lyrics, another grouping reviewers have found effective. Two come out of the war experience, and two deal with its aftermath.

SONNET TO THE PAST.

Thy presence hath been grateful—thou hast brought
  Toil and privation, which have tutor'd me,
  To strength and fit endurance;—set me free
From vainest fancies,—and most kindly wrought
On the affections which had else run wild,
  Untrained by meet denial of their thirst.
  What though I held thee yesterday accurst,—
Believe me not the vain and erring child
Still to remember chastening by its pain,
  More than its uses;—True, that to my home
  Thou hast brought grief, and often left it gloom;—
But that I do not of thy deeds complain,
Is proof that they have done no bootless part—
Have hurt my house, perchance, but help'd my heart.

(1825, 1849)

SUMMER, *WRITTEN IN THE CHOCTAW NATION.*

Now, in her glowing livery of flow'rs,
New sprung, and fresh created from the bow'rs,
Where Spring pours forth her horn of fruits and teems
The valley with its flowing rills and streams,
Comes forth the laughing eye, flush'd cheek and streaming hair,
That curls and wantons o'er a neck as fair,
Of gay and revelling summer. At her glance
Winter recedes, and from his icy trance
New freed, bounds forth the torrent and asserts his sway
O'er the old furrows of a former day.
The mountain wears no more the brow of age,
And nature leaves her wither'd hermitage,
To live 'midst fruits and flow'rs and freshen'd stems,
And kindles at the streamlet's moon-made gems,
Whose banks support a grassy fringe of green,
Reflected in the pebbly bed, that's seen
Rippling in smiles, and whispering to the trees,
Thro' which steals gay and gladly, the young breeze,
Playfully murmuring like a swarm of bees.
The lizard steals upon the freshest flow'rs,
As death gives shadow to our sunniest hours;
And the gay butterfly on varied wing,
Pursues the insect that it cannot sting:
And all is life and fragrance; let us fly,
My gentle steed, to that far distant sky,
Where nature seems more lovely, as more dear,
The lowliest flower that I meet with there!
Away, my stag-eyed deserter, we'll greet
The home of childhood, made by change more sweet!
Away, thou sluggard! I would hail again
The cheek of pleasure, made more dear by pain!
Swifter than summer's pinions let us flee,
Where much shall then be thine, and more for me—
My steed, the sun grows fervid, and the day
Is long—we can o'ercome much space, away, away!

(1827)

SONG OF THE IRISH PATRIOT.

i

Patriot, weep not, the chain that has bound her,
  The country so dear to thy heart and thy pride—
The shackles which tyrants have woven around her
  The strong arm of freedom shall shortly divide.
Weep not, the hour is gone forever,
  When years had been proper for brave men to shed;
And now is the time for achievement or never
  When the spirit calls, is the voice of the dead.

ii

Your Currans, your Emmets indignantly starting,
  Now burst through the cearments of death and arise;
To the vigor of Freedom and Erin imparting
  A spirit, that Tyranny proudly defies.
Can theirs sons in their servitude shamefully slumber
  Is the spirit that glowed in their fathers no more
No, Liberty, no—for they champions outnumber,
  And will die for each grain of the sand on thy shore.

iii

Let the shout of the kindred soul, cordially flowing
  Ascend with the mighty who've sworn to be free;
And thy sympathies grateful, to freemen bestowing
  America, waft o'er the dark rolling sea.
And in long years to come when with freedom attended
  The green-shore of Erin shall smile on the sight
Her prayer with the winds and the waves will be blended
  That thou may'st for ever be first for the right.

(1828)

ADDRESS *WRITTEN FOR THE BENEFIT*
OF THE "ASSOCIATION OF THE FRIENDS
OF IRELAND IN CHARLESTON."

Where is that sacred Harp, whose anthem broke
The Freeman's slumbers, and the Tyrant's yoke?—
Those living sounds, whose wild and matchless pow'r,
Hailed Freedom's birth, in Nature's morning hour:—
Fill'd with unearthly freshness, all the breeze
That gaily bore it, o'er unnumber'd seas;
And, where God's image, on his creatures, stood,
Bore it in conquest—worshipped it in blood!

To Greece it came—yet not with Greece it dwelt,
But fled afar, when Greece no longer felt;—
Barbarians won the guerdon of the free,
And savage nations bow'd to Liberty!
The Gaul received it—the wild Hun was bless'd,
The savage Tartar hail'd the friendless guest,
And barren altars, proved, how ill bestow'd,
Upon the brute, the presence of the God!

To other shores, that sacred presence came
And lands unknown, at last received a name—
Bow'd with strange fervor, to her witching lore,
And broke the chains, that never pain'd before!
The mountains roll'd her anthems to the vale,
Which caught the sound, and murmured back the tale;
The grey ribb'd rocks, shook off their apathy,
Caught the high spell, and shouted Liberty!

One little island in the deep appeared,
And there, awhile, her shamrock shrine, she rear'd:
Rich was her homage in that favour'd spot—
And long remember'd, when herself forgot!
When Brian's harp was dumb, and Brian's sword
No more obey'd—no longer owned a lord—
And Connaught fell, and Ulster lived no more—
And sorrow had a voice thro' all that shore!
Ay she forgot—how much adored she stood,
Her sacred garments dyed in Erin's blood,
Where, 'neath her car, delighted votaries knelt,

And, in their triumph, scorn'd the death they felt—
Proud to be martyrs, at her shrine, alone—
Witness her Emmet, Fitzgerald, and Tone!

Through trackless years of gloom, that people came,
And bow'd in silence, for they bow'd in shame!
No bannered crowd, nor consecrate array,
Gave her high worship to the eye of day!
A stolen pray'r, a shrinking sacrifice,
That trembled, as it saw the smoke arise,
Lest other eyes, less honest than the few,
Should idly look, and chance to see it too!
Their Temple's ruins heard alone their prayer,
The shrine was prostrate, and the altar bare—
The *Holy* overthrown, the spirit gone—
Silence and Ruin—dwellers there alone!
Fierce War and ruthless Tyranny had spread
Their bristling steel and torches blazing red—
Whence Freedom flew, assiduous to explore
Some unpolluted shrine on some fair shore—
And her true followers, still unsubdued,
Watch'd her high flight, and where she fled, pursued,
And when she came, America, to thee,
Stood in the cause of man—and perished for the free!

Here have their children worship'd at the shrine,
Our fathers built—your altar-piece, and mine!
Their arm uprear'd its columns, and their hands,
Chosen by Freedom, from an hundred lands,
Raised up this common temple, not to be
For any special sect, but for the free!
Their blood was pour'd upon it—and their tears,
Wrung forth by toil and danger were their prayers
For this—for these high favors, do we claim
The voice of gratitude, and honest fame,
Nor these alone! Americans! We dare
Point to the chains, our father's people wear,
Bid you review their deeds in Freedom's cause,
And ask for wrong'd Hibernia, equal laws!

A cry of anguish comes across the main,
And shall we hear that cry and hear in vain!

Shall we refuse *our sympathies* to those
Who met, and bled, and battled with our foes!
Shall we not speak, while all the world shall hear,
How nobly freemen think, how bravely dare—
When scepter'd tyranny, grown old in crime,
Strikes at the tree of Freedom in its prime,
Shall we look bravely on while brave men bleed,
And barely start with horror at the deed,
When one united voice would quell the wrong,
Strengthen the weak, and dissipate the strong.

The flame is spreading far; the rights of man,
Once felt and known, shall burst away each ban,
What shall restrain, what madness man the breach,
When Freedom's voice, is in O'Connell's speech—
And all the gathering spirits of the past,
Rush, like assembled cataracts, at last!
When Erin claims her liberty, nor kneels
But speaks in actions what her spirit feels;
And men are roused by oft repeated wrong
To be themselves, and battle with the strong.

Send forth thy voice, America! The sound,
Born for the world, the world shall hear around,
Men shall arise as when a Volcan speaks,
And feel the hot blood rushing thro' their cheeks,
While startled Albion, bending o'er the sea;
Herself shall say—RISE IRELAND! BE FREE!

(1829)

SONG IN MARCH.

i

Now are the winds about us in their glee,
Tossing the slender tree;
Whirling the sands about his furious car,
March cometh from afar;
Breaks the seal'd magic of old Winter's dreams,
And rends his glassy streams;

Chafing with potent airs, he fiercely takes
Their fetters from the lakes,
And, with a power, by Queenly Spring supplied,
Wakes the slumbering tide.

ii

With a wild love, he seeks young Summer's charms,
And clasps her to his arms;
Lifting his shield between, he drives away
Old Winter from his prey;—
The ancient tyrant whom he boldly braves,
Goes howling to his caves;
And, to his northern land compelled to fly,
Yields up the victory;
Melted are all his bands, o'erthrown his tow'rs,
And March comes, bringing flow'rs.

(1832, 1840, 1846)

THERE'S A GORGEOUS GLOW ON EARTH.

i

There's a gorgeous glow on earth,
    In the valley, on the grove;
'Tis a night to wander forth,
    With a song of truest love:
Thou shalt speak for me the flame
    Burning in my bosom now—
Thou shalt give my love its name,
    Help my lip to breathe its vow,—
Thou shalt bear her praises far,
Thou, my gentle, sweet guitar.

ii

As I murmur, sing for me—
    Tell her that my spirit roves,
Ever sleepless, never free,
    Sighing through her garden groves,
That, beneath her lattice now,
    With a song to feeling dear,

I am breathing many a vow
  Of a true love for her ear;—
Send thy tender plaint afar,
Tell her all, my sweet guitar.

      iii

Tell her that the heart which pleads,
  Hopeful, nor unworthy quite,
May be won by glorious deeds,
  Guided by her eyes of light—
That, if she but once approve,
  It will seek the paths of fame;
Let her eyes but look in love,
  It will win a deathless name—
Let no wanton discord mar,
Speak her sweetly, sweet guitar.

(1840)

FRIENDSHIP.

Though wrong'd not harsh my language. Love is fond
  Though pain'd,—and rather to his injury bends,
  Than chooses to make shipwreck of his friends
By stormy clamors. He hath nought beyond
  For consolation, if that these be lost,—
  And rather will he hear of fortune crost
Plans baffled, hopes denied,—than take a tone
  Resentful,—with a keen and quick reply
  To hasty passion, and the angry eye,
Such as by noblest natures may be shown,
  When the mood vexes.— Friendship is a seed,
  Needs nursing,— You must keep it free from weed,
Nor if the tree hath sometimes bitter fruit
Must you for this lay axe unto its root.

(1842)

BEAUTY IN SHADE.

I mark a sadness on thy brow,
Not meet in one so young as thou,
And as I hear thy accents now,
    There's sorrow in each tone;
And hast thou felt the heavy chain,
The venom of love's shaft—the pain—
The dream that wakes to weep in vain,
    The life forever lone?

Like some rich waters pour'd to waste,
With few to seek, with none to taste,
Do thy heart's fountains vainly haste
    To desert sands and seas?
Oh! Flow'rs thy hope in friendless sky,
Beneath no fond and feeling eye,—
Or like some harp that hangs on high
    Among forgotten trees.

                                        (1842)

WOOING; BY A BASHFUL GENTLEMAN.

Hear the tale of a boyish heart,
    Hear and be wise ere ye go to woo;
Ever with boldness play your part,
    Nor weakly sigh, nor timidly sue;—
    Hear the tale of a boyish heart:
As I drew near to my lady's bow'r,
I sung her a song that might win a flower;
Song so gentle and sweet to hear,
It had suited well in a fairy's ear;
Lowly and soft at first it rose,
And touching the sigh at its dying close.

Hear the tale of a boyish heart,—
    Vainly I sung to my lady's ear;
A minstrel came with a bolder art,
    And he sung in an accent loud and clear;—

He sung not the tale of a boyish heart;
His spirit was high, and his soul was proud,
His song was eager, and wild, and loud,—
And, O! methought, how worse than vain,
The chorus strong and the swelling strain,—
Song so stormy and wild to hear,
Will never suit for a lady's ear.

Hear the tale of a boyish heart—
   Never you sing in your lady's ear,
As if your soul were about to part,
   And you stood on the edge of a mortal fear—
    Tell her the tale of a manly heart!—
A maid is a woman and not a flower,
And she loves, in her lover, the proofs of power—
His eye must be ardent, his spirit high—
For her the soft note and the tender sign
She may be timid and tremulous still,
But he must be one who must have his will.

(1845)

THE DYING CHILD.

i

Dim at this solemn hour,
Thick midnight round us,
Dimly the taper burns
Low in the socket:—
But even more dimly yet,
Fleeting and flick'ring fast,
Is the sweet life of her,
Whom we have cherish'd.

ii

Father, relight the lamp,
Take not the sacred oil,
From the pure fountain
Of life thou hast given us;—
Leave us not, blessed Father,

To our own darkness,
Darkness most sad and dreary
When thou hast taken from us,
That young flame that, to our hearts,
Brought the first sunlight.

      iii

Not to our pride of heart,
Vain hope or vain glory,
But in thy mercy only,
Yield to our prayer.
To our tears, to our weakness,
To the sad love that crouches
Dumb o'er the cradle,—
Humbled in heart and lonely;—
Give to the wretched mother,
She who has borne the pain,
Oh! Sire, still let her keep,
The dear gift that came with it.

                      (1847)

BALLAD — "YES, BUILD YOUR WALLS."

      i

Yes, build your walls of stone or sand,
    But know, when all is builded—then,
The proper breastworks of the land
    Are in a race of freeborn men!—
The sons of sires, who knew, in life,
    That, of all virtues, Manhood, first,
Still nursing peace, yet arms for strife,
    And braves, for liberty, the worst!

      ii

What grand examples have been ours!—
    Oh! Sons of Moultrie, Marion,—call
From mansions of the past, the powers,
    That pluck'd ye from the despot's thrall!
Do Sumter, Rutledge, Gadsden, live?—

Oh! For your City by the Sea,
They gladly gave, what men could give,
   Blood, life and toil, and made it free!

     iii
The grand inheritance, in trust,
   For children of your loins, must know,
No taint of shame, no loss by lust,
   Your own, or of the usurping foe!
Let not your sons, in future days,
   The children now that bear your name,
Exulting, in a grandsire's praise,
   Droop o'er a father's grave in shame!

                             (1863)

SACRIFICE FOR LIBERTY.

'Tis evermore the same! The usurper's need,
Demands the brave shall fall—the noble bleed;
Yet, tutor'd by the examples which they leave,
The living should avenge them, and not grieve!
Their blood prepares the soil for Freedom's tree,
And hallows all that's dear to Liberty.
Honor and great renown attend the brave,
Who die their homes and fatherland to save;
Their children flourish in an honored name,
And triumph nobly in a father's fame.
But keen the pang when woman falls the prey,
To passions fouler than the wish to slay,
And, hapless gain to freedom when she dies,
Stricken on the hearth, the last, best sacrifice!

                             (1863)

WAIL.

i

Oh! ye shrubs and flowers,
   Golden bells and trailing vines,
   Purple-eyed and orange twines,
Wandering wild o'er sunny bowers
Where the bird-song made the hours,
   One long joy from dawn to dark;—
Never more unfold your buds!—
   Well may ye go weep! go weep!—
Weep in show'rs—weep in floods—
   She that loved ye, as the lark
Loves the skies at morning peep,—
   Soaring upward, as to mark
   Where the night and morning meet;—
She is lying fast asleep,—
In a slumber dread and deep!—
Oh! That dreary, dreary sleep,
Terrible, beautiful, dreary, sweet!—
As a star that has fallen from happy skies,
And downward prone, on the green bank dies,
But with ever a light in its fading eyes,—
Such a beautiful light,—
That earth and death cannot wholly blight,
And that hallows the bank where the lost one lies!

ii

Oh! that dread and beautiful sleep—
While the bells are tolling with tones so deep,
And the bird-song's hush'd, and the blossoms weep!
Ever since yesternight,
She saw the last of light,
And the last white rose that the garden bore,
Sleeps on her bosom forevermore!

iii

Oh! pleasaunce of walks and bowers,
   Green creepers and purple twines,
And bells of blue which told the hours,
As they sped in light through the mazy lines,

Fringed with the sunset flowers,
And each innocent bloom that, from smiling, shines
   As if wooing a place in the maiden's hair,
And speaking with look that says "We are fair,"
And more—"We are pure—come ye, and be
The purity, bright and bloom, ye see!"—
Ah! me! Ah! me!—
Ye bloom no more for her who sleeps,
   And ye bloom no more for me!—
The soul of the eye that weeps, and weeps,
   Hath an eye no more for ye!—
Yet, though she is gone,
And I am alone,
Yet bloom ye on!—yet bloom ye on!—
Bloom for the brighter and happier eyes,
That have suffered no blight, no dread surprise,
   And know not the woe,
   Which they soon shall know,
That the bright star flies,
From the sweetest skies,—
That the beautiful dies! The beautiful dies!

                       (1863)

VOICES OF SOLITUDE.

   The heart that never had a taste of grief,
Hears never a voice of solitude. She sings
For sorrow and thought, with song beyond belief,
Perchance, by sense of desolation taught.

   The comforter lies buried in the oak,
The solace in the brook. The meadow heaves
With sympathy; and, in shadows of the wood,
Lurk sweet reflective aspects, that persuade,
Through breathings, that might be of summer winds,
Were a leaf shaken!

   In lone hills and dells,
Methinks there lurks a tribe of tiny elves,

That, with a proper ministry, unseen,
Beguile the wanderer to forgetfulness;
And solitude, the mother of them all,
Brooding in depth of shadow, sends them forth
Each with becoming office, for the heart,
Too long a trembler, in a fearful watch
With Dread and Death, and at the couch of Pain,
Knowing to suffer only—not to save!

   Solicitous, though silent, she hath spells
So to recal the perished hours and forms,
That never to our hearts brought solitude,
Until they perished.

     To my spirit's sense,
Lone, wandering through these groves, arise the shades
Of many who, with fingers clasped in mine,
Went, singing of the sunshine, 'till each leaf
Took on a twiring motion, as in dance
To music, in whose every string a heart
Grew to vibration; and within mine own
Waken'd all thoughts to singing.

     Once again,
Methinks, I have them back; all living still,
In absence of the living! "*Do* they live?"
I murmur, with a doubt uprising still,
Even though I feel each presence of the Past
About me, and hear, singing in mine ears,
The dear sweet music of the first love, making
Its music for itself; for the first time
Beholding the glory in the sky,
Bloom in the flower, and fragrance in the breeze,
Down on the peach, and, in every fancy
Wings wrought in looms of rainbows.

    We are far
From the dear homes that knew them, where, so long
It needed not the reassuring thought,
That I am still in the beloved embrace,
With all her dear, sweet music in mine ears,
With all her brooding charms before mine eyes,

And with a finger's touch receiving thrill,
As from the subtle fluid of the cloud!

Those homes are far away—the glorious plains
That nursed my hope, from fond conceptions fresh,
To the fruition of a bliss, whose flight
Was winged with fire, and found relief in tears—
Themselves a rapture—and mine eye, perchance,
Shall look upon their glad vintages no more,
That gave me wine in roses, songs on wings,
And beauty and bliss in common bread and meat!

Alas! That I should wander, when the voice,
Through thousand tracts and realms of solitude,
Still follows, and with ever-during prayer,
Implores me back to gardens, where the blooms
Still make the glory for the waste, and crown
The silence with a starry canopy,
Whose birds sing wanton of a blest condition,
That fears no future, suffers from no change,
While the free will, no more a wanderer,
Anchors with faith, and knows for once content.
Where am I? Wherefore wander, when these voices
Entreat me to the folding up of wings,
And the realization of a bliss
Which leaves the Ideal to a sad despair?

Deep wastes surround me where the Choctaw roves,
And the wolf howls, along the untrodden way.
Are these the fit exemplars for a life
That took its lesson in Italian groves,
By classic fountains, under skies of Hellas,
And from the clear, deep voices of the Muse,
Whose pipes were of Apollo? Shall this realm
Of barrenness compensate for the lyres
Of those, who, full a thousand years ago,
Sate on Pierian summits, and taught songs
That built grand temples to the gods, on heights
Made sacred to all ages by their shrines?
And shall there be a power in any song
For these grand solitudes, which shall summon Pan
To teach the hidden secrets of his pipe

To the wild hunters of this wilder realm,
Making them ministers in those holier arts,
That win the way to peace through melody?

   I know not! Not for me the office set
To shape the moral of the nomad tribes,
That here have range most ample, but no home—
And yet, even here, that inner sense of soul,
So taught by ancient song, divines the true,
And feels the way to every dear possession
As certain as if memory were at fault,
In record of her losses.

     They are here,
With leaf and breeze at ministry; gray shades,
And giant trees, and colors that, like words,
Read to me from the lichen of the rock,
In lines of red and orange, till, methinks,
The voices grow to audible speech of love,
And what is only a soul consciousness
Asserts itself in meaning to the ear,
Quickened by each emotion of the Past
To a new life in Hope.

   Yes, they are here,
Sweet presences of love, the gay, the good,
Graceful and ever tender, in the shrub,
That bends towards me, like a nymph of summer,
And waves me with a palm branch in her hand.
They come in groups, in troops, and through the forest,
Send song with fragrance, blessing every sense
That once had birth in rapture! They are here,
The heart that loved them, and must ever love,
Pursuing as their own.

    'Tis no solitude,
Where common life is voiceless, that wakes love,
With all her summer voices of gay birds,
Happy with wings, and mated in their flight,
Through gardens of the tropics, where the bloom
Makes still the being.

'Tis solitude,
That memory wakens, with her scriptural tongue
Telling of what we did at Easter-tide,
By that sweet murmuring river near the sea,
Where first I sang my ballad from the heart
Seeking another's; trembling like the seeker,
For that she felt that she alone was sought.

What then was said, what sung—what murmured only,
Having a fate in it—precious as a blessing
Which yet enshrines a fate.

So memory takes,
Tutored by solitude to be the seer,
Prophetic virtue on her tongue of tears,
And what is past of the delicious hours
Grows to be present, shorn of every aspect
That might make memory fearful.

With her smiles
She sweetens sadness, and, along the waste
Pours her unwasted sunshine.

Sudden, the way
Grows bright before me.
Blue the arching sky
Springs from each hoary tree-top.
Soft, the smile,
Diffused, as from the opening porch of heaven,
Streams in upon the waste, with flowery tints
That carpet earth with beauty, flinging fresh wreaths
Of loveliness, in grace, o'er withered stems,
Which cover up decay, and on their brows,
Plants with a diadem, made up of stars,
That care that sorrows in their streaming moss.

Sweet glory, and the rich delight of love
Glow in each aspect, that in sterile realm
Hath found a bosom, profligate in wealth,
In which to plant the rose and rear the bloom!
And, what a sudden flood of merriment,
Discourseth that one bird, who from the bush,

Leaps out with swift gyrations, whirl on whirl,
Still caroling wildly with a clarion throat,
As Love, in very dawning of its day,
Telling my heart of all those gleeful hours,
When boyhood scarce knew heavier toil or task
Than just to sing and lose itself in play.

(1866)

THE COMING CHANGE.

Still Winter howls, but, in his cry,
  A plaining wail declares his fate;
He sees a sign in earth and sky,—
    He hears a tiny voice, elate,
    With hope for Spring a better state.

He dreads the songs that, from the earth,
  With thousand numerous voices rise;
They tell him of a coming birth,—
    An eye that blooms, a wing that flies,
    And hosts, that all his powers despise.

Ay, Spring at hand, with all her flowers,
  Her sunny blooms, her genial rays,
Sufficient to o'erthrow his powers;
    In very songs, in idlest plays,
    To shake the throne from which he sways.

The moonlight creeps from plain to grove,—
  The green to silver turns, and, soon,
The bird of Spring, made free to love,
    As grateful for Love's generous boon,
    Pours out, on midnight air, his tune.

The song finds echoes for the heart,
  But moves us not, like him, to sing;
For we have seen our hopes depart,
    Our moonlight, with our dreams, take wing,
    And leave no promise of our Spring.

Yet glorious memories still we keep,
   Of seasons that our souls have known;
These lift us up, though still we weep,
   And though the flowers they brought are gone,
   The pure sweet scent remains our own!

Ay, grateful memories yet are ours,
   The pride, the worth, the virtuous fame;
More precious than all blooms of flowers—
   The souls that Fate could never tame,
   The memories grand that know not shame.

Shall these not bring, in other years,
   The freshness of a Spring that glows
Triumphant through long terms of tears?
   Shall not our homes, made free of foes,
   Even as the desert, bring the rose?

Even for our hearts, as for our skies,
   I hear a voice of coming Spring;
The blight to other regions flies;—
   Our bird shall once more find his wing,
   And songs of sweet deliverance sing.

Even from the graves of buried years,
   The shrines of glorious actions gone,
Prophetic strains now fill mine ears,
   That tell of tyrannies o'erthrown,
   The felon foile'd, the Despot down.

God's works of grand revenges, rise,
   In his own seasons, sure as these,
That now with beauty crown our skies,
   Make fruitful earth, and, with the breeze,
   Bring blessings o'er a thousand seas.

(1867)

Explanatory and Textual Notes

Abbreviations Cited in Explanatory
and Textual Notes

For complete publication data and information on where to find the nineteenth-century periodicals cited in the Explanatory and Textual Notes, see James E. Kibler, *Pseudonymous Publications of William Gilmore Simms* (Athens: University of Georgia Press, 1976), pp. 15–29.

ARCHIVAL SOURCES

Scrapbooks A–H
Simms kept these eight large scrapbooks lettered A through H as a collection of his writing. Here he pasted more than seven hundred signed, unsigned, or pseudonymously published poems clipped from various periodicals, as well as numerous manuscript copies. These scrapbooks are a part of the Charles Carroll Simms Collection in the Manuscripts Division of the South Caroliniana Library, University of South Carolina. For a description, see James E. Kibler, *The Poetry of William Gilmore Simms* (Columbia, S.C.: Southern Studies Program, 1979), pp. 461–62.

Don Carlos Manuscript
Simms's manuscript of his unfinished drama. On the verso of the sheets, Simms pasted clippings of his poems from 1841 on. This document is also in the Charles Carroll Simms Collection, cited above.

Personal and Literary Memorials
A ledger in the Charles Carroll Simms Collection containing manuscript poems and clippings in the manner of the scrapbooks.

Manuscript Poetry Box
A file box in the Charles Carroll Simms Collection containing various manuscript poems.

Printed Poetry Box
A file box in the Charles Carroll Simms Collection containing clippings of poems from various periodicals.

PUBLISHED WORKS BY SIMMS

Poems (1827)
Lyrical and Other Poems. Charleston: Ellis & Neufville. 1827. The volume was in press by September 1826.

Early Lays (1827)
Early Lays. Charleston: A. E. Miller, 1827.

Vision of Cortes (1829)
The Vision of Cortes, Cain, and Other Poems. Charleston: James S. Burges, 1829.

Atalantis (1832)
Atalantis: A Story of the Sea. In Three Parts. New York: J. & J. Harper, 1832.

Book of My Lady (1833)
The Book of My Lady. A Melange. Philadelphia: Key & Biddle, 1833.

Guy Rivers (1834)
Guy Rivers: A Tale of Georgia. New York: Harper, 1834.

The Yemassee (1835)
The Yemassee. A Romance of Carolina. New York: Harper, 1835.

Southern Passages (1839)
Southern Passages and Pictures. New York: George Adlard, 1839. The volume was actually published by December 1838.

Donna Florida (1843)
Donna Florida. A Tale. Charleston: Burges & James, 1843.

Grouped Thoughts (1845)
Grouped Thoughts and Scattered Fancies. A Collection of Sonnets. Richmond, Va.: William Macfarlane, 1845.

Areytos (1846)
Areytos: Or, Songs of the South. Charleston: John Russell, 1846.

Atalantis (1848)
Atalantis; A Story of the Sea. Philadelphia: Carey & Hart, 1848. The volume did not actually appear until 1849.

Cassique of Accabee (1849)
The Cassique of Accabee. A Tale of Ashley River. With Other Pieces. Charleston: John Russell, 1849.

Father Abbot (1849)
Father Abbot, or, The Home Tourist. Charleston: Miller & Browne, 1849.

Sabbath Lyrics (1849)
Sabbath Lyrics; or, Songs From Scripture. Charleston: Walker and James, 1849.

The City of the Silent (1850)
The City of the Silent. A Poem. Charleston: Walker & James, 1850. The volume did not actually appear until 1851.

Egeria (1853)
Egeria: or, Voices of Thought and Counsel, for the Woods and Wayside. Philadelphia: E. H. Butler, 1853.

Poems (1853)
Poems Descriptive, Dramatic, Legendary and Contemplative. 2 vols. Charleston: John Russell, 1853. It is understood that vol. 2 is referred to unless otherwise signified. The volumes did not actually appear until 1854.

The Forayers (1855)
The Forayers or the Raid of the Dog-Days. New York: Redfield, 1855.

Eutaw (1856)
Eutaw: A Sequel to The Forayers. New York: Redfield, 1856.

The Cassique of Kiawah (1859)
The Cassique of Kiawah. A Colonial Romance. New York: Redfield, 1859.

Areytos (1860)
Simms's Poems Areytos or Songs and Ballads of the South with Other Poems. Charleston: Russell & Jones, 1860.

Letters, vols. 1–6
The Letters of William Gilmore Simms. Edited by Mary C. Simms Oliphant et al. Columbia: University of South Carolina Press, 1952–82.

Explanatory and Textual Notes

SONNET — TO MY BOOKS.

Simms reported that he published verses in the local Charleston papers at the age of fifteen and was a regular contributor by sixteen (*Letters,* 1:161, 285; 2:221). Although "Sonnet" is probably not Simms's first published poem, it is his first proved one. Written at the age of sixteen, it appeared in the *Charleston City Gazette,* 20 March 1823, under the proved pseudonym "16."

As one might expect of the work of so young an author, the poem is somewhat derivative, showing the influence of Shakespeare both in theme and in verbal echoes in the couplet, and of Keats's "On First Looking into Chapman's Homer" in subject matter and the way in which the simile is used in the sestet. The influence of Keats is in itself significant because it is the first known instance of influence in America, predating by six years the English poet's so-called "discovery" in America at Harvard, as related in Hyder Rollins, *Keats' Reputation in America* (Cambridge, Mass.: Harvard University Press, 1946). There is, however, freshness in the imagery throughout. Books, as "chaste" creators, father the spiritual side of man, an image which the poet then elaborates upon by saying he will likewise "foster with a filial care" the "pleasures" and "scenes" of such books which recreate the past for their readers, implying that he will likewise become a foster parent of such scenes. If so, this first known published poem is also his earliest announcement of his future career as fictional historian. The "foster-filial" image suggests, considering his own father's abandonment of him in 1808, that books have taken the place of parents. The first line thus becomes: Books, as "chaste creators" of his "youthful mind" have been his spiritual parents. Father and foster-father images are among the commonest images in both his poetry and fiction. Here is an early instance of his use of a concern in his own life as the raw material from which he creates art, a situation which was to be the case throughout his career.

One of the work's most significant aspects is its revelation that Simms was already devoted to antiquarian history at this early age, an interest which would remain strong throughout his life. Here, too, is a major theme—that even though "nations fade," the written record through high art is of "endless date"—an idea expressed throughout his career to his last poem, in which he similarly states that though cities and temples perish, a poet's song endures. This, of course, is the venerable old theme of *Ars longa.*

The work also serves as a period piece reflecting the new interest in things classical. Greek Revivalism would soon be in vogue in both art and architecture in the South.

"Sonnet" exists in only one version and is printed here under Simms's name for the first time. One emendation has been made:

3. your's] yours

9. Pompeii: Identified in 1763 after excavations were begun in 1748. The discovery of this city was an important factor in stimulating a renewed interest in the antique and is thus a topically significant as well as an artistically effective, appropriate image.

THE EVENING BREEZE.

The poem's speaker is an enchanted sea breeze luring the listener to a magic realm made beautiful through imagery, but one that would most certainly destroy the mortal. The "Battery" of the subtitle is the promenade at the tip of the peninsula city of Charleston, overlooking the harbor and the Atlantic Ocean beyond. As a native of Charleston, the poet always had a strong affinity for the sea and often used it for subject matter and imagery. At an early age he wrote that the ocean, of all the objects of nature, affected his imagination most powerfully. He longed to voyage alone beyond sight of land in order to commune "as with a mysterious being." Such was its powerful effect upon him throughout his career.

This lyric was published three times before becoming a part of Simms's fanciful verse drama *Atalantis:* first in the *Charleston Courier,* 26 May 1824, then in his *Poems* (1827), pp. 89–90, and finally in the *Charleston City Gazette,* 12 May 1830. It was heavily revised in both the 1832 and 1848 editions of *Atalantis.* The 1848 version has much to recommend it, but the text chosen for printing here is the original 1824 *Courier* poem with two emendations taken from the 1827 *Poems* text:

  5. breathed] breath'd
  23. taste] taste of

OH! SWEET GUITAR.

Published when Simms was eighteen, this youthful lyric is an example of Simms's musical poetry in the manner of the Cavaliers, an important group of poems in a highly varied canon. The poem's musicality exhibits one of the real strengths of early Southern poetry, in fact, the chief characteristic by which it is traditionally distinguished, thereby inviting comparison to the works of such Southern lyricists as Pinkney, Wilde, Cooke, Chivers, Poe, and Lanier. In keeping with Simms's Celtic heritage, there are affinities with Thomas Moore's *Irish Melodies.* Simms spoke highly of Moore throughout his career.

This poem was published three times: *Charleston Courier,* 9 October 1824; *Early Lays* (1827), pp. 90–91; and *Magnolia* 1 (May 1840): 264. The *Magnolia* version is expanded, thereby losing some of the lyrical beauty of the original. The text printed here, therefore, is the 1824 *Courier* version with one emendation:

  4. lovely] lonely (1827 reading, correction of a typesetting error)

ADDRESS FOR NEW-YEAR'S DAY.

This occasional poem was an unsuccessful entry for the *Charleston Courier* New Year's poetry prize of 1 January 1825. Its opening description is a humorous treatment of the Romantic's starving-artist cliché, which places the poet (in the manner of Thomas Chatterton) in a drab room which he heats by burning the legs of his cot. Here the young artist is "deified by nectar," in other words drunk, when he receives his *Courier* announcing the contest. The tone of the last three stanzas becomes serious, as the speaker voices his devotion to a calling that will bring bitterness and suffering. He is resolved, despite poverty and other hardships, to remain devoted to his craft. His greatest reward comes in knowing that he will learn to laugh at Time, which can only grant the true and honest artist Immortality. This is a venerable old poetic theme that Simms treated on many occasions throughout his career. The first and last poems in this collection, in fact, play variations on it.

The poem also contains some of Simms's developing views of life: that death often steals the soul's "first fire" and the "heart's first homage," that at the least "joy is a shadow" soon to disappear, and that to live is to suffer loss. These are gloomy assertions of reality that dominate some of his earliest poems and are expressed often in his letters: "Set your heart on nothing mortal! The most precious things are the first to be taken from us!" (*Letters*, 6:210).

The poem appeared only once (*Charleston Courier*, 12 January 1825). It is collected here under Simms's name for the first time, with emendations:

21. plate] Plate
60. our's] ours.

Simms claimed authorship in a manuscript note (P 1540, Manuscripts Collection, South Caroliniana Library, University of South Carolina) and in his Scrapbook A.

Notes

18. Piece of Plate: This was the award promised to the winner of the *Courier* poetry contest.

26. old Will: Shakespeare, of course, from the famous soliloquy in *Hamlet*.

27. Hence, horrible shadow: *Macbeth*, III. iv. 106.

THE BROKEN ARROW.

A very significant poem both historically and artistically, "The Broken Arrow" is Simms's first known work on an Indian subject, predating his initial fictional treatment of the red man by two years and *The Yemassee* by a decade. In a handwritten note in his Scrapbook G, Simms reveals that "this dirge was in my 19th year, written while travelling through the nation." The date of composition can be further pinned down to be mid- to late May 1825, for in his essay also entitled "The Broken Arrow" (*Ladies Companion*, January 1844, pp. 110–19), Simms writes that he passed through the Creek nation "a few weeks after the assassination of General William Macintosh," an event which occurred 1 May 1825. He goes on to say that he "picked up, as well from Indian as from white authorities, sundry small particulars relating to the event." The poem and essay thus contain firsthand accounts which historians have not used.

"The Broken Arrow" provides the first proof of Simms's statement to the Indian scholar Henry Schoolcraft, in 1851, that he possessed "an early and strong sympathy with the subject of the Red Man, in moral and literary points of view," a sympathy which has "rendered me in some degree a fit person to insist upon their original claims and upon what is still due them by our race" (*Letters,* 3:101).

As an artistic creation, the poem is interesting for its use of the epic caesura at mid-line to suggest the sound of Indian speech. It is Simms's first known narrative poem, a form which was to become one of his fortes, a fact which Simms himself perceptively discerned (see *Letters,* 2:257). It also qualifies as his first dramatic monologue—written long before those of Tennyson and Browning, whom he has heretofore been unjustly accused of imitating. Its narrator is likely the old sad chief identified in Simms's fifth note as one to whom the poet talked on his journey. "The Broken Arrow" is an important example of effective narrative poetry from the early career.

It was published four times: *Charleston Courier,* 31 May 1826; *Poems* (1827), pp. 7–9; *Book of My Lady* (1833), pp. 124–25; and *Old Guard,* 6 November 1868, pp. 863–67. The 1826 and 1827 versions are substantially alike. The 1833 text is an intermediate version which adds a 28–line verse introduction, expanded to 107 lines in 1868. The 1826 version is the text printed here, while the expanded 1868 version also appears in this volume. The following emendations have been made to the 1826 text:

Title. ROKEN] BROKEN

    [Bracketed material removed from beneath title and placed as footnote 1, as in the 1827 version.]

    [Numbering of footnotes with superscript numbers rather than symbols, as in the 1827 version.]

    8. view] view.

Notes

Title. Broken Arrow: A major Coweta town, the place of meeting for the signing of the Georgia Treaty of 1825.

    2. Chief: General William McIntosh, a Lower Creek (or Coweta) Indian awarded the rank of general for his service to the U.S. government, and in opposition to the Upper Creeks, who opposed deeding away their lands to the whites. He was bribed on several occasions to betray Creeks and Cherokees through cession of land and was assassinated 1 May 1825 by a party of Upper Creeks.

    20. In the 1827 text Simms added a note to this line: "This is but partially true, Mackintosh did attempt a defence, but his aim and not his rifle, was defective."

Footnote 1. Mackintosh: The correct spelling was McIntosh.

Footnote 2. In the 1827 note Simms has added that Madwolf exclaimed that McIntosh was "to die by the laws he had himself made."

Footnote 3. Menawe: Ogillio Heneha, commonly known as "Menawa," former

Red Stick leader, one of the Upper Creeks and an Okfuskee chief, who was placed in command of the two hundred warriors for execution of McIntosh.

Footnote 4. In the 1827 note Simms adds: "I have good reason for the line. Of the Plum they are passionately fond. I have ridden for an hour under one continued orchard, that fringed the road."

Footnote 5. In the 1827 note Simms identifies the Indian to whom he talked as "an old Chief of the Mackintosh party" to whom he read the articles of the Georgia Treaty of 1825, "which was received while I was in the Nation." Simms commented to him "that he would find good hunting grounds in the west—plenty of buffalo, deer, &c. 'Ah!' said he, after a momentary brightening of countenance at the intelligence; 'yet when we get good settled there, and the pipe smoke well, whiteman will want more land.' This needs no comment." The old chief is thus likely a model for the poem's narrator, if not the narrator himself.

WRITTEN IN MISSISSIPPI.

This lyric, first published in *Poems* (1827), grew out of Simms's travels to Mississippi in 1824–25. As the 1836 version reports in its title, it was written "in the Choctaw Nation." The poet was correct in saying that in 1825 he was resting where the white man "has scarcely ever come." As this and the previous poem indicate, these western journeys inspired many of his works of poetry and were thus among the most important events that shaped his career.

The poem is successful in its lyricism and concreteness, using details from the natural scene like the mockingbird, wind in the pine tops, the "bee-tree," and red deer, all particulars Simms would have seen on the Southern frontier. In the last line of stanza 2 appears a skillful use of onomatopoeia.

The poem was published twice: first in *Poems* (1827), pp. 73–74, and then in *Southern Literary Journal* 2 (June 1836): 272–73, entitled "The Traveller's Rest, Written in the Choctaw Nation, Mississippi." In the second, Simms turned his tetrameter lines into pentameters, thus weakening the poem by altering its swiftness and its light, energetic tone. The version printed here is the 1827, without emendation.

In 1849 Simms published a sixteen-page work which used this poem as its basis. It appears as "The Traveller's Rest" in this volume.

Notes
    16. bee-tree: The linden or basswood, an important tree for honey production.

TO A WINTER FLOWER, *WRITTEN IN THE CREEK NATION.*

This poem exists in two main versions: the one printed here, from *Poems* (1827), and an expanded version which appeared in four variant texts from 1832 to 1860: *Charleston City Gazette*, 27 January 1832; *Southern Literary Messenger* 3 (October

1837): 619; *Southern Passages* (1839), pp. 156–58; and *Areytos* (1860), pp. 70–72.

The *Southern Literary Messenger* appearance is dated November 1825, the year of Simms's return from his first journey to Mississippi. The expanded version, also printed in this volume, omits reference to the red man, a primary subject of this version.

No emendation to the 1827 copy text has been necessary.

Notes

    20. Last of thy train: Likely an allusion to his own lonely situation.

SONG. "I HAVE NO HEART TO SING."

Another of Simms's Cavalier lyrics, this poem exists in three forms and is here printed for the first time under his name. It was first published in *Album,* 10 December 1825, p. 194, signed "Almirez." The second form is a manuscript in Scrapbook G, which precedes the final version in *Magnolia,* n.s., 1 (July 1842): 50, signed "Spiridion." The *Magnolia* version has been chosen for copy text over the manuscript because as editor of the *Magnolia* Simms was likely responsible for the changes, even in matters of punctuation.

The copy text is here printed without emendation.

SONNET. — "IF FROM THE MORNING OF THY DAYS."

The sonnet was to become one of Simms's favorite forms. This, one of his earliest successful examples, was first published in *Poems* (1827), pp. 48–49, then revised for the *Magnolia* 4 (May 1842): 275, and dated 1826. The text printed here is from the *Magnolia* with one emendation based on the 1827 text:

    2. illumed] illum'd

Notes

    12. sweet fever-balm: Likely the colloquial term for lemon balm, an herb used for the cure of melancholy.

THE SLAIN EAGLE. (SALUDA.)

Although perhaps somewhat repetitious, this poem has memorable descriptive passages and shows its author's skill in handling the technicalities of verse. It is written in Spenserian stanza (eight iambic pentameter lines and an alexandrine, rhyming *ababbcbcc*).

It is one of Simms's few didactic poems. In the last stanza, the speaker calls the eagle an "examplar" and a "human homily" to teach mankind the important lesson of what great loss and destruction for all men results from a little man's envy of the aspiring, noble spirit. As the poet puts it in his final stanza, the eagle becomes the "type," or emblem, of Genius. It is interesting to note that the crest Simms created for himself was the eye and wing, the first symbolizing close observation, the latter representing the flight of poetic imagination—the heart of artistic genius.

The poem exists in essentially two main versions: a shorter one published in the *Southern Literary Messenger* 3 (October 1837): 666–68, dated 1826; *Southern Passages* (1839), pp. 83–88; and *Poets and Poetry of America*, ed. Rufus Griswold (1845), pp. 304–5; and a longer, final version published in *Areytos* (1860), pp. 264–71. The text printed here is from *Areytos,* with one emendation:

    31.5. villany] villainy

Notes

Title. The Saluda of the title was first added to the poem in 1860. It refers to the Saluda range of mountains on the South and North Carolina border, a favorite haunt of the poet.

12.7. Eblis: Or Iblis, Mohammedan devil, identical with Satan, tempter of man.

TO THE MOUNTAINS.

Although the poem first appeared in 1826, it was not until 1845 that Simms particularized his descriptions of the mountains beyond vague effusions. In 1845 he gives the setting as the Saluda mountain range between South and North Carolina, a fact which indicates the poet had visited this scenery by that time.

The poem was a favorite of Simms's, being published seven times: *Poems* (1827, that is, 1826), pp. 36–37; *American Monthly* 5 (August 1835): 475, titled "Serenade"; *American Museum of Science* 2 (May 1839): 421, titled "Mountain Serenade"; *Southern and Western* 2 (December 1845): 381; *Areytos* (1846), pp. 85–86, titled "To the Mountains"; *Southern Literary Messenger* 26 (May 1858): 358–59, titled "To the Mountains"; and *Areytos* (1860), pp. 272–73, titled "Wander, Oh Wander Here." Each appearance shows minor revisions.

The text published here is the *Southern Literary Messenger* version of 1858, with no emendations.

THE LOVE OF MACKINTOSH.

Another poem growing out of Simms's journeys west, "The Love of Mackintosh" was published only in *Poems* (1827, i.e., 1826), pp. 57–59. Here he dramatizes the statement made earlier in his note to "The Broken Arrow" that the Indian apprehends "to its fullest extent, the miseries of leaving the home of childhood, associated so firmly by the ligament of a past eternity," a sentiment Simms understood fully himself when he refused to leave his birthplace for the West.

A longer second version, entitled "The Widow of the Chief," was published in *Southern Literary Journal* 1 (September 1835): 31–32, and *Southern Passages*

(1839), pp. 225–28. In this expanded version the widow states finally that the red man will be forgotten by the pale race: "A people will succeed who shall not know / The race they robb'd of home and heritage / . . . the great nation vanish'd and forgot."

No emendations have been made except to supply the title "The Love of Mackintosh" to the untitled poem, to indent line 32, in keeping with the practice in the remainder of the poem, and to supply the final quotation mark in the last line.

Notes

1. Mackintosh: General William McIntosh, a chief of Coweta, assassinated 1 May 1825. See notes to "The Broken Arrow" (1825).

8. O-co-ne: A river in northeast Georgia.

34. desert Arrow: The town of Broken Arrow, an important Coweta village in north Georgia, through which Simms passed in May 1825. The site was deserted soon thereafter.

THE WILDERNESS.

This, one of Simms's earliest blank-verse poems, contains what also might be his first use of the natural scene as mirror for the interior landscape. Beginning at line 13, the poet creates two contrasting scenes that reflect two responses to life: the icy, impersonal intellectualism of Neoclassic Reason versus the familiar, warm, local, and emotional approach of Romanticism. These two manners correspond to conflicting attitudes toward nature: the clinical, bookish, and scientific versus the personal and heartfelt. The poet opts for the latter.

The poem's primary subject is the discovery of nature and the beginning of converse with her in her wilderness form. For this topic Simms appropriately chooses a wilderness setting, in fact, two wilderness settings. It is at the initial one (a contemporary "deep Indian forest" on the frontier) that the speaker has a vision which takes him back two centuries to the second setting, the original coastal wilderness of the "new found land" first seen by the colonists as they debarked onto the Atlantic shore. Like the contemporary narrator, early discoverers are "awe-fill'd" and struck with wonder at the fresh, green breast of the New World. In the last lines of the poem, the colonists, in praising the world's Creator, merge with nature itself, for unspoiled nature likewise echoes their praise of the Creator. There is thus achieved a oneness among all things: man and man; man and nature; and man, nature, and Creator. This "wilderness" experience thus becomes an archetypal discovery of unity and leads to the poem's conclusion, where, in "sweet communion," the men are moved to tears. Complicating this optimism are the contradictory image of the approaching ship as a specter hand on the wall at midnight and the description of the ship's energy and threatening power as it advances unchecked upon the land, image and diction patterns that likely suggest man's future destructive impact upon this same wilderness. "The Wilderness" is an early milestone in the history of American Romanticism.

This work was published only once: *Poems* (1827, i.e., 1826), pp. 163–66. It is here reprinted without emendation. The poem likely grew from the author's experiences on the frontier, 1824–26. It was composed no later than September 1826, when *Poems* had gone to press.

Notes

66. hand at midnight: An ominous image, perhaps suggesting man's destructiveness.

79. blue: The color of hope.

82. Ophir: Biblical land of gold and wealth, here juxtaposed to the giant trees, the stumps of which Simms wept over on the frontier.

INVOCATION.

This poem first appeared in *Early Lays* (1827), pp. 17–18. In lines 3–4 it shows the unmistakable influence of Philip Freneau's "The Wild Honeysuckle." (Simms's scarlet-flowered variety must be either the coral honeysuckle or *Bakeri* azalea, and not the *Rhododendron arborescens* which Freneau described.) When Simms revised the poem in its five future appearances, he altered these lines to remove all traces of Freneau.

The text here printed is from *Early Lays,* with one emendation: the generic title "Sonnet" is changed to "Invocation," the title of the versions in the *Family Companion,* 15 October 1841; *Southern Literary Messenger* 10 (July 1844); *Grouped Thoughts* (1845); and *Southern Home Journal* 2 (26 September 1869).

THE GREEN CORN DANCE.

Another of Simms's poems using the Indian as the subject, "The Green Corn Dance" describes the Busk, or *boos-ke-tan,* an important seasonal ritual of harvest for the Southeastern Indian, attended by entire chiefdoms. The place of ceremony was usually a square ground (given as the council house in the 1827 version) where the celebration lasted several days; on the fourth a feast was prepared and the warriors danced in war dress. Contemporary sources all suggest that the time of celebration was when the corn, called "green corn," had ripened in summer, not when coming from the ground in spring as Simms has it. Simms describes an initiation ceremony, called "A-boos-ke-tan," in his *The Cassique of Kiawah* (1859), p. 252.

The poem was published twice: *Early Lays* (1827), pp. 27–29; and *Book of My Lady* (1833), pp. 257–58. A twenty-one-line manuscript in Scrapbook D is a very different fragmentary version. The text here printed is the 1833 version, with one emendation: Simms's introductory paragraph has been made a footnote. Its meter—iambic heptameter—was first used in the 1833 text, replacing the pentameter of the *Early Lays* version. This rarely used meter was to become a favorite of Simms's and is represented by several poems in this edition.

ROSALIE.

"Rosalie" was first published in *Early Lays* (1827), pp. 64–65, then revised in *Knickerbocker* 10 (December 1837): 479, signed "G. B. Singleton," before final revisions in *Southern Literary Messenger* 6 (June 1840): 445. The *Knickerbocker* text is printed here with the following emendations from the 1827 and 1840 publications:

    0. [*Placement of numerals before stanzas, as in 1840 and Simms's usual practice. Simms seldom used periods after the numerals.*]

    1. bower] bow'r
    3. flower] flow'r
    4. flower] flow'r
    5. spring] Spring
    21. bower] bow'r
    23. flower] flow'r
    24. flower] flow'r

TOKENS AND PLEDGES.

This effective early lyric on the theme of mutability was published in *Early Lays* (1827), pp. 72–73; *American Monthly* 5 (May 1835): 170, signed "Linus"; and *Magnolia*, n.s., 1 (October 1842): 256, signed "Childe Hazard." The second appearance reveals Simms's marked improvement as a poet, for the 1827 version lacks the skillful diction, polish, and careful structuring of imagery exhibited in the 1835 appearance. One must conjecture that Simms had lost his 1835 text when he went to publish again in the *Magnolia* (an 1835 clipping does not appear in his scrapbooks); and his second rewriting, much closer to the 1827 version, is this time not as successful. Therefore the text printed is from the *American Monthly* of 1835, with two emendations taken from the 1827 text:

    1. to night] to-night
    7. flowers] flow'rs

Simms parodied the poem's idealistic theme that his lover's vow will last when nothing else does, in a poem entitled "Guaranties" (1860), also published in this edition. In the latter, the poet says that the pleasure of the kiss itself is treasure enough even if the vow that the same lips utter "be fidelity or fudge."

THE APPROACH OF WINTER.

This poem, collected here for the first time, appeared only in the *Charleston Courier,* 25 August 1827, in this form. For a later, rewritten version, see "The Close of the Year 1861." The *Courier* text is emended as follows:

29. do] no

Notes

9. broad Indias: Pride of India trees (*Melia azedarach*), called locally china-berries, favorite street trees in Charleston during Simms's day.

38. *Mercury, Gazette:* Two Charleston newspapers. The *Gazette* is the *City Gazette.* Simms published the poem in a third paper, the *Courier.*

58. "Woollens Bill": Refers to a duty on wool and woolens, a series of tariffs, begun in 1816, for the protection of the American wool industry.

60. "Tartan Plaid": A woolen cloth in Scottish plaid.

77. Tripping once more: Charleston was deserted during the summer fever season, and the natives returned with cooler weather.

78. Broad-street . . .: Three of the primary streets of the city.

85. Chupein's: Lewis Chupein operated a mineral water establishment at 13 Broad Street in 1827; Chupein's was obviously a favorite gathering place for "loungers."

SERENADE.

This was one of the poet's favorite lyrics; he published it six times: *Courier,* 5 September 1827; *New York Mirror,* 10 October 1829, p. 112; *Southern Literary Messenger* 6 (January 1840): 37; *Areytos* (1846), pp. 66–67; *Southern Literary Messenger* 27 (May 1858): 357; and *Areytos* (1860), p. 274. The text chosen here is that of the *New York Mirror,* with one emendation from the 1827 text:

21. when thou] the moon

Notes

20. Simms makes the *Courier's* "Carolinian maid" more regional as a "southern maid" in the New York paper, thus perhaps reflecting the poem's new place of publication.

SONNET. — THE PORTRAIT.

This poem was published four times. The first two are similar: *Magnolia* 3 (November 1841): 523, dated 1827, and *Southern and Western* 2 (August 1845): 94. The texts in *Russell's* 3 (July 1858): 334, and *Areytos* (1860), pp. 147–48, are both expanded into three sonnets in a sequence entitled "Sonnets.—To My Friend with My Portrait." The version published here is from *Southern and Western* (1845), with three emendations from the *Magnolia* text which reflect Simms's usual practice:

2. memory—] memory,—
5. glance—] glance,—
7. fixed] fix'd

THE MINIATURE.

The miniature portrait of a loved one or close relative was particularly popular in Charleston from the late eighteenth century to Simms's own day. Owing to their smallness, these portraits had a special intimacy; they were worn as jewels by some, but carried about and viewed privately by others. This poem is another example of his effective use of native material. The miniature's oval shape, its smallness and delicacy, and especially the luminous quality of "pearl and gold" painted on ivory, are appropriate to the metaphor of the star in line 3. When the reader learns that the miniature is not literal at all, but instead an image set in the poet's heart, the star metaphor becomes even more effective because, like the star, his loved one becomes the emblem of an eternal ideal which guides him. The poem thus provides a good example of chivalric romanticism.

"The Miniature" was published three times: a twelve-line version in *Southern Literary Gazette* 1 (October 1828): 89; an expanded version in *Southern and Western* 2 (April 1845): 86, which was in turn polished in *Poems* (1853), pp. 117–18. The version published here is the *Poems* text of 1853, with two emendations from the *Southern and Western* text, reflecting Simms's usual practice:

17. Wouldst] Would'st
20. couldst] could'st

SONNET.

One subject of this richly suggestive poem is the magic power of the artist to strike universal chords in the heart and to cast spells and charms, even to the point of "securing" love against loss. Simms was fond of advising young poets to "extort from every subject its inner secret—for the Poet is a Seer" (*Letters*, 4:236). In the couplet, the chords swept by wind refers to the aeolian harp.

Two versions of the sonnet are published in this edition. The first, printed here, is from the *Southern Literary Gazette* 1 (October 1828): 128, signed "Amand." The second version, entitled "Sonnet.—I Will Breathe Music" (1841) is printed in this volume.

There is one emendation:

11. love's] loves

SUMMER NIGHT WIND.

This poem first appeared in the *Southern Literary Gazette* 1 (December 1828): 220, then *Vision of Cortes* (1829), pp. 102–3. It was subsequently expanded in *Southern Literary Journal* 2 (April 1836): 90–91; *Southern Passages* (1839), pp. 4–6; *Southern Literary Gazette* 3 (13 July 1850); and *Poems* (1853), pp. 127–31. The text printed here is the 1828 version, with the following emendations from the 1829 and 1836 texts.

2. wave] waves

3. breaks] break

28. shoulds't] should'st30.   and] and feel

Notes

Compare William Cullen Bryant's "To the Evening Wind" in *Poems* (Boston, 1831), p. 26. Bryant reviewed *Vision of Cortes* and thus knew Simms's poem.

THE STREAMLET.

The poet has taken an object from nature and made it into a complex personal emblem which serves as the work's central focus. The stream symbolizes (1) continuity and eternity, (2) the "soul" of nature in its manifold roles, and (3) memory. The last of these Simms made clear in a couplet which appears only in the *American Monthly* version: "Mine is the stream that must forever roll, / Memory's my name—my waters feed the soul." The significance of the stream develops from a specific memory of his father, who walked with the lad along these same banks, the experience culminating in nature's performance of all the services it could perform for the Romantic. These include a teacher of essential truths of the heart, spiritual guide, inculcator of morality, friend, aid to reflection, giver of life, restorer of youth and innocence, means of escape from the worries of the world, soother of tired spirits, opponent of materialism, firm anchor for belief in the midst of a chaotic, unstable world, and aid to recovery of a lost loved one through memory. The poet's choice of stream as symbol is remarkably apt, for though the stream flows like both memory and life, it remains inexhaustible in its deep banks from age to age. This important poem and "The Slain Eagle" are two of the first to show that Simms viewed nature as emblematic.

It is also quintessentially Southern in its recognition of the importance of place, with all its complex fabric of associations, here from the speaker's own personal family past. The man remembers that as a child his father told him of the stream's "voice," which the youth could not then hear. Now, with age his heart "not ear" discerns the mingled voices of both stream and father: "It is his language,—I should know it well,— / He speaks through these sweet waters which he loved / In boyhood, and where still our footsteps roved."

The poem was first published in twelve stanzas in the *Southern Literary Gazette* 1 (February 1829): 280–81, signed "Amand"; then revised (adding stanzas 1, 6, 13, and 18) and entitled "The Voice of the Streamlet" in *American Monthly* 5 (April 1835): 95–96. Its last appearances were an expanded version of twenty-two stanzas in the *U.S. Democratic Review* 8 (August 1840): 109–12; and *Poems* (1853), pp. 292–97. Stanzas 2, 3, 5, 7–12, and 22 appear here for the first time. The text printed in this edition is from *Poems*, with two emendations from the 1840 text:

9.3. plunged] plung'd

10.6. back] back,

Notes

Compare William Cullen Bryant's poem "The Rivulet" in *Poems* (Boston: Russell, 1831), p. 35.

7.2. Santee to Savannah: Two rivers in Carolina.

7.3. laurel: Local name for the *Magnolia grandiflora*, a tree native to the Carolina lowcountry.

10.1–2. His grave: A reference to the poet's father, who was buried in Mississippi. He died several years after the short version of this poem was written. Stanza 10 was first added in the 1840 expansion as a tribute to the elder Simms's wisdom and sensitivity, now more fully appreciated by the grown son.

TO ———.

This poem was published in the *Charleston Courier*, 5 February 1829, signed "Lyricia," then in *Southern Literary Gazette*, n.s., 1 (1 September 1829): 175, signed "†." It was never collected. The text is here published under Simms's name for the first time from the *Courier* without emendation.

BALLAD. THE SLEEPING CHILD.

This poem was published twice, but never signed or collected. It here appears under Simms's name for the first time. Its first publication (*Southern Literary Gazette*, 15 July 1829) was entitled "To My Little Daughter," thus identifying its subject as Anna Augusta Singleton Simms, born 11 November 1827. The *Russell's* version of December 1857 is much revised and improved. The text is from *Russell's*, the only emendation being a reduction to lower case of all numerals, in keeping with Simms's usual manner.

TO MY FRIEND.

This sonnet, again showing Simms's devotion to high artistic mission, first appeared in *Vision of Cortes* (1829), pp. 135–36; and then was revised for *Southern Literary Messenger* 2 (July 1845): 442; *Grouped Thoughts* (1845), p. 43; and *Poems* (1853), p. 99.

The text used is the *Grouped Thoughts* version with one emendation from 1853:

3. affliction] affection

THE PEACE OF THE WOODS.

This pastoral poem has as its theme the superiority of the simple life in nature and the values associated therewith. The statement that man's true aim should be to strive for the golden mean becomes a central theme of Simms's canon: one must balance the passions with reason, and let neither dominate. The Horatian mean had also been an important theme in the colonial poetry of the South. The simple man who is never ambitious for wealth and fame is rewarded by peace of mind. His life is thus like placid water undisturbed by storm. The raging wind that could "disturb" or "deform" the waters is a metaphor for being overthrown from high position, attacked by the envious, or simply the restlessness caused by one's own envy, ambition, and greed. An external landscape thus becomes a metaphor for the state of mind of the subject—and, by contrast, of the state of mind of the speaker, who admires and longs for such calmness, but does not quite have it in his life. The theme is thus effectively dramatized through metaphor.

The poem was published in *Vision of Cortes* (1829), pp. 140–41; *Family Companion* 1 (15 January 1842): 200–201; *Southern Literary Messenger* 11 (September 1845): 557; *Grouped Thoughts* (1845), p. 60; and *Areytos* (1860), p. 416. The text here is from *Areytos* with two emendations:

   [*The title is taken from* Grouped Thoughts *rather than the first line, as was the practice in* Areytos.]
      1. enamored] enamor'd

Notes
      3. scaith: Dialect for *scathe,* harm, injury.

CONFOUNDED BORES.

"Confounded Bores," written in iambic tetrameter, rhyming *aabccb,* is an early example of Simms's humorous verse, one of the best and least-known groups of his poems. Through its satire is revealed the poet's daily routine as a newly married young lawyer and author and the difficulty he is having in settling down to write. His wife of stanza 3 is the former Anna Malcolm Giles, whom he married in 1826. The poem's serious side involves the proper use of time in order to leave meritorious work that time "shall not shame to see." Simms was thus already considering how he might make a lasting contribution to literature.

The poem exists in two versions: *Southern Literary Gazette,* n.s., 1 (15 August 1829): 160, entitled "My Time," and an undated, unidentified clipping in Simms's scrapbooks, probably from around 1830. The version printed here is the 1830 text, with the following emendations based on *Southern Literary Gazette* readings:

      10. power] pow'r
      17. husband] 'husband
      18. hat!] hat!'

The poem is here published under Simms's name for the first time.

AT PARTING.

This lyric consisted of only one stanza in all its publications: *Southern Literary Gazette*, n.s., 1 (15 September 1829): 206; *American Monthly* 5 (March 1835): 43; *Southern Literary Messenger* 6 (April 1840): 292; *Southern and Western* 1 (February 1845): 134. It was never signed or collected. The two-stanza text printed here is from an undated manuscript in Scrapbook A, with two emendations:

> [*The title, which in the manuscript repeats the first line, is here taken from the 1835, 1840, 1845 texts.*]
> 1.8. &] and

Notes

2.3. old Moultrie's isle: Sullivan's Island, north of Charleston, on which stands Fort Moultrie, site of an important battle in the American Revolution. The Carolina name is pronounced with an *o* as in *shoe*.

FRAGMENT.

The subject of "Fragment" is the brief return of some red men to the home of their childhood, after a forced removal. Here, the poet shows that the Indian, like himself, attaches more value to home than does the average white man. Considering the fact that his other poems on Indian subjects grew out of experience, one might assume that Simms witnessed such an event as described here. The poem provides another early example of a skillful use of blank verse.

"Fragment" was published unsigned in *Southern Literary Gazette*, n.s., 1 (15 September 1829): 212, and *Southern Literary Journal*, n.s., 3 (April 1838): 299. The text, published here for the first time under Simms's name, is from the *Southern Literary Journal*, with one emendation from the 1829 version:

> 2. father's] fathers'

BALLAD — STANZAS.

This poem was first published in the *Southern Literary Gazette*, n.s., 1 (1 October 1829): 240, then slightly revised in *Southern Literary Journal*, n.s., 3 (May 1838): 329–30. Under the title "Monna" a revised version appeared in *American Review* 11 (December 1845): 622–23; *Atalantis* (1848), pp. 114–16; and *Poems,* vol. 2 (1853), pp. 190–92. "Ballad" sounds remarkably like Poe; but its 1829 publication date makes it impossible for Simms to have borrowed from that poet. Parallels exist in Poe's "Ulalume" (1847), "The Raven" (1845), and "Annabel Lee" (1849). It is thus not surprising that Poe was an early champion of Simms's poetry and was very possibly influenced by him. Of particular note is Simms's attempt to reveal the psychology of the first-person narrator. This is one of his earliest poems in which he tries to do so, and, as such, it bears some similarities to the next work, "The Modern Lion."

The text here printed is from 1838, with one emendation from the *Southern Literary Gazette:*

5.3. rapt] wrapt

Also, roman numerals have been reduced to lower case, in keeping with Simms's usual manner.

THE MODERN LION.

Another of Simms's early comic poems, "The Modern Lion" is a playful monologue that satirizes the fop. There is also a serious side to the poem. Simms laments what he sees to be a loss of strength in modern man. His fiction likewise demonstrates that the founders of the nation were men of greater character than those of the American present, when wealth, fashion, and show are held to be more important than substance. The poem's epigraph suggests that the strutting beau of the period is a kind of comic Bottom, who can mimic and play a part, but rarely be the thing imitated. For example, the speaker's vanity has led him to write a book, the existence of which is to him of secondary importance to the portrait that will accompany it. Simms's scorn for the dilettante writer was always acute.

The poet here pays attention to the sound of his poem and, with some success, has attempted to make it reinforce sense. The diction, syntax, and punctuation (as in 2.1) suggest the fop's language. The singsong meter, short jingling lines, and silly rhymes are all appropriate to the subject. The result makes for a pleasant light poem of some polish, a type of which there are few in American verse of Simms's time. The poet's creation of a fictional first-person narrator who reveals his character through his speaking the poem, and whose character is actually the poem's primary focus, would alone make the poem noteworthy. The work has much in common with Simms's recently discovered first work of fiction, "Light Reading" (*Courier,* 27 July 1824), which is told by a foppish first person narrator who had been much favored by the city ladies.

The poem, here printed under Simms's name for the first time, was first published in Simms's *Charleston City Gazette,* 22 December 1830, signed "*E.*" and entitled "A Modern Beau." Its other publication was in the *Southern Literary Messenger* 3 (August 1837): 473, signed "***." The *Southern Literary Messenger* version adds the lines from 4.5 through the end of the poem. In Simms's Scrapbook D, he has penciled the following corrections to his *Southern Literary Messenger* text:

1.8. walk about the] switch my way
3.7. yellow] lilac

The text printed here is from the *Southern Literary Messenger* with Simms's two corrections from the Scrapbook and the following emendations:

Epigraph. Line 1. too will] too. I will [*Correction of a typesetting error.*]

1.5. tidiness] tidyness [*Spelling in the 1830 text.*]

1.8. town] 'bout town [*In correcting, Simms mistakenly canceled his preposition.*]

2.1. me terribly,] me, terribly—[*1830 reading.*]

In addition, all roman numerals have been made lower case, in keeping with Simms's usual practice.

Notes

Epigraph: Altered from Shakespeare's *A Midsummer Night's Dream,* I.ii.

3.7. lilac: Simms had originally written *yellow,* but revised to *lilac* some time after 1837, when apparently yellow was no longer associated with foppishness. It is interesting to note that Charleston artist Charles Fraser, in depicting "Beau Nasty" around 1796, gave him yellow britches. In Fraser's "Sketches from Nature," actors and men of fashion wear yellow.

6.3. Inman: Henry Inman (1801–46), looked on by his contemporaries as the leading American portrait painter of his day. A miniature of Charlestonian Thomas Fenwick Drayton, dated and signed "Inman 1828," is held by the Gibbes Museum of Art. Drayton, a member of Charleston high society, is here pictured as a delicate-faced young gentleman with black tresses.

6.7. "Mirror' and the 'Star': Likely the *New York Mirror,* begun 1823, whose forte was its comments on fads, foibles, and popular enthusiasms. It was richly illustrated. The "Star" is unidentified. There had been a *Charleston Star* in the 1790s.

STANZAS AT EVENING.

This poem appeared in only one version (*U.S. Democratic Review* 9 [July 1841]: 58–59) and was never collected. As its title reveals, its setting is the Southern frontier, which Simms was again visiting in 1851. It contains some striking visual images.

No emendations have been necessary.

SONG.

This lyric was published five times: *Charleston City Gazette,* 29 June 1831, signed "Vidal"; *Southern Passages* (1839), pp. 155–56; *Southern Literary Messenger* 27 (September 1858): 192; *Areytos* (1860), pp. 189–90; and *Magnolia Weekly* 2 (28 November 1863): 65, signed "Adrian B. Beaufain." Each time the text was altered slightly (for example, the "blue eye" of his first wife, Anna, judiciously became a "dark eye" in 1839, after Simms's second marriage, to the dark-eyed Chevillette, in 1836), until major revisions were made in the *Magnolia Weekly.* This final version, while showing skill at handling an elaborate form, is not as good a poem as the simple version of 1831. The 1831 text is therefore printed here with one emendation which appeared in all the later versions:

5. moonlights] moonlight's

THE WINTER FLOWER.

This poem, dated November 1825 in the *Southern Literary Messenger,* was origi-
nally inspired by Simms's visit to the Creek Nation in 1824–25. Whereas the short
early version published in 1827 had stressed the plight of the red man, the ex-
panded version of 1832 (after his most recent visit to the West the year before)
omits the Indian and implies the wilderness is now devoid of all human life.
Stanza 7 perhaps develops the "pale flow'r" as a symbol of the white man, who has
outlasted his vanquished brethren. If so, Simms asks what is the "secret spring of
life" or "favor" that has allowed his survival. This question, however, is only a
minor consideration in light of the primary theme that all life is transient. The dis-
appearance of the red man strengthens the Romantic emphasis on mutability; and
the pale flower, with the frosts of winter already upon it, is also doomed to die in
short time. Simms hints strongly on many occasions that the white man, through
the destruction of nature, will bring about his own destruction. This idea seems
implicit here.

The recent death of both grandmother and father perhaps explains the last
stanza's emphasis on the loss of loved ones and the painful condition of being the
last left to mourn their deaths. Simms's 1831 trip to the West, in fact, was taken to
settle his father's estate; and he was, indeed, now the last remaining member of
his immediate family. He had thus learned the truth of the final stanza from hard
experience. The poem, accordingly, has been revised from its early short version
to incorporate emotion occasioned by recent events in his life. Thematically, the
poem's last stanza resembles the final lines of "Broken Slumbers."

This expanded version was published four times: *Charleston City Gazette,* 27
January 1832: *Southern Literary Messenger* 3 (October 1837): 619; *Southern Pas-
sages* (1839), pp. 156–58; and *Areytos* (1860), pp. 70–72. The text printed here is
from *Areytos,* with three emendations restoring readings from the earlier appear-
ances in order to eliminate what is probably housestyling:

7.1. thine?] thine,
8.4. skies?] skies.
9.2. alone—] alone,—

BROKEN SLUMBERS.

This poem, like "Elegiac" which follows, probably grew out of Simms's grief over
the death of his first wife, Anna Giles Simms, from tuberculosis. Line 16 is a real-
istic portrayal of the effects of the disease, and line 39 is accurate in stating that
the poet's mother and father had also died, the first in 1808, the latter in 1830. In
addition, he had lost his brother and the grandmother who had reared him. His
only remaining family was his four-year-old daughter, Anna Augusta. Never before
collected or published under Simms's name, the work appeared twice: first in
the *Charleston City Gazette,* 29 March 1832, and finally in *Magnolia,* n.s., 1 (July
1842): 52. The text here printed is from the *Magnolia,* which lightly revised and

improved the *City Gazette* appearance. Only one emendation to the *Magnolia* text has been necessary: the restoration of an 1832 reading in order to correct what was likely a typesetting error:

34. thy] the

ELEGIAC.

This effective elegy reveals Simms's early belief in spiritualism, or the ability of the souls of the departed to commune with their loved ones. Simms's Christianity was never orthodox, demonstrated by the fact that from the mid-1820s he speaks often of spirits and mediums (see, for example, *Letters*, 3:431, 491). The initial date of publication of "Elegiac" came shortly after the death of his first wife, Anna Giles Simms, from tuberculosis in February 1832; and the poem is thus at least partly autobiographical. Its re-publication in 1858 came after a renewed interest in spiritualism which led him to consult mediums. At one point during this time he could write: "I am now personally attended by representatives from the spirit world; that my dreams are shaped by them." It is important to note that this subject, common in his verse, does not derive from an imitation of the supernatural element in Poe, as demonstrated by his early belief in spiritualism and the date of publication of such poems as "Elegiac."

The poem was published three times: *Charleston City Gazette*, 14 April 1832: *Magnolia* 4 (March 1842): 154; and *Charleston Mercury*, 28 September 1858, signed "Il Penseroso." It always appeared anonymously and was never collected, perhaps because of its too-personal nature. It is thus published here for the first time under Simms's name. The *Magnolia* version is the copy text for this edition and incorporates six corrections Simms made to the clipping of the poem pasted in his Scrapbook D:

4. Re-animate,] Re-animate
9. Does] Doth
12. delight;] delight,
14. see;] see,
15. had] hath
15. waste] waste,

The title comes from the 1858 *Mercury* text. The *Magnolia* version had read "Sonnet—'The Beautiful, The Silent'" with Simms canceling "Sonnet" in his scrapbook clipping.

STANZAS BY THE SEA-SHORE.

The genesis of this poem came in "Lines Written at Sea," published in *Southern Literary Gazette*, n.s., 1 (15 September 1829): 201. The first six lines of the *Gazette* poem are retained with revisions in an otherwise completely rewritten work. The new work likely expresses Simms's grief at the loss of his wife. The dreary ocean landscape is a metaphor for his restless, desolate state of mind. It was published in the *Charleston City Gazette*, 25 April 1832, signed "M.E.S.," a few months after her death. Simms, although he never collected this poem, revised and published it again in *Southern Literary Gazette*, n.s., 2 (7 August 1852): 54, and as "Helmless— Adrift!" in *Southern Home Journal* 2 (23 May 1868). The 1852 poem is datelined "Sullivan's Island," an island north of Charleston from which Simms wrote several poems. The Moultrie House was a fashionable spa there. The text printed here is from the *Southern Literary Gazette* of 1852, with no emendations.

Notes

1. Roll on . . . roll: Adapted from Byron's *Childe Harold's Pilgrimage*, canto 4, stanza 179: "Roll on, thou deep and dark blue Ocean—roll!"

THE FEARFUL MEMORY.

This monologue in blank verse is spoken by a guilt-haunted narrator. As in "The Broken Arrow," "Ballad—Stanzas," and "The Modern Lion," Simms creates a speaker who is obviously not meant to be the poet himself and whose poem reveals his character, a feat rare in Simms's day. It is worth repeating that the poet's interest in psychology, especially its morbid aspects, points ahead to Poe, who will in such a work as "The Black Cat" (1843) also make use of the guilt-ridden narrator. In Simms's own canon, the poem bears close similarities to *Martin Faber* (1833), "Confessions of a Murderer" (1829), and *Confession* (1841), all treatments of criminal psychology narrated in the first person. The poem owes much to William Godwin, Schiller's "Der Verbrecher," and Goethe's *Sorrows of Werther;* the paragraph "rendered from a German romancer of repute" which formed the basis of the poem cannot be designated with assurance. "The Fearful Memory" is yet another example of Simms's prevailing interest from 1829 to 1833 in criminal psychology, a preoccupation which produced his first novel, *Guy Rivers,* in 1834.

There are also similarities to two preceding poems, "Broken Slumbers" and "Elegiac," which also treat the return of a dead loved one to the living. The speaker here is, however, a very different sort of man.

"The Fearful Memory" appeared only once, in *Book of My Lady* (1833), pp. 239–43. No emendations have been made except the placing of the prose paragraph, which introduced the poem, in a footnote.

THE EXILE. — A BALLAD.

A strongly autobiographical poem, "The Exile.—A Ballad" is interesting chiefly for several memorable lines and images and for its biographical information. The *Areytos* (1860) version notes that the poem was written "At Sea—1833," likely on Simms's journey to take up residence in the North. He had just barely escaped bodily harm when he and his Unionist newspaper office were assailed by a mob of

Nullifiers. With his wife's recent death, Charleston held painful memories for him. He felt his works were not sufficiently appreciated in his native place and thus decided to leave it. Of the works in which he is self-conscious, this is one of his best, although he is never his most effective in any poem in which he indulges in self-pity. Despite this weakness, the work is successful in demonstrating a conflict in the speaker. Through all his protest, his love for the place of his birth is obvious. It is this dialectical tension which saves the work; and it is not surprising that in the next poem of this edition, he will decide to return home. "The Exile" is also technically interesting. It is one of Simms's several works with heptameter lines. The pause which occurs within each line at varying places eliminates the inevitable monotony of stanzas each consisting of four long couplets without variation.

Although the bulk of the poem was written in 1833, the last stanzas were either added or altered in 1859 to apply to the current political scene in pre-war South Carolina. In 1833 there would have been no great need to call emigrated Carolinians back from the West to her defense; and in the sixth stanza, he likely refers to his Revolutionary romances, all of which postdate 1833.

The poem first appeared in *Russell's* 6 (December 1859): 205–6; then finally in *Areytos* (1860), pp. 103–6. The *Areytos* text is printed here with these emendations:

Title. [*As is usual in* Areytos, *the title is a repeat of the first line. The* Russell's *title has, therefore, been reinstated.*]

6.8. honor] honour

9.5. favor] favour

Both the above spellings are from the *Russell's* text and are Simms's customary ones. The replaced forms are likely housestylings from the Redfield *Poems.*

Notes

3.2. fathers: Simms's great-grandfather, Thomas Singleton, was a locally celebrated Patriot of the American Revolution.

3.5. prison-ship: During the Revolution, his great-grandfather was kept in a prison ship off Saint Augustine by the British.

5.8. noble talent: Simms is likely voicing here his theory of the *natural aristoi,* or Jeffersonian aristocracy of talent. He used both term and concept frequently. See, for example, *Letters,* 5:150, and his depiction of Dory Bostwick in *Woodcraft.*

STANZAS. *WRITTEN ON THE NORTH RIVER IN 1833.*

This poem, published here under Simms's name for the first time, has its basis in the poet's homesickness after his move north in 1833 following the death of his first wife. His love of home was soon to bring him back again, this time to stay. In theme, imagery, setting, and subject, the poem has much in common with "The Grape Vine Swing."

The poem appeared only once, in *Southern Literary Journal,* n.s., 1 (August 1837): 524, signed "G——." There are no emendations.

Notes

Title. North River: An estuary of the Hudson River.

7. urns: Probably alluding to his wife's and father's recent deaths.

25. wild strain: The black Congaree boatmen's signal horn. (See Simms's poem on the subject, "The Congaree Boatman's Horn.")

32. Hudson: River in New York.

32. Congaree: River in central South Carolina.

SONG.

Although Simms must have valued this lyric, he never collected it. It was published six times, each version being slightly revised: *Knickerbocker* 2 (November 1833): 340; *Magnolia* 2 (January 1843): 8, signed "Spiridion" and entitled "Myrrha"; *Broadway Journal* 2 (October 1845): 190; *Floral Offering* (1847), n.p.; *Charleston Mercury,* 5 August 1858; and *South Carolinian,* 6 April 1864, entitled "Love's Plea in Spring."

The *Knickerbocker* text is here published without emendation.

Notes

9–10. flower . . . hour: An obvious borrowing from Philip Freneau's "The Wild Honey Suckle," a line which Simms eliminated in all five versions that follow.

SONG. — I HAVE LIVED IN FANCIES.

The text of "Song" is from its only publication, in *Southern Field* 2 (14 July 1860):

57. Here it is dated 1834, two years after his wife's death and two years before his second marriage. Its first two stanzas provide a remarkably full autobiography of the poet. No emendations have been necessary.

FAREWELL STANZAS.

A good example of Simms's large group of occasional poems, or album verse, "Farewell Stanzas" is addressed to the sisters Cornelia, Caroline, and Mary Lawson, daughters of Simms's good friend and literary agent, James Lawson of 136 Twelfth Street, New York. Its only appearance, in *Rose Bud,* 27 December 1834, requires emendations:

Title. Standardizing capitalization.

6. Doomed] Doom'd

30. —— street] Twelfth-street

"COME BACK SOON."

Written during Simms's courtship of Chevillette, who was to become his wife the following year, this poem exists in four printed versions and in a manuscript pre-dating 1840: *American Monthly* 4 (1 February 1835); sheet music published in 1842 by George Willig of Philadelphia and Samuel Hart of Charleston as no. 7 of the "Songs of the South" series; *Southern Literary Messenger* 6 (April 1840): 292; and *Russell's* 3 (April 1858): 20.

The text is from *Russell's* with two emendations:

    1.1. then] thus [*Manuscript reading.*]
    2.6. soon?"] soon"?

THE AWAKENING.

This lyric exists in two major forms, a two- and a three-stanza version. The three-stanza version was first published in the *Charleston Mercury*, 21 February 1859, and reprinted in *Areytos* (1860), p. 143, reflecting some interesting biographical details, but marring the lyricism of the short version. The two-stanza poem appeared in *Knickerbocker* 5 (June 1835): 534; *Orion* 4 (May 1844): 132; and *Areytos* (1846), pp. 94–95, its subject possibly being Simms's grief over the loss of his wife in February 1832. The *Areytos* (1846) version is printed without emendation.

STANZAS TO A LADY WHO ASKED WHY MY VERSES WERE ALWAYS SAD.

This poem seeks to explain in striking imagery the basis for his melancholy themes. A barren external landscape of tempest and "shock" describes both the speaker's inner life and his poetry's tone. This is achieved through implicit metaphor in the third and fourth stanzas. The poem was published in *Rosebud* 4 (31 October 1835): 38; *Boston Notion* 2 (10 April 1841); and *Southern Literary Messenger* 27 (July 1858): 21. The text is from the *Boston Notion* with one change which repairs a damaged line with the 1835 and 1858 reading:

    3.1. mine] mine,

CAROLINA WOODS.

This poem, describing the red man's forest spirits that enliven nature and expressing the very Southern theme of the past's continued existence in the present, appeared as the epigraph to Simms's short story "Logoochie" in the *Magnolia Annual* (1836), p. 36. It was later expanded into a long poem in *Southern Patriot*, 30 January 1847, entitled "Carolina Woods"; and in *Poems* (1853), pp. 75–77, entitled

"Haunted Woods. A Fragment." The *Magnolia* version had no title, and the title is here taken from the *Southern Patriot.* There are no further emendations.

THE PRAYER OF THE LYRE.

This poem reveals Simms's concept of poetry as essential humanizing agent. Nature led a divinely inspired Bard to invent music, which "harmonized" earth, "made the stern heart gentle," and prepared the soul for eternity. The narrator finds modern man, "the changed shepherd," to have fallen from the old ways into harshness, selfishness, materialism, and isolation, and thus to be again in need of the ancient faith and lore, the old Bard's music from "nature's antique lyre," which would "win us with ancient lures to ancient worship still." Like "Moral Change" and "The Brooklet," this poem is another significant work written in 1836 which sets forth essential Romantic theory of a Coleridgean cast.

"The Prayer of the Lyre" was published in *Magnolia Annual* (1836), pp. 98–104; *Southern Passages* (1839), pp. 134–39; and *Magnolia Weekly* 11 (26 March 1864): 206. Simms revised it each time, making his most significant change in 1864, when he added stanzas 8, 10, and 21. The version printed here is this 1864 text, with the following emendations from the previous versions in keeping with sense and the poet's usual practice:

2.2. vexed] vex'd
2.3. those] these
4.5. When] Then
4.6. claimed] claim'd
6.5. Down—brought] Down-brought
7.2. fresh] forest-
12.3. sooth] soothe
16.5. unlift] uplift
19.4. spirits'] spirit's
25.3. cottag] cottage

LANDSCAPE.—SALUDA IN MIDSUMMER.

This poem was published four times, first in the *Magnolia Annual* (1836), signed "Claude" and entitled "Kaatskill," then in *Southern and Western,* November 1845, still signed "Claude," but now with a subtitle: "In Illustration of a Picture by Cole." For its third appearance, in *Charleston Mercury,* 17 November 1855, Simms changed the mountain setting to the Saluda range along the South and North Carolina border, one of Simms's favorite mountain spots. Simms first acknowledged his authorship on its last appearance in his collection *Areytos* (1860), the poem now revised and entitled "Landscape.—Saluda in Midsummer."

The "Landscape" of the title reveals that the poet still had in mind the influence of landscape painters like Thomas Cole in bringing the life of the mountains to the city drawing room and salon. In the poem both painter and nature poet perform the same task and become allied. The author here paints in words a similar scene with the same result of instilling a reverence for the natural, now graced and enhanced by the harmonies of art.

In the *Mercury* text Simms has offered this note: "Saluda—the reader will understand this as including the entire range of the Saluda mountains, with all their varieties of height and plain, rock and cataract."

The text printed here is from *Areytos,* with one emendation from the 1855 version:

    58. The] That

DEAR HARP OF THE FOREST.

In good Wordsworthian fashion, this poem treats a renewed love of nature after a period of despondency, and thereby a rekindling of poetic inspiration. The poem is likely autobiographical: the speaker's sorrow perhaps resulted from his first wife's death, and now his inspiration stems from his joy in Chevillette, who was soon to become his wife. The year 1836 was a happy time for Simms. He had just published *The Yemassee* and *The Partisan,* both very popular, and was being hailed as the great new American novelist. After his marriage he would also move to Woodlands plantation, a spot he grew to love very much. The large number of good poems which were written in this year marks it as one of his most fruitful.

There are two main versions of this poem: a short one, published four times, in the *Southern Literary Journal* 1 (February 1836): 442, as a series of "Carolina Melodies"; in *Magnolia* 1 (March 1840): 230; in *Areytos* (1846), pp. 8–9; and in an unlocated issue of the *South Carolinian* of 1866. The long version first appeared in the *Southern Literary Messenger* 6 (April 1840): 290; then as sheet music (2 March 1842); *Areytos* (1846), pp. 73–74; *Charleston Mercury,* 4 March 1859; and *Areytos* (1860), pp. 5–6. The text published here is the short version from *Magnolia* (1840), with three emendations from *Areytos* (1846):

    [*Reinstatement of numerals for stanzas, as was Simms's habit.*]
    3.5. nearer] dearer
    3.7. dearer] clearer

THE BROOKLET.

This blank-verse poem, like "The Streamlet," has as its central theme the uses of nature. It exists in a thirty-line version, published in the *Southern Literary Journal* 1 (April 1836): 90, and in *Southern Passages* (1839), pp. 1–2. The expanded version, printed here, appeared in *Cassique of Accabee* (1849), pp. 45–47, and *Poems* (1855), pp. 7–10. "The Brooklet" is a good example of how Simms could take a short poem and expand it successfully by the addition of effective descriptive passages. The text is from *Poems* (1853), with two readings from the *Cassique* text of 1849 in order to remove probable modernization by the editors of *Poems* (the last shows the kind of senseless grammatical tinkering made by the editors):

29. flowers] flow'rs
48. ? Squirrels] ; squirrels

Notes

43. the genius of the place: Simms learned from Indian lore that particular locales had spirits residing there as a result of past events which occurred therein. The red man honored this "genius of the place" with reverence, and sometimes with offerings. See *Early Lays,* p. 105. The importance of the living spirit of place and the past was equally strong in Simms.

COTTAGE LIFE.

Although the genesis of this poem came no later than 1828, its first stanza dates from 1836, the period when Simms wrote some of his best blank verse. The opening extended description of the cottage in the forest was added only after Simms's marriage to Chevillette, at whose country seat Simms took up residence in 1836. The bucolic setting described here is a pastoral landscape of the middle ground, poised between wilderness and city, a landscape whose peace is broken only by the occasional sound of mill machinery. As "Quiet's especial temple," the scene allows few rude sounds to break the "ancient ordering," in which there is none of the "doubt" or "despair" of crowded city life. In its use of imagery, tone, and soft, restful sounds which reinforce the tone, the poem is effective.

"Cottage Life" was printed five times: *Southern Literary Gazette* 1 (September 1828): 8; *Charleston City Gazette,* 22 October 1831; *Southern Literary Journal* 2 (April 1836): 92; *New Yorker* 6 (27 October 1838): 81; and *Southern Passages* (1839 [i.e., 1838]), pp. 20–22. The last of these is the text printed here, without emendation. A section of the first stanza appeared slightly revised in *Oracles from the Poets,* ed. Caroline Gilman (New York: Wiley & Putnam, 1844), pp. 225–26.

Notes

19. bee tree: The basswood or American linden.

THE SHADE-TREES.

This poem is another good example of Simms's growing preference for blank verse, a form which yielded some of his best poetry, although here, Simms's lines are not always pentameter. "The Shade-Trees" reveals the poet's early view of the inexhaustibleness of nature, a view which he later altered after seeing man's wanton destruction of forests on the frontier. It also suggests one basis for his displeasure with Christianity as often practiced. Simms styled himself a freethinker who, rather than disputing meanings of biblical texts and following the letter of the law, would seek to honor its spirit, which to him (in this poem, at least) meant a demonstration of one's love of mankind through self-sacrificing deeds of kindness. This he defines in "The Shade-Trees" as the "true religion." The poem's accurate, careful description of the heat of a lowcountry summer is also noteworthy.

"The Shade-Trees" was published in the *Southern Literary Journal* 3 (June 1836): 273; *Southern Passages* (1839), pp. 25–27; and *Poems* (1853), pp. 173–75. It underwent fewer revisions than most of his verse, for other than punctuation changes, the primary revision for *Poems* came in the final lines, which in the earlier texts had read:

> Happy, for mankind,
> Were such the toil of most who clamor much,
> And mouth in sacred texts,—vexing the heart
> With disputation. Better far to seek
> The distant wayside, and with kindly hand,
> Sink deep the shade-tree's roots whose friendly leaves
> The pilgrim blesses, while he blesses them.

The text printed here is from *Poems* (1853), without emendation.

MORAL CHANGE.

Another good poem of 1836, "Moral Change" relies heavily on Romantic philosophy imbibed largely from Coleridge. Lines 23–27 are, in fact, a close rendering of the following lines from "Dejection: An Ode": "O Lady! we receive but what we give, / And in our life alone does Nature live." In this poem, Simms demonstrates that nature is created through the mind which views it. If the mind is corrupt (as with materialism or cold scientific theory), nature too becomes corrupt. The result of an unfeeling or "unsympathetic" response to nature results in a fallen world, and isolation and "incompleteness" for the individual.

Simms here is working toward a looser form than blank verse, without either a basic iambic rhythm or fixed line length (although still primarily pentameter). Structurally the poem consists of two stanzas of thirty lines each. The last line is truncated, mirroring nicely the incompleteness described in the line.

The word *green* to describe *wand* symbolizes the green world of youth. Nature is now darkened by the dark views of the speaker, but he has moments when he can recall the green nature of his childhood. Memory waves her wand and raises the veil which had obscured the past and its imaginative time. The poem may thus be influenced by "Tintern Abbey."

"Moral Change" was published in *Southern Literary Journal* 3 (December 1836): 277–78; *Southern Passages* (1839), pp. 3–10; and *Poems* (1853), pp. 204–6. Like "The Shade-Trees," it differs from most of Simms's other verse in not being significantly altered in re-publication. Except for punctuation, the 1853 text is very close to that of 1836. The text here is from *Poems* (1853) with two emendations from the 1836 and 1839 appearances:

35. naught] nought
50. seasons] season

THE INDIAN VILLAGE.

This poem is one of Simms's most interesting for a number of reasons. First and foremost, it is effective satire. It also provides a hard, realistic look at the "noble savage" philosophy, a view which had influenced his creation of Indian character several years earlier in *The Yemassee*. His depiction of the red man in his first poems a decade before had also been sympathetic and colored by the romanticism and idealism of his youth. Here, the poet shows a totally different picture.

The poem was first published in the *Southern Literary Journal* 3 (January 1837): 343–44. It was then revised for *Southern Passages* (1839 [i.e., 1838]), pp. 49–53, from which this text comes, with the following emendations from the 1837 text and a manuscript written ca. 1868:

1. freedom] Freedom
26. wove] wore
38. Turkey Foot] Turkey-Foot
40. Flat] Fat
45. from] on
46. The "] "The
47. double dealing] double-dealing
52. cape positive] Cape Positive
75. 'gainst] gainst
75. shattered] shatter'd
105. Flat] Fat

Around 1868 Simms wrote a much-expanded manuscript, doubling the poem's length, setting the poem in a particular Indian village, and creating two characters who present contrasting views of the Indian. The realistic speaker, who has views similar to those expressed in "The Indian Village," is Simms's father, an experienced soldier who had fought the Creeks under Jackson; whereas the idealistic youth of the longer poem is likely the young poet himself. Simms then published the long poem in *Old Guard* in 1869; it is collected in this edition as "Chilhowee, the Indian Village."

Notes

5. "Burnt Corn" settlements: Settlements along Burnt Corn Creek of the lower Alabama River in southern Alabama. This was the site of the Battle of Burnt Corn in the Creek War of 1813. Simms's own father served in Coffee's Brigade in this war. It is likely his voice that we hear as narrator of the poem.

8. Yazoo: A river in western Mississippi which flows into the Mississippi River.

13–14. Hangs rocking: Unlike here, in his 1827 version of "The Green Corn Dance" Simms presents this custom as a pleasant idiosyncracy and implies there is virtue in it: "By this means, the form acquires that arrowy straightness and beautiful symmetry, for which the North American Indian is so very remarkable" (*Early Lays*, p. 105).

52. "Cape Positive": In English legal practice, a judicial writ touching a plea of lands or tenements. It was divided into *cape magnum* and *cape parvum*. Servitudes are also classed as *positive* or *negative*.

53. "non-committal": Another legal term having the common meaning of the adjective.

FIRST DAY OF SPRING.

In the poem's fifth stanza, the poet goes from a description of externals to show how spring makes him "feel." His emotions "bound," "break chains," and "leap" in parallel to "bursting buds," "leaping birds," and the "tender shoots" that "spring to birth." Thus the external landscape mirrors the internal one. Just as his feelings "bound" high after long suppression, spring renews life in all of nature's visible forms. The external landscape thus becomes the metaphor by which these feelings are effectively expressed.

The poem's tone reflects Simms's happiness in his new marriage and life at Woodlands. The poems of 1836 and 1837 mark a turn from the dominant Byronic melancholy of much of his youthful verse, a mood from which he would be largely free now for a decade.

The poem appeared first in *Knickerbocker* 9 (May 1837): 487, entitled "Spring" and datelined 1 April 1837, Orangeburg, South Carolina, a town near Woodlands. The *Southern Passages* (1839) and *Poems* (1853) texts differ in a few substantives from the *Knickerbocker*, and their meter is improved. The 1853 text is therefore reprinted here without emendation.

BOY LOST IN THE WOODS.

"Boy Lost in the Woods," while certainly not a profound poem, shows Simms at his best in a relaxed, conversational style. His blank verse is skillfully done, seeming very natural; and he is conscious of sound as a means of reinforcing sense (as at 6.15–21, where he uses the confusion of complicated syntax to suggest the boy's own confusion in the forest maze). His images are effective: for example, the waning sun grieving over his forced departure from the earth, the lengthening shadows "cast, like old men's dreams, upon the longer past," or the editor as a monster who sits on a tribunal mound made of the skulls of slaughtered authors. Perhaps the poem's greatest strengths however are its genial humor and the successful creation of an easy, casual tone of amused detachment which helps reveal the personality of the narrator, who, as a grownup, clearly recognizes that as a youth he was proud, fastidious, hardheaded, and vain. Yet, too, the man knows that his present resolve and strong will grew out of the boy's will to freedom. The child, in this respect, did become father to the man.

The autobiographical details of the poem are accurate in describing young William's situation at the time: being without a father, living in the city, and being fascinated by nature and woodmen's realistic tales, which he hopes one day to translate into stories in the woodman's "self-same language . . . nor abate a jot / Wherein his speech was rude, for any ear." (Simms, in fact, was soon to publish his first frontier novel, *Guy Rivers*.) Also highly significant are the comments in stanza 19, added in 1837, about current "insidious" literary fashions "warp'd away from nature,"—fashions which favor "rash" romances and find such tales as the woodman's out of date.

All in all, the poem reveals Simms to be a genial Southern Wordsworth reflecting on childhood, but in a far different manner from the poet of the "Intimations" ode. This is not a philosophical poem and musters its strength instead from the good-natured warmth, down-to-earth realism, concreteness, frankness, and humor of its extroverted narrator. It is quintessentially Southern in many ways, including its casual, conversational, relaxed tone.

"Boy Lost in the Woods" was published twice, first in short form in *Southern Literary Gazette* 1 (November 1828): 135–37, signed "Jonathan," and second in the *Southern Literary Messenger* 3 (August 1837): 505–7—and signed "Quince," likely after Peter Quince of *A Midsummer Night's Dream*. It was never collected and appears here under his name for the first time. Simms pasted it in his Scrapbook A, thus proving his authorship. The *Southern Literary Messenger* text is expanded from the *Southern Literary Gazette* by the addition of stanzas 1, 3, 5, and 18, and most of stanzas 17 and 20. In stanza 19, the image of the editor and the important last five lines are added in 1837. The poem's other lines are heavily revised. The 1828 version had not been divided by stanza numerals. A prefatory note to the 1828 text explains that the poem was "intended to hit off the peculiar character of the writings of Coleridge. The subject is well adapted to the rambling manner of that eccentric author; and the occasional points of antithesis may serve to bring Hood's more sentimental efforts to the reader's recollection." The 1837 text is published here with the following emendations:

[*All large roman numerals are changed to small ones in Simms's habitual manner in his manuscripts.*]
    1.3. eveving] evening
    5.8. as] an
    15.3. her's] hers

Notes
    3.5. close city: Probably a description of his native Charleston, with its "suburbs" of "white houses."
    3.15. mother: Likely *grandmother* in actuality; his mother died in 1808, when he was two.
    11.15. Confusion worse confused: After John Milton, *Paradise Lost*, book 2, line 996: "confusion worse confounded."
    17.1–4. An accurate description of the Southern pioneer cabin.
    18.8. Hoe-cake: Simms is accurate in describing its derivation.

20.38. *sub-rosa:* A legal term for "covertly."

LINES IN THE ALBUM OF THE LATE MISS M. T. R——.

Simms may have deemed this occasional lyric either too personal or too ephemeral to collect under his name. It was published only once, under the proved pseudonym "Alceus," in *Southern Literary Messenger* 3 (August 1837): 514. The lady is unidentified. The text is from *Southern Literary Messenger* without emendation and appears here under Simms's name for the first time.

ANACREONTIC.

This lyric was published twice, but not under Simms's name, and was never collected, perhaps because it deals with the passion of love too explicitly for the time. The first appearance was signed "G. B. Singleton" in *Knickerbocker* 10 (September 1837): 173. Simms then made minor improvements in *Southern Literary Messenger* 7 (July 1841): 470, the text published here with these emendations: "I." and "II." become "I" and "ii" in keeping with Simms's habitual practice in his manuscripts. The title "Wilt Thou Then Leave Me?" is changed to the *Knickerbocker*'s "Anacreontic" because the *Southern Literary Messenger* version was published as part of a series in which all titles were standardized to first lines.

The title alludes to the Greek poet Anacreon; and "Anacreontic" has come to describe any light lyric, particularly of an amatory tone.

TWILIGHT MUSINGS.

This poem was never signed or collected under Simms's name. It was first published in *Knickerbocker* 10 (October 1837): 301, under the pseudonym "G. B. Singleton"; then in *Magnolia,* n.s., 1 (December 1842): 374, signed "Spiridion"; and finally unsigned in *Richards,*' 15 September 1849. The *Magnolia* version is an improvement over the *Knickerbocker,* but the *Richards'* text has lost life through overpolishing. The version printed here is the *Magnolia* with these emendations from an early manuscript version in Scrapbook A:

> [*Numerals are added to mark the stanzas.*]
> 7. pow'r] power

ASHLEY RIVER.

When in the second stanza of "Ashley River" the poet alludes to the loved ones he has left, he likely means his parents, brothers, grandmother, and first wife, all lost to him through death. From the banks of Ashley, a favorite haunt of his youth in

Charleston and the subject of one of his first poems while still a child, he must now move inland to another stream, the Edisto, and to the "other clime" of Woodlands plantation. In essence, the speaker is saying that he will no longer be obsessed by past griefs, and will instead seek to begin a new life. His last stanza reveals a conflict, however, when the narrator says he can never forget what he had loved so well—the river being tied to the memories of the lost loved ones for which it becomes an effective symbol.

This simple lyric is one of my personal favorites. It illustrates well the themes of loss, exile, and remembrance that so dominate the first two decades of Simms's poetic career.

The poem reveals much polishing in the five times it was published: *Southern Literary Journal*, n.s., 3 (March 1838): 175; *Southern Literary Messenger* 6 (December 1840): 837; *Areytos* (1846), p. 58; *Southern Literary Messenger* 27 (September 1858): 196–97; and *Areytos* (1860), pp. 194–95. In polishing, however, the poet often robs the work of spontaneity, thus marring the lyric more than its small imperfections had. Therefore the text printed here is of the first publication of 1838, with one emendation:

2.1. blessed] bless'd

THE HUNTER OF CALAWASSEE.

The hunt of a fabulous animal that takes on supernatural attributes is a motif long established in folklore. Here, the obsessive nature of the hunter foreshadows works like *Moby-Dick* and T. B. Thorpe's "The Big Bear of Arkansas."

"The Hunter of Calawassee" is an excellent example of Simms's large group of narrative poems. Like "The Green Corn Dance" and "The Exile.—A Ballad," it is written in iambic heptameter couplets, the lines all having caesurae, a very appropriate technique for the telling of an ancient tradition. William Elliott likewise recounts this folk legend in his *Carolina Sports* (1846). It is interesting to note that Simms's poem first appeared in the same issue of the *Southern Literary Journal* in which Elliott's "Devil-Fishing" was published, thus suggesting Elliott was likely aware of Simms's tale before writing his own famous prose version.

Kedar's character is carefully delineated. His disrespectful treatment of the old and faithful Lauto is mirrored in his irreverent attitude toward nature—as seen in his cruelty to his "noble" steed and in the mad rush to kill this special deer. That Kedar himself dies in the process leads to the poem's chief theme that to destroy nature invites self-destruction. This is a common thematic thread throughout Simms's poetry, fiction, and essays. The poem has much in common with Coleridge's "Rime of the Ancient Mariner," where he "prayeth well, who loveth well / Both man and bird and beast." The outcome of Kedar's story is far different from the mariner's, however; and Simms's tale is both darker and less hopeful in that the power over nature exterminates the man who does not learn the lesson of the proper reverence for creation "both great and small." Kedar, very much the willful modern man, is the monomaniac whose obsessive quest brings annihilation.

Simms understands that there must be bounds to the quest and that man's willfulness has to have curbs.

Simms himself was a hunter who knew that there must be a time not to hunt at all. Not to heed these laws was sacrilege, for proper hunting was sacramental and had to be done with reverence. Kedar fails on all counts.

The buck likely represents more than nature, perhaps the mysterious and unfathomable nature of life itself. Too close a pursuit and rashly ignoring bounds to it may plunge the pursuer to his death. Like Kedar, modern man's arrogance in placing himself over nature and its creator will lead inevitably to destruction. Delphi's oracle had cautioned that man should know his place—that is, that he is the created, not the Creator, and should not try to assume more than his finite position. Lauto, a humble slave, through his very humility, has learned that wisdom. His master, arrogant to his death, never does.

For a treatment of this poem, see Doreen Thierauf, "Ancient Wisdom versus Material Progress in Simms's 'The Hunter of the Calawassee,'" in a forthcoming issue of *Mississippi Quarterly*.

The poem was published three times: *Southern Literary Journal*, n.s., 3 (April 1838): 277–80; *Southern Passages* (1839), pp. 99–108; and *Poems* (1853), 1:288–93. There are few variants among these texts, remarkably few considering the usual high number of revisions. The text is from *Poems* (1853) with the following emendations from the earlier versions to replace broken lines or eliminate what appears to be housestyling:

> 5.7. w] we came,
> 5.8. s] shame!
> 6.4. again] agen
> 12.6. race;] race;—

The second and third sentences of Simms's note on the fall of the leaf are from the 1838 text. All symbols to mark Simms's footnotes have been changed to superscript numerals.

Notes

Title. Calawassee: Spelled *Caliwasee* on the Mills *Atlas* map of Beaufort County, South Carolina (1825). It is an island in a cypress swamp between the Colleton and Chechessee rivers in lower central Beaufort County. The *Atlas* shows the area to be uninhabited.

2.2. Ocketee: A river and creek of this name flow by Caliwasee Island into the Colleton River. They are surrounded by cypress swamp.

5. footnote 2. Gascoigne's "Commendation of the noble Arte of Venerie": Poems attributed to George Gascoigne, first printed in 1575.

7.4. Rollo's pack: Unidentified. Rollo was a Norman king.

16.1. Che-che-see: A wide river near Caliwasee Island surrounded by cypress swamp.

SONNET—THE WREATH.

This poem's speaker, a true Romantic, praises the simpler, local, and more famil-
iar over the showy, exotic beauty of the "wide wood" which calls attention to itself.
The universal application comes in mankind's failure to value those objects clos-
est to home. The poem is a verse counterpart in some ways to Simms's literary
creed that the artist should use and take inspiration from the local. It gives spe-
cial significance to his statement that "I have been the first to reveal the latent and
romantic uses which lay in the soil" (*Letters*, 6: 199). "Sonnet" bears close thematic
similarity to "The Beauty of Departing Objects."

The poem varies the rhyme of the Shakespearean sonnet but retains its octave-
sestet-couplet structure. Its text is printed without emendation from its only
appearance, in *Southern Literary Journal*, n.s., 3 (April 1838): 273, a clipping of
which is in his Scrapbook A. It is collected here for the first time under Simms's
name.

MEMORY.

As a result of effective imagery and diction, this poem is noteworthy. An external
scene of barren winter is skillfully used to portray an interior landscape of a deso-
late heart, in a manner reminiscent of modern verse. With its emphasis on the
death of a loved one and its eerie imagery, "Memory" again indicates why Poe was
an early admirer of Simms's poetry and was perhaps influenced by him.

"Memory" was published in *Southern Literary Journal*, n.s., 4 (December 1838):
437, and *Atalantis* (1848), p. 142, the latter being the text printed here without
emendation.

INVOCATION.

"Invocation" was addressed to the poet's second wife, Chevillette, whom he had
married two years earlier. It was first published as "Invocation: A Southern Pic-
ture" in the *Knickerbocker* for October 1838, with a dateline of Charleston, Sep-
tember 1838. The "quiet grove" away from the bustling world is Woodlands on the
Edisto River, where the couple lived. Simms's recognition that Eden's blisses can
last only for a brief moment provides a nice touch of reality to the idyllic picture
and creates an effective dramatic tension and balance, especially because in the
background of the poem is the "coarse discord" and "violence" of the world that
lies just outside their fragile bower. Parts of the work contain some of Simms's
most charming descriptions of his life at Woodlands and a particularly lovely trib-
ute to his wife, who, as the imagery effectively suggests, was noted for her gentle-
ness. The imagery of harmonious sound is also appropriate because Chevillette
was a talented singer and musician. The poem's composition originated during a
very happy time in Simms's life and a period which produced some of his best

poetry, a time valued even more dearly because the speaker realizes, from what experience has taught him, that this happiness will not last forever, as it truly did not.

The text printed here is from the only other publication of the poem, *Southern Passages* (1839 [i.e., 1838]), pp. 88–89, with one emendation from *Knickerbocker* in keeping with the poet's usual practice:

11. Filled] Fill'd

TAMING THE WILD HORSE.

Written largely from the point of view of the horse, this vigorous poem is a remarkable instance of negative capability. It also trumpets the great zeal for untrammeled freedom so dear to the Romantic. As a song of praise for wilderness, it bears similarities to "The Slain Eagle."

The setting is probably the prairie of the Southern frontier, which Simms knew from his travels of 1824–31.

This poem appeared only once, in *Southern Passages and Pictures* in 1839 [i.e., 1838]. In his Scrapbook D. Simms has made one correction on a clipping from *Southern Passages*. At line 24 he has deleted "—imperious" after "his." The text printed here is from *Southern Passages* with the sole emendations being Simms's correction and the addition of a space in *if twere*, line 24.

LAY OF LEONORA.

This sprightly poem's tripping meter and close and jingling rhyme again show that Simms was aware of the value of sound as a means of reinforcing sense. The poem's light humor provides another example of a strength which Simms shows in abundance in both his fiction and verse. The poem's underlying theme, learned from observation, is that actions and not words will win a lady fair.

The poem first appeared in *Roberts'* 2 (15 June 1841): 563; then *Magnolia*, n.s., 2 (March 1843): 171; and Simms's *Donna Florida* (1843), p. 45. The text printed here is the last, with no emendations other than lowercasing the numerals.

THE LAND OF THE PINE.

This lyric is almost prayerful in its speaker's expression of love for the Southern homeland and his desire never to be separated from it. It was published in *Southern Literary Messenger* 7 (July 1841): 470, before being expanded to four stanzas in *Areytos* (1846), pp. 10–11, and *Poems* (1853), 2:103–4. The text for this edition is the short 1841 version with the following revisions from *Areytos*:

1.1. Pine] pine

1.6. hope] song

2.3. its] the soul of its

2.3. vanish and die] die

2.4. Let me still see] Still let me see

2.5. the] its

2.6. odors] blessings

The *Areytos* text, it should be noted, was expanded as a call to arms in the war with Mexico. The poem's emphasis is thus changed greatly.

MY LOVE, LOVES ME.

The lightness, simplicity, unpretentiousness, and sincerity of this poem are all strengths that make it one of Simms's best love lyrics. Unlike the works of so many of his contemporaries, this poem is unencumbered by romantic sentimentality and artificial diction. Simms was apparently still enjoying his happy life at Woodlands.

The poem is here printed from its only appearance in the *Southern Literary Messenger* 7 (July 1841): 471. The sole emendation has been to make all numerals lower case.

An early version of this poem ("You Ask Me How I Love Thee") appeared in *Godey's* 4 (June 1832): 289, and was incorporated in *Beauchampe* (1842), pp. 363–64.

SONNET. — I WILL BREATHE MUSIC.

The early version of 1828 appears at p. 30 of this edition. The second version printed here is from the *Ladies' Companion* 16 (November 1841): 39. The early version's "rose" has become a more interesting flower of "blue cells," this change perhaps suggesting the influence of German Romantic poetry, in which *die blaue Blume* was a primary symbol.

Simms then published the poem three more times in revised forms: *Southern Literary Messenger* 10 (July 1844): 422–23; *Grouped Thoughts* (1845), p. 6; and *Areytos* (1860), p. 406. The *Ladies' Companion* text has been judged superior and is here printed with one emendation:

14. flower] flow'r

SOLACE OF THE WOODS.

This variant of the Shakespearean sonnet voices a central Romantic theme. Nature is the restorer of the soul of an individual who has become tainted by the materialism and tedium of city life or, as the poet puts it, "the narrowing toils of trade."

This poem was published in *Magnolia* 4 (May 1842): 275; *Southern Literary Messenger* 10 (July 1844): 423; *Grouped Thoughts* (1845), pp. 10–11; *Poems* (1853), p. 12. The text here printed is the last, with three emendations taken from early versions in keeping with Simms's usual practice and considering the housestyling of the *Poems* volume:

> 4. care—] care,—
> 8. listener—] listener,—
> 8. unafraid—] unafraid,—

LOVE'S TOUR FOR THE PICTURESQUE.

The place names of this poem are actual; they exist in the mountain region of northeast Georgia. Guy Rivers is Simms's character from his novel of that title set in this area.

The poem's only appearance was in *Magnolia*, n.s., 2 (July 1842): 29, signed "Childe Hazard," a proved pseudonym appropriate to the subject matter, which is reminiscent of Byron's *Childe Harold's Pilgrimage*. Two emendations have been made:

> 18. Torrora's] Toccoa's
> 42. Torrora] Toccoa

The poem's publication in the July issue of the *Magnolia* was appropriate, because as editor, Simms was bidding farewell for the summer season and would "see" his readers again in the fall, precisely as the poem says. That the poet emphasizes "the living for love, not the dying" marks a shift in both attitude and tone from his early verse. His tone had been lightening now for several years, and his emphasis shifting to physical rather than romantic love.

DREAMING OR WAKING.

This Byronic lyric was never published under Simms's name possibly owing to its suggestiveness. It is another poem that emphasizes the physical side of love. It was signed "Childe Hazard" in *Magnolia*, n.s., 1 (August 1842): 109, then expanded, although not for the better, in *Magnolia Weekly* 1 (8 August 1863): 268. The early text is here printed without emendation.

NIGHT SCENE: MOULTRIE HOUSE—
SULLIVAN'S ISLAND.

This poem is set on Sullivan's Island, near the city of Charleston. In stanza 4, therefore, the two rivers are the Ashley and Cooper, which find their "sleep" in the bay, that is, Charleston Harbor. Looking westward from the island, the view is that presented in the poem. To the east is the Atlantic, hence the description of white-caps. "Night Scene" is thus a poem which describes a particular setting carefully and accurately.

The poem was first published in *Magnolia*, n.s., 2 (January 1843): 40; then in the *Charleston Mercury,* 7 August 1858; and lastly, in *Areytos* (1860), pp. 59–61. The text is from *Areytos* with these emendations. Capital numerals are reduced to lower case; and the subtitle is changed from "How Still Is Nature Now!" to the *Mercury*'s "Moultrie House—Sullivan's Island."

SONNET. — BY THE SWANANNOA.

There are two main texts of this poem, that of *Magnolia*, n.s., 2 (March 1843): 197, and *Southern Literary Messenger* 11 (August 1845): 485. The latter was collected in *Grouped Thoughts* (1845), p. 46, and *Poems* (1853), p. 17. The text published here is from *Poems* with no revisions.

The primary difference between the two versions is the couplet, which in 1843 had read: "And skirts the gentle slope, the Grace's seat, / Where Dickson muses in his calm retreat." In the earlier couplet, Simms is likely referring to fellow Charlestonian Samuel Henry Dickson (1798–1872), to whom he dedicated *The Yemassee*. Dickson held the chair of medicine at the Medical College of South Carolina for many years and was a poet and essayist. He purchased tracts of land on the Swanannoa River near Asheville from Dr. J. F. E. Hardy (also a native South Carolinian) in 1837 and 1843 and built a home, "Swanannoa Hill." His brother Dr. John Dickson (1795–1847) also resided in Buncombe County, North Carolina.

The poet particularly emphasizes the use of sound to reinforce sense in this poem; the enjambement in the first line and the lengthened last line effectively suggest the flowing river.

Notes

    4. Ausonian: Frequently used in poetry to mean "Italian," after Ausonia in southern Italy.

SHAKSPEARE.

This tribute to Shakespeare is a very fine one indeed. It was first printed in the *Magnolia*, n.s., 2 (May 1843): 287–88, which text is reprinted here without emendation. Subsequent versions in *Graham's* 33 (September 1848): 170–71; *Cassique of Accabee* (1849), pp. 82–83; and *Poems* (1853), pp. 155–56, are expanded to include an emphasis on Shakespeare as poet of nature by the banks of Avon. While the revised versions are interesting as revelations of the Romantic view of the Bard, the early text is a superior poem. Simms's knowledge of Shakespeare was extensive and was a great influence on his career. His *A Supplement to the Plays of Shakspeare* (1848) included a biography of the dramatist.

INFANT SMILING IN SLEEP.

The text is taken without emendation from the poem's only appearance: *Magnolia*, n.s., 2 (May 1843): 307. The unsigned work is known to be by Simms owing to its inclusion in the poet's scrapbooks. It later became the basis of a three-part poem, "Sonnets. Sleeping Infant Smiling in Its Mother's Arms," in *Russell's* 3 (June 1858): 222.

FOREST WORSHIP.

Simms's basic images in this poem depict God as the great architect with nature as his temple (here a localized Southern structure whose pillars are tall pines). It then follows that owing to its architect, the forest is the most appropriate place of worship and that God favors the prayer offered here by the "child of misery," over the worship of fortunate ones who seek gilded altars. Simms again shows his dissatisfaction with organized religion.

Like the "child of misery" whose loved ones sleep in forest graves, Simms chose a forest plot at Woodlands for his dead, a logical extension of the metaphor of forest as temple, for its burial sites would thus be hallowed ground in close proximity to the house of worship.

The view of God as architect sounds Neoclassical, particularly because he appears to be a Neoclassical or Greek Revival builder. The forest, as Simms pictures it, is a classical temple with pillars, not a cathedral with arches and spires; and although the forest as temple of nature was to become a Romantic cliché, Simms created a structure which departed from the Gothic cathedral of the stereotype. (See, for example, William Cullen Bryant's "Forest Hymn.") Perhaps the poem's most significant line contrasts the gold altar with the forest of "rude scatter'd emblems," a phrase which shows once again that the poet was aware of the emblematic or symbolic nature of the world.

"Forest Worship" was first published in *Godey's* in November 1843. The text is from the second and final appearance, in *Sabbath Lyrics* (1849), with two emendations from the *Godey's* version in keeping with Simms's usual practice:

13. offered] offer'd
15. proffered] proffer'd

NOTES FROM BARTRAM.

Simms quotes from William Bartram's *Travels* in his *Early Lays* (1827), p. 107. He began taking notes on Bartram's *Travels* around 1844 in a ledger which he entitled "Notes from ." The precise date of these jottings is uncertain. The only indication of their time of composition is Simms's statement in the *Charleston Courier* of 9 May 1867 that he wrote them "twenty odd years ago." Interpreting this phrase as meaning a few years more than twenty, I have assigned the poem's date as around 1844. Simms's practice in the ledger was to borrow a striking Bartram image, or "word picture" as Simms called it, and to render it in blank verse, using, as the poet reports, Bartram's imagery "and amplifying his suggestions with my own, the better to perfect his pictures."

Some of these ledger entries he used as the basis for a series of *Russell's* poems in 1858. In 1867 he went back to his ledger to create one number of a twelve-part travel series (entitled "Flights to Florida") for the *Courier* of 9 May 1867, in which the ledger entries are only slightly altered. The *Russell's* versions had had short introductions such as "Here you see" or "I bring you here to see" in order to allow the poems to stand alone. In the *Courier* series, however, these are unnecessary, for its introduction tells the reader from the outset that these are related images, sketches, and vignettes, not separate titles. It is the *Courier* text which is printed here, with corrections of numerous compositorial errors based on the manuscript and *Russell's* versions.

Numbers 19 ("The Pompous Palms of Florida"), 24 ("The Forest of Agave"), 38 ("The New Moon"), 40 ("Forest Lunch"), and 57 ("Keowee") do not appear in the *Courier.* Numbers 24 and 57 come from the ledger manuscript and are published here for the first time. Numbers 19, 38, and 40 are from *Russell's* 3 (April 1858): 35, (May 1858): 137, and (May 1858): 168, respectively. Because the *Courier* text was signed "Clytus," the entire "Notes from Bartram" is published here under Simms's name for the first time.

The following emendations have been made to the *Courier* text:

[*Title taken from ledger in Charles Carroll Simms Collection, South Caroliniana Library. The* Courier *title, "Flights to Florida," applies to the twelve-part travel series and not to the series of poems.*]

3.2. arched] archéd [Russell's *text.*]

3.4. dried] Druid [*Manuscript of this poem in Scrapbook B.*]

3.6. fraternal] paternal [*Ledger manuscript and* Russell's.]

3.7. old] eld [*Manuscript of this poem in Scrapbook B and a penciled revision by Simms on a clipping in Scrapbook B.*]

4.6. badges] hedges [*Manuscript of this poem in Scrapbook B.*]

4.8. warrior legions] warrior-legions [Russell's *clipping in Scrapbook B revised by Simms.*]

7.4. bottom] hollow [*Ledger manuscript.*]

8.7. Pale,] Pale [*Ledger manuscript.*]

12.1. wave] move [Russell's *text.*]

14.0, 2. Azalee] Azalæa [Russell's *text.*]

16.3. your] yon [Russell's *text.*]

17.5. flame glance] flame-glance [Russell's *text.*]

17.8. Charges] Clangs [Russell's *text.*]

19.0–7. [*The text comes entirely from* Russell's. *It is placed in this position because in Bartram's* Travels, *it is in this position.*]

20.0. Chionea] Chironia [*Ledger manuscript.*]

21.0. Ockrys] Ophrys [*Ledger manuscript.*]

22.0. Leeds] Seeds [*Ledger manuscript.*]

24.0–2. [*The text comes entirely from the ledger manuscript.*]

25.2. drowsing] drowsy [Russell's *text.*]

33.0, 1. Andronada] Andromeda [*Ledger manuscript and* Russell's.]

34.0. Ephonskya] Ephouskyca [*Ledger manuscript and* Russell's.]

38.0–4. [*The text comes entirely from* Russell's *and ledger manuscript.*]

40.0–20. [*The text comes from* Russell's *and ledger manuscript.* Russell's "green palms" *at 40.2 is emended to* "great palms" *as in ledger manuscript.*]

43.3. centenels] centinels [*Ledger manuscript.*]

43.5. Swell] Swells [*Ledger manuscript.*]

44.1. acorn] acorn, [*Ledger manuscript.*]

45.0. Evandiflora] Grandiflora [*Ledger manuscript.*]

51.0, 3. Xanthoxilus] Xanthoxilon [*Ledger manuscript.*]

54.1. gray] gay [*Ledger manuscript.*]

57.0. [*Title supplied by editor in absence of title.*]

57.1–3. [*The text comes entirely from the ledger manuscript.*]

Notes

In the introduction to the poems in "Flights to Florida" (*Courier,* 9 May 1867), Simms writes: "I propose to give you, in this, my last chapter, [notes] such as I made from the pages of that dear old enthusiast, William Bartram, twenty odd years ago. Of this famous and fine old traveler . . . I have something said already. He was not merely a naturalist, but possessed of a decided fancy and enthusiasm, which perpetually lifted him into the purple atmosphere of Poesy. He colored richly; dipped his brushes in the rainbow, and borrowed wings for vision from the imagination, which enabled him to rise always above the clouds. In making notes from Bartram, I have, almost insensibly, been beguiled by his fancy into the exercise of my own. I have made my notes mostly in a metrical form—in blank verse—using his imagery and amplifying his suggestions with my own, the better to perfect his pictures. His phrases and epithets are sometimes exquisitely happy; and the scraps that I shall quote to you, from these, my notes, may hereafter be employed, with equal propriety, by the enthusiast naturalist, as he roves the forest, and by the lovely damsel as she turns over the leaves of her Album or Herbarium."

11.2. coracle: Bartram's boat, a gift of Henry Laurens of Charleston.

40.3. bay: Simms notes in the *Old Guard* text of this section (October 1866, pp. 603–8) that the bay is the "Dwarf Laurel," that is, the *Magnolia virginiana.*

41.0. Compare the poem "The Palmetto Royal."

1–57. The page numbers of the references to Bartram's *Travels* (reprint, New York: Dover, 1955) that form the bases for Simms's poems are: no. 1, p. 16; 2, p. 61; 3, p. 94; 4, unlocated; 5, p. 17; 6, p. 19; 7, p. 18; 8, p. 93; 9, p. 66; 10, pp. 65 and 137; 11, p. 65; 12, p. 65; 13, p. 60; 14, p. 17; 15, p. 62; 16, p. 19; 17, unlocated; 18, p. 16; 19, p. 17; 20, p. 17; 21, p. 17; 22, p. 20; 23, p. 35; 24, unlocated; 25, p. 34; 26, p. 35; 27, p. 35; 28, p. 37; 29, p. 37; 30, p. 42; 31, p. 43; 32, p. 43; 33, p. 47; 34, pp. 65 and 137; 35, unlocated; 36, p. 65; 37, pp. 65 and 44; 38, p. 66; 39, p. 71; 40, p. 73; 41, p. 81; 42, p. 88; 43, p. 89; 44, p. 90; 45, p. 91; 46, p. 90; 47, p. 92; 48, p. 105; 49, p. 106; 50, p. 106; 51, p. 107; 52, p. 111; 53, p. 126; 54, p. 129; 55, p. 189; 56, p. 190; 57, p. 363.

57. In commenting on the poems at the end of "Flights to Florida," Simms wrote: "These specimens, drawn mostly from the pages of old Bartram, will suffice to suggest to the naturalist, the poet and the painter, the resources of Florida, in material history, and the picturesque; and the elements of fine poems and fine pictures [that] abound in all sections of this peculiar country. It will be seen that many of the descriptive epithets employed by Bartram, in his delineations of natural objects, whether bird, or beast, or fish, shrubs, trees, or plants, are singularly felicitous in their truthfulness, and fanciful in their choice. I could multiply their number indefinitely, but if these shall persuade the reader to a perusal and study of the charming volume of this spirited old traveler, I shall be quite satisfied. ... He traverses some of the most picturesque regions of Georgia and South Carolina; passes into our mountains, when they were still tenanted by the Cherokees; along our seaboard and middle regions, while they were still occupied by the remnants of the Yemassee, the growing tribes of the Seminole, and while the Muscoghee and Choctaw, were still in power, and capable of sending their thousands of warriors into the field, such as subsequently forced old Hickory to his hardest fighting and made all his triumphs costly. In all Bartram's wanderings, no matter in what region, or among what people, whatsoever the scene, circumstance, or situation, he never once foregoes his keen faculty for observation, search, or analysis; nor loses, at any time, that fine felicitous fancy which fills his volume with *word* pictures, appealing to the eye as well as to the mind, and suggesting corresponding and sympathetic fancies to the mind which travels with him." Simms too was a careful and perceptive observer of nature, as shown in James Kibler, "Simms as Naturalist," *Mississippi Quarterly* 31 (Fall 1978): 499–518.

SHADOWS.

The genesis of "Shadows" is an *Album* (27 August 1825) publication of the same title, which was slightly revised for *Poems* (1827), pp. 52–55. The version printed here, from *Orion* 3 (January 1844): 194, is an extensive rewriting, possibly in light of his first wife's death in 1832.

A still later version, published in 1865 after the death of his second wife, also appears in this edition, under the same title.

WITCH OF ELLANO.

The meter of this poem appropriately suggests the incantation. It was first published in *Godey's* 28 (February 1844): 76, as "Witchcraft," then in *Areytos* (1846), pp. 28–29, and *Areytos* (1860), pp. 334–35. It was not until 1860 that Simms added lines 2.5–3.4. The *Areytos* (1860) version is here printed with the following emendation from the earlier texts in keeping with Simms's usual practice:

    3.5. glance—] glance,—

In addition, roman numerals are all made lower case.

PARTING. A FRAGMENT.

This poem, written in ottava rima, carries one elaborate figure throughout: an extended metaphor which likens the speaker's heart to a harp, whose musician is Ianthe. The use of the name Ianthe (from Byron's poem to Mary Harley) and of ottava rima both suggest Lord Byron's strong influence. The work's primary merits are lyricism, competence in handling the metaphor, and pleasant, effective diction.

"Parting" appeared only in *Orion* 4 (July 1844): 225, unsigned. Simms never collected it except in his scrapbooks, and it appears here for the first time under his name. Only one emendation, the kind of housestyled punctuation he customarily removed when revising, has been necessary:

4. play'd,] play'd

FLOWERS AND TREES *AND* THE SAME SUBJECT.

"Flowers and Trees" is one of Simms's most skillfully constructed sonnets. The three quatrains lead logically to the couplet in which Simms explains why he prefers the live oak over spring flowers: through its survival, the oak teaches him the meaning of endurance. It thus becomes a symbol, again demonstrating Simms's awareness of the world's emblematic nature. The poem also makes effective use of personification, with the ancient oak becoming a Druid patriarch, a particularly appropriate image considering that the oak was especially venerated in Druidical religion. In both poems, Simms takes his subjects from the local scene which he knew well. The description of the live oak as "hoary-headed" signifies that it is draped with Spanish moss—an accurate description rather than a poetic affectation.

The purpose of "The Same Subject" is to describe and to advocate an esthetic approach to nature over a scientific or mechanical one. Simms's knowledge of the "species" of plants was extensive (his interest in naturalists like Bartram has been demonstrated); but his emphasis here is on their deeper lessons, never taught by books.

Both poems were published in *Southern Literary Messenger* 10 (July 1844): 423; *Grouped Thoughts* (1845), pp. 8–9; and *Poems* (1853), p. 11, and are printed here from *Poems* without emendation.

Notes

The Same Subject.
3–5. The maple and redbud, both showy in the early spring in the Carolina lowcountry, are accurately described.
7. laurel: The common name in Simms's day for the *Magnolia grandiflora,* a tree native to the Carolina lowcountry.

RELIGIOUS MUSINGS.

The subject of this sonnet is the symbolic nature of creation. In physical nature reside hidden spiritual springs and powerful meanings. The simile of nature as a Jacob's Ladder which lifts the speaker to spiritual truths is appropriate because both the poet's view of nature and the biblical phenomenon involve divinely inspired visions of transcendence.

"Religious Musings" was published in *Southern Literary Messenger* 10 (July 1844): 423; *Grouped Thoughts* (1845), p. 10; and *Poems* (1853), p. 12. The text is from *Poems* with one reading from the earlier versions representing Simms's habitual spelling:

3. naught] nought

SONNET. POPULAR MISDIRECTION.

This poem presents basic tenets of Simms's philosophy: modern man, in worshipping idols of gold and in placing his altars in the marketplace, has broken his ancient covenant with God. Pomp, show, and respectability have replaced genuineness in religion. A central image calls for restoring the teraphim, or Semitic household gods, and of thus reestablishing the covenant by returning to the "sweet humility of our home desires" instead of flaunting "foreign fashions." By "home desires," he means the genuineness and reverence of place that would lead to the true virtue and peace of the poem's first line.

"Sonnet" was published in *Southern Literary Messenger* 10 (August 1844): 483; *Grouped Thoughts* (1845), pp. 20–21; and *Poems* (1853), pp. 73–74. The text is from *Poems* with one emendation from the earlier versions representing the poet's usual practice:

1. recall] recal

HARBOR BY MOONLIGHT.

The setting is Sullivan's Island, across the harbor from the city of Charleston. As the poem accurately details, the viewer would see the open Atlantic before him, and to his right, the city, long noted for its church spires. The "ramparts" are of Fort Moultrie on Sullivan's Island, a popular resort for Charlestonians (the Moultrie House Spa was located there—hence the women strolling and children playing along the beach), a fact which must have been a pointed irony for Simms the poet-historian. As so many of his poems reveal, Simms had learned that such beauty and happiness as are depicted in this placid scene are transient, for its delicate charm depends partly on an insubstantial romantic haze of moonlight, both literally and figuratively. The moonlight's unreality symbolizes the romantic views of the "thoughtless" strollers along the beach who do not contemplate this beautiful mask which hides scenes of violence owing to battle and tempest. The children play beneath the fort's ramparts "As if 'twere safe from carnage ever more"; and all those on holiday act as if they had "assurance 'gainst to-morrow's wo." Behind the moonlight mask and the most smiling aspects of life lies the truth that existence is fraught with violence, pain, struggle, and woe, traits far more common than beauties such as these. The poem reveals Simms's sense of the sadness at the core of life, and the essentially thoughtful nature of the poet, who is constantly seeking the reality behind the appearance and the meaning beneath the surface. All this is done subtly and by implication, never through open and obvious statement.

The poem's sestet moves to a description of the city itself. Like the women and children of the octave, the placid town is also innocently deluded. The moonlight "seems" brighter as it plays over it, as if it is in an honored, "queenly" spotlight. That these *seemingly* "intenser fires" are evidence of divine favor is, however, only an illusion akin to those that might be held naïvely by a maiden protected by her mother. The city, deftly symbolized in the couplet as a virgin star sheltered at the side of the matron moon, thus *appears* safe from life's shocks as a favored object of heaven, whereas in reality time's "tempest" and war might easily destroy her beauty and peace. History and his own life have taught the poet how fragile and fleeting happiness usually is; no one and nothing can ever be safe from loss.

Both this poem and "Heedlessness" reveal that the poet feels most men in their "thoughtlessness" are unable to see beneath the surface of things in order to comprehend these realities and are thus unaware of the abundant lessons residing in the physical forms. Only the heedful "Seer-Poet" can be an interpreter. The sonnet turns prophetic in light of what was to occur on this same scene less than two decades later. For many reasons, this is one of Simms's best sonnets. It is an effective, realistic descriptive poem and at the same time has a quiet and graceful simplicity that belies a complexity of universal meaning presented without a trace of overt moralizing. All its meanings are transmitted through symbolism, diction, comparison, and ironic juxtaposition.

"Harbor by Moonlight" was published in *Southern Literary Messenger* 10 (August 1844): 484; *Grouped Thoughts* (1845), p. 14; and *Areytos* (1860), p. 412. The text is from *Grouped Thoughts* with no emendations.

THE NATAL STAR.

As with other Romantics, the star to Simms represents divine influence, hence its place as the central image of this poem. In presenting it as a heavenly counterpart of mankind, Simms shows the close link between humanity and nature by using the relationship of inner and outer landscape.

"The Natal Star" was published in *Southern Literary Messenger* 10 (September 1844): 521; *Grouped Thoughts* (1845), p. 15; and *Areytos* (1860), p. 414. The text is from *Areytos* without emendation. The title is taken from *Grouped Thoughts* owing to the standardizing of first lines into titles in *Areytos*.

PROMISE.

"Promise" was first published in *Southern Literary Messenger* 10 (September 1844): 521, and *Grouped Thoughts* (1845), p. 21, before heavy revision in *Areytos* (1860), p. 413. The superior *Areytos* version is here printed with one emendation from the earlier texts in keeping with Simms's usual practice:

14. ended,] ended,—

The title is taken from *Grouped Thoughts* owing to the standardizing of first lines into titles in *Areytos*.

SONNET. — THE AGE OF GOLD.

The poem's theme is similar to that of "Sonnet. Popular Misdirection," also first published in 1844. "The Age of Gold" further develops the earlier poem's theme by emphasizing the role of the poet as minister to man, a seer who would guide mankind along spiritual paths in a time of materialism. Simms makes an ironic play on the phrase "Golden Age," the period of the highest achievement of Greek art and intellectual endeavor, by contrasting it to his own age in America wherein "cash is conqueror," an era that too often takes money as the measure of all things. The poem's last two lines are another criticism of organized religion, which Simms here feels to be likewise corrupted by secularism and materialism, and thus also serving golden idols.

In his anti-materialism, a theme that he had expounded upon since the early 1820s, Simms is closely akin to his fellow Southerner Edgar Allan Poe, and influenced the young Charleston school of Timrod and Hayne, whose acknowledged master he was. There is thus a deep demarcation between the Simms school and such writers to the northward as Emerson and Whitman who in the wake of Franklinian business ethics could celebrate industrial villages and factories as subjects worthy of poetry. Simms, on the other hand, strongly felt materialism in any form to be counter to the Creator's true intentions for man. This is one of the chief themes throughout the entire canon of fiction, poetry, and essays.

"Sonnet. — The Age of Gold." was published three times: *Southern Literary Messenger* 10 (September 1844): 521; *Grouped Thoughts* (1845), p. 18; and *Poems* (1853), p. 146. The text is from *Poems* (1853), with no emendations.

AH! TURNING O'ER THE CLASSIC PAGE.

This work shows the poet's growing disenchantment with his "degenerate" times and praises the unselfish heroism and devotion demonstrated in classical literature. Simms's criticism of American greed and materialism was particularly widespread in the poems of this decade. His concern was so deep that it would soon lead him to become engaged in politics by serving in the South Carolina state legislature. In many ways the poem's themes epitomize an entire culture.

The poem appeared in *Southern and Western* 1 (February 1845): 134, and *Columbia Phoenix*, 1 May 1865. The text is from the *Phoenix*, with no emendations beyond the lowercasing of the stanza numerals. It is published here under Simms's name for the first time.

The poem's last twelve lines are particularly appropriate to its wartime publication and likely thus occasioned Simms's inclusion of it in his newspaper in 1865. The first lines of the third stanza anticipate Henry Timrod's ode to the Confederate dead.

THE LONELY ISLET.

This haunting poem once again reveals Simms's belief in spiritualism. Although one might suspect the influence of Poe on the subject matter and tone, knowledge of Simms's very early similar poems reveals that he had written this manner of work long before Poe. If there is influence, it is of Simms on Poe.

The grass of the setting is likely the marsh grass of the Carolina lowlands. The eerie quality of this coastal landscape would thus be suited to the tone. Simms has here effectively captured the melancholy beauty of the scene.

The poem was published four times, each appearance basically unchanged: *Southern and Western* 1 (March 1845): 165; *Southern Literary Messenger* 12 (April 1847): 249–50; *Atalantis* (1848), pp. 119–20; and *Poems* (1853), pp. 195–96. The text is from *Poems* (1853) with no emendations except the lowercasing of the stanza numerals.

Notes

3.8. make constant moan: Perhaps an echo of Keats's "La Belle Dame," who is said to make "sweet moan," or of Tennyson's Lotos-Eaters, who "make perpetual moan" ("The Lotos-Eaters," line 62).

CLARICE.

This psychological study has a nicely turned final stanza. The poem was published in *Southern and Western* 1 (April 1845): 255–56; *Southern Literary Messenger* 12 (May 1847): 306; and *Atalantis* (1848), p. 106. The text is from *Atalantis*, with no emendations except the lowercasing of the stanza numerals.

ACCABEE — A BALLAD.

"Accabee" is the germ of Simms's finest narrative poem, "The Cassique of Accabee," also collected in this edition. The poet is here drawing on a traditional tale which is recounted in full in the longer poem. The text is from the poem's only appearance, in *Southern and Western* 1 (June 1845): 378–79, without emendation. It is here published under Simms's name for the first time.

Notes

Title. Accabee: The ruins of an early plantation and garden on Ashley River. See notes to "The Cassique of Accabee."

SYMPATHY WITH NATURE.

The poet here speaks of a transcendental release from self through a merging with nature. His "We are a part of all we see and hear" is perhaps an echo of the famous line from Tennyson's "Ulysses" (1833, 1842): "I am a part of all that I have met."

The poem was published in *Southern Literary Messenger* 11 (July 1845): 442; *Grouped Thoughts* (1845), p. 41; and *Areytos* (1860), p. 414. The text is from *Grouped Thoughts*, with no emendations.

HEEDLESSNESS.

Here the poet elaborates on the theme of mutability by showing that man is a heedless creature unaware of his mortality even when the voice of death is whispering in his ear. The one "near me now" of line 14 might refer to any of the many loved ones Simms had lost by this time. Man's refusal to see beneath the literal surface here mirrors Simms's general belief that literalness had become the cardinal sin of the era. It also shows Simms's understanding of the essential seriousness beneath the casual surface. To quote Vergil, there are tears in the very nature of things. This understanding lined up well with the Celtic melancholy that Simms often displays.

The poem's first lines recall "The Winter Flower," and the last four are close in theme to "Harbor by Moonlight." Nearing the age of forty, Simms was becoming even more preoccupied with the passage of time.

The sonnet is one of the poet's best and measures favorably against any written in America during its day. Its density of good imagery and felicity of expression are greatly responsible for its success. It deserves wide recognition.

"Heedlessness" was published twice only: *Southern Literary Messenger* 11 (July 1845): 442, and *Grouped Thoughts* (1845), pp. 44–45. The texts are identical and are here printed without emendation.

THE SOUL IN IMAGINATIVE ART.

These sonnets, which attest to Simms's faith in the creative power of the imagination and its ascendancy, were published in *Southern Literary Messenger* 11 (September 1845): 556; *Grouped Thoughts* (1845), pp. 55–56; and *Poems* (1853), pp. 107–8. The text is unemended from *Poems*, where the works formed two in a series of sonnets.

THE BEAUTY OF DEPARTING OBJECTS.

This poem, again on the theme of mutability, states the universal truth that one seldom fully appreciates the familiar until about to lose it and that things reveal themselves passing away. Mortality is a subject on which the poet wrote frequently to the end of the decade. In celebrating the local and how one often fails to value it properly, the poem bears similarities to "Sonnet—The Wreath."

The poem appeared only twice: *Southern Literary Messenger* 11 (September 1845): 556, and *Grouped Thoughts* (1845), p. 57. The texts are identical and are here reprinted without emendation.

IMAGINATION.

A major Simms poem on a subject central to Romantic thinking, "Imagination" reflects the poet's continued interest in Coleridgean philosophy (especially at 6.35–39). Simms's image of imagination as the "creature of wing and eye" was very important to him; he chose this emblem to stand for his art (and as the hall-mark on his signet). The winged eye represented to him two facets of the imagi-nation: "impassioned" free flight coupled with careful, realistic observation and perception, thus bringing into balance and integrating the two sides of his person-ality: the romantic and the realistic. The poet's increased emphasis on escape from the material world seen in this poem was to continue well into the 1850s.

The work's three appearances are *Southern Literary Messenger* 12 (November 1846): 681; *Atalantis* (1848), pp. 91–96; and *Poems* (1853), pp. 252–58. The text is from *Poems* with the following emendations from earlier texts in order to restore Simms's habitual practices:

1.1. god] God
1.1. power] pow'r
1.4. flower] flow'r
3.35. naught] nought
4.4. oh] O
4.14. oh] O
5.17. god] God
6.33. god's] God's

In addition, all roman numerals are made lowercase, in keeping with the poet's usual manner.

Notes
5.17. wayward God: Cupid.

LOVE SONG IN SPRING.

A lyric reminiscent of the poet's early verse in which a lover urges compliance, this poem was published in the *Charleston Southern Patriot,* 17 April 1847, appropriately signed "Eros"; the *Southern Literary Messenger* 26 (May 1858): 356, signed "Adrian Beaufain"; and *Charleston Daily South Carolinian,* 14 April 1866, signed "Werter." The text, collected here for the first time under Simms's name, is from the *Daily South Carolinian* with one emendation restoring an earlier reading:

   13. sad if,] sad, if

PROPER UNDERSTANDING.

This poem was published in *Literary World* 1 (5 June 1847): 421, signed "Pierre Vidal"; *Charleston Mercury,* 31 May 1859, signed "L'Allegro"; and *Areytos* (1860), p. 17. The text is from *Areytos* with the following emendations from the *Mercury:*

   1.4. caught?] caught:
   1.8. good-by] good-bye
  1.10. good-by] good-bye
   2.8. clear!"] clear"!

Roman numerals are made lowercase.

THE MEMORIAL TREE.

This poem is centered around a complex symbol that represents both mutability and continuity. The memorial tree, in its spring leaves, represents youth; in its summer foliage, symbolizes first love; in its autumn garb, emblemizes grief over loss and death of loved ones. It thus stands for transience. At the same time, because it is an ancient "record" tree, it preserves the accounts of lives long past— in fact, the history of an entire race, the vanquished race of red men who have long since disappeared. (The Indian himself, here as in Simms's earliest verse, also represents transience.) The speaker, like the red man before him, leaves his record on the tree and knows that it will remain after he is in the grave to be read by other generations to come. Through nature, therefore, the record of man is preserved. The human story of birth, love, death, and rebirth, is likewise closely mirrored in her own forms and cycles. Nature thus bears the message of continuity and immortality transcending the short-term shifting and vanishing forms of the individual mortal's life. She therefore remains as a constant emblem from generation to generation, and her lessons are not subject to time.

   The poet may have had in mind as subject the famous "Angel Oak" of Johns Island, near Charleston, said to have been worshipped by the Indians as a deity, and, like the tree of the poem, left standing when its surrounding forest was cleared for tilling. It bears many initialed "records."

The poem's only appearance came in *Graham's* 32 (January 1848): 11–12, and is here printed with one emendation:

89. others] others'

The poem is collected here for the first time.

SPIRITUAL SYMPATHIES.

This remarkable group of sonnets is similar to poems published ten years earlier on the death of the poet's wife. Unlike its earlier counterparts, however, it concludes that one errs if he seeks the spiritualist's way of keeping a departed one near, when the loved one already resides within: "How should I dream to have thee or to see, / Save in this heart." Perhaps Simms's recent loss of his daughter occasioned the poem's writing.

The text is printed without emendation from the poem's only appearance, in *Godey's* 36 (January 1848): 60, and is published here for the first time under Simms's name.

THE GRAPE VINE SWING.

This poem was first published in *Godey's* 36 (June 1848): 363. It was reprinted the following year in *Cassique of Accabee* (1849), pp. 110–11, before being collected in *Poems* (1853), 2:79–80. The text published here is from *Godey's*, incorporating the two substantive changes made in *Poems*—the change of "a condor" to "the condor" and the insertion of "still" in the poem's last line. William Cullen Bryant collected the piece in his *Family Library of Poetry and Song* (New York: Fords, Howard, & Hulbert, 1870), p. 456.

"The Grape Vine Swing" is a poem of recollection. The key to remembrance is the speaker's association of the ship's "cordage" (which he now holds as he sails at sea to the northward) with the memory of the "cordage" of the grape vine of the Southern forests of his memory. It is an effective descriptive poem, but as well presents (through diction and personification) a dual view of nature as being both fearsome (as in the vine as serpent, cougar, boa, and condor) and lovingly familiar and sheltering (as in lover's "embrace," "soft cheek" on "lover's breast," and the maiden sheltered "in thy drooping fold.")

Even more important, the poem contrasts two cultures and ways of life: the Southern nature-based culture and the Northern urban and machine-based one. The steam-powered vessel "strains" against nature, and the culture with which it is identified is tidy and ordered in contrast to the powerful life force, which the vine represents. The poem ends with the deceptively simple question that is far from innocent: will the Southern nature-based culture survive this modern new way? Even more significant, will nature itself survive it? "The Grape Vine Swing" is one of the most sophisticated American poems of its time.

This poem was selected to represent Simms by Alfred Kreymborg in his popular *An Anthology of American Poetry* (New York: Coward-McCann, 1930). Even though Kreymborg's text mars the sense and imagery of the first stanza by supplying "beach" for "beech," and thereby changing a tree to a coastline, the poem still stands up well in the context of the anthology. The beech-condor image no doubt describes the effect of the vine's "spanned" covering of the tree's crown, as if beneath a condor's wing of dark. Simms obviously intended the last two lines to be parallel; condor and boa should thus destroy oak and beech, both trees.

OH! WELCOME YE THE STRANGER.

This poem's theme, the importance of hospitality, shows the poet's Southern heritage. It was published, set to music, in *Godey's* 37 (July 1848): n.p.; then revised in *Poems* (1853), pp. 175–76, and *Arthur's* 3 (April 1854): 309. The musicality of the *Godey's* text is more effective and is thus printed here with two emendations from the later versions in keeping with Simms's usual practice:

2.7. deferred] deferr'd
3.8. blessed] bless'd

Roman numerals are made lowercase, in keeping with Simms's usual practice.

SUMMER AFTERNOON, IN MY STUDY.

Simms published this poem in *American Review* 8 (October 1848): 346, then revised it for *Southern Literary Gazette* 3 (19 October 1850): 1, as "Summer Evening in My Study." In 1867 he extensively reworked it as "From My Study Windows."

With a "soul that only dreams of doom," the speaker is a pessimist who is fated "to doubts that pain." If the poem is autobiographical, it is particularly accurate in describing his life during this period. Tempering his pessimism is always the knowledge that there is respite in nature "commission'd thus by power above" (line 38, *Southern Literary Gazette* version), and hope and joy when least expected.

The text is taken from *American Review* with one emendation from later versions:

25. doomed] doom'd

See also the 1867 text, "From My Study Windows."

Notes

1. ailanthus: A genus of trees, sometimes called "Heaven Trees," native to the East Indies and cultivated in America.

3. jasmine: Likely the yellow jessamine (*Gelsimium sempervirens*). Its "golden gems" appear in early spring, which is thus the setting.

Simms's reworking of this significant poem over several decades culminated in this final version of 1853. It began as the short lyric "Written in Mississippi," published in *Poems* (1827), pp. 73–74. An expanded version, titled "The Traveller's Rest, Written in the Choctaw Nation, Mississippi," appeared in *Southern Literary Journal* 2 (June 1836): 272–73. Six years later a further expanded version was published in *Magnolia*, n.s., 1 (November 1842): 285–88, followed by still further revisions in *Cassique of Accabee* (1849) and *Poems* (1853).

The *Magnolia* version of 1842 notes the poem had its inception ten to twelve years earlier.

This highly autobiographical blank-verse poem grew out of Simms's experience in the Southwestern wilderness, 1824–30. The identity of "the benevolent old master," the "veteran of the forest and true friend" is unknown. Simms made trips to the frontier home of his father, and it is likely the elder Simms, since the description fits him. The phrase "Boy as I was" is probably a reference to the poet's own age at the time of his first trips. Simms was in his late teens and no doubt was "speaking still through books." The setting is the prairieland of Alabama.

The lesson taught from the experience begins with a strong emphasis on mutability—especially man's vulnerability to change. The red man has vanished, and the white race too may pass away, for those nomads that fail to build lasting monuments and instead leave ruins will surely destroy themselves. Such was the wandering red man; and the guide sees a similar weakness in the white man, who wantonly is laying waste to nature in his westward migration, as witness the denuded landscape and barren soil. A more personal message comes home to the young narrator, who sees his own situation described in his father's statement that the "gray usurpers Death and Change" have left him solitary, with no family, and an exile, now loving only woods and streams as a wanderer in the wilderness. The elder Simms fears that in running to the wilderness to escape past griefs he has himself been guilty of leaving no monument for his kind to benefit man and further the chances of his kind's survival. He wonders what "moral monument" will remain to preserve his memory after death. The sire's questioning of his own deeds leads the boy to ask the same questions of himself. Though he makes no answer, indeed never articulates the question, one may with reason infer that his confrontation of his father's question may have been an important turning point in the young man's life that influenced him to stay in his native city rather than uproot to the West, and therefore also to choose writing as a career. His "moral monument" would thus be his art. Further, he would learn to face the past and bear its griefs rather than flee from them. The poem ends with the father's hymn of thanks to the Creator for providing guidance and sustenance in a difficult life of toil and pain. It is a message of trust that God will not desert his creation, a message that perhaps provides the courage for the youth to make his choice and then remain true to his artistic calling.

The poem was published in *Cassique of Accabee* (1849), pp. 53–69, and *Poems* (1853), pp. 22–35. The text is from *Poems* with the following emendations from the *Cassique* text in keeping with the poet's usual practice:

17. recall] recal
21. succor] succour
22. vigor] vigour
107. succor] succour
117. flower] flow'r
136. flowers] flow'rs
150. flowers] flow'rs
151. Brightening] Brightning
165. flowers] flow'rs,
172. sovereign] sov'reign
173. eyed] ey'd
193. through] thro'
208. flowers] flow'rs
220. flowers] flow'rs
231. flowers] flow'rs
236. flowers] flow'rs
238. mid] 'mid
308. Askelon] Ashkelon
361. erewhile] ere while
416. flowers] flow'rs
418. succor] succour

For the short version of the poem published in 1827, see "Written in Mississippi," pp. 8–9. For a discussion of the changes between the 1842 and 1849 versions, see James E. Kibler, "Stewardship and *Patria* in Simms's Frontier Poetry," in *William Gilmore Simms and the American Frontier*, ed. John Caldwell Guilds and Caroline Collins (Athens: University of Georgia Press, 1997), pp. 209–20.

Notes

162. Hyacinthus: Simms correctly reports the legend. Apollo accidentally slays Hyacinthus with a discus. The crimson-purple of the blood from the wounded forehead of Hyacinthus is Simms's reason for making the allusion.

297–98. Talladega . . . Tallas-hatchie: The two streams of this name joined the Coosa River on its eastern side, in the upper Creek settlements of present-day northeast Alabama. The Talladega and Tallas-hatchie settlements were the scenes of Andrew Jackson's campaigns against the Indians in 1813. Simms's own father fought with Jackson in this campaign. If he is indeed the "old master" of the poem, then his account of the Indian defeat would be firsthand.

299. Emuckfau: Imukfa (meaning "shell"), a tributary of the Tallapoosa River (in a horseshoe bend of the river) in northeast Alabama. The settlement of this name was the site of a victory of the whites over the Creeks in March 1814, in which 557 Creeks were killed.

300. Autossee: Atasi or Atassi (meaning "warclub") was an Upper Creek place-name for stream and settlement on the east side of the Tallapoosa River in east central Alabama. It was the site of a battle in November 1813.

306. Monohôee: The Creek chief who was defeated in the Battle of the Horseshoe (or Imukfa) in March 1814. This battle was the final stand of the Creeks, who were massacred by Jackson, and thus it marked the end of the Creek War.

308. Ashkelon or Ashdod: The first is a place of battle in Judges 14:19; the second, a strong place of Judah in Joshua 15:46.

310–11. iron-soul'd old chief . . . from Tennessee: Andrew Jackson, the elder Simms's commander in battle.

314. Choctawhatchie: River in southern Alabama that flows into the Gulf of Mexico.

335. Saladanha: Unidentified.

THE CASSIQUE OF ACCABEE; A LEGEND OF
ASHLEY RIVER.

Cassique is the Indian word for "chief." The setting (the ruins of the home and gardens of the plantation called Accabee) is an actual site on the Ashley River; and the plot of the work comes from folk legend. (For "one of the many legends" about Accabee, see Simms's "The Spectre Chief of Accabee" in *Literary World* 11 [31 July 1852]: 74–76. In "The Spectre Chief," Simms relates that the house is off the Dorchester Road. Records in *South Carolina Historical Magazine* 16 [January 1915]: 1–49, and 19 [January 1918]: 45–47, show two Accabee plantation houses, both in ruins in 1915.) In an interview with the editor in 1968, Simms's granddaughter Mary C. Simms Oliphant recalled that Accabee was, at the time of the poem's composition, owned by the poet's friend Colonel Walton. An early owner during Colonial times was William Elliott (1696–1766), the son of William and Catherine Schenckingh Elliott. Loutrel Briggs, in his *Charleston Gardens* (Columbia: University of South Carolina Press, 1951), describes plantations of the Accabee area, with their ruins of fisheries, statues, and pleasure grounds, much in the same way that Simms does here. According to "The Spectre Chief of Accabee," the chief's wigwam stood precisely where the plantation house was built. In this tale, the chief haunts the land because he resents its appropriation by the white man. It is said to be under the proprietorship of a Mr. Brown, a great raconteur, "who talks like a Trojan" and accuses the author of getting many of his published stories from him.

The finest of Simms's narrative poems, "The Cassique" is permeated with the strong sense of place and the power of the past to brood over and shape the present. The past is depicted as a mysterious, unfathomable, yet tangible force which does not die; and those who lived long ago still leave their impress on the land. Men's deeds, for good or ill, remain after them in legend and, more importantly here, in the "genius" or spirit of the place. Their lives become a part of the land itself. Hence, a dead landscape is humanized and enlivened to its greatest degree through human associations. For the poet, a knowledge of the past and its legends and traditions is a means of turning one's eyes outward. Such a knowledge creates the perspective necessary to see one's small position in the broad span of time, thus placing his life in a context which prevents self-centeredness. It is fitting that all the travelers by Accabee are hushed and awed by the story. They show humility and reverence, a respect for the place and those who have come before them. Their sense of the past, in allowing transcendence of ego, has led to the identical result of the successful process of Imagination, and is, in fact, directly dependent upon it. Simms, the good Southern Romantic, shows that the physical is less than half of reality, and that only in man's transcendence of self are the greater possibilities of life open to him. In its emphasis on place and the past, "The Cassique" is a very Southern poem.

Another related theme is the depiction of "fate" as weakness of character. Man has free will as long as he chooses to exercise it. For example, the chief at the poem's end masters what would have surely been his "fate" through a "resolute will" (lines 646–48). His mastery of passion in rejecting the faithless girl stands in direct contrast to her easy yielding to the peddler. The key lines for this theme occur in the latter scene when the narrator says,

> There is a fate beside us day and night,
>> Obedient to the voice within our hearts;
> Boldly we summon, and it stands in sight;
>> We speak not, and in silence it departs;—

(Lines 365–68)

It is at this point that she "roves with aimless will" into the forest and speaks the peddler's name, and he materializes. Thus begins the chain of events that eventually results in tragedy. Further, these choices have a bearing on the landscape long after the participants have passed away. The gloom of sad and tragic lives has made a mark on Accabee which cannot be removed. This tension between the concepts of free will and determinism thus becomes a dramatic conflict in the poem, which shows that a strong character and dynamic exertion of will always make their impress and are again necessary to triumph over powerful external influence. For a virtual restatement of this theme, see stanza 10 of "The Close of the Year 1861."

The form of the work, original to Simms, is worth noting. Carried consistently throughout the 101 stanzas is the seven-line stanza, rhyming *ababccb*. The first four lines are pentameter, the couplet is trimeter, and the seventh is hexameter. The poet's technical skill in carrying it out over so long a poem is considerable. It is never tedious, largely owing to the forceful drama of the swiftly moving plot. Above all, the poem tells a good story.

The genesis of "The Cassique" came in 1845 in a five-stanza poem entitled "Accabee—A Ballad," published at p. 137. The cassique, who is the central figure of the longer poem, plays no role in the earlier version. In 1849 Simms expanded the work to one hundred stanzas and made it the title piece of his collection of the same name. Here, the full story of the cassique is told. The first four stanzas of the ur-Accabee serve as an introduction, and its last stanza becomes the conclusion.

In the 1855 *Poems* edition, Simms added stanza 31 for the first time, to bring the work's total to an odd-numbered 101. There are substantive changes in the 1853 edition over the 1849. For example, the last line of the 1845 text (which had contained "dream'd of yore" and was changed to "known of yore" in the 1849 text) finally becomes "felt of yore" in the 1853 version, an excellent revision for a Romantic poet intent on strengthening his theme.

The text is the 1853 version, with these emendations taken from the 1849 text in keeping with Simms's usual practice:

  45. lagoon] lagune
  57. till] 'till
  57. white man] white-man
  64. neighbors] neighbours
  84. declared] declar'd
 102. flower] flow'r
 106. reached] reach'd
 107. till] 'till
 153. surprise] surprize
 205. white man] white-man
 249. Till] 'Till
 261. flowers] flow'rs
 322. her] He drew her [*Replacement of a broken line of type.*]
 390. bowers] bow'rs
 444. woe] wo
 495. flower] flow'r
 512. woe] wo
 522. white man's] white-man's
 532. showers] show'rs
 555. woe] wo
 575. didst] did'st
 579. power] pow'r
 580. dower] dow'r
 583. white man's] white-man's
 600. red man] red-man
 650. woe] wo
 664. While] Whilst
 683. welcomed] welcom'd
 691. Till] 'Till

Notes

  00. An unidentified Charleston painter did a portrait of the chief and the orphan girl. The portrait is in the collection of Mary Simms Furman of Greenville, South Carolina.

70. Helena Bay: Bay of Santa Helena or Saint Helena, at the present town of Beaufort on the extreme southern coast of South Carolina.

74. Gaelic chief: Henry Erskine, third Baron Cardross. His Scotch settlement, begun in November 1684 near the present town of Beaufort, South Carolina, was destroyed by Spanish and Indians 17 August 1686, as told in Simms's *The Cassique of Kiawah*. Lord Cardross is a character there. There were several murders, and the Indians took hostages.

99. Albyn: Albion, ancient name of Britain.

175. maid: Desdemona in Shakespeare's *Othello*.

200. casina tea: Tea of the *Ilex vomitoria*, a favorite of coastal Indians.

229. stream divides: The Edisto divides into a north and south fork near the site of Simms's plantation, Woodlands.

335. Hunter's Star: Orion.

521. Eutaw: In Simms's day, a swampy creek fed by Eutaw Springs and flowing into Santee River in upper Charleston County. Eutaw is the setting of Simms's novel *Eutaw*.

670. purchaser: Possibly William Elliott (1696–1766), son of William and Catherine Schenckingh Elliott, who owned Accabee in the mid-1700s.

673–79. An accurate description of the Ashley River plantations of the Colonial era. See Loutrel Briggs, Charleston Gardens (Columbia: University of South Carolina Press, 1951), pp. 111–13.

694. native genius: Simms wrote in 1827: "When passing any dangerous reef, or point of land, in their frail canoes, the Indians invariably offer to the Spirit of the Place" a token of homage (*Early Lays*, p. 105). Simms often refers to the *genius loci* in his poetry. It is a concept that he found both important and meaningful.

STANZAS.

This tender lyric was perhaps suggested by the death of the poet's fourteen-month-old daughter, Valeria Govan Simms, on 21 September 1846. If so, the place of burial is Woodlands, in the forest setting described in the poem. The work's slant rhyme helps create a melancholy tone and provides relief from what would otherwise be a jingling monotony. Its simplicity, sincerity, and vivid imagery make the lyric memorable. Here is another example of a good poem which Simms never collected or claimed as his own, perhaps because he considered it too personal.

The text of "Stanzas" is printed without emendation from its only publication: *Richards'* 2 (6 October 1849), signed "Parish Saxon, Desilla, S.C." It is here published under Simms's name for the first time.

SOUTHERN ODE.

The text is from the *Charleston Mercury* of 7 February 1850. The poem was written in reaction to the sectional crisis of 1850. It speaks of invasion and usurping rights and is a spirited call to arms. The poem is signed "Tyrtæus" after the Spartan war poet (ca. 684 B.C.) whose war lyrics roused the fainting spirits of his countrymen in war. The image of the last stanza impresses the idea that the argument for peace is specious, in that there can be no peace as long as Southern rights are continuously in danger and there is no mutual faith among the sections. Simms reasons that in a sense the nation is already at war.

"Southern Ode" was later republished as four separate "Lyrics of the South" in the *Charleston Mercury* from 1859 to 1860. These appearances remain largely the same, except in the accidentals, and are quite pertinent to the immediate pre-war period. The 1850 text has been reprinted, however, without emendation. This is the first time the poem has appeared under Simms's name.

Notes

41–44. These lines refer to the Mexican War, largely fought by Southerners. After the victory, Northerners stepped in to try to determine what would be done with the conquered territory. This was a big issue in the sectional crisis of 1850. (The proposal by Wilmot of New York was that slavery be excluded from all these territories, a ploy that would eventually result in further weakening of Southern strength in Congress.) Simms also presents this same view of the Mexican War and its aftermath in his satire "The Father Abolitionist."

45–48. From the *Arabian Nights*. The image is that the North is getting a free ride on the back of the South. The plea of "riding together," or of union, is seen as being actually only a trick for the North to keep the free ride.

FROM *THE CITY OF THE SILENT.*

This excerpt is stanza 13 of the twenty-nine-stanza poem. *The City of the Silent* is written in stately heroic couplets on the theme of burial traditions and varying concepts of death throughout history. An ambitious work, it is a kind of ultimate "graveyard" poem, being delivered by Simms at the dedication of Magnolia Cemetery in Charleston, South Carolina, 19 November 1850. It was begun in early November and completed by the twelfth of that month (*Letters*, 3:73). The poem's local success prompted Simms to bring the work out in pamphlet form later that year with copious notes by his friend James Warley Miles. The last line of the excerpt exhibits a skillful mating of sound and sense. The text of this excerpt is from *Poems* (1853), p. 336, without emendation.

Notes

22. "in love with death": Likely an echo of Keats's "Ode to a Nightingale": "I have been half in love with easeful Death."

HORACE IN DISHABILLE. TO MY MAN TOM.

Simms adapted a number of odes from the Latin poet Horace. This one is a translation of book 1, ode 38, "To His Servant," changed to a Southern setting. It was signed under the pseudonym "Musæus," the name of the Greek poet (ca. 410 B.C.) in Vergil's *Aeneid.*

The poem is here published for the first time under Simms's name from its only publication in *Southern Literary Gazette* 3 (15 March 1851). The "dishabille" of the title means "stripped" or "naked." Simms also published adaptations of Horace's odes 9, 11, 15, 16, 18, 23, and 32. For no. 11, see p. 268.

"LA BOLSA DE LAS SIERRAS."

This work presents the poet's vision of a prelapsarian ideal in which the unity of creation has not yet been fragmented by man's greed. The exotic landscape of flamingo and palm reflects a preindustrial world and a vision of perfect beauty where there is neither strife nor ambition and man lives a simple life. In this setting all nature exists in perfect communion and harmony, and each "requites" the other in a symbiotic relationship. The poet thus at moments desired escape to a haven of primitive peace which he had not found in a fallen world. With the death of more loved ones and other sorrows later in this decade and the next, this impulse to escape the prison of empirical reality was to become even stronger. (See, for example, "Fancy in Siesta.")

"La Bolsa" was first published in *Sartain's* 10 (May 1852): 441. In *Southern Literary Gazette,* n.s., 1 (26 June 1852): 305–6, it is expanded from eight stanzas to fourteen. The final text in *Poems* (1853), pp. 241–44, lightly revises and improves the *Southern Literary Gazette.* The text is from *Poems,* with the following emendations based on the *Southern Literary Gazette* and Simms's usual practice:

1. flowers] flow'rs
3. towers] tow'rs
14. footsteps] footstep
22. flowers] flow'rs
35. empire] Empire
38. favor] favour
50. day-star] Day-star
61. harbors] harbours
68. beauty] Beauty
68. harbors] harbours
80. peace] Peace

Footnote 1 had appeared as a note after the title.

Notes

20. Mezquite: *Prosopis juliflora,* reaching its largest size (above fifty feet) in southern Texas along the Rio Grande.

BALLAD.

Appropriately signed "Il Penseroso" in its only appearance, "Ballad" is here pub-
lished for the first time under Simms's name from *Southern Literary Gazette*, n.s.,
1 (19 June 1852): 293, without emendation. It is a good lyric that expresses the poet's
philosophy of melancholy verse, affirming that a sorrowful poem, while some-
times painful, still strengthens. It comes from the poet as a "love-commissioned
thing" to minister to its reader. Thus, as the poet says, "sorrow's song is holy."

HARMONIES OF NATURE.

An important blank-verse poem on several of Simms's favorite themes, "Har-
monies of Nature" shows the need of man's surrender to nature. The second
stanza again depicts nature's opposing forces, ambition and materialism, as im-
pediments to the soul. In the third stanza, a Coleridgean emphasis appears in the
poet's making nature fade as man's own soul fails to discern its beauties. In the
eleventh stanza, Simms makes the important statement that nature is the "type"
or symbol of the eternal, thus summing up the philosophy which in a host of ear-
lier poems had led him to use natural objects as symbols of eternal truths. The
final stanza contains the effective image of the woods and other physical manifes-
tations of nature as merely the "robes" that dress the spirit, and the mirror to
man's inner self. The poet is thus demonstrating through metaphor that nature's
visible forms express man's innermost feelings.

First published as "Forest Music" in *Southern Literary Messenger* 22 (March
1856): 211–13, it next appeared in *Old Guard* 4 (November 1866): 679–82. The text
is from *Old Guard* and is here collected for the first time. An undated manuscript
version in Simms's scrapbooks is used in the following instances as the authority
for emending the *Old Guard* text when that version's readings (likely the result of
housestyling) contradict Simms's habitual practice:

    3. gladness!'] gladness.
    11. fear;] fear;—
    13. things;] things;—
    15. soul] Soul
    25. for ever] forever
    26. palls] pales
    27. everywhere] every where
    27. nature] Nature
    31. are;] are;—
    32. whisper—] whisper,—
    34. self] Self
    50. beauties;] beauties;—
    57. season] seasons
    59. soul] Soul
    60. hours] Hours

66. passions;] passions;—
84. notion;] notion;—
109. winged] wingéd
114. green-fringed] green-fringéd
121. awhile] a while
124. strain—] strain,—
126. custom;] custom;—
127. hark] Hark
129. beguiled] beguiléd
130. ours;] ours;—
134. Heaven] heaven

Notes

Lines 48–62 show the influence of Wordsworth's "I Wandered Lonely as a Cloud" (1804).

SONG OF THE SOUTH.

This lyric first appeared in a short version in *Southern and Western* 1 (April 1845): 261–62, which was collected in *Areytos* (1846), pp. 38–39. It was then expanded in a livelier and more impassioned version in 1857 (*Southern Literary Messenger* 25 [December 1857]: 465–66), now declaring total commitment and a love of homeland so strong that he would sacrifice life for her sake. In 1858 (*Charleston Mercury,* 16 June) he made several substantive changes which are not improvements. In *Areytos* (1860), pp. 9–10, he made still another over the 1858. The *Areytos* (1860) text was then printed largely unchanged in *Southern Literary Messenger* 32 (January 1861): 5; *DeBow's* 31 (August 1861): 205; *Southern Monthly* 1 (September 1861): 10–11; *War Songs of the South* (Richmond, Va.: West & Johnson, 1862), pp. 15–16; and *Rebel Rhymes and Rhapsodies,* ed. Frank Moore (New York: G. Putnam, 1864), pp. 285–86. The text chosen here is the superior long version of 1857. Its title, however, comes from the 1858 *Mercury* text, as the 1857 used only the first line, from a series entitled "Songs of the South." Otherwise there have been no emendations.

Notes

1.6. Simms here acknowledges that his region honors him, thus providing still more evidence to contradict William Trent's influential thesis that Simms felt that the South neglected him. There could hardly be a stronger expression of commitment to native place than exists in this poem.

THE CHIMNEY CRICKET.

This poem of iambic tetrameter couplets and triplets could have as well been entitled "Winter Night at Woodlands." It is an accurate description of the domestic scene with wife and children, down to the detail of old grandsire (probably Simms's father-in-law) nodding by the fireside. The poem's evocation of mood is its chief strength. The singing cricket is a didactic variety rare in Simms; its moral lesson is a theme that the poet is often repeating during this time: man is happiest when leading the simple rural life of modesty and "homely duty" away from the urban and industrial whirl. The poem also emphasizes the value of constancy and loyalty and the need of continuity from generation to generation.

The poem was published in *Russell's* 3 (May 1858): 151–54, and *Areytos* (1860), pp. 173–79. The text is from *Areytos* with these emendations:

Stanza numerals are made lowercase.

5.17. Prison] Prism [*The* Russell's *reading.*]

Notes

Compare also "The Cricket. At Midnight, in the Chamber of Death," *Richards,'* 26 January 1850, which contains these lines:

That chirping cricket watches like myself;
He hath his song, and, were its burden known,
It were, perchance, a song of Thanksgiving
To the Great Father! His untiring hymn
Narrates the gifts, inordinate or mean,
He wins in his short life. A week of stir,
A rest in the old crevice while the day
Burns fiercely, and a progress safe by night,
Near the old mantel, in the hollow wall—
And for these boons he blesses. Should he prate,
O such were not the burden of his chaunt,
Thus jolly, with his click-clack, thro' the night,
In sounds that strike at vacancy, and pierce
The drowsy ear of silence, mocking mine!—
Oh, God! be merciful! From him I learn
All things that live have cause of thanksgiving;
For life itself is privilege:—its pains,
When felt the most, are proofs of its dear worth.

THE POET.

This work defines one aim of the poet. As author of delight, beauty, and intuition, his role is to uplift man's spirit from the material to a view of the eternal.

The text is unemended from the poem's only publication in *Russell's* 3 (July 1858): 353, and is published under Simms's name for the first time.

BALLAD. — COME, LET US DISCOURSE.

This poem is an outpouring of grief barely kept in bounds by the tight form of the poem. The rawness of grief expressed in the work rises from the poet's likely having written it within hours of his son Sydney's death from yellow fever on 22 September 1858. Line 3, "For what shall be our waking to-morrow" when the child will no longer answer a call, suggests that it is still the night of his death. And the fact that the poet writes of only one death, when a second son would die twelve hours later, is strong evidence of the immediacy of the event. After both children had died, Simms wrote his friend James Henry Hammond on 24 September 1858: "Oh! dear Hammond, weep for me! I am crushed to earth. I have buried in one grave, within twelve hours of each other, my two beautiful boys, Sydney, & your namesake, Beverley Hammond, two as noble little fellows as ever lived. . . . It is a terrible stroke of fate, leaving us almost desolate. I feel heart broken, hope crushed, and altogether wretched. I can write no more" (*Letters*, 4:93).

This poem appeared only in *Areytos* (1860), pp. 364–66, and is printed here unemended except by lowercasing the stanza numerals.

Notes

4.5. This line echoes the opening of Simms's "Stanzas to ——" in *Southern Literary Journal* 3 (December 1836): 289.

BALLAD. — OH! MY BOYS!

This poem was written after the death of both sons, Sydney and Beverley, 22 and 23 September 1858, and succeeds in showing the poet's sense of loss and bewilderment. It is a highly personal poem relying on small particulars. The children's names appear, and the poet focuses on the familiar objects of their play. An unpretentious work, its basic ordering rests on two contrasts: the children's former liveliness versus the still of death, and the noise of toy trumpets and drums versus the silence of grief. Its rhythm and close rhyme suggest the nursery rhyme, in keeping with the age of the subjects.

One of the poem's greatest strengths is Simms's refusal to idealize the children, who appear realistically as makers of deafening "racket," a description which must have particularly suited Beverley, whom Simms had described the preceding year as a "stout, powerful, good humored, rowdy Saxon" (*Letters*, 3:504). The poem ends quietly with the father sitting among the objects which remind him most of them.

The work is printed without emendation from its only appearance in *Areytos* (1860), pp. 366–67.

SONNET. — TO W. PORCHER MILES.

This poem was occasioned by the faithful attendance of W. Porcher Miles as the poet watched for twelve days over his dying sons. One notes an even more impressive depth and maturity in much of the poet's writing from this time on — particularly in *The Cassique of Kiawah* (1859), thus perhaps explaining why some critics feel this novel to be his best. His children's deaths, like his first wife's, were among the events in his life which had the strongest influence on his writing.

This work (dated Woodlands, 2 April 1859) was first published as the preface to *The Cassique of Kiawah* (1859), and the following year in *Areytos* (1860), p. 364. The text is from *Areytos* with two emendations from *Cassique,* restoring Simms's habitual practice:

9. !] ! —
10. evermore —] evermore, —

Notes

Title. W. Porcher Miles: The younger brother (1822–99) of Simms's close friend the Reverend James Warley Miles, of Charleston. He was professor of mathematics at the College of Charleston and a lawyer.

For a consideration of how the poem shares similarities to the novel it prefaces, see David Aiken, Introduction to *The Cassique of Kiawah* (Gainesville, Ga.: Magnolia Press, 1989).

'TIS TRUE THAT LAST NIGHT I ADORED THEE.

Both the meter and rhyme of this poem are appropriate to its light subject matter. The theme concerns how romantic influences like moonlight and song are akin to wine in their distortion of reality. The poet thus shows he is well aware of the difference between love's romance and its reality and here treats this difference with the characteristic Simms humor so lacking in other poets of his day.

The work was published in the *Charleston Mercury,* 16 May 1859, signed appropriately "L'Allegro," and in *Areytos* (1860), p. 282. The text is from *Areytos* without emendation. In *Areytos* Simms himself appended the following explanatory notes:

7. *bender:* "Our Collegiate naturally uses what is supposed to be flash dialect. But, in truth, flash language, not to be guilty of a pun, is very often the language of the fancy. Here, the word *bender* is simply figurative; signifying the rather circuitous progress, snake fashion, which a young blood is apt to take, after the professors have all retired for the night."

10. *spree:* "*Spree,* is simply an American contraction of the French word *esprit,* which, freely rendered in our idiom, means 'on the wing.' "

12. *Cottons:* "*Cottons* — clings closely; a figure drawn from the now general use of cotton wool in the manufacture of chemise and shirt."

RAISONS IN LAW AND LIQUOR.

This comic student drinking song was published as "Dithyrambic—A College Lyric" in the *Charleston Mercury,* 8 July 1859, signed "Blox," Columbia, South Carolina, appropriately the site of South Carolina College. Simms incorporated it in his *Paddy McGann* (1863). The text is from *Paddy McGann* without emendation. The "Raisons" of the title is Paddy's Irish dialect for "Reasons."

Notes

21. Blackstone and Vattel: Two famous law commentaries, *Commentaries on the Laws of England* (1813) by William Blackstone, and *Le Droit des Gens* (1758) by Emmerich de Vattel.

FRAGMENT, FINALE OF THE DANDY-LION *AND* THE FINALE OF THE FLIRT.

The text of these satirical poems is unemended from their only appearance in *Russell's* 6 (October 1859): 56, 72. They are published here for the first time under Simms's name.

PROMISE OF SPRING.

This carefully constructed poem presents the prophetic vision of tombs and a "Horror worse than Death" hidden behind the blossoms of spring. For the speaker, who yokes the opposites in the rhyming pair "blooms" and "tombs," spring on the verge of war is the saddest of shams and illusions. The title is therefore ironic.

The imagery of the first stanza prepares the reader for the spring war disguise in that the street trees of the city (Charleston) have put out buds in the shape of spears and their "helms" or helmets appear "plumed," as in medieval battle dress. Stanza 4, which stands at the center of the poem as a pivot from spring to "Horror," is particularly thoughtful. The poet realizes the loss and deprivation that must accompany any such conflict. This is a work of sound artistic merit with universal application. Henry Timrod's justly famous "Spring" (1863) may well have been indebted to it for inspiration.

The text is from *War Poetry* (1866), pp. 329–30, which is a polished version of the first appearance in the *Charleston Daily South Carolinian* of 1 February 1860. In a headnote to this poem, the *Carolinian*'s editor writes that "one of our city Poets brought us" this work yesterday—that is, 31 January 1860. The poem appears here under Simms's name for the first time. It is proved to be his by his inclusion of it in his scrapbooks.

CICADA—THE KATY-DID.

This simple lyric appeared in *Areytos* (1860), p. 135, and in a slightly altered, inferior version in *Southern Home Journal* 2 (4 July 1868). The text is from *Areytos* with one emendation (the making of "summer" uppercase in keeping with the *S.H.J.* and Simms's usual practice). The subject is from the poet's local scene. The live oaks at Woodlands are still made musical in deep summer by the cicada's song.

GUARANTIES.

This deftly handled poem is a spoof of youthful Romantic idealism. It is a humorous version of "Tokens and Pledges" (1827), published at p. 25. The speaker now calls for the physical demonstration of love, not "musical vows."

The text is from the poem's only known appearance, in *Areytos* (1860), p. 141, with one emendation:

> 9. vo] vow

THE PALMETTO ROYAL.

This poem grew from a three-line jotting in Simms's notes taken on William Bartram's *Travels,* ca. 1844. Its symbolic import, considering the war preparations under way at the time of its writing, is clear. The palmetto royal is the old local name for the yucca, or Spanish bayonet. (See Sam Stoney, *Charleston:Azaleas and Old Bricks* [Boston: Houghton Mifflin, 1937].) Simms's note, however, seems to merge it with the sabal palmetto, the true "badge of our Country"—that is, an independent Carolina.

The sabal palmetto in South Carolina history has long been recognized as the emblem of the successful resistance to the British in the Revolution. Fort Moultrie, which repelled the British fleet in 1776, was made of palmetto logs, and the tree therefore became synonymous with the sovereign State of Carolina from that time onward—hence "The Palmetto State" and the palmetto as emblem on the state flag. "Palmetto Badges," mentioned obliquely in the poem's note, were being made of palmetto leaves by the ladies of Charleston for the soldiers of the state who were preparing to defend their homes at the time Simms wrote his poem. These badges were worn on jackets and kepis by the Carolinians during the war.

"The Palmetto Royal" exists in three texts: an early version in *Russell's* 3 (May 1858): 164; *Charleston Mercury,* 14 February 1861; and a manuscript in Scrapbook D, written ca. 1861. The manuscript version is printed here, with one change: the note which appears bracketed in the manuscript after the title is placed as a footnote. It is here published under Simms's name for the first time.

Notes

The Southern poet "of long ago" in the footnote is unidentified. The poem's true main source, as stated above, is William Bartram, and perhaps it is he to whom the note refers. Bartram, however, was a Pennsylvanian. See "Palmetto Royal" in "Notes from Bartram."

KING'S MOUNTAIN.

This blank-verse poem celebrates the "brave mountain men" who defeated the enemy in this famous battle of the Revolution, 7 October 1780. Although Simms notes that the poem was written "many years ago, on a visit to the battle field," it is appropriately placed in 1861, when Simms himself felt it appropriate to revise and publish the poem for the first time in acknowledgment of the new threat to his region. As he writes in the note to the poem, its purpose is to inspire, through a recital of the heroic deeds of the past, noble actions in the present. Simms visited the battlefield in 1855; but it is likely that he had been there earlier, so the poem's date of initial composition is impossible to fix precisely.

The poem was published only once in the *Charleston Mercury* of 13 September 1861, signed "Gossypium," the Latin word for "cotton" and a proved pseudonym. It is here published for the first time under Simms's name, with the following emendations to the *Mercury* text:

6. breathe] breathes
21. hunter's] hunters
103. their's] theirs

Notes

Another poem on Kings Mountain appears in *Areytos* (1860), pp. 322–24.

THE CLOSE OF THE YEAR 1861.

The chief theme of this important poem is whether man has the freedom to rise above circumstance. As in "The Cassique of Accabee," the poet's answer is that a person is determined only in the degree to which he lets his animal nature dominate him; "but, as he rises to the rank of man," with will, thought, courage, and purpose, he has power to "baffle fate." The speaker states that since the nature of the world is change, no one can count on happiness if he bases that happiness on transient earthly things. Chance and an uncontrollable dark fate do control the world's externals (its animal, or physical side). Yet, in this uncertain world, what matters chiefly is the manner in which one lives his life in the face of the death which "confronts us from each quarter." "We *live* but as we *do!*" the poet says; and if "*well* we do," then neither "chance nor change" can affect what is truly important. The poet's conclusion is that life is finally worth little; but that the courage with which one faces it is everything. His final lines state that true meaning in life is found only in the strife that "tries true manhood." Here in 1861, Simms was voicing basic existential theory. In addition, he has moved from his early Romanticism in saying that man must be *over* nature now, not one with it. The poem thus reflects an important shift in view.

The poem's central image is the shifting "winds," which represent the change and circumstance which buffet man. In stanzas 20 and 21, the winds become the destructive storm of war, now raging "over all," a "dark fate" which uproots the giant tree and blackens the horizon like the hurricane. In fact, the storm is a favorite metaphor for war throughout Simms's poetry and fiction. (Simms may have had in mind the seal of his native state, which pictures an uprooted oak in a Revolutionary War context.) Throughout the poem, the physical landscape is a mirror of the inner one.

The genesis of this work came in "The Approach of Winter," *Charleston Courier,* 25 August 1827, published in this edition; but the poem is so changed as to be new. The text of "The Close of the Year 1861" is from its only publication, in the *Charleston Courier,* 25 March 1862, signed "Senex," or "old man," and is published here under Simms's name for the first time. In two clippings in the poet's scrapbooks, Simms made the following corrections, which have been incorporated in the text (along with the lowercasing of the stanza numerals):

> 7.5. dead] dread,
> 8.3. scorn] scan
> 8.5. harm,] harm—
> 12.3. soul—superior] soul-superior
> 12.6. rain] vain

Notes

13.5–6. Simms knew this truth from his own experience; and the line is prophetic in light of the death of Chevillette, only months away.

14.4. Likely an echo of Tennyson's famous lines from "Ulysses": "To strive, to seek, to find, and not to yield."

16.1. My country: Simms, of course, means either the Southland or Carolina.

21.1. An echo of the first line of one of Simms's favorite poems, "The Storm Is Gathering."

ELEGIAC. R. Y., JR.

All but the last lines of this elegy might as well have been written for Simms's own sons, Sydney and Beverley, whose deaths in 1858 were still on his mind. The poem's immediate subject was Richard Yeadon, Jr., the adopted son of Simms's lifelong friend. He had been killed in action at the Battle of Seven Pines in Virginia the preceding month. The poet develops the image of the child as tree throughout the work. In the second stanza, the tempest (as metaphor for war) which uproots the tree recalls that same image both in "The Close of the Year 1861" and in his Revolutionary romances. The agricultural imagery in this and other poems reveals the extent to which Simms had become a planter.

The text is from the poem's only publication, in the *Charleston Courier,* 24 July 1862, signed "Philo." It is published here under Simms's name for the first time. In a clipping in his scrapbooks, the poet has made the following corrections, all of which have been honored in this text:

2.23. arms] aims

3.12. And now has] Has

3.12. its] it

3.16. more] most

3.26. reaches] es [*Here Simms cancels the first five letters, but fails to insert others. "Sallies" is an editorial substitution, chosen because Simms used the word in other poems and because it alliterates.*]

3.38. Remote,] Remote

Stanza numerals have been made lowercase in keeping with Simms's usual practice.

ODE — OUR CITY BY THE SEA.

This rousing narrative of the Southern repulse of Northern invaders in the Battle of Charleston Harbor, 7 April 1863, is one of Simms's most intricate poems from a technical standpoint. Each of the twelve-line stanzas rhymes *ababcccdeeed*. Lines 5, 6, and 12 are dimeter; line 8 is hexameter; and the remainder are tetrameter. The result of the poem's short lines and many rhymes is an energetic, almost breathless quality that carries well the poem's buoyant emotion. "Ode" is an effective martial lyric in the classical tradition and exhibits a skillful use of the technical arts of poetry. Its defiant tone is blended with epic grandeur in the description of Colonel Rhett's valor and victory against great odds. The personification of Forts Moultrie and Sumter in stanzas 2 and 3 as the brave old Revolutionary generals Moultrie and Sumter themselves, rising up in defense of the harbor, adds a nice touch.

The poem exists in two versions: *Charleston Mercury,* 22 June 1863, and *War Poetry* (1866), the first appearing only months after the battle that occasioned the poem. The technically superior text printed here is from the *Mercury,* with one emendation: the addition of the question mark in the final stanza (taken from *War Poetry*). It was probably intended in the *Mercury,* as no mark of punctuation appears there.

Notes

1.9. Fort Sumter was never taken even after many Federal attempts and the longest siege of the war.

2.1. Old Moultrie: Fort Moultrie, near the northern entrance to the Harbor, the site of General William Moultrie's important repulse of British warships in 1776.

3.3–4. "His" refers to Fort Moultrie; "Sumter," to Fort Sumter.

8.10. scaith: harm

9.8. Turrets: turret guns on the Northern ironclads.

10.12. "Keokuk": A Yankee double-hulled warship with double turrets, heralded to be invincible but ripped by shells and sunk by Southerners. Her guns were salvaged by Confederates and used in Fort Sumter and on Sullivan's Island. Simms's description of battle is historically accurate. One of the "unsinkable" Keokuk's guns is on display at White Point Gardens, Charleston.

FANCY IN SIESTA.

This poem, in good Romantic fashion, is written in praise of the fancy, dream, spontaneity, and naturalness. The poet advocates pure and complete freedom for the imagination with no bounds or strictures, hence the primary images of "unclipt" nature and of a boat without sail drifting down a river, while its occupant eats the lotus of forgetfulness. This freely wandering fancy has no cares of "Thought," "Time," "Greed," or any worries of the world. Specifically in stanza 11, these cares are the "Dragon forms of Fear, / Blood-red on wings of sable flying," which represents war. As the dateline states, the poem was written in the midsummer of 1863 at Woodlands.

"Fancy in Siesta" shows the poet's even more heightened desire for complete escape from the world. His despair is clearly stated in stanza 7 in his definition of life: "Half life is but a dream, and blest / Is he who dreams away the rest." Here the poem departs from a familiar Romanticism and more closely parallels the poetry of the decadence in tone, subject, and imagery. The poem's lotus and white lilies strongly bring to mind the Pre-Raphaelites (and more specifically the Lancelot and Elaine sequence of Tennyson's *Idylls of the King*), while the sailless, drifting boat most assuredly prefigures Rimbaud's "The Drunken Boat" of the 1890s. The closest parallel to the work, however, is Tennyson's "The Lotos-Eaters" (1832–42). The poem is very rich with the sensuousness of the young Tennyson's Keatsian period. It is important to note that while Tennyson's Lotosland is a creation purely of his mind, Simms's setting is based firmly at Woodlands, with close realistic description of the natural scene, heightened by the colors of the imagination.

Simms published the poem twice: *New York Mercury* 28 (13 January 1866): 4, and *XIX Century* 3 (April 1870): 832. The final publication is revised and expanded with the addition of stanzas 1, 2, and 12. The text is from the *XIX Century* with these emendations: the lowercasing of all stanza numerals and the incorporation of Simms's holograph corrections (as follows) from a copy of the *XIX Century* in his Printed Poetry Box, Charles Carroll Simms Collection:

2.2. there] these
2.3. there] these
2.4. Gul of Bulbul] Gul and Bulbul
3.4. slumbrous] slumberous
5.2. Lurk] Lush
6.9. 'blent] y'blent
8.9. brew] knew
8.10. more!] more!—
10.9. possession] perversion
10.10. gain,] gain.
10.14. laid,] lain
10.17. And] And,
10.17. gleam] gleam,
12.4. Open] Opes
12.9. rose hue] rose-hue

The poem is collected here for the first time.

Notes

Epigraph. From *Cymbeline*, III.iii.33–34, 47–49.

2.2. Caliph's garden: Likely the garden of Haroun-al-Rashid of the *Arabian Nights*. "Caliph" was the title given the sultan of Turkey.

2.4. Gul and Bulbul: The Princess Perizadah in the story "The Two Sisters Who Envied Their Cadette" in *The Arabian Nights* mentions a speaking bird called "Bulbul."

2.8. Haroun: Haroun-al-Rashid, caliph of Baghdad, introduced in the *Arabian Nights*.

5.9. Arachné: In classical mythology, a maiden who, having surpassed Minerva in weaving, was changed into a spider.

7.20. "play i'the plighted clouds": Milton's *Comus*, line 301.

14.2. oaks: The live oaks at Woodlands.

THE GAME COCK OF THE REVOLUTION. (SUMTER.)

This is one of many war poems in the canon which invoke the Revolutionary War past as inspiration for valor and revenge for the invader's wrongs inflicted on civilians. It is based on the life of General Thomas Sumter (1734–1832) of South Carolina. As Simms says in his preface, the "Past has lessons which should teach . . . the Present." The war was now become a desperate conflict for the South; and this poem is typical of the manner in which Simms used his knowledge of the past to draw pertinent parallels to his own day. The poem uses the ballad stanza but with skillfully rendered alternating tetrameter and trimeter lines. It moves swiftly, has vitality, and tells a good story. The form of the narrative is actually a frame story, in which the first and final stanzas introduce and comment on the inner monologue delivered by Sumter himself.

The text is from its only appearance, in the *Charleston Courier*, 14 November 1863, and is unemended. It appears here under Simms's name for the first time.

Notes

19.1–4. Cowpens and Hanging Rock were Revolutionary War battles fought January 1781 and August 1780 respectively. Tarleton was the English Lieutenant Colonel Banastre Tarleton (1754–1833), often called "The Butcher" by Carolina patriots.

BALLAD. "THE DREAMS OF OTHER DAYS."

"Ballad" was first published in the *Charleston Mercury* for 20 April 1864, signed "Alcæus" (Greek lyric poet, 620–580 B.C.). It then appeared revised in the *Columbia Phoenix* of 5 May 1865, before being revised a final time in the *Charleston Courier* for 2 February 1870, less than five months before the poet's death. This last version was datelined Vidalia, North Carolina, a fictitious place-name, and signed Philip Marston, Jr. (after the English novelist and poet). The work, like so many from this period, expresses the poet's loneliness after the death of Chevillette and recalls a love from the past.

The text is from the *Courier* and has required no emendations other than in making the numerals lowercase. It is here published under Simms's name for the first time.

THE TEMPLE AT ÆGINA.

A tribute to classical art and imagination, this poem, perhaps because of its rhyme, was not included in his blank-verse series, "Sketches in Hellas," to which it otherwise has many affinities. The poem's last lines are addressed to the defeated South. Interestingly, the adjacent column in the newspaper in which the poem appears relates the burning of Atlanta and charts Sherman's progress toward South Carolina. The poet focuses on Troy's vanquished heroes and her weeping daughters, who meet their tragic end with dignity and courage and thus find a kind of triumph in the immortality of song. Simms's depiction of art as that magical power of genius which "shapes" the "stubborn" stone "to form" and draws forth "waters" of life and meaning from dry rock in order to sustain humanity is a highly significant statement of artistic process and worth. Simms's own artistic rendering of Southern courage and faith in the immortality of the human spirit exemplified in both defeated Troy and his own land will be his means of bringing from dry rock the water of life to sustain future humanity and, thus, clearly foreshadows William Faulkner's conception of the artist as one of the pillars that help man endure and prevail by reminding him of eternal verities such as honor, courage, compassion, and sacrifice. On many counts, this is among Simms's most effective poems.

The text is unemended from its only publication in the *Columbia Daily South Carolinian*, 19 November 1864, signed "Adrian P. Beaufain," a favorite pseudonym. It is here published for the first time under Simms's name.

Notes

Title. Ægina: A small island near Athens.

28. Homer's Heroes: From the *Iliad*.

29. Cassandra: Daughter of King Priam of Troy, gifted with the power of prophecy. From Homer's *Iliad*.

30. Ilium: The poetic name for Troy. "Ilium's daughters" is a direct reference to the women of the South.

30. Andromache: The wife of Hector in Homer's *Iliad*, whose final parting with her husband before battle is one of the most memorable passages of the poem.

THE STORM PETREL.

This poem is unusual in the canon owing to its didacticism. It has as its subject a familiar coastal object, which Simms uses as the means for setting forth a universal truth. The sea bird's mission traditionally has been as a warning to sailors that a storm is imminent. Here Simms denies this, as well as the message of his own early Bryant-inspired version, "To a Bird at Sea" (1827), which states that God sends the bird as a cheerful guide. In "The Storm Petrel" the bird now teaches the lesson of total trust in God for sustenance. Now that Woodlands has been destroyed by war, the poet sees that the bird's homelessness parallels his own; and yet the bird survives through God's care.

"The Storm Petrel" has its genesis in Simms's own "To a Bird at Sea" and in Barry Cornwall's "The Stormy Petrel," but is a marked improvement over both. There is also a short, inferior version entitled "The Sea Bird," *Godey's* 35 (October 1847): 179. The text published here is of the expanded, improved last version in the *Columbia Daily Phoenix,* 12 April 1865, with one emendation:

59. Rocks] Rock

The poem is here published for the first time under Simms's name.

THE BELLE OF THE BALL ROOM.

This poem was published three times: *Columbia Daily Phoenix,* 15 April 1865; *Old Guard* 4 (December 1866): 752; and *Charleston Courier,* 4 February 1870. The setting copy is the superior revised *Courier* version, with one emendation:

1.7. guild] gild

as appeared in all the earlier versions. It is collected here for the first time.

In the first stanza the speaker comments that it is all well and good for the heedless belle of the ballroom to feed her "hunger of heart and soul" through the pleasures of dance, song, beauty, and show. The diction of the second stanza, however ("wanton," "gilded," "insects," and "giddy") shows this hedonistic philosophy to be severely limited and childishly selfish because it focuses only on surfaces. As for the speaker, he has the darker "fate" to live in the "toils of Care" and "Thought." As author, his life's purpose has been and will be to use his "gift" of soul and his "Powers" in "long conflict with human woes." The poem is a clear late statement of artistic purpose.

Notes

The "Caroline P****——*" of the title remains unidentified, as is the epigraph. One possibility for the belle is Caroline Paine, whom Simms noted as a desirable, pretty, young woman in the *Charleston Mercury,* 11 August 1859. A possible source for the epigraph is the thirteenth-century Persian poet Saadi. In 1866 Simms signed a copy of Saadi's *The Gulistan, or Flower-Garden,* trans. James Ross (London: J. M. Richardson, 1823). Ahrimanes and Ormusd are ancient Persian Zoroastrian deities said to be manifestations of evil and good, respectively, and in perpetual conflict.

1.3. golden fleece: In Greek myth, the object of the search of Jason.

THE VOICE OF MEMORY IN EXILE, FROM A HOME IN ASHES.

As the title notes, the poem was written while Simms was "in exile" from Woodlands. Woodlands had been burned, and Simms was in Columbia, where he was working as editor of the *Columbia Daily Phoenix*. The poem centers on his internal conflict of whether or not to return to the ashes of his home; or, in or other words, whether to live in the past or to break from it. The poem provides no resolution, but instead dramatizes the internal struggle and gains intensity thereby.

It is published here for the first time under Simms's name from its only appearance, in the *Columbia Daily Phoenix*, 19 April 1865, with one emendation which restores the poet's habitual spelling:

7. Recall] Recal

A longer version of this poem, published in 1868, appears in this edition as "Heart-Omen."

Notes
5. blossoms: As Simms's letters and the records of Pomaria Nurseries (Pomaria, South Carolina) reveal, Simms had long enjoyed planting ornamental shrubs around the house at Woodlands. The poem faithfully relates that these were destroyed during the war, as recounted by one of the destroyers who relates the soldiers' "making away with the evergreens and rose-bushes of his artistically arranged walks, flower-beds, and drives . . . and making brooms of his pet shrubs." (Major George Nichols, aide-de-camp to Sherman, in *The Story of the Great March* [New York: Harper, 1865]. Reprinted in *Simms Review* 4 [Winter 1996]: 40–41.) For Simms's orders from Pomaria, see James E. Kibler, "Simms the Gardener: Reconstructing the Gardens at Woodlands," *Simms Review* 1 (Summer 1993): 17–25.

WHAT'S LEFT.

This poem is a good example of an effective lyric from Simms's last years. His wife, Chevillette, had died a year and a half before, and at this point he decides he will not love again, for to become involved would inevitably assure another loss. Philosophically, as the poems of this collection reveal, Simms had believed since youth that happiness is only a temporary respite from pain, which is the dominant mode. He reconciles himself to the fact that he will now travel his remaining short "weary way alone." If any man ever had cause to feel loss, it was Simms in 1865.

He was seriously ill; he had buried his two favorite sons, four other children, and his wife; he had lost mother, father, father-in-law, brothers, and the grandmother who brought him up; and he had seen his home burned twice. In addition, he lost his best friend and confidant, James Henry Hammond, the year before, and had witnessed the defeat and destruction of the South, whose history he had spent much of his life chronicling and whose literature he had almost single-handedly attempted to found. It must have appeared that he was doomed to lose all that he valued; hence the poem's title.

The poem appeared unsigned in the *Columbia Daily Phoenix*, 13 April 1865, then revised and signed "Philip Marston, Jr." in the *Charleston Courier*, 3 February 1870, a few months before his death. The text is from the *Courier* with the following emendations based on the *Phoenix* text:

1.1. expelled] expell'd
2.1. though] tho'
2.6. woe] wo
3.4. strains] spells

The poem is here published under Simms's name for the first time.

Notes

2.5. Circean: After Circe, the voluptuous sorceress in Homer's *Odyssey* who turns men to swine.

SHADOWS. — .

This fine lyric of the poet's last years is a very personal expression of faith in the strength of love. It is possible that the spiritual presence of the loved one to which he refers is of his deceased wife, Chevillette. The early version of the same title (1825) had also described loss by death. The great difference between the two is that in the 1865 version Simms has concluded that his loss is so great that he will no longer and in no way seek consolation in this world.

"Shadows.—I" was published in the *Columbia Daily Phoenix*, 25 April 1865, then revised in the *New York Mercury*, 6 January 1866, p. 51. The text is from the *Mercury* with emendations based on the *Phoenix* in accordance with the poet's usual practice, and is here collected under Simms's name for the first time.
Title. Shadows.] Shadows.—I.

21. blessed] bless'd
23. sorrowed] sorrow'd
26. coming] coming,
28. tears.] tears:
31. cheered] cheer'd

One of the poet's most poignant lyrics, whose subject is likely again the spiritual presence of his deceased wife. The imagery descriptive of the dead one is remarkably concrete and realistic, and comes as something of a shock. The text is from the poem's only appearance, *Columbia Daily Phoenix,* 26 April 1865, with one emendation:

19. woe] wo

The poem is here collected under Simms's name for the first time.

MIDSUMMER FOREST LUNCH. A SCENE IN FLORIDA.

This blank-verse poem probably grew out of experiences from a trip Simms made to Florida in late 1865 or early 1866. In a letter of 7 July 1866 describing the poem, Simms implies that he experienced such a feast and was sketching from life a particular host in a particular locality. Neither the editors of the *Letters* nor I have been able to identify either (see *Letters,* 4:562–63, 577); but one good possibility is William Hayne Simmons (1784–1870), an old Charleston friend who had moved to his orange grove on the Saint Johns River and then to Saint Augustine many years earlier and who had frequently contributed to Simms's magazines over the years. Although the poem was written by 7 July, Simms stated that he would soon begin the process of revision before it would be submitted for publication. Simmons and Simms were reunited in Charleston soon after the poem was written, and Simms wrote that he called on Simmons frequently for reminiscences of the olden times. Both Simmons and Simms died in 1870 and are buried in Magnolia Cemetery.

Parts of the work echo Simms's "Notes from Bartram." Several of its sections are in fact particularly close: for example, lines 83–95 (which also appeared as "The Cypress" in *Russell's* 3 [May 1858]: 137) and lines 181–225 (which appeared in *Russell's* 3 [May 1858]: 168).

The text is from the poem's only publication, in *Old Guard* 4 (October 1866): 603–8, and is here collected for the first time. The following emendations have been made:

54. coolneas] coolness
84. arches] archéd [*Russell's and the manuscript reading.*]
115. Idumean] Idumea
122. Fyoridian] Floridian
Symbols marking Simms's footnotes have been changed to superscript numerals.
Note 3. when] where

Notes

34. reduced of fortune: An apt description of Simmons at the time. He returned to Charleston, ruined financially.

59–62. Likely a description of Simms himself. These lines present a theme that is prominent in Simms's verse during this period.

80. Tigris: River in the Arabia of Haroun-al-Rasheed of *The Arabian Nights.*

96. consciousness: Simms here states the likelihood of sentience in the plant kingdom, as he had in earlier poems. The proud cypress is sentient but silent, thus providing a lesson to boastful man, in the same manner that the live oak had been the symbol of endurance in "Flowers and Trees."

115. Idumea: Isaiah 34:5: "My sword shall come down upon Idumea, and upon the people of my curse, to judgement."

125. Aidenne: Or, Aidenn, the name for the Mohammedan paradise.

146. Houri: Among the Mohammedans, nymphs of paradise. In the Koran, the houris are virgins of unfading youth.

172. paroquets: The Carolina paroquets, now extinct.

184. bay: As Simms notes, the "Dwarf Laurel," or *Magnolia virginiana,* commonly known as sweet bay.

211. nonpareil: The painted bunting, a small brilliantly colored coastal bird. Simms wrote of one such bird, who, caged and taken north, would not sing. See his *Egeria* (1853), p. 275.

216. Puck: A celebrated fairy of the Middle Ages, depicted in Shakespeare's *Midsummer Night's Dream.* Also called "Robin Goodfellow."

217. Ariel: The spirit of air, a servant of Prospero in Shakespeare's *Tempest.*

THE KISS BEHIND THE DOOR.

As the third stanza reveals, the poet was sixty years old when he wrote this poem. The work shows Simms during a bright moment in dark years. In the first version, published in the *Charleston Courier,* 17 December 1866, the young beauty is named Annie, and the singer is Alice. In the poem's other publication (*Courier,* 1 February 1870), Annie becomes Rosalie and the singer is unnamed. If there is an actual subject, which is very likely, she remains unidentified.

There also exists in the scrapbooks a manuscript, ca. 1870, which is a rough early version of the 1870 text. The text here is from the 1870 *Courier* with no emendations except the lowercasing of stanza numerals; it is here published under Simms's name for the first time. Its first appearance came under the pseudonym "Claude"; its second under "Yorick" (appropriate in light of the poem's frivolous tone).

"AY DE MI, ALHAMA!"

This lyric appeared only once (*Charleston Mercury,* 11 January 1867) and never under Simms's name. In *Letters,* 5:7, Simms writes that he composed it "while strolling among my ruins," the remains of his plantation, burned by the invader. Its title and first line are taken from the refrain of a Spanish ballad included in Gines Perez de Hita's *Guerras civiles de Granada* (1595). (Lord Byron translated it as "A Very Mournful Ballad on the Siege and Conquest of Alhama.") The effect of the original ballad was such that it was forbidden to be sung by the Moors, on pain of death. Simms, as he had always been, was still aware that his own native scene was the best subject for art. The poem is at the same time an elegy of loss, a strong statement of faith in the continuation of principles, and a lyric of commemoration as equally fitting as Henry Timrod's famous Confederate "Ode." Its fifth stanza makes use of the "Lost Cause" motif, but denies that any cause is truly lost as long as there are those who "hold the Faith" and vigilantly "keep their post." The poem ends on a strong note of conviction. It contains some of the better lines occasioned by the war, both North and South. Its text is from its only appearance, with no emendations, and is here published under Simms's name for the first time.

Notes

The title translates "Woe Is Me, Alhama." In stanza 2, the "blooms of snow" probably are ripened cotton bolls, which Henry Timrod had similarly imaged as the "snow of Southern summers" in his "Ethnogenesis." In stanza 4, a "glaive" is an old term for "broadsword."

TO MY FRIEND TOM GREENE, ON HIS DOULEURS ABOUT MISS QUITA.

This light lyric shows that despite his losses, the poet had maintained his sense of humor. It says that even in the midst of the recent disaster, life goes on, people fall in love, men have to work. The strong message is of courage, duty, and responsibility. The profession of the pseudonymous author, given as "Late Planter" now "Scissors Grinder," is a grimly humorous comment on the times. The poem is published here without emendation from its only appearance: *Charleston Courier,* 14 February 1867. It appears here under Simms's name for the first time.

SONNET. — EXHAUSTION.

Despite exhaustion and cancer, the poet was making a courageous stand. The text of this poem is unemended from its *Southern Opinion* appearance, 12 October 1867. It had been published a few months earlier in the *Charleston Courier,* 5 April 1867. It is here collected for the first time.

AMONG THE RUINS.

This effective poem is autobiographical. The ruins are of Woodlands, burned two years earlier. The thicket on the hill across the brook is the plantation burial place of his wife and children. As the poem states, he and his "famishing brood" of remaining children (stanza 5) had been living in the burned-out frame of the home, but are now forced to leave "the grand old woods" of the plantation and wander on the "road of exile." It is one of the last poems written from Woodlands, whose ruins here effectively symbolize all Simms's losses. Throughout the canon, the frequent appearance of the word *ruin* has meant loss through time. The poem also returns to the favorite motif of exile and the forced departure from family graves.

Although on the verge of losing control of the poem while describing the "Fiend" who has starved his children, the poem's conclusion is restrained. This is one of the better poems to come out of the war experience, a far cry from the many sentimental effusions, North and South.

"Among the Ruins" was published in *Southern Society* 1 (19 October 1867): 21, and signed by Simms from Woodlands. The *XIX Century* appearance of September 1869 must have been a reprinting, with no textual authority, since the few variants were not typical of Simms's manner and the poem is still signed from Woodlands. The text published in this volume is from *Southern Society* and incorporates Simms's pencil corrections of a *Southern Society* clipping pasted in his scrapbooks:

> 6.26. Ruth] ruth
> 7.2. wither] hither

In addition, the following editorial change has been made to restore the poet's habitual spelling:

> 3.10. woe] wo

The poem is here collected for the first time.

Notes
1.4. Shorn of flowers: Simms's ornamental plantings were now destroyed. See previous notes to "The Voice of Memory in Exile."

FROM THE STUDY WINDOWS.

This is a longer version of "Summer Afternoon, in My Study" (1848). The poet composed this new work when his study windows no longer existed except in memory. Perhaps because the poem could not be dated from the burned Woodlands, Simms datelines it from Vidalia, North Carolina, a fictitious place-name. The first two and the last stanzas are added for the first time.

The text is from its only appearance, in *Southern Society* 1 (23 November 1867): 16, signed "Adrian B. Beaufain," a favorite pseudonym. There is one emendation of what was likely a typesetting error:

> 23. features] patines

The poem appears under Simms's name for the first time.

Notes
See notes to "Summer Afternoon, in My Study."

For notes on the early short version of "Chilhowee," see "The Indian Village." In this longer version, the poet creates a dialogue between a young, idealistic traveler whose knowledge has heretofore come from books, and his father, who is acting as an experienced guide on the frontier. The naïve youth is most certainly young Simms himself; and the guide is the elder Simms, who had moved from Charleston to the Mississippi wilds in 1808, when Simms was a small boy, and whom the poet likely is now visiting. The setting of the poem is probably one of the trips Simms made to the frontier some time before his father's death on 28 March 1830. In the short version, no Indian village is named; the speaker relates that the description which follows could take place anywhere along the ancient military trace from Georgia to Mississippi territory. In the long version, Simms has given his village a name, one which is usually associated with the Cherokees of southeastern Tennessee. (Chilhowee was a Cherokee village on the Little Tennessee River.) By 1868 the other setting had no natives.

The work is much improved over the short version by the addition of the contrast between idealized and realistic views of nature and the Indian. In the early version, only the father's realistic view is presented, and it is presented as if it is the poet's own; it is not voiced by a character. In "Chilhowee" the poet creates a dramatic tension which yields a more sophisticated poem. This tension is based essentially on the conflict between a primitivist's bookish ideal (spoken by young Simms) and a realistic view of man and society gleaned from experience (voiced by the father). Simms also shifts his primary emphasis in the longer version. The Indian's fate now serves as the example of the degrading results of unchecked license and provides the father with proof of his realistic theories about unrestrained "Nature and Freedom," proof which later saves young Simms from sentimentalizing the "noble savage" and from anarchy-primitivism in general. The poem's themes are thus greatly broadened, and the work itself is made more universal. Its central movement, in fact, precisely fits the pattern described by Leo Marx (*The Machine in the Garden* [London: Oxford University Press, 1964]) as the basic symbolic action of our American fables: a journey that begins with the "corrupt city, passes through a raw wilderness, and then, finally, leads back toward the city" with the result being that "what is learned . . . is *not* the lesson of primitivism" (p. 71).

Simms concluded early that when nature and man's natural urges go unchecked, destruction results. The young poet therefore begins his journey as a sentimental primitivist fleeing the city but ends it as a realist who will head back home again. The mature poet's ideal is a life in which wild nature and civilization coexist in balance, or as Leo Marx defines it, the pastoral ideal of the middle ground. The poet's own early Romantic views of the supremacy of "Nature and Freedom," imbibed from European philosophers such as the ones listed in the poem and expressed in his Indian poetry of the 1820s, are here contradicted by the examples of the results of unchecked nature and freedom on the frontier, where "no law, no limit" is the only rule, and, more recently in his own society, the destruction wrought by the recent war of militant egalitarianism. To Simms, savage nature requires the gentling hand of sensitive, honorable men to create harmony and bring it to its full potential through art, learning, feeling, and intellect. In light of the chaos of the late war under the popular cause of "Freedom," Simms, in 1869, could indeed see the truth in the lines he had written in 1837: "Nature and Freedom! These are glorious words / That make the world mad." It is perhaps for this reason that he, after thirty years, returned to this poem and republished it in a strengthened, augmented version.

The long version exists in four texts: a partial manuscript (ca. 1868); a complete manuscript (ca. 1868); *Old Guard*, February 1869; and a clipping from the *Old Guard* in Simms's Manuscript Poetry Box, revised in his hand. The text printed here is from the *Old Guard*, with all Simms's autograph corrections inserted. Both manuscripts have also been consulted and have supplied readings. Emendations to the *Old Guard* text follow. All emendations (except those marked in brackets *"Manuscript reading"*) are Simms's own corrections to his *Old Guard* clipping:

  3. crowned] crown'd
  4. 'till] till [*Manuscript reading.*]
  5. blue;] blue;—
  6. Spreading] Speeding
  7. Full-blooded,] Full-blooded
  8. Commencing] Commercing
  8. dawn;] dawn;—
 12. wild—] wild!—
 15. sight,] sights,
 20. happiness—] happiness;—
 30. renews,] renews;
 31. it,] it;
 33. spoke] spake
 36. both] both,
 53. 'till] till [*Manuscript reading.*]
 57. seest] see'st [*Manuscript reading.*]
 59. poesy!] poesy!—
 71. Ironoclast] Iconoclast
 75. life,] life;—
 76. abashed] abash'd
 78. Montaigue] Montaigne
 80. dared to] dared
 81. better] bitter [*Manuscript reading.*]
 99. all,] all.
129. Behold] Survey
140. Stretched] Stretch'd [*Manuscript reading.*]
173. The 'Crooked] 'The Crooked [*Manuscript reading.*]
181. do vote] double [*Manuscript reading.*]
189. wasted] tasted [*Manuscript reading.*]
221. break] burst

221. pigs] pigs—

222. barbecue] barbacue [*Manuscript reading.*]

238. or] and

245. words,] words—

Notes

Title. Chilhowee: The only town of this name which I have been able to find is a Cherokee village in southeastern Tennessee, but the setting suggests Mississippi Territory.

33. my sage companion: Simms's father.

39. Burnt-Corn Settlements: Settlements along Burnt Corn Creek of the lower Alabama River in southern Alabama. This was the site of the Battle of Burnt Corn in the Creek War of 1813. Simms's father served in this war in Coffee's Brigade.

43. Yazoo: River in western Mississippi flowing into the Mississippi River.

62–63. Chateaubriand: François René Chateaubriand, French Romantic writer and statesman (1768–1848), whose writings were widely read in America. He came to the United States in 1791 attempting to discover the Northwest Passage but getting no farther west than Niagara, though he wrote about the Mississippi and West as if he had. Simms also takes issue with him on the habits of songbirds in "Maize in Milk" (1847).

67. Louis Quatorze: King of France (1638–1715). The grand monarch noted for the splendor of his court.

69. St. Pierre: Charles Irénée Castel Abbé de Saint-Pierre (1658–1743), French social theorist, reformer, and critic of Louis XIV. He advanced ideas on constitutional government, free education, government care for the poor, and taxes on income.

70. syllabub: A sweet, frothy dessert much loved in the South in early days.

70. Rousseau: Jean-Jacques Rousseau, French philosopher (1712–78) whose works influenced the French Revolution and much "liberal" thinking.

71. Voltaire: François Marie Arouet (1694–1778), poet and philosopher.

77. Rabelais: François Rabelais, French satirist (1483–1553).

78. Montaigne: Michel de Montaigne, French essayist (1533–92) whose essay "Of Cannibals" has been called one of the fountainheads of modern Primitivism.

86. wild flowers: In Simms's *The Forayers* (1855), p. 485, Peyre St. Julien comments that the reason wayside flowers have no odor is that they should not delay the traveler.

127. *coup d'œil:* Comprehensive grasp.

132. Hangs rocking . . .: In his 1827 version of "The Green Corn Dance," by contrast, Simms presents this custom as a pleasant idiosyncracy and implies there is virtue in it: "By this means, the form acquires that arrowy straightness and beautiful symmetry, for which the North American Indian is so very remarkable" (*Early Lays,* p. 105).

For a treatment of this poem, see Charles Sigman, "Simms's Vision: The Beginning of American Poetic Romanticism and Realism in 'Chilhowee, the Indian Village,'" *Simms Review* 2 (Winter 1994): 18–23.

THE TWO UPON THE HEARTH.

This poem, one of the last Simms wrote, is also one of his most poignant, and in some ways among the finest, of his autobiographical lyrics. In fact it stands in company with the best poems occasioned by the war. The poet's restraint and control of tone are impressive, especially considering his subject matter. It is a quietly dramatic work growing out of suffering and grief, from which the only relief is through memories willed into being by the imagination. The work is made concrete through well-chosen details which describe his wife and children, particularly his sons Sydney and Beverley, who died in 1858. It is another of Simms's dialectical poems, the conflict within the speaker being a struggle between the happy memories of the past and sorrows of the present. These are personified as the sole two visitors at his hearth. One wakes while the other sleeps, and these states are constantly shifting.

There is some deftness in the poet's handling of rhythm. For example, the sharp spondee "Wo wakes" in the last line is very forceful in suggesting the harshness of waking to the present.

The embryo of the poem is "Shadows" in *Early Lays* (1827), pp. 62–64. It was completely reworked for the *Southern Home Journal* 1 (March 1868), thus providing a good example of Simms's ability to keep a mediocre poem in eddy in his mind until creating an effective poem from it.

The text is from the *Southern Home Journal*. There exists an undated manuscript in Simms's Manuscript Poetry Box, a rough version of the polished *Southern Home Journal* rendering. Only one emendation based on this manuscript has been made to the *Southern Home Journal* text:

10.4. hushed] hush'd

The poem is here collected for the first time under Simms's name.

Notes

4.2. orange bloom: This is not a poeticism but rather an accurate description; the Carolina lowcountry had groves of citrus in Simms's day. Orange Street in Charleston, for example, was the site of a large grove in the eighteenth century.

6.1–5. She . . . large dark eyes: A description of Simms's wife, Chevillette.

9.5. My noble boys: Sydney and Beverley Simms, who died of yellow fever, 22 and 23 September 1858.

HORACE IN DESHABILLE. TO JEDEDIAH QUIRK, ESQ., POLITICIAN.

Simms adapted a number of odes from Horace. This humorous poem, an adaptation of book 1, ode 11, "Ad Leuconoü," was published in Charleston during the Federal occupation. It tells its politician addressee that the less involved with politics he is, the better. As in the Latin model, the speaker advises to seek pleasure, regardless of the morrow. Ode 1.11 contains the famous line "carpe diem quam minimum credula postero.")

The poem was published first in the *Charleston Mercury,* 24 March 1868. The following day it appeared with a note stating it is republished "to-day as corrected by the author" owing to errors in printing. The text is from the corrected version of 25 March, without emendation. It is here published for the first time under Simms's name. The *Mercury* texts are signed "Quevedo," after the Spanish satirical poet of that name (1580–1645).

Notes

Title. Deshabille: "Stripped" or "nude." Simms also spelled the word *dishabille* on other occasions.

6. Mesmer: Friedrich Mesmer (1734–1815), a German physician known for his theories of animal magnetism, called mesmerism. The *pass* is the movement of the mesmeriser, or hypnotist. This allusion fits well the original ode by Horace, in which the speaker tells Leuconoü, from a race of famous fortune tellers, to leave off looking in the book of Fate or astrology.

18. Bureau: The Freedman's Bureau, set up after abolition to implement reconstruction.

20. President: Andrew Johnson.

THLECATHCHA; OR, THE BROKEN ARROW.

A shorter version of lines 108–96 had been published as "The Broken Arrow" in the *Charleston Courier* in 1826 and in Simms's *Poems* (1827), and is collected in this edition. In *Book of My Lady* (1833), the poet added to this short version, a new 28-line introductory section, which he has here expanded to 107 lines in the present text. The notes in the *Courier* version are omitted in 1833 but in 1868 become an expanded prose explanatory paragraph, here placed as footnote 1.

The depth, maturity, and stately movement of the newly written blank- and free-verse lines attest to the effectiveness of Simms's mature poetry. Line 66 provides evidence of the wisdom learned from the events of the war. Here he identifies with the Indian people who in defeat are forced from their homes, much as he himself was from Woodlands. Since both were conquered peoples, Simms realized that the Southern and Indian nations had much in common. This knowledge served to heighten his already strong sympathies with the red man.

In the clipping of the poem pasted in his scrapbooks, Simms has written above line 108: "This dirge was in my 19th year, written while travelling through the nation," hence May 1825, That Simms would rework this, one of his first poems, into one of his last indicates the high regard he had for both the subject and poem. It contains some of his best descriptive verse.

The text is from *Old Guard* 6 (November 1868): 863–67. In a clipping in his scrapbooks, Simms has carefully corrected typesetting errors and has made some final revisions of his own, all of which have been honored:

33. stripes] strifes
38. poisons] passions
41. band] haunt
51. irregulur] irregular
55. if] of
70. whine] volume
73. Tall] With
87. Hung] Hang
128. was] were
148. o'er] through
148. when the] when
151. hiss] tongue
152. one] me
154. subtlely] subtly
158. triumph] triumph;
179. and the] and

In addition, there are two editorial changes which restore Simms's spelling present in the preceding versions and in the prose note:

71. MICCO] *Micco*
151. Menawee] Menawe

Notes

See notes to "The Broken Arrow."

Footnote 1. assassination of Mackintosh: 1 May 1825. In his essay in *Ladies Companion*, January 1844, pp. 110–19, Simms states that he passed through the Nation "a few weeks" after the assassination.

HEART-OMEN.

An expanded version of "The Voice of Memory in Exile" (1865). The text is from *Southern Home Journal* 3 (26 December 1868), with two emendations:

2. pleasing] pleading
23. Recall] Recal

It is collected here for the first time under Simms's name.

Notes

7. hillock: In other poems, this "hillock" is identified as the family cemetery at Woodlands.

14. ruins: The ruins are, of course, of Woodlands. See the notes to "The Voice of Memory in Exile."

Although Simms first conceived the Hellas series as early as 1842, he did not complete the poem until 1870 as his last poetic project. Its final section, in fact, was published the month before his death. The poem began as a series of eighteen miniatures on Greek scenery in Simms's *Magnolia,* July 1842–April 1843. Subsequently, other miniatures appeared in *Richards'* and *Southern Literary Gazette* in 1850 and 1851. Then in the fall of 1862 Simms began grouping and expanding his earlier works into the form here printed. The project continued to occupy his mind in 1864 and 1865, when he published in the *Columbia Phoenix* two new "scenes," both of which he expanded and revised in 1870. The series was to some extent inspired by Pausanias, Greek geographer of the second century A.D. Both he and Simms take the position of a tour guide, pointing out the chief places of interest.

In a letter which prefaces the 1862 series (dated 20 September 1862 and reprinted in *Letters,* 4:412–14), Simms notes the difficulty in achieving the calm concentration necessary for literary composition, "when the whole country is heaving with the throes of a mighty revolution—when we are arming our sons for battle—when every dwelling presents daily a scene of parting—and when, from so many thousands, a voice of wailing is sent up from mothers and sisters." As for himself, he notes his "household troubles," one of which is the rebuilding of Woodlands, which had burned shortly before. From "amidst the din of saw and hammer, and in hourly communion with my workmen," he sends these poems to recall classical lore and tradition because he feels the subjects are timely: "the histories of Greece, in the conflict of that Confederacy with the Median invader, are not dissimilar, in detail and character, to that which our young Republic is waging with our enemy," and therefore "these poems may be found not so far foreign to our present moods as the general topic might seem to suggest." The 1870 additions are likewise timely for their period in that they present the long view, in which the lives of those who suffer tragedy find immortality through portrayal in art. Using the saga of the Trojan War for a parallel, the poet attests to the truth that the story will continue to live when both victor and defeated lie in dust. The following exclamation near the end of the poem's final section is Simms's envoi, in which he declares his undiminished faith in the value of poetry:

> That a tale should live,
> While temples perish! That a poet's song
> Should keep its echoes fresh for all the hills
> That could not keep their cities!

Simms follows this statement with the affirmation that art alone can stand in effective opposition to "the promiscuous mausoleum of Nothingness." His last stanza envisions the meeting of the spirit of the poet with the souls of those men whose names he has kept living, and who now bestow him appropriate honor. The final lines reveal a quiet optimism which, coming at this most difficult time of his life, shows a triumph over adversity and the melancholy that had been so large a part of his personality. The image of Electra singing in the Apollo Chamber a song of hope, offers the promise of a future dawn of joy and contentment after the "long night" of this worldly existence. "Sketches in Hellas" is a distinguished last work which shows no diminution of the poet's mature strengths.

In a letter of 17 July 1863 (*Letters,* 4:434), Simms notes that the editors of the *Illustrated News* have an additional six sketches which they have not published and fears that the reason they have not is that, being in blank verse, the sketches lack "the aid of rhyme—the cunning artifice of octo-syllabic jingle." What happened to these six is unknown. It is likely that three of them appear in revised form in this edition as nos. 6, 7, and 9 of the series. But the other three, which in 1862–63 alluded to "the present condition of our affairs," and which Simms felt would be ineffective if not brought out immediately, were never published in the *Illustrated News* and have not yet surfaced.

I. ARCADIA.

This section exists in three forms: an undated manuscript in Scrapbook B which consists of the first twenty-three lines; *Russell's* 3 (September 1858): 507, which also covers the first twenty-three lines; and *Southern Illustrated News* 1 (October 1862): 2. The following emendations have been made to the 1862 text:

1. we] wé [*Manuscript reading.*]
2. rise,] rise [*Manuscript reading.*]
4. GENIUS LOCI] Genius Loci [*Removal of housestyling.*]
10. recall] recal [*Simms's usual spelling.*]
16. OLD GODS] old Gods [*Manuscript reading.*]
18. FAITH to POWER] *Faith to Power* [*Manuscript reading.*]
20. their] these [*Manuscript reading.*]
21. While] Where [*Manuscript reading.*]
22. fulfilling] fullfilling [*Manuscript reading.*]
37. STATE] *State* [*Removal of housestyling.*]
39. LYCÆUS] *Lycœus* [*Removal of housestyling.*]

Notes

Title. Arcadia: The central region of Peloponnesus, surrounded by a ring of mountains which form a natural barrier.

4. *Genius Loci:* That is, the spirit of the place.

39. *Lycœus:* According to the Arcadian legend, recorded in Pausanias, the birthplace of Zeus.

45. Olympian Sovran: Zeus.

47. Pan: The Greek god of forests, pastures, flocks, and shepherds.

II. SALAMIS.

An eleven-line miniature in *Magnolia*, n.s., 1 (August 1842): 116, has become lines 5–9 and 26–33 of this version, published from *Southern Illustrated News* 1 (11 October 1862): 2. In Scrapbook G, Simms revised a clipping as follows:

35. hoary] desperate
52. beneath] below
63. pursuing] eager

All these changes have been honored, with one further addition:

8. PERSIAN DESPOT] *Persian Despot [Removal of housestyling.]*

Notes

Title. Salamis: Site near Piræus of the Greek naval victory over the Persian invader in 480 B.C.

8. *Persian Despot:* Xerxes, who placed his throne on Mount Ægaleos overlooking Salamis.

28. Satrap: Persian ruler.

35. desperate Despot: Xerxes.

56. Sharp beaks: The pointed Greek ships effectively pierced the hulls of the Persian boats.

III. CASTALY.

Published from its appearance in the *Southern Illustrated News* 1 (18 October 1862), with one emendation: the replacing of a symbol with a superscript numeral to mark Simms's footnote. A sixteen-line miniature had first appeared in *Magnolia,* n.s., 1 (July 1842): 34.

Notes

Title. Castaly: Stream formed from the spring of Castalia, at Parnassus in central Phocis.

18. Priesthood . . . Muse: The priesthood of Apollo at Delphi. Castalia's waters were the Muses' waters of inspiration.

20–21. Yonder shrine . . . Apollo's: Apollo's shrine at Delphi.

22. Parnassus: Apollo's shrine is built on a ledge of this mountain, home of the Muses.

22. chasm: The priestess sat on a tripod over the chasm, and the influence of the uprush of winds gave inspiration to prophesy.

33. Poet's fount: Spring of Castalia. The Muses brought *mousika* (which included poetry) down to earth from Parnassus.

50. Thulé: In Greenland. In ancient geography, the northern most habitable region; any distant, unknown region.

IV. THESSALY.

A five-line miniature in *Magnolia*, n.s., 1 (October 1842): 240, became lines 4–6 and 129–31 of this poem. The twenty-seven-line "Thessaly—A Fragment" appeared in *Richards*,' 27 April 1850, signed "Gessner." The text is from *Southern Illustrated News* 1 (18 October 1862), with the following emendations taken from Simms's clipping, revised in his hand in Scrapbook G:

22. silence] hence
34. They] It
34. fierce] fiery
55. Alcestes] Alcestis
101. wood-down] wood-dove
105. muse] Muse
111. Legion] Legend
123. lap] lapt
Footnote 1. Alcestes] Alcestis

Symbols to mark Simms's footnotes have been changed to superscript numerals.

Notes

Title. Thessaly: The richest and largest plain in Greece.

14. Syrinx: Musical instrument of reeds joined with beeswax; the shepherd's pipe, associated with Pan, named for the nymph Syrinx, whom Pan loved, and who, while fleeing from him and at the moment of being seized by him, was turned into a tuft of reeds by her sister nymphs.

44. Centaur: Creature half man, half horse.

45. Cyclops: Gigantic creature with one wheel-sized eye in the middle of his forehead.

45. Calydonian Boar: The terrible boar which laid waste to the country of Calydon; killed by Atalanta and Meleager. The hunt is alluded to in the *Iliad*, Ovid, and Apollodorus.

46. Alcides: The name of Hercules in his early years. He is usually pictured carrying a club.

50. Wife of . . . Admetus: Alcestis, the wife of King Admetus, in Euripides' drama *Alcestis*, gives her life for her husband. She is brought back to life by Hercules.

52. Hebe: The daughter of Hera, who becomes the wife of Hercules. Here her role is as the goddess of youth.

55. Alcestis: See note on line 50.

61. Hercules: Brings Alcestis back to life by rescuing her from Hades.

62. Euripides: Greek dramatist, the youngest of the three great tragedians, who died at the end of the fifth century B.C.

70–71. Ossa . . . Olympus . . . Peneus: The river Peneus separates the Ossa mountain range from Mount Olympus to the north and flows into the sea, hence the reference at line 69 to Neptune (Poseidon), god of the sea.

74. Vale of Tempé: The Peneus valley between Olympus and Ossa.

98. lentisk: The mastic tree, *Pistacia lentiscus.*

98. Bay: Or laurel, the *Laurus nobilis.*

99–100. sacred Bay . . . shoot . . . Castilian rills: To escape Apollo, the virgin huntress Daphne was changed into the laurel tree by her father, the river god Peneus, on the banks of the river. Apollo, dismayed at his loss, decided that she would at least become his tree and its leaves crown his victors. "Wherever songs are sung and stories told," vowed Apollo, "Apollo and his laurel shall be joined together." The tale is told in Ovid.

Footnote 3. Ford's "The Broken Heart": No such poem appears in *The Broken Heart,* although the drama is set in Greece and has a character dying to the sound of music. Simms is actually referring to *The Lover's Melancholy,* I.i, in which such a contest is reported to have taken place in Tempé by the character Menaphon.

V. THE TEMPLE OF MINERVA, AT SUNIUM.

The twelve-line miniature "Sunium," in *Magnolia,* n.s., 1 (July 1842): 43, becomes lines 72–73, 102–6, and 142–45 of this text, published from *Southern Illustrated News* 1 (1 November 1862). An intermediate version in *Southern Literary Gazette* 3 (8 June 1850) had been revised and expanded to form the 1862 text. Simms corrected a clipping of the *Southern Illustrated News* in his Scrapbook G. These revisions have all been incorporated in this text:

5. the] this
7. genius] Genius
9. drank] drunk
11. drank] drunk
24. eaves] caves
29. power] powers,
33. so well] well
44. natural] material
51. month ago,] month
52. Western] western
54. muse] Muse
55. powers] pioneer,
64. long] gay
69. mammon] Mammon
77. tables] trebles
95. realms] worlds
98. realms] witness
101. and o'er] o'er
108. ever eager] eager
109. with] o'er
122. re-people] re-peoples

In addition, in keeping with Simms's usual practice and the *Southern Literary Gazette:*

102. honors] honours

Notes

Title. Sunium: Or Sounion, a cape south of Athens, where are located the ruins of a temple to Minerva.

19. Prometheus: The Titan who stole fire from heaven as a gift for man.

47. Pericles: Athenian general and statesman during Greece's Golden Age in the fifth century B.C.

47. Timon: Athenian ruler, the type of despair, made the main character of a play by Shakespeare. Simms proposed to the actor Forrest, on the basis of Forrest's personal misfortunes, writing a play for him using Timon as a central figure.

66–68. Romeo . . . Juliet . . . Jessica . . . Shylock: All characters from Shakespeare.

136–45. hosts . . . sacrifice: Reminiscent of the description of the urn's frieze in John Keats's "Ode on a Grecian Urn."

VI. THERMOPYLÆ.

Begun as a three-line miniature in *Magnolia*, n.s., 1 (September 1842): 190, this poem was expanded in *Cassique of Accabee* (1849), p. 104; *Southern Literary Gazette*, n.s., 1 (19 June 1851): 185; *Poems* (1853), p. 60; and the *Columbia Daily Phoenix*, 11 May 1865. The text is from *Southern Home Journal* 1 (4 April 1868), without emendation. It closely resembles the *Daily Phoenix* text, whose appearance in early 1865, when the South was being invaded, was appropriate considering the poem's subject matter.

Notes

Title. Thermopylæ: The narrow pass lying between the lofty mountain ridges of Oeta. This was the site of the famous defense of Greece against the Persians under Xerxes in 480 B.C.

5. 'Three Hundred.': The three hundred Spartans who were slain defending the pass.

7. The 'immortals' of the Median: The ten thousand Persian barbarians who served as Xerxes' guard. The Spartans were attacked from front and rear.

9. Leonidas: The Spartan king who defended Thermopylae. He gave his life rather than retreat. The account is given in Herodotus.

19. Œta: Mount Oeta was the scene of Hercules' apotheosis. From here, he was taken in a cloud to Olympus, where he was received as one of the immortals.

VII. THE PEACE IN ELIS.

"Elis," a thirteen-line miniature in *Magnolia*, n.s., 1 (August 1842): 92, corresponds roughly to lines 16–35 of this text. In the 27 May 1865 issue of the *Columbia Daily Phoenix*, Simms published an intermediate version, before heavily revising and expanding it into the version published in the *New Eclectic* 6 (January 1870): 8–12.

The *New Eclectic* is the text printed here, with the following emendations based on the *Daily Phoenix* and Simms's usual practice:

> 5. Gulf] gulph
> 16. Hallowed] Hallow'd
> 21. Honored] Honor'd
> 27. schooled] school'd
> 36. looked] look'd
> 44. dressed] dress'd
> 60. watched] watch'd
> 60. weighed] weigh'd
> 141. Selene] Selenæ
> 153. pressed] press'd

Notes

Title. Elis: The region between the western barrier of Arcadia and the Ionian Sea. It contains several plains. In the country's center is the plain of Olympia, through which the Alpheus flows.

1. Taÿgetus: Mountain in the range of the same name in southern Greece separating Laconia and Messenia. The capital of the "stern Laconian race" was Sparta.

4. Corona: Mountain on the coast of the Messenian gulf, to the southwest of Taÿgetus.

9. Peace delights: Warring cities honored a sacred truce during the Olympic games, and the territory of Elis itself was considered especially sacred during the games, when no armed force could enter it.

12. Alpheus: The river that flows through the plain of Olympia.

51–55. This section on peace was appropriately added in 1870.

113. Prytaneum: A building where met the administrative body.

115. Altis: The sacred grove of Jove at Olympia, an area hallowed by the temples of Zeus and Hera and the place from which the competitors filed toward the stadium.

125. Jove's . . . temple: In the Altis at Olympia. Here was located Phidias's statue of Zeus, one of the seven wonders of the world.

129. Phidias: Most famous Greek sculptor, who was known for his sculptures of gods and goddesses. The sculpture on the Parthenon is attributed to him.

136. Endymion: The shepherd whom the moon goddess, who loved him, made to sleep eternally in youth.

138. Aphesis: The starting post for horses in a race.

141. Selenæ: The moon goddess, who fell in love with Endymion.

147. Latmos: Or Latmus, the mountain glade where Endymion kept his sheep.

VIII. SCENE AT ACTIUM.

The "Actium" of *Magnolia*, n.s., 1 (September 1842): 139, is revised to become lines 16–33 of this text. The poem's intermediate version in *Southern Illustrated News* 1 (25 October 1862): 7, was heavily revised and improved in *New Eclectic* 6 (February 1870): 173–76. The *New Eclectic* is the text here printed, with the following emendations based on the *Southern Illustrated News* and Simms's usual practice:

14. Gulf] gulph
21. gulf] gulph
27. poets] Poets
27. linked] link'd
29. gods] Gods
36. bannered] banner'd
59. beggared] beggar'd
70. flower] flow'r
81. limned] limn'd
82. Gulf] gulph
95. empire] Empire
110. death] Death
122. honor] Honor
127. poets] Poets

Symbols to mark footnotes have been changed to superscript numerals.

Notes

Title. Actium: The scene of Mark Antony's defeat by Octavian in 31 B.C., which precipitated his and Cleopatra's suicide in Egypt shortly thereafter. Actium is on the northwest coast of Greece.

14 Ambracian gulph: Below Actium, the site of the naval battle.

119. Ventidius: First century B.C. Roman general favored by Antony. See Shakespeare's *Antony and Cleopatra*, III.i.

127. Happy for us that have the Poets left us: Simms comments here on his own situation. One of his last requests to a New York friend was to haunt the cheap bookstalls for volumes of poetry to send him.

IX. THE LIONS OF MYCENÆ.

The germ of this poem was a six-line miniature in the *Magnolia*, n.s., 1 (August 1842): 103. Its intermediate version in the *Columbia Daily South Carolinian*, 9 October 1864, was revised and expanded for *New Eclectic* 6 (May 1870): 532–34, from which this text is published with the following emendations based on the *Daily South Carolinian* text and Simms's usual practice:

4. Gulf] gulph
6. Drama,] Drama [*Simms canceled the comma in a clipping of the* South Carolinian *text in his Scrapbook G.*]

30. Lions] lions

35. king of men] King of Men

77. seaside] sea-side

87. bard] Bard

95. fate] Fate

95. passion] Passion

96. king of men] King of Men

Notes

Title. Lions of Mycenæ: One of the earliest extant specimens of Greek sculpture, located above the ancient gate at Mycenae. The city now exists only as massive ruins rising above the plain of Argos. Mycenae was the home of King Agamemnon during the Greek Bronze Age.

3. site . . . Acropolis: The speaker likely stands at the ruins of Argos, at the head of the Argolic Gulf. A few miles to its north rises Mycenae.

4. Argolic gulph: An inlet of the Sea of Crete.

7. Danaus: According to Greek legend, the Egyptian founder of Argos, who fled there with his fifty daughters to escape the persecution of their suitors.

9. Lernean pool: Home of the Lernean hydra.

15. Pausanias: Greek geographer, fl. ca. 150 A.D., who wrote a second-century *Description of Greece,* likely an important source for Simms's poem in that one intention of both authors was to act as tour guide, pointing out chief places of interest.

16. Thucydides: A Greek historian of the fifth century B.C.

33. City of the Atridæ: Mycenae, home of the House of Atreus, to which Agamemnon belonged.

35. King of Men: King Agamemnon.

36. Agamemnon: Mycenaean king of the Bronze Age whose story is told by Homer in the *Iliad* and by Aeschylus in the Oresteian trilogy.

38. son: Orestes, who avenged his father's murder.

39. Pylades: The close friend and cousin of Orestes, who helped Orestes avenge his father's murder.

41. Electra . . . urn: In the *Choëphorae* of Aeschylus, Orestes, on his return to Mycenae after his father's death, recognizes his sister seated by their father's tomb.

46. Clytemnestra: Wife of Agamemnon, who, with her lover, murders her husband. Her portrayal by Aeschylus as a woman of indomitable will is the source for Simms's comparison of her to Lady Macbeth, a parallel drawn frequently by nineteenth-century critics.

51. Iphigenia: Daughter of Agamemnon and Clytemnestra, sacrificed to the gods by Agamemnon for favorable winds to Troy. Based on his sources, Simms is correct in portraying Clytemnestra's use of this reason for murder as a pretext only.

58. "Resembled . . . slept": A paraphrase of *Macbeth,* II.ii.13–14.

63. Cyclopean walls: Gigantic walls, generally called *Cyclopean,* because posterity could not believe them to be the works of man.

75. blind old man: Homer.

83–84. *Vixere fortes . . .:* "Many brave men lived before Agamemnon," Horace, *Odes,* 4.9.25–26. The context of these lines by Horace also applies to the greater argument in Simms's poem—that it is the poet alone who bestows immortality.

92. Mæonides: Homer.

93. Æschylus: Greek dramatist born in 525 B.C. His Oresteian trilogy is based on the history of the family of King Agamemnon.

104–7. Electra . . . song of joy: Electra sings a song of joy after her father's death is avenged at the end of the *Choëphorae.* Although it will require the actions of the third play of the trilogy, the curse on the House of Atreus will finally be lifted; and Simms's last lines are therefore correct in imaging future joy after long sorrow.

[UNTITLED]

This previously unpublished sonnet appears only in manuscript in Simms's Scrapbook D. It candidly states the poet's view of contemporary religion, echoing in its octave Wordsworth's sonnet "The World Is Too Much with Us" (1807), a poem whose theme is close to that of several of Simms's works. Both poets shared essentially the same criticism of the materialistic times in which they lived.

Simms's most explicit treatment of religion came in a letter of 1856 which states that although he is a religious man, he has always "stubbornly opposed every creed of every Christian church extant. I rejected the Old Testament as a religious authority altogether, & satisfied myself that the New was, however true and good, & wise & pure in many things, a wonderfully corrupt narrative. Spiritualism as a philosophy is in more complete accordance with my own speculations, felt & pursued for 30 years" (*Letters,* 3:431). In 1847 he had written that his "theology" was not "orthodox," but was still "without a shade of irreverence" (*Letters,* 2:385). Simms clearly shows affinities with Celtic religions, especially that of his father's native Ireland.

Because the sonnet's date cannot be determined, it is placed here. It is printed without emendation from Simms's manuscript, except for replacing ampersands in the first and third stanzas with *and.*

Notes

8. unknown God: Named in Wordsworth's sonnet as Proteus (who rises from the sea each midday) and Triton (the son of the sea god Neptune).

EPIGRAMS.

This selection from Simms's large group of epigrams was written from 1829 to 1867. They do not appear in chronological order but are arranged instead as Simms placed many of them in several short, numbered groupings (of from four to six poems) extant in manuscript in his scrapbooks. The system of numbering before the title is Simms's own in his manuscript groupings. Only here, the groups are combined; and the numbers run consecutively to thirty. The first epigrams deal with women, the next ones with men, and the final ones with the professions and topical matters. The great majority of the titles are Simms's own; the few that have been supplied are identified in the notes.

Epigram 1: Published from Simms's undated manuscript in Scrapbook G without emendation. It first appeared in *Magnolia* 3 (December 1841): 539, where Simms describes it as "an excrutiating piece of Spanish flattery." It was then published in *Magnolia* 4 (March 1842): 187; *Southern and Western* 1 (April 1845): 256; *Broadway Journal* 2 (1 November 1845): 261; *Godey's* 38 (March 1849): 159; *Egeria* (1853), p. 112; and *Areytos* (1860), p. 89. The Spanish source is unidentified.

Epigram 2: Published here for the first time from the undated manuscript in Scrapbook G without emendation.

Epigram 3: The text of this, one of the poet's first epigrams, is from *Egeria* (1853), p. 185. The poem was first published as "Epigram on a Young Lady Who Looked Witty Things, but Never Spoke Them" in *Southern Literary Gazette*, n.s., 1 (1 November 1829): 269, then in the *New York Mirror*, 20 October 1832, p. 128; and *Magnolia* 3 (December 1841): 535.

Epigram 4: The text of this poem is from an undated manuscript in Scrapbook G. It is published here for the first time, without emendation. The title is editorially supplied. The Gotham of line 2 is New York.

Epigram 5: The text of this poem is from the undated manuscript in Scrapbook D. It is here published for the first time. The title is editorially supplied and the following emendations have been made:

2. growld] growled
2. &] and
2. fortune's] fortunes

Epigram 6: Published without emendation from its only appearance, in *Magnolia* 3 (December 1841): 538.

Epigram 7: Published without emendation from *Egeria* (1853), p. 101, where Simms writes that the poem is "from the Portuguese." It first appeared in *Rambler* 1 (11 October 1843): 19, as "The Garden and the Flower, Epigram—From My Old Port Folio." It was also published in *Broadway Journal* 2 (1 November 1845): 261, and *Areytos* (1860), p. 263.

Epigram 8: Published as "from the Scotch"; with one emendation (a supplying of the final quotation mark) from *Broadway Journal* 2 (8 November 1845): 270. It first appeared in *American Monthly* 4 (1 February 1835): 384, and *Magnolia* 3 (December 1841): 538.

Epigram 9: Published from *Broadway Journal* 2 (8 November 1845): 270. It first appeared in *Magnolia* 3 (December 1841): 538. One emendation has been made:

4. lover's] lovers'

Epigram 10: Published without emendation from *Areytos* (1860), p. 306. Its earlier appearances were *Godey's* 37 (December 1848): 360; an unlocated clipping from Scrapbook D, entitled "Bows and Beaux" and signed "Quince"; and *Egeria* (1853), pp. 272–73.

Epigram 11: Published without emendation from *Egeria* (1853), p. 71. It also appeared in *Southern Literary Gazette* 3 (1 June 1850); and *Areytos* (1860), p. 337. In *Egeria* Simms writes that "many of our virtues are not even skin-deep: we put them on and off with our clothing; and, to prepare for God, we too often pursue the same course which we employ in preparing for company. The first Eve put on fig-leaves for concealment. The modern Eve, for the same object, has only to keep hers well washed. Soap and water, and French perfumes, suffice." In *Areytos,* Simms noted that the poem's source was Proverbs. The original manuscript of the poem is on a page of Simms's copy of J. G. Herder's *The Spirit of Hebrew Poetry,* trans. James Marsh, 2 vols. (Burlington, Vt.: Edward Smith, 1833). Here Simms notes that vol. 2, p. 207, was the source of the poem's inspiration: "Such also is the way of an adulteress, / She eateth, and then wipeth her mouth, / And saith, 'I've done no wrong.'" Proverbs 30:20. For a fuller treatment of Simms's annotations in Herder, see James E. Kibler, "Simms and *The Spirit of Hebrew Poetry,*" *Simms Review* 12 (Winter 2004): 4–7.

Epigram 12: Published here for the first time from its only text, an undated manuscript in Scrapbook D. It is unemended but for an editorially supplied title.

Epigram 13: Published from *Egeria* (1853), p. 184, with one emendation from the earlier text in *Magnolia* 3 (December 1841): 539:

    2. end;–] end!"–

Simms in *Egeria* writes the history of Pacuvius: "They tell a scandalous story of Pacuvius, the Roman dramatist. He had three wives, all of whom hanged themselves;–a remarkable felicity of fortune, it was said by the Stoics–but not more remarkable than the additional circumstance, that they all hanged themselves on the very same tree. Pacuvius one day lamented this fortune to his friend Attius, another poet, who had never had but the one wife; and she, it seems, had never shown the slightest disposition to hang herself anywhere, unless around the neck of her husband. Attius confounded the complaining bard by earnestly begging for a slip of the same tree, that he might set it out in his own garden."

Epigram 14: The text is from a manuscript in Scrapbook D, without emendation except for an editorially supplied title. It is here published for the first time from its only source.

Epigram 15: The text comes without emendation from *Southern Literary Messenger* 3 (July 1837): 428, signed "Q." It is published under Simms's name for the first time.

Epigram 16: The text comes from its only appearance in *Southern Literary Messenger* 17 (April 1851): 211, signed "Ichabod." It is published under Simms's name for the first time. The only emendation has been to supply a title.

Epigram 17: Published without emendation from *Southern and Western* 1 (June 1845): 411, identified here as "An Epigram from the Old English." Its only other appearance was in *Areytos* (1860), p. 332.

Epigram 18: Published from *Broadway Journal* 2 (8 November 1845): 270, with one emendation:

    1. death"!] death!"

A note states that the epigram is "from the Italian." Its earlier appearance was *Magnolia* 3 (December 1841): 537.

Epigrams 19–21: Published from the manuscripts in Scrapbook D, with editorially supplied titles and replacement of the ampersand with *and*. These poems are published for the first time.

Epigram 22: Published without emendation from *Egeria* (1853), p. 127, and said to be of Saxon origin. It also appeared in *American Monthly* 4 (1 September 1834): 168; *Magnolia* 3 (December 1841): 537; and *Broadway Journal* 2 (8 November 1845): 270.

Epigram 23: Published without emendation except for an editorially supplied title from the *Charleston Mercury*, 15 June 1860, signed "Quip." It appears here under Simms's name for the first time.

Epigram 24: Published here for the first time from an undated manuscript in Personal and Literary Memorials. The title is editorially supplied, and the ampersand at line 8 is changed to *and*. The date of the poem is uncertain, but the tone of the triplet points toward the postwar period.

Epigram 25: Published from an unidentified clipping in Scrapbook A, with one emendation:

8. Deliver."] Deliver.'

Epigram 26: This epigram first appeared in *Southern Literary Journal* 2 (March 1836): 66, then in *Magnolia* 3 (December 1841): 535. The text here is from *Broadway Journal* 2 (8 November 1845): 270. A revised last version in *Egeria* (1853), p. 186, is said to be rendered from the French of Boileau.

Epigram 27: Published first in *Magnolia* 3 (December 1841): 536, this poem is unemended from *Broadway Journal* 2 (6 December 1845): 331.

Epigram 28: Published from its only appearance, in *Southern Literary Journal* 1 (December 1835): 273. The title has been editorially supplied.

Epigram 29: First published in *Charleston City Gazette* (9 November 1830), this poem later appeared in *Magnolia* 3 (December 1841): 538, and *Egeria* (1853), p. 238. The text is unemended from *Egeria*.

Epigram 30: Published from an undated manuscript in Scrapbook G. The title is editorially supplied; the quotation mark is added in line 3; and the ampersand in the last line is changed to *and*. The poem is published here for the first time.

SONNET TO THE PAST.

"Sonnet to the Past" was first published in *Album*, 8 October 1825, p. 120, and signed "Wilton." Simms collected it in *Poems* (1827), pp. 43–44. Extensively revised, it appeared in *The Cassique of Accabee* (1849), p. 88, and *Poems* (1853), pp. 160–61. The text is from *Cassique* without emendation. The 1853 printing is the 1849 text, but with housestyling of accidentals, so has been rejected as copy text.

The poem was first published in *Poems* (1827), pp. 26–27, then expanded as "The Approach of Summer," *Southern Literary Journal,* n.s., 1 (May 1837): 239–40, where it was dated 1 May and signed "G.B.S." (short for Simms's proved pseudonym "G. B. Singleton"). The shorter *Poems* version is printed here with two emendations:

 Title. ummer] Summer
  14. streamlets] streamlet's

SONG OF THE IRISH PATRIOT.

Never appearing under Simms's name, this important lyric's only appearance was in *Southern Literary Gazette* 1 (December 1828): 215. It was signed "Vidal," a proved Simms pseudonym.

 Simms here commemorates the great men who died in the cause of Irish freedom in the risings of 1798 and 1803. The only emendations have been to make Simms's arabic numerals into roman numerals, in keeping with Simms's usual practice.

Notes

 2.1. Currans . . . Emmets: John Philpot Curran (1750–1817), Irish lawyer, orator, and statesman, who said, "Eternal vigilance is the price of liberty." Robert Emmet (1778–1803) participated in the rising of 1803 and was executed by the English. After being hanged, Emmet's head was severed and held up to the crowds as the head of a traitor. His moving speech at his execution helped keep the spirit of Irish freedom alive into Simms's own day. He declared, "When my country takes her place among the nations of the world, then, and not 'til then, let my epitaph be written." For a treatment of Simms's understanding of the fight for Irish independence and Emmet's involvement therein, see James Everett Kibler, "Simms's Irish," *Simms Review* 9 (Winter 2002): 1–7, and Kibler, "Simms's Celtic Harp," *Studies in Literary Imagination* 42 (Spring 2009): 168–80.

ADDRESS *WRITTEN FOR THE BENEFIT OF THE "ASSOCIATION OF THE FRIENDS OF IRELAND IN CHARLESTON."*

Printed here from its only appearance, in the *Charleston Courier,* 21 April 1829, with the following emendations:

 2. Tyrants] Tyrant's
 4. Freedoms] Freedom's

Notes

 Title. "Association of the Friends of Ireland": The title has a byline stating "by William Gilmore Simms, Jun. Esq. and spoken by Mr. J. J. Adams, of the Charleston

Theatre." Irish societies had been organized in Charleston from the mid-1700s onward. The first was the Irish Society of Charleston in 1749, followed by the Friendly Sons of St Patrick in 1779, and the Friendly Brothers of Ireland in 1786. The rising of 1798 inspired the formation of the Irish Volunteer Company in 1798 and the Hibernian Society in 1799. Simms became a member of the latter society in 1849. The St. Patrick's Benevolent Society was founded in 1817.

1. Harp: The ancient symbol of Ireland and Irish freedom.

29. Brian: That is, Brien Boru (947–1014), first high king of Ireland. King Brien breathed life into Celtic culture as a leader, warrior, and harpist. Brien defeated the invading Vikings at the Battle of Clontarf in 1014, thus ending Viking power in the land. There was, however, no comparable leader to fill his shoes, and the next century saw the beginning of eight centuries of foreign domination.

31. Connaught fell, and Ulster lived no more: Probably meant to suggest the Red Branch Knights of Ulster, who, like King Brien, were successful in repulsing Viking invaders. In 1169 the Normans were invited to settle a dispute between tribes of Ulster and Connaught but, instead, came as conquerors. England followed in the sixteenth century, and under Elizabeth I, the last of the Gaelic chiefs were defeated and their lands in Ulster were planted with the Scots who troubled James I. Simms was correct in saying that at this point "Connaught fell, and Ulster lived no more." Ulster, formerly the province least under English influence, became the region least Gaelic. This is the ancestral home of Simms's father. The poem thus shows that at age twenty-three, Simms was already knowledgeable about the long span of Irish history and its struggles for freedom.

38. martyrs . . . Emmet, Fitzgerald, and Tone: For Robert Emmet, see notes to "Song of the Irish Patriot." Fitzgerald is Sir Edward Fitzgerald, executed by the English for his part in the rising of 1798. Tone is Theobald Wolfe Tone, an Irish revolutionary who died in prison by his own hand to cheat the English hangman. Tone was a friend of the Simms relatives in Belfast.

71. the chains, our father's people wear: The poet is being most literal here. His father hailed from outside Belfast in county Antrim.

88. O'Connell's speech: Daniel O'Connell (1775–1847), who agitated for Catholic voting rights in the 1820s. He created the first mass movement of the Irish people that forced Parliament to grant them right to vote in 1829. As his career progressed, he became insistent upon Irish independence. Simms gauged him correctly as a charismatic leader in the Irish cause. That Simms had singled him out this early in his career shows just how aware he was of current events in the Irish movement.

SONG IN MARCH.

This poem was often reprinted in Simms's day. It first appeared in the *Charleston City Gazette*, 15 March 1832, then *Southern Literary Journal* 1 (March 1837): 63; *Southern Literary Messenger* 6 (June 1840): 446; *Areytos* (1846), p. 63; and *Poems* (1853), p. 24. The poem shows minor revisions from 1837 to 1840. Subsequently only one substantive change appears. In line 5 "around" becomes "about" in 1846. The 1853 text is the same as the 1846, but with further corruption of the accidentals. The text here printed is from 1846 with accidentals from 1840, when, it appears, Simms had recopied his text for submission to the *Southern Literary Messenger*. The 1853 poem remained largely a polished version of its effective first appearance of 1832. When one considers Simms's usual method of revising, expanding and rewriting, this fact alone is noteworthy and likely argues that the poet found this work solid.

THERE'S A GORGEOUS GLOW ON EARTH.

This lyric appears only once: *Southern Literary Messenger* 6 (January 1840): 37. Here the speaker addresses his guitar and hopes his talent will persuade and enchant the listener. It is a simple and unaffected poem, reminiscent of Thomas Moore's *Irish Melodies*. The only emendations are a lowercasing of the roman numerals to mark the stanzas, in keeping with Simms's usual practice.

FRIENDSHIP.

This sonnet appeared four times: *Magnolia* 4 (May 1842): 275; *Southern Literary Messenger* 11 (March 1845): 177; *Grouped Thoughts* (1845), p. 36; and *Poems* (1853), p. 206. The text printed here is the 1842 edition with one emendation of a typesetting error in the 1842 text:

    4. sought] nought

The *Poems* text modernizes the diction and spelling, in violation of Simms's habitual manner. Simms revised the text in the 1845 publication, but the revisions are not effective.

BEAUTY IN SHADE.

This lyric shows metrical sophistication of no small order. It was published four times: *Magnolia*, n.s., 1 (September 1842): 140, signed "Spiridion," a proved pseudonym; *Broadway Journal* 2 (11 October 1845): 203; *Areytos* (1846), pp. 89–90; and *Charleston Mercury*, 4 May 1864, signed "Adrian B. Beaufain," a proved pseudonym. There is also a full manuscript in Simms's hand in his Scrapbook A.

    The poem is carefully structured. In the initial four lines, the speaker notes the beautiful one's sadness. The rest of the work consists of his posing three questions suggesting possible reasons for her sorrow. Each question consists of four lines. The lyric thus demonstrates Simms's ability to create a perfectly controlled and ordered poem. When he chooses not to, one must grant that it is not for lack of skill or proficiency in his craft, which this poem demonstrates he obviously had in great degree.

The rhyme scheme of each eight-line stanza is *aaabcccb*. The lines are iambic tetrameter, tetrameter, tetrameter, trimeter, tetrameter, tetrameter, tetrameter, trimeter. The two trimeter lines are the *b* rhymes. Simms used ottava rima (see, for example, "Parting. A Fragment" on p. 128), and his verse form here shows some affinities with it. The form is of Simms's own creation and shows his frequent innovation within a loosened traditional form. Simms's verse form, with its tercets and complicated tetrameter-trimeter foot, is more complicated and difficult than ottava rima. The truncated lines 4 and 8 are effective in creating in dramatic fashion the proper tone of loss and incompleteness. "Beauty in Shadow" is typical of Simms's fine verse in which he exhibits versatility and mastery of metrics.

The poem is printed here from its 1842 appearance, with two emendations from the manuscript:

1.8. trees!] trees?

Lowercase roman numerals to mark the stanzas.

Simms revised the poem heavily in its last appearances but did not improve it.

WOOING; BY A BASHFUL GENTLEMAN.

This humorous poem appeared in Simms's *Southern and Western* 1 (February 1845): 99; *Areytos* (1846), pp. 53–54; and *Areytos* (1860), pp. 326–27. The first-person narrator, with an implied listener, and the revelation of the narrator's character through his telling create a poem akin to a dramatic monologue. Simms uses the poem's diction skillfully to help portray the narrator. The poem is published here from its 1845 text without emendation.

THE DYING CHILD.

This touching personal lyric was first published in the *Charleston Southern Patriot* around 1847. The issue in which it appears is not extant, but fortunately Simms clipped the poem from the newspaper and pasted it on the verso of his *Don Carlos* manuscript, now at the South Caroliniana Library. It is a three-stanza original version that Simms expanded to seven stanzas in *Southern Literary Gazette* 3 (12 October 1850): [n.p.]. The latter was clipped and pasted in Simms's scrapbooks B and D, and on the verso of the *Don Carlos* manuscript. The text printed here is the shorter and artistically superior *Southern Patriot* version, which is emended only by a lowercasing of Simms's roman numerals, in keeping with his usual manner. Simms's handling of the imagery of dimness and darkness and of candle, lamp, and sunlight is deft and an organizing principle lacking in the longer version.

The poem likely grows out of Simms's own loss of a child. The last stanza provides a view into Simms's domestic life, particularly his devotion to and appreciation of his wife: "She who has borne the pain" of childbirth. Simms prays that the child be spared most especially for the devoted mother who hangs "Dumb o'er the cradle,— / Humbled in heart and lonely." For the wrong-minded biographer who makes much of Simms's callousness toward his wife, the final stanza should give pause. (See also Tom Fleming's perceptive comments in "More Than a Statue," *Chronicles of American Culture* 36 [April 1993]: 25–27.)

The poem "Wail," also collected here, is another personal lyric that Simms never collected or claimed as his own—again perhaps because he deemed it too personal. "Wail" also treats his wife and pays proper tribute to Mrs. Simms at her death in 1863. This pair of lyrics should stand at the center of the significant body of poems that Simms wrote from experience, composed during the immediate time of grief, when that experience was raw.

BALLAD — "YES, BUILD YOUR WALLS."

This poem was first published in the *Charleston Mercury*, 4 August 1863, signed by Simms, then reprinted with no substantive changes in *Southern Field and Fireside*, n.s., 1 (29 August 1863): 213, and *War Poetry* (1866), pp. 466–67. The text is from its first appearance in the *Mercury* with only a lowercasing of the stanza numerals. The *War Poetry* text shows housestyling of the accidentals and is thus rejected.

"Ballad" repeats Simms's view, frequently expressed in his war verse, that the new conflict resembled the American Revolution—hence his invocation of Moultrie, Marion, Sumter, Rutledge, and Gadsden, all Revolutionary War heroes of Carolina. He does so in order to remind present-day Carolinians of the glory of their past in the hope that they will again exhibit bravery defending their freedom. The "City by the Sea" is, of course, Charleston.

SACRIFICE FOR LIBERTY.

This sonnet appeared in the *Charleston Mercury*, 29 October 1863, unsigned. It is here collected under Simms's name for the first time, and without emendation. Simms clipped and pasted it in his scrapbooks D and G. The patriot's blood preparing the soil for "Freedom's tree" may be a paraphrase of Thomas Jefferson's famous statement that in every generation the tree of liberty must be watered by the blood of patriots.

WAIL.

Unsigned and never acknowledged by Simms, "Wail" is another of the excellent mature works growing out of the poet's own experiences, here the sudden death of his wife on 10 September 1863. Its only appearance is in the *Charleston Mercury*, 5 December 1863. A manuscript of the poem in a hand other than Simms's appears in Scrapbook B. In a letter to Paul Hamilton Hayne, dated 23 September 1863, Simms wrote about his state of mind at his wife's death: "I was, I think, insane. I neither slept nor ate for four days and nights. Fever seized me, and I should have gone mad but for the administration of timely opiates. I am once more on my legs, but very weak. Today, is the first that I have given to the desk, and this I could do only in snatches of brief period. . . . [E]very thing seems blank, & waste, & very cheerless. I am alone! Alone!" (Note the "I am alone" in both letter and poem.) If the poem's "yesternight" is credited as the time of composition, the work was at least begun on 11 September, following his wife's death on the tenth. The verse is raw—the intense grief is barely kept in control—and thus argues for the immediacy of composition. Simms had had practice in writing such poems of terrific anguish from the loss of children. He must have found the process a means of dealing with personal tragedy and too personal to acknowledge or collect under his name.

The rhyme scheme is intricate. The poem's tetrameter lines often make use of tercets in a complicated pattern that gives the poem the mystic power of chant or incantation. It is difficult not to see Simms's Celtic heritage at work in the versification.

The only emendation to this poem is the lowercasing of the roman numerals, in keeping with the poet's usual practice.

Notes

2.6. the last white rose that the garden bore: Likely, an accurate detail. Simms had planted many ornamentals at Woodlands. Roses were among his and his wife's favorites.

VOICES OF SOLITUDE.

This poem's only appearance was in *Old Guard* 4 (December 1866): 723–26. Simms pasted and revised it in his Scrapbook B. The text here incorporates all Simms's scrapbook revisions:

23. veil] recal
42. this] the
43. pink] peach
62. wonder] wander
76. chortah] Choctaw
85. Perian] Pierian
95. home] home—
113. even] ever

Even though this poem was written during the darkest period of the poet's life, it still affirms nature's ability to cheer and heal. It opens, in fact, by stating that the heart that has not felt grief can never appreciate the true beauty of nature. The poem has much in common with Simms's earlier verse. The poet notes being far away from home in the Choctaw wilderness; he laments the loss of his first love, presumably his first wife, Anna, whom he courted by the Ashley River. It may thus be an expanded version of a work first composed on his trips to the Southwest. Because Woodlands now lay in ashes, Simms was once more a wanderer. In its blank verse, the poem resembles his fine works of the 1830s. The section beginning at line 80 has the same subject as "Sketches in Hellas" (p. 277).

THE COMING CHANGE.

Simms published this poem in the *Charleston Mercury*, 11 February 1867, signed "Hampden–Sydney," a proved pseudonym. He pasted it in scrapbooks A, B, D, and G, without revision. The *Columbia Daily Phoenix* reprint of 13 February 1867 makes obvious errors and has no authority. Stanzas 4–7, apparently favorite lines, had an earlier incarnation as "Moonlight in Spring," *Southern Literary Gazette* 3 (11 May 1850): [n.p.]; *Southern Literary Messenger* 26 (May 1858): 355; and *Columbia Daily South Carolinian*, 30 March 1864. The stanzas of 1867 are much altered. The poem is metrically sophisticated. Its eleven stanzas have tetrameter lines rhyming *ababb*. The poem is here collected and appears under Simms's name for the first time, with one emendation:

2.5. power] powers

Index of Titles

Index of First Lines